Power of...
FRAME MAKER 4
for Windows

David B. Doty

First Edition—1993

ISBN 1-55828-314-5

Printed in the United States of America.

10 9 8 7 6 5 4 3 2 1

MIS:Press books are available at special discounts for bulk purchases for sales promotions, premiums, fund-raising, or educational use. Special editions or book excerpts can also be created to specification.

For details contact: Special Sales Director
MIS:Press
a subsidiary of Henry Holt and Company, Inc.
115 West 18th Street
New York, New York 10011

Development Editor: Cary Sullivan
Production Editor/Design: Joanne Kelman
Associate Production Editor: Stephanie Doyle
Copyeditor: Peter Bochner

Contents

3 Creating and Editing Text 35

10 Using Cross-References 177

11 Checking Spelling and Usage 191

14 Anchoring Graphics: Working with Anchored Frames ...239

15 Working with Color 249

16 Creating Tables of Contents and Other Lists 265

17 Creating Indexes 275

18 Building Complex Documents ("Books") 297

19 Working with Footnotes 313

Acknowledgments

Thanks to Frame Technology and especially to the following Frame personnel for their cooperation and assistance: Juliana Lensing, Rennet Fletcher, Dave McLaughlin, Kristin Viis, Carol Kaplan, Lisa Clear, Katie Doweling, Brenda Fathom, Craig Apart, Al Banally, and any technical support engineers whose names I neglected record.

Thanks to Laurie Pulsing, Chris Glazed, Hal Lewis, and Rich Gold for their advice, comments, and suggestions on publication design and/or FrameMaker techniques.

Thanks to Carol McClelland of Waterside Productions and to Cary Sullivan and Joanne Kelman of MIS:Press for their indispensable assistance in the creation of this book.

To my mother, who read to me
(fortunately, not from computer books)

CHAPTER 1

Introduction

What Is FrameMaker?

Frame Technology describes FrameMaker as "a complete publishing solution designed to meet all of your word processing, graphics, page design, and long-document building needs." Although this claim may involve a bit of marketing-department hyperbole, it is not too far from the truth. FrameMaker is a powerful desktop publishing program that incorporates more extensive text editing and drawing capabilities than have heretofore been available in such applications, plus unique features found in no other PC publishing application.

FrameMaker was first developed for UNIX platforms, and this environment still represents 60% of the program's installed base at the time of this writing. About two years ago, FrameMaker was ported to the Macintosh, and most recently, in 1992, the first version of FrameMaker for Windows was released. In mid-1992, Windows accounted for 25% of the program's installed base and represented its most rapidly growing market segment.

FrameMaker shows its UNIX ancestry in its features. UNIX has long been the operating system of choice in the scientific and engineering professions and in academia, and FrameMaker is well-equipped with features suited to scientific, technical, and academic publishing, such as a powerful equation editor, extensive table formatting capabilities, and sophisticated cross-referencing abilities. Another way in which FrameMaker may reflect its UNIX origins is in its attempt to combine word processing, drawing, and layout features in a single package. Traditionally, UNIX has been well-equipped with programming and communications tools, but has not had the abundance of shrink-wrapped word processors and graphics programs found in the PC and Mac environments; hence, the necessity of providing all of the tools in a single application. In the PC environment, we are more likely to write and edit text in Microsoft Word or WordPerfect, create illustrations with Adobe Illustrator or CorelDRAW, and then reach for a desktop publishing program to combine these disparate elements into a finished publication.

How FrameMaker Differs from Other Desktop Publishing Programs

The three other leading contenders in the PC/Windows desktop publishing wars are Xerox Ventura Publisher, Aldus PageMaker, and QuarkXPress. Ventura Publisher and PageMaker are old antagonists, having both been on the scene since the advent of PC desktop publishing in the mid-1980s. QuarkXPress is a recent migrant from the Macintosh environment. Of these three programs, FrameMaker most closely resembles Ventura in both its feature set and orientation, but it far surpasses Ventura in terms of power and flexibility. FrameMaker is quite unlike PageMaker and QuarkXPress, both of which use a "pasteboard" metaphor, and are therefore more suited for one-of-a-kind, graphically driven design tasks.

Frame Technology stresses FrameMaker's orientation to "structured, content-driven publications," for example, technical books, manuals, and reports, as distinct from graphically driven publications, such as advertisements and brochures. FrameMaker excels at creating and maintaining large, structured documents or groups of documents that must maintain a consistent appearance and organization while undergoing frequent revisions and updates. Prior to the release of Frame-Maker for Windows, Ventura was generally the tool of choice for producing this kind of publication on the Windows platform. FrameMaker, however, has much more powerful and practical text editing features than Ventura. Ventura assumes that text originates in another word processing application, and maintains text in its original format so you can go back to that word processor when extensive editing is required. Although FrameMaker *can* import text created in other Windows word processors (and from other platforms as well), it also incorporates complete WYSIWYG (What You See Is What You Get) word processing capabilities. Ventura's editing facilities are adequate for minor editing tasks, but painful for anything more extensive. Creating a large document *from scratch* in Ventura would be out of the question. Further, FrameMaker is free of the modes that can make Ventura such a hassle to use: In Ventura, you must be in Text Mode to edit text, in Paragraph Mode to format paragraphs, in Graphics Mode to create or edit graphics, or in Frame Mode to move or resize frames. In FrameMaker, you can keep whatever tools you want on the screen and use them as needed. There are no modes standing in the way of your using the tool you want when you want.

In a feature-for-feature comparison, FrameMaker and Ventura appear rather similar: Both have an equation editor, table editor, footnotes, cross referencing, user variables, and book-building capabilities. However, when it comes to actually using these features, FrameMaker surpasses Ventura in terms of power and flexibility in most cases.

FrameMaker is not the ultimate desktop publishing application. There are some areas, most notably the flexibility of typographic controls, where Ventura still appears to have the edge. However, FrameMaker 4.0 has corrected many of the shortcomings of the previous version, and has to be considered a serious contender for any publishing project involving long structured documents or document sets.

Several features set FrameMaker apart from all other desktop publishing and word processing applications:

- **Cross-platform compatibility**—FrameMaker runs on PCs with Windows, on the Macintosh, and on UNIX systems from vendors such as Sun, Hewlett-Packard, Apollo, NeXT, DEC, SCO and several others. Documents can be exchanged among these different platforms without modification.

- **Conditional Text**—this feature allows you to create and print multiple versions from a single base document. Text or graphic elements that are given conditional tags can be selectively shown or hidden when generating different versions of a document.

- **Hypertext**—FrameMaker can create locked, read-only versions of documents for electronic distribution in conjunction with a companion product called FrameReader. These documents can contain hypertext links for easy navigation through related topics.

- **Mixed Page Orientations**—these give FrameMaker the ability to mix portrait (vertical) and landscape (horizontal) pages in the same document.

Who This Book Is For

Like any full-featured desktop publishing application, FrameMaker is rich and complex, with many layers of functionality. This complexity is unavoidable, since the process of creating a publication involves a great many distinct tasks: writing and editing text, laying out pages, typesetting, creating and placing illustrations and other graphic elements, building books from many disparate elements, creating tables of contents and indexes, and othcrs. All of these tasks must be coordinated and their results combined smoothly to create a successful publication.

Once upon a time (in a galaxy far away?) all these tasks were performed by trained specialists. Writers wrote, editors edited, graphic artists designed publications, typesetters set type, illustrators illustrated, paste-up artists put it all together, camera operators made color separations, and so forth. Maybe this process still goes on in some large organizations with big publication budgets and staffs, but more and more frequently, as a result of both the desktop resolution and of shrinking budgets, people who are not and never planned to be graphic artists, typesetters, or publication designers are being called upon to perform all aspects of publication design and production with the aid of programs such as FrameMaker and its competitors. *Power of...FrameMaker 4.0 for Windows* is written especially for these people. If you are a writer, editor, programmer, engineer, scientist, manager, or academic, and you find yourself, voluntarily or involuntarily, in the role of a one-person publication department, help is at hand. (If you are a graphic artist, typesetter, designer, or illustrator, but a newcomer to FrameMaker or to desktop production tools in general, you too may find this book useful.)

How This Book Is Organized

As with many programs, FrameMaker's ease of learning is in inverse proportion to its depth and complexity. FrameMaker has a tool (or several) for almost any task you may want to perform, but which tool to use and how to use it effectively may be far from self-evident to the inexperienced user. Fortunately, almost no one will need *all* of FrameMaker's features, and certainly no one will need to use all of them at once. The sane approach to learning FrameMaker (or any complex computer program) is to learn the fundamentals so you can find your way around in the program (made simpler in this case by the Windows interface), then learn those skills that are necessary to do your job on a daily basis. As new tasks come along, learn how to perform them. Don't try to memorize all the commands in the program before you start working—this will lead only to confusion and frustration. You should, however, try to become familiar in a general way with all the major features in the program, so that when a new problem crops up, you will be aware that a tool exists to solve it (this schedule needs to be formatted in rows and columns...time to learn about the Table Designer...the ideas in this paragraph could be expressed more clearly in a formula...time to learn the Equation Editor...).

This book is organized along similar lines. Chapter 2 covers the fundamentals: how to navigate in FrameMaker, load, save, and print files, configure your working environment, and the like. The next three chapters deal with the skills you are likely to need in creating any publication: writing, editing, and importing text (Chapter 3); creating, designing and using page layouts (Chapter 4); and creating and using paragraph and character formats to control the appearance of type (Chapter 5). Chapter 6 contains tips on how to make the best use of the controls described in Chapter 5.

Chapters 7-11 deal with additional text-oriented features that are useful to know but which you may not need on a daily basis: controlling the flow of text and creating multi-flow publications, such as newsletters or magazines (Chapter 7); finding and changing objects, which is a more sophisticated version of the usual search and replace feature (Chapter 8); using variables, i.e., place holders for text strings that can be expected to change (Chapter 9); using cross references (Chapter 10); and using the spelling checker and thesaurus (Chapter 11).

The next four chapters deal with graphics: how to create illustrations and other graphics using FrameMaker's built-in drawing tools (Chapter 12); how to import, position, and edit graphics created with other programs (Chapter 13); how to anchor graphics so they move with the text flow (Chapter 14); and how to use spot and process color and create color separations (Chapter 15).

Chapters 16–18 deal with the FrameMaker features that are usually required in larger publications: tables of contents and other generated lists (Chapter 16); indexes (Chapter 17); and "book building," the combining of multiple files to generate a single publication (Chapter 18).

Chapters 19–21 deal with features that will be of interest primarily to those working with technical, academic, and scientific publications, namely footnotes (Chapter 19); tables (Chapter 20); and equations (Chapter 21). The final chapters, 22–24, deal with unique FrameMaker features: using conditional text to generate multiple versions from a single document, creating hypertext documents for electronic or on-disk distribution, and creating reports.

About the Tips and Techniques Icon

However sophisticated FrameMaker may be in manipulating the textual and graphic elements that make up a publication, there is one thing it can't do: make aesthetic judgements. The design of publications in the West is a tradition that goes back at least as far as Gutenberg in the 15th century (far longer if you consider the scribes who worked with pen and brush and the craftsmen who chiseled letters in stone). Until recently, however, the aesthetic principles of design and typography were the concern of a small number of trained professionals. Then the desktop revolution placed powerful typographic and design tools in the hands of many people (including the author) who had hitherto given little thought to the aesthetics of publication design. Many of the early results were, not surprisingly, less than inspired. Although the worst excesses are, it is to be hoped, past, there is still much we non-artists can learn by studying the work of professional designers, graphic artists, and typesetters. Therefore, I have consulted a number of such design professionals and have included their suggestions wherever practical. These suggestions are identified by the icon at the head of this paragraph. These are not, for the most part, suggestions on how to use FrameMaker as such, i.e., what commands to use to perform a particular task, but advice for the novice on such matters as choosing fonts, setting line length, line spacing, and word spacing, and the dozens of other small decisions that go into the design of a publication. It is hoped that by this means, at least a little of the knowledge and tradition of typography and publication design will be passed on to FrameMaker users, and that better-looking publications may result.

New Features of FrameMaker 4.0

FrameMaker 4.0 includes many new or modified features. The following section provides a broad overview of the changes in version 4.0. This information is provided for users of previous FrameMaker versions. If you are just starting out with FrameMaker 4.0, feel free to skip this section.

For detailed accounts of the new and/or changed features described here and of minor changes too numerous to mention, consult the chapters devoted to the features of interest to you. Throughout the book, new or changed features will be identified as such.

New Templates

FrameMaker 4.0 includes a variety of new document templates. An option in the Files>New dialog box allows you to browse through the standard templates and see thumbnail views of them before selecting one for opening. The New dialog box also offers predefined "blank sheets of paper" in portrait and landscape orientations for starting new documents, in addition to the Custom option available in previous versions.

Changes in the Document Window

New Tool Bars

The FrameMaker 4.0 document window (the work space in which you write, edit, and format documents) has two conspicuous new features: the Quick Access Bar and the Formatting Bar. The Quick Access Bar provides buttons or icons that you can use to select many of FrameMaker's most frequently used features without opening a menu. The Formatting Bar allows you to set line spacing, alignment, and tab stops, and to apply paragraph formats, without using the Format menu or the Paragraph Designer. Both the Quick Access Bar and the Formatting Bar can be turned off or on from the View menu; in addition, the Quick Access Bar can be switched from a horizontal to a vertical format and moved freely around the screen.

New Menu Options

FrameMaker 4.0 comes with two sets of menus: A complete menu set that makes all the program's features available, and a quick menu set that provides the features needed by those who write, edit, and format documents, but don't need to design new layouts or create new text formats. In addition, FrameMaker 4.0 gives you the ability to create a custom menu set that meets your personal or company needs by creating a configuration file.

Good-Bye Page Menu

The Page menu has been eliminated in FrameMaker 4.0. Its commands have been redistributed to the View, Format, and Special menus.

Quicker Loading of Your Most Recent Work

The five most recently loaded documents are now listed at the bottom of the File menu; you can load any of these documents by opening the menu and clicking on the file name or pressing the file number on the keyboard.

New Page Layout Features

When you modify a master page, body pages based on that master page are now updated automatically, i.e., it is no longer necessary to *apply* the edited master page to the body page. You can now change the basic page size and layout of an existing document more easily. The Page option on the Format menu opens the Normal Page Layout dialog box, in which you can specify page size, margins, and columns for the current page. The Format menu also includes a new Page Breaks command that allows you to control the position of any paragraph, by allowing it to be freely placed or forcing it to the top of the next available column or page. The process of using variables in headers and footers has been simplified by the inclusion of a Headers and Footers command on the Format menu.

New Formatting Features

The Paragraph Format window and Character Format window have been redesigned and renamed the Paragraph Designer and the Character Designer, respectively. The Paragraph Designer, in particular, has undergone major changes. The Tabs Properties group has been eliminated and its features have been incorporated in the Basic Properties group. The process of setting a series of evenly spaced tabs has been simplified. The Leading property in the Basic group has been renamed Line Spacing. It is now possible to set single, one-and-one-half, and double spacing, as well as a line height in points. A new properties group called Pagination has been added. This group includes two new paragraph types: Side Heads (headings that hang in the margin) and Run-In Heads (headings that appear as part of the first line of a body paragraph, but are really independent paragraphs for the purposes of formatting and table of contents generation). The Character Designer and the Default Font group in the Paragraph Designer both include new underline options (double and numeric) and capitalization options. Both designer windows now have tag menus so you can apply format tags without having to switch to the format catalogs. The operation of the Apply button in both designer windows has been simplified.

The Table Format window has also been redesigned and renamed the Table Designer. Its apply and update operations have been simplified like those in the Character and Paragraph Designers.

Document Comparison and Reporting

FrameMaker includes a Document Comparison utility (on the File menu), which compares two files and generates a summary indicating the differences and a composite document that shows the common and different features of the two. It also has the capability of using user-created report generators to report on whatever document properties may be of interest. A sample report generator that counts the words in a document is provided with FrameMaker.

Thesaurus

In addition to its spell checker, FrameMaker 4.0 includes a thesaurus, which includes definitions, synonyms, and antonyms. Hypertext links make it easy to look up related words.

New Graphics Features

Dashed Lines

The drawing tools on the Tools Palette now support dashed lines. You can select one of eight predefined dash styles or create your own pattern by modifying the configuration file (not exactly the easiest way I could think of to create a new pattern).

Free Rotation

You can now rotate graphic objects freely, either by grabbing a handle and dragging with the mouse, or by specifying an angle and direction of rotation (clockwise or counterclockwise) in a dialog box. (In FrameMaker 3.0, graphic objects could only be rotated in 90° increments.) You can also set a fixed increment for rotation by setting a Snap Rotate factor in the View Options dialog box.

More Complete Color Support

FrameMaker 4.0 supports four-color process, in addition to the spot color support available in version 3.0. Several different color models are available, including CYMK (Cyan, Yellow, Magenta, Black) for four-color process printing; RGB (Red, Green, Blue) and HSL (Hue, Luminance, Saturation) for precise color control on video displays; and Pantone colors for the precise matching of spot colors.

New Features for Hypertext Documents

FrameMaker 4.0 allows the use of a greater variety of character format options to identify active areas in hypertext documents. (Active areas are the areas you click on to jump to new topics.) You can now create hypertext links to jump to specific pages in a document other than the first, last, next, or previous page. FrameMaker 4.0 can automatically add hypertext links when generating a table of contents, index, or other list.

New Math Features

A new Positioning page on the Equations palette allows more precise positioning of the elements in equations. You can now use a variety of special math fonts in your equations if they are available on your system, in addition to the standard PostScript Symbol font. You can also apply character formats to many elements in equations.

CHAPTER 2

FrameMaker Fundamentals

Navigating in FrameMaker

FrameMaker is a Microsoft Windows application, and conforms fairly closely to the standard Windows user interface, so much about FrameMaker's appearance and operation will be familiar to you if you have used other Windows applications, especially word processing and desktop publishing programs. This book assumes that you are familiar with the basics of Microsoft Windows and know how to open and close dialog boxes, move and resize windows, select commands from menus, and the like; if not, consult the *Microsoft Windows User's Guide*. FrameMaker differs from most other Windows applications in one minor but noteworthy respect: Rarely in FrameMaker will you find the ubiquitous **OK** button for activating changes to the settings in a dialog box. FrameMaker typically uses Set or Apply, or another term appropriate to the context, to label this button.

In this book, we will sometimes use the shorthand **Command1>Command2** to describe a menu selection. This means select **Command1** from the menu, then select **Command2** from the submenu that appears.

N O T E

Starting FrameMaker

You start FrameMaker by double-clicking its icon in the Windows Program Manager or by dragging a FrameMaker document onto the FrameMaker icon from the File Manager. The program initially displays the FrameMaker logo, then opens a window like that in Figure 2.1. This window, like that of any Windows application, has a title bar at the top, with a control-menu box on the left and minimize and maximize buttons on the right. Below the title bar is a menu bar with headings for nine pull-down menus. Only four of the pull-down menus are available when you first start FrameMaker: **File**, **View**, **Window**, and **Help**. The remaining menu titles are "grayed out," indicating they are not active. All of the menus will become active once you load an existing document or begin to create a new one.

Figure 2.1 FrameMaker Program window

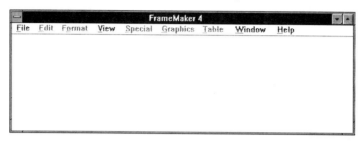

The Page menu, found in previous versions of FrameMaker, has been deleted and its commands have been moved to other menus, primarily the Format, View, and Special menus.

N O T E

Starting a New Document

To load an existing document or create a new one, use the File menu. When you first open the File menu (Figure 2.2), most of the options are again grayed out, indicating that they are unavailable. However, the first two options, **New** and **Open**, which are the only ones that concern us at the moment, are available.

Figure 2.2 File menu

When you select **New** from the File menu (keyboard shortcut **Ctrl+N**), the dialog box in Figure 2.3 appears. From this dialog box, you can start a new document in one of several ways:

Figure 2.3   New File dialog box

```
┌─────────────────────────────────────────────────┐
│                      New                         │
│  Use Blank Paper:                                │
│   ┌──────────┐  ┌───────────┐  ┌──────────┐      │
│   │ Portrait │  │ Landscape │  │ Custom...│      │
│   └──────────┘  └───────────┘  └──────────┘      │
│                                                  │
│  Use Template:            Directories:           │
│  [*.*            ]        c:\maker4\samples\special │
│   activtbl                 c:\                   │
│   colortbl                 maker4                │
│   finantbl                  samples              │
│   math                       special             │
│   resume                                         │
│   travlfrm                                       │
│                                                  │
│  List Files of Type:      Drives:                │
│  [All Files (*.*)  ]      [c: delta_tp  ]        │
│                                                  │
│   ┌──────┐    ┌────────┐    ┌──────┐             │
│   │ New  │    │ Cancel │    │ Help │             │
│   └──────┘    └────────┘    └──────┘             │
│   ┌──────────────────────────────────────┐      │
│   │     Explore Standard Templates...     │      │
│   └──────────────────────────────────────┘      │
└─────────────────────────────────────────────────┘
```

■ You can select a predefined sheet of blank paper in either portrait or landscape orientation (new in FrameMaker 4.0).

■ You can create a custom blank page, by filling in the specifications in the dialog box in Figure 2.4.

■ You can select one of FrameMaker's standard templates (or a template that you have created) using the drive, directory, and file selection boxes.

■ You can also examine FrameMaker's templates by selecting the **Explore Standard Templates** button at the bottom of the dialog box (new in FrameMaker 4.0). This opens a FrameMaker hypertext document that describes the purpose and features of each template and displays a thumbnail version. You can load a selected template into FrameMaker from the online document by pressing the **Create** button.

You can still use your FrameMaker 3.0 templates with FrameMaker 4.0 if you wish.

N O T E

Figure 2.4 Custom Blank Paper dialog box

When you start a new document, whether custom or from a template, FrameMaker names it NoName#, where # is its ordinal number in the series of new documents started in the current work session. To change the name, save the document using the **Save** or **Save As** command, typing the name you want.

For details about using templates and creating custom documents, consult Chapter 4.

Opening an Existing Document

Open an existing document by selecting **Open** from the File menu (keyboard shortcut **Ctrl+O**). This opens a dialog box with drive, directory, and file lists, such as that in Figure 2.5, from which you can select a file to open. FrameMaker can open several types of files:

Figure 2.5 File Open dialog box

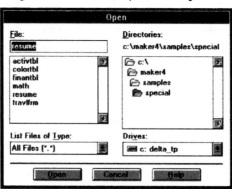

- Normal FrameMaker document files.

- Maker Interchange Format (MIF) files.

- Maker Markup Language (MML) files (MML is a text markup language that makes it possible to create FrameMaker documents with a conventional word processor.)

- Documents created in other major PC and Macintosh word processing applications, including Microsoft Word, WordPerfect, and MacWrite. FrameMaker attempts to retain as much of the original document's format as possible.

- Standard ASCII text files.

NOTE

If FrameMaker is uncertain of the format of a file that you are attempting to load, it will display the Unknown File Type dialog box (**Figure 2.6**). Pick the type of file you want to from the list of filters, then click on **Convert**.

Figure 2.6   Unknown File Type dialog box

Unknown File Type
File: c:\wp\techproj\bg\draft1
Convert From:
MS Word Mac 4.0
MSI
RTF
Text
Ventura Publisher 1.0-4.0
WordPerfect 5.0
WordPerfect 5.1
Convert   Cancel   Help

When you attempt to open a document, FrameMaker makes sure that all the fonts the document uses and all the graphics files imported by reference are on your system and in the appropriate locations. If it fails to find any of the fonts, it will alert you and offer you the options of canceling or continuing to load the document. If you opt to continue, FrameMaker will replace the missing fonts with the best substitutes it can find on your system. If you save the document, the new fonts will permanently replace the originals. If it fails to find any of the linked graphics, FrameMaker opens a dialog box in which you can specify the location of the missing file. (See Chapter 13 for more information on importing graphics files.)

Loading ASCII Text Files

If the document you are attempting to open is an ASCII text file, FrameMaker will offer you two choices as to how the document should be broken into paragraphs:

1. Combine adjacent lines into paragraphs and break paragraphs only at blank lines.

2. Make each line a separate paragraph.

For most cases the first choice is more practical. Use the second option only for line-oriented material, such as program code.

Quicker Loading

FrameMaker 4.0 maintains a list of the five most recently opened documents at the bottom of the File menu. These files are numbered from most recently opened to least recently opened. You can load any of these documents by selecting it from the menu or pressing the corresponding number key.

Document Window

When you open or create a document, a document window opens. Initially, the document window is distinct from the main program window, but if you click on the document window's maximize button, the two windows combine into a single window, as in Figure 2.7. This eliminates one title bar, giving you more screen space in which to view and work on your document.

Figure 2.7   FrameMaker document window

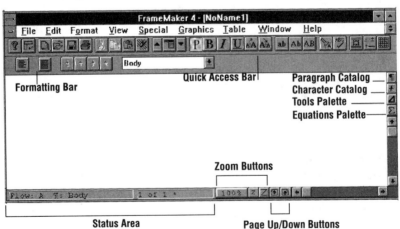

NOTE You can have several different FrameMaker documents open at one time. Each appears in its own document window. You can switch among the several document windows either by clicking on their respective title bars or by opening the Window menu and selecting the document name from the list that appears there.

The document window is the work space in which you create, edit, and format documents, so it is important to become familiar with all of its features, especially those unique to FrameMaker. Each of these features will be described briefly here, and in depth in the appropriate chapter.

The document window in FrameMaker 4.0 includes two conspicuous new features: the Quick Access Bar and the Formatting Bar. When you first install FrameMaker and open a document, these two tool bars appear at the top of the document window, between the menu bar and the horizontal ruler (see Figure 2.7). Either or both of the bars can be turned on or off via commands on the View menu (described later in this chapter), and the Quick Access Bar can optionally be switched to a vertical orientation. When the Quick Access Bar is oriented vertically, it becomes a free-floating palette that you can place anywhere on the screen.

Quick Access Bar

The Quick Access Bar initially appears as a horizontal row of buttons or icons above the document window. These buttons are designed, as the name indicates, to give you quick access to some of FrameMaker's most frequently used features. The Quick Access Bar is organized as five groups of buttons. The first ten buttons on the left (or on top in a vertical orientation) are called the *common access* group and are always available. These buttons are:

- Help with the Quick Access Bar
- Switch the Quick Access Bar between horizontal and vertical orientation
- New (start a new document)
- Open
- Save
- Print
- Cut
- Copy
- Paste
- Undo

The next two buttons switch among the four pages or groups of buttons that fill the remaining 14 positions on the bar. The four groups consist of one group for text editing, two groups for creating and editing graphics, and one group for working with tables. The functions of these buttons will be described in the appropriate chapters.

Formatting Bar

Below the Quick Access Bar is the Formatting Bar. The Formatting Bar can be turned on or off from the View menu, but it cannot be relocated. The Formatting Bar has tools for setting paragraph alignment, line spacing, and tab stops, and for applying paragraph format tags. The operation of these tools will be explained in Chapters 3 and 5.

Right-Margin Buttons

Along the upper right margin of the window, below the maximize/restore button, is a vertical row of four buttons:

- **The Paragraph Format Catalog button (¶)**—FrameMaker stores formats (sets of characteristics that can be applied to text) in catalogs. Paragraph formats control features such as the default font, line spacing, alignment, indentation, tabs, and the like. When you click on the ¶ button, a Paragraph Format Catalog window for the active document, such as that in Figure 2.8, opens. Paragraph formats are applied by clicking an insertion point in a paragraph, then selecting a format from the catalog. For a detailed discussion of paragraph formatting, consult Chapter 5.

Figure 2.8 Paragraph Format Catalog window

- **The Character Format Catalog button (ƒ)**—character formats work similarly to paragraph formats, except that they are applied to selected text within a paragraph, rather than to entire paragraphs. Character formats are used to apply characteristics such as boldface, italics, superscript, subscript, underline, strikethrough, and the like to selected text. When you click the *f* button, a Character Format Catalog window, such as that in Figure 2.9, appears. To apply a character format, select one or more characters, then select a format from the catalog. For a detailed discussion of character formats, consult Chapter 5.

Figure 2.9   Character Format Catalog window

■ **The Tools button** (△)—opens the Tools Palette (Figure 2.10) used for creating and editing graphics. For a detailed discussion of the Tools Palette and FrameMaker's graphics features, consult Chapter 12.

Figure 2.10   Tools Palette

■ **The Equation button** (∑)—opens the Equations Palette (Figure 2.11), used to create and edit equations and mathematical formulas. For a detailed discussion of FrameMaker's equation features, consult Chapter 21.

Figure 2.11 Equations Palette

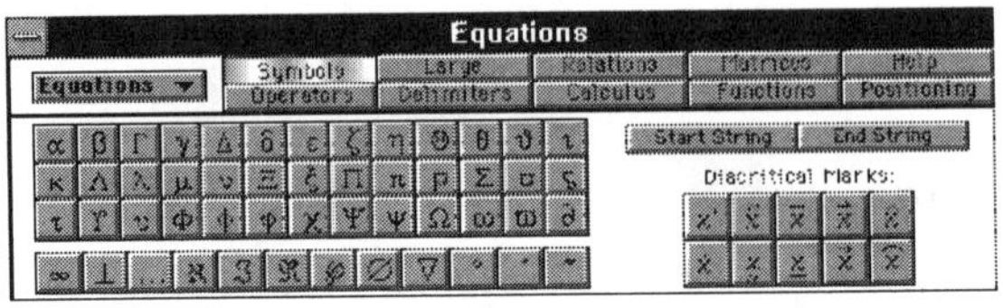

Below the Equation button are the up/down scroll arrow and scroll box for the document window. These control vertical scrolling, as in any Windows application. The scroll bars in FrameMaker behave a bit differently from those in most Windows applications, as they cause the screen to scroll through *all* the pages in the current document, not just the current page. The various methods for navigating through the pages of a FrameMaker document will be described in detail later in this chapter.

Lower-Margin Buttons

Along the lower margin of the window are the status bar and several more control buttons. The status bar displays information about your current location in the document. If an insertion point (the text cursor) is active, the left section of the status bar displays the flow tag and paragraph format tag for the paragraph where the insertion point is located; otherwise, this area is blank. (For an explanation of text flow, see Chapter 7; for paragraph format tags, see Chapter 5.) To the right of the tag area, the current page number and page count for the document are displayed.

Zoom Buttons

To the right of the status bar are three Zoom buttons that control the scale at which your document is displayed in the document window. The first, which displays a percentage indicating the current scale of the display, allows you to select one of ten different percentage scales from a pop-up menu (Figure 2.12). This menu includes three additional options:

Figure 2.12 Zoom pop-up menu

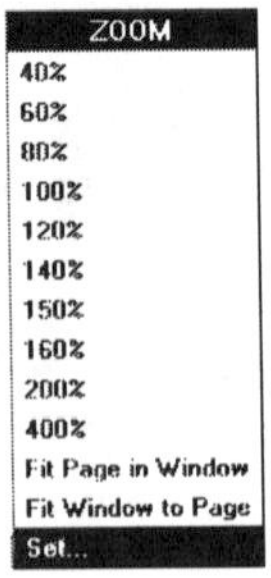

- **Fit Page in Window**—scales the display so that one complete page fits in the document window at its current size.

- **Fit Window to Page**—if possible, scales the document window to the size of one full page. This is possible only if the scale for the document is such that a full page fits entirely on the screen.

- **Set**—selects the scaling percentages that appear in the pop-up menu. The acceptable range of percentages is from 25% to 1600%. This is an extremely useful feature that I have not seen in any other desktop publishing application.

To the right of the %-scaling button are two more buttons labeled z and Z. Use these two buttons to step sequentially down or up through the same set of scaling options that are displayed in the pop-up menu.

Page Buttons

To the right of the three zoom buttons are two buttons for selecting the previous and next page, respectively. You can also move backward and forward through the document using the Page Up and Page Down keys on the cursor-control keypad or the scroll bars. To the right of these two buttons is the horizontal scroll bar for the document window. Yet another way to get around in a FrameMaker document is to use the **Go to Page** command on the View menu. This command opens a dialog box such as that in Figure 2.13, which you can use to jump to a specific page, the page with the insertion point, or a specific line number.

Figure 2.13 Go To Page dialog box

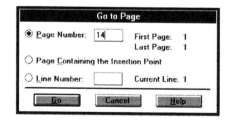

Rulers

Rulers are displayed along the top and left sides of the document window. The rulers are on by default, but you can turn them off by unchecking the **Rulers** option on the View menu. By default, the rulers are calibrated in inches, but a number of other measuring units can be selected via the **Options** item on the View menu (described next).

Keyboard Shortcuts

FrameMaker has keyboard shortcuts for most menu commands and other operations. These will be described throughout the book in Shift+ conjunction with their respective commands or operations. FrameMaker uses two kinds of keyboard shortcuts: standard Windows-type **Control**, **Alt**, and/or **Shift** key sequences, such as **Ctrl+V**, and Escape sequences, such as **Esc x Y z**. In the first example, you would press and hold the **Control** key and then press **v**. In the second example, you would press and release the **Escape** key, then press **x**, **Shift+Y**, and **z** in secession. Escape sequences are case sensitive; that is, **Esc x Y z** is not the same as **Esc x y z**.

View Menu

Several aspects of the appearance of the Document Window can be controlled from the View menu (Figure 2.14). The View menu contains the following options:

Figure 2.14   View menu

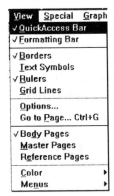

- ■ **Quick Access Bar**—toggles the Quick Access Bar on or off, as described earlier.

- ■ **Formatting Bar**—toggles the Formatting Bar on or off, as described earlier.

- ■ **Borders**—turns the dotted borders around text columns and picture boxes on and off.

- ■ **Text Symbols**—makes nonprinting characters such as tabs, paragraph marks, line breaks, frame anchors, and the like visible.

- ■ **Grid Lines**—displays a dotted grid to help you align objects on the page.

The spacing of the grid lines can be set with the **Options** command (see following).

■ **Options**—opens the View Options dialog box (Figure 2.15). The View Options will be discussed in the following section.

■ **Go to Page**—use this command to jump to another page in your document, as described previously.

Body Pages, Master Pages, and Reference Pages

The next three items on the View menu switch the display among the three types of pages that make up a FrameMaker document: Body Pages, Master Pages, and Reference Pages. Body pages are the actual pages of your document, containing the text and graphics that will be printed. Master pages are guides that control the layout of body pages. A master page typically includes text columns and elements such as headers, footers, and page numbers. A document can have as many as 100 different master pages. When you make changes in a master page, for example, changing the size and position of text columns or the page numbering format, all the body pages based on that master page will change accordingly. The third type of page, a reference page, is a storage space for frequently used page elements, such as rules, other recurring graphics, and the like. The elements stored on a reference page can be imported *by reference* into body pages, saving you the trouble of creating or importing multiple copies of these frequently used items. Reference pages also perform special functions in generated lists, indexes, and hypertext documents. All FrameMaker documents have body pages and master pages. Reference pages are optional. When you first load a FrameMaker document, the view will be set to body pages.

We will examine the creation and application of master and reference pages in detail in the next and subsequent chapters.

Color

This item determines how colors will be displayed in multi-color publications and allows you to select a color model and create new colors. These operations will be described in detail in Chapter 15.

Menus

A new feature of FrameMaker 4.0, this command opens a submenu with three options: **Complete**, **Quick**, and **Modify**. The **Complete** option displays all the available commands on the FrameMaker menus. This is the default setting when you install FrameMaker. If you need to use all of the program's features, this is the setting to use. The **Quick** option displays a more limited selection of commands. If you write and/or format documents but don't design them (for example, you work as a writer or editor in a company where an art or design director creates the templates and paragraph formats), the commands provided by the **Quick** option will probably be adequate for your needs. Use the third option, **Modify**, to load an alternate set of menus if one is available. FrameMaker comes with a sample alternate menu set called SAMPLE.CFG, which is located in your \FMINIT directory. To create your own alternative menu set, you must write an ASCII text file with the appropriate commands. Examine the SAMPLE.CFG file and consult the on-line manual *Customizing Frame Products* for details.

View Options

The checkboxes in the View Options dialog box (Figure 2.15) duplicate many of the commands on the View menu and reflect their current settings. The dialog box contains additional settings that reflect the appearance and behavior of the document window.

- **Display Units**—selects the unit of measure used throughout the program. The options are centimeters, millimeters, inches, picas, points, didots, and ciceros. The type-specific units of measure are defined in Table 2.1.

This option does not change the unit of measure displayed on the rulers; that is controlled by the setting in the Rulers list box (see later).

N O T E

Figure 2.15 View Options dialog box

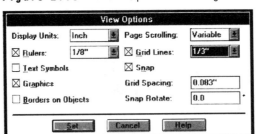

Table 2.1 Definitions of units of measure

Point	the basic unit of measure for type; one point = 0.01384 inch, or approximately 1/72 inch.

Pica   12 points, or approximately 1/6 inch.

Didot   a unit of typographic measure used in continental Europe in place of the point; equal to 0.0148 inch

Cicero   a unit of typographic measure used in continental Europe, equal to 12 didots or 0.178 inch. Slightly larger than a pica (first used in a 1485 edition of Cicero).

N O T E   Regardless of the unit of measure you select in the list box, you can specify any unit of measure when typing in dialog boxes elsewhere in the program and FrameMaker will translate to the unit you specified in the Display Units list box. To type another unit of measure, follow the conventions in Table 2.2:

Table 2.2   FrameMaker abbreviations for units of measure

To specify	Type after the number
centimeters	cm
inches	" or in
picas	pc, pi, or pica

To specify	Type after the number
millimeters	mm
didots	dd
ciceros	cc or cicero

■ **Page Scrolling**—controls movement from page to page in the document window. There are four options:

   Variable—displays the pages in a grid, depending on the scale at which you have chosen to view the pages and the size of your screen, and scrolls either horizontally or vertically, as necessary, when you select the next or previous page or a specific page number.

   Vertical—displays the pages in a vertical column and scrolls up or down to move to the next or previous page or a specified page number.

   Horizontal—displays the pages in a horizontal row and scrolls left or right to move to the next or previous page or a specified page number.

Facing Pages—displays two pages side by side in the document window. You may need to rescale the page size using the zoom buttons and/or resize the document window to accommodate two pages on the screen.

When more than one page is displayed on the screen, the active page is surrounded by a heavy black border. When you scroll to a different page that is already fully visible on the screen, the display doesn't move, and the black border simply moves to the new page.

- **Rulers**—the check box turns the rulers on and off for the active document, as does the separate Rulers menu item, described earlier. The drop-down list box to the right of the check box allows you to select from a number of different calibrations for the rulers.

- **Grid Lines**—the check box turns the grid on and off for the active document, as does the separate Grid menu item, described earlier. The drop-down list box to the right of the check box allows you to select from a number of different settings for the spacing of the grid lines.

- **Snap**—the snap grid is an invisible, "magnetic" grid, distinct from the one controlled by the Grid Lines settings. The snap grid is used in conjunction with the drawing tools on the Tools Palette (see Chapter 12 for a detailed explanation). Use the check box to turn the snap grid on or off, and type a number and unit of measurement in the text box at the right to specify the spacing of the snap grid lines. You can also set a snap rotate property. This number, expressed in degrees, causes graphic objects to rotate by the specified increment. If the number is zero, graphic objects will rotate smoothly, with no snap.

- **Text Symbols**—turns the display of nonprinting characters on and off, as does the separate Text Symbols menu item described previously.

- **Graphics**—turns the display of graphics on and off. Turning off the display of graphics speeds up the redrawing of pages when scrolling or paging through the document, and may be helpful when you are interested primarily in editing or formatting text.

- **Borders on Objects**—turns the borders around text columns and picture boxes on and off, as does the separate Borders menu item described previously.

Printing Your Documents

One of the minor joys of using Windows is that you don't have to install and configure a printer driver for every new application you install (nor do applications developers have to spend their time writing drivers for every printer on the market). If you have a PostScript or PCL printer installed and working properly under Windows 3.1, printing from FrameMaker should be hassle-free.

As with most Windows applications, FrameMaker's Print command can be found on the File menu. When you select this command, the Print Document dialog box (Figure 2.16) appears. Most of the options in this dialog box will be fairly self-explanatory to experienced users. The options in the Print Document dialog box allow you to do the following:

- Print the full document.

- Print a selected range of pages.

- Select the number of copies to print.

- Select the scale at which to print the document.

- Print your document as a series of thumbnails—reduced pages printed four or more to the page. (The maximum number of thumbnails per page is 256.)

- Print to a file. (Use this option to send output from FrameMaker to a remote printer or a service bureau.)

- Print only odd- or even-numbered pages, or both (allows a double-sided document to be printed on a normal printer by running the pages through once for the odd-numbered pages then flipped and run through again for the even numbers).

- Collate multiple copies of your document.

- Print your document in reverse page order (useful if your printer delivers pages face up or if you are printing a double-sided document in two passes).

- Print low-resolution images for quicker printing (this affects graphics only, not text).

- Print your document with registration marks and crop marks (this requires that your document size be smaller than the physical page you're printing on—if this is not the case, FrameMaker will warn you and ask for your permission to continue).

- Print spot colors as black and white.

- Print or set up color separations.

(Operations involving spot colors and color separations will be explained in Chapter 15.)

Figure 2.16 The Print Document dialog box

Print Document

Print Page Range:
- ⦿ All
- ○ Start Page: 1
- End Page: 1

Copies: 1
Scale: 100%

☐ Thumbnails · Rows: 2
Cols: 2

☐ Print Only To File: [   ]

☒ Odd-Numbered Pages
☒ Even-Numbered Pages
☒ Collate
☒ Last Sheet First
☐ Low-Resolution Images
☐ Registration Marks
☐ Skip Blank Pages
☐ Spot Color As Black/White

☐ Print Separations
[Set Up Separations...]

[Print] [Cancel] [Setup...] [Help]

Setup

When you click the setup button in the Print dialog box, you open the standard Windows Printer Setup dialog box. This is the same dialog box you see when you select **Printers** from the Windows Control Panel and then click the **Setup** button in the Printers dialog box. You can use this dialog box to select your paper source, paper size, orientation, and number of copies to print, if the default settings for these parameters are not satisfactory for your document. More detailed settings can be found behind the **Options** button, but if you have set up your printer correctly under Windows, there will be no need to change its configuration from within FrameMaker. For more information on printer installation and setup, consult the *Microsoft Windows User's Guide.*

NOTE Wherever there is a potential conflict between settings in FrameMaker's Print dialog box and the Windows Print Setup dialog, the FrameMaker settings take precedence. For example, if you specify three copies at a scale of 75% in the FrameMaker Print dialog box, that is what you will get, even though the Windows Print Setup calls for one copy at 100%. Also, unlike most desktop publishing or word processing applications, FrameMaker permits portrait and landscape pages to be mixed in a single document. The settings of the individual pages will take precedence over the portrait/landscape setting in the Print Setup dialog.

NOTE Frame Technology's release notes indicate that there were a variety of printing problems using the drivers supplied with Windows 3.0, so if you have not already done so, you should probably upgrade to Windows 3.1. Although I hate to act as a salesman for Chairman Bill, it is probably a good idea to upgrade to 3.1 on general principles. Windows 3.1 is an altogether more robust program, handles DOS programs better, and is far less prone to those irritating "Unrecoverable Application Errors."

Saving Documents—Four File Formats

When you save a FrameMaker document for the first time, or save it under a different name with the **Save As** option, you are offered four choices of file format shown in the list box at the bottom of the Save As dialog box (Figure 2.17).

- **Normal**—this is the basic FrameMaker document format, and the one you should use in most situations. It incorporates all formatting and graphics in the most compact format and can be opened by versions of FrameMaker on all platforms.

Figure 2.17 The Save As dialog box

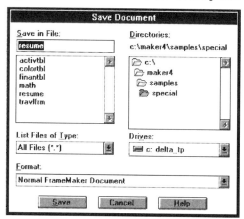

- **View Only**—this option is used to lock a document so that it can be loaded and read in FrameMaker or FrameReader but not edited. This is the option you would use to save a hypertext document for on-line or on-disk distribution (see Chapter 23 for information on creating hypertext documents). When you lock a document, or load a previously locked document, the catalog and palette buttons disappear from the right margin of the document window and the menu titles on the menu bar change to File, Edit, Navigation, Window, and Help. Use the commands on the Navigation menu to move around in the locked document.

N O T E

You can unlock a locked document in FrameMaker by pressing **Esc F 1 k** (press the keys successively, do not hold them all down at once, and press **Shift** with the **F**).

- **Text Only**—saves only the text from your document, in ASCII format. This option strips all formatting information and graphics from the document. If you use it, be sure to give the document the .TXT extension— FrameMaker does not do this automatically—to avoid overwriting an existing version of your document.

- **Interchange Format (MIF)**—This option saves the file as a Maker Interchange Format (MIF) file. A MIF file includes the complete FrameMaker document, with all formatting information and graphics, in an ASCII format. MIF files are used when it is desirable or necessary to transfer files in ASCII format, for example over standard phone lines or on certain networks that use communications protocols that may corrupt FrameMaker binary files. MIF files are also useful when you want to write a program to perform some operation on a large number of FrameMaker documents. For example, some third-party database publishers that work in conjunction with FrameMaker manipulate FrameMaker documents in MIF format. If you save a file in MIF format, *be sure* to give it the MIF extension—FrameMaker does not do this automatically. It is *not* necessary to save files in MIF format to move them to versions of FrameMaker running on different hardware platforms or operating systems, although it may be useful to do so if you experience difficulties with such transfers.

Reverting to the Previous Version

If you make changes in a FrameMaker document that prove unsatisfactory, you can revert to the last saved version of the document by selecting **Revert to Saved** from the File menu. If you have selected the **Autosave** option in the Document Preferences dialog box (described later in this chapter), the program will revert to the last version you *manually* saved, *not* to the autosaved version.

Undoing the Last Command

Most FrameMaker commands can be reversed by selecting **Undo** from the Edit menu or using the keyboard shortcut **Ctrl+Z**. You must use the **Undo** command immediately after the command you want to reverse, without any intervening commands. Some FrameMaker commands cannot be undone, but the program will give you adequate warning before executing one of these commands. If you are uncertain about the outcome of such a command, be sure to save your work before using it, so that you can use the **Revert to Saved** command, as described previously.

Setting Your Preferences

Selecting the **Preference** option on the File menu opens the Preferences dialog box (Figure 2.18). The settings in this dialog box control several minor aspects of the program's behavior.

Figure 2.18 Preferences dialog box

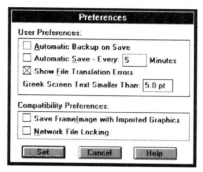

In addition to those in the Preferences dialog box, many aspects of FrameMaker's operation are affected by settings in the FRAME.INI file, an ASCII file created when you first install FrameMaker and updated by the program periodically.

N O T E

Automatically Saving or Backing Up Your Work

Two options in the Preferences dialog box allow you to automatically save the last version of your document as a backup whenever you save a new version and/or to automatically save your work periodically, after a time interval you specify. If you check the **Automatic Backup on Save** box, whenever you save your work, the previous version is saved with the name %FILENAM.DOC, where FILENAM represents the first seven letters of the original file name. If you check the **Automatic Save–Every: __ Minutes** box, FrameMaker will periodically save your work with the file name $FILENAM.DOC, where FILENAM again represents the first seven letters of the original file name. The latter option is particularly helpful if you tend to become engrossed in your work and forget to save regularly—it can save you a lot of frustration if a power failure or a mysterious Unrecoverable Application Error brings your system to a halt. When you save your work manually, using the **Save** or **Save As** command, FrameMaker automatically erases the autosave file.

Show File Translation Errors

Use this option if you import text created in other programs into your FrameMaker documents. If any errors occur when importing a file, FrameMaker displays them in a FrameMaker Console window.

 If you use TrueType fonts with Windows 3.1, you will get a console window showing the font substitutions every time you open a file with PostScript fonts. This happens even in totally irrelevant cases, such as the FrameMaker Help files and online documents. As a result, you may **N O T E** want to disable this option.

Greeking Text

To *Greek* text, in this context, means to display small text on the screen as a series of gray bars, rather than trying to render the characters accurately. Specify a point size below which text will be Greeked. The size you choose will depend on the size and resolution of your display. Six-point type may be perfectly legible on a 17" screen at 1024 × 768, but quite hopeless on a 640 × 480, 14" standard VGA monitor. Don't waste your computer's processing power trying to render text that will be illegible anyhow.

Creating a FrameImage Facet for Imported Graphics

Checking this option creates a FrameImage facet, a cross-platform compatible graphics format similar to the Sun Raster format, for imported graphics that use a format that is unique to Windows, such as a Windows Metafile. This ensures that when you transfer your FrameMaker documents to other platforms, your graphics will be displayed and printed correctly. FrameMaker also creates FrameImage facets for graphics imported via OLE (Windows Object Linking and Embedding). If your documents will be edited and printed only on the Windows platform, you can dispense with this option. To see the facets used for an imported graphic, select the graphic, then open the Graphics menu and select **Object Properties**. The Facets text box will show the facets for the selected graphic.

Locking Network Files

When several users have access to the same FrameMaker documents over a network, two or more might try to edit the same document at the same time, resulting in confusion and wasted effort. You can prevent another network user from editing the same document that you are currently working on by checking the **Network File Locking** box. When this option is active, FrameMaker creates a special file with the name of the document you are currently editing and the extension .LCK. When other users attempt to open the same document, FrameMaker will warn them that the document is already open for editing. It will allow them to open a view-only version of the document, but will not prevent them from opening and editing the original if they so choose.

CHAPTER 3

Creating and Editing Text

There is nothing special about creating and editing text in FrameMaker, and that's good news. Other PC/Windows desktop publishing programs assume that you will create text in a separate word processing program and then import it into the publishing application for layout and formatting. As a result, these programs have rather limited and, in some cases, cumbersome text editing facilities. FrameMaker has no such limitations. Although you can import text into FrameMaker from all major PC word processing applications (an essential feature for freelance editors such as the author, and for those who are emotionally attached to their word processors), the program was designed to be a complete WYSIWYG word processor, not just a layout and formatting program with limited editing facilities.

Creating Text

To begin entering text in a FrameMaker document, open an existing document or start a new one with the **New** option on the File menu (**Ctrl+N**). Click with the mouse in a text column (represented on-screen by a dotted outline) to create an insertion point, which appears as a blinking vertical line, and start typing. If there is already some text in the document, you can place the insertion point anywhere in the text. If the document is empty, the insertion point will automatically appear at the top left margin of the first text column, before the end-of-flow symbol (§).

NOTE

You may encounter text strings in a FrameMaker document in which you cannot place an insertion point. For example, you will probably not be able to place an insertion point in a header or footer in most documents. This is because these elements are in the background—

they are entered on master pages and are echoed on body pages based on those master pages. To create or edit headers and footers or other background elements, you must work on the appropriate master pages, as explained in Chapter 4. Other text strings in which you can't place an insertion point include variables and cross-references. If you attempt to place an insertion point in a word and a whole word or phrase is highlighted, it is probably a variable or cross-reference. To work on a variable or cross-reference, open the Special menu and select the appropriate command, then follow the instructions in Chapter 9 or 10.

As you type, the text will flow and wrap as you would expect in a word processor. If there are multiple text columns on the page, text will flow from the bottom of the first column to the top of the second, and so on. When the page is full, a new page will be automatically created.

Actually, how text will flow from column to column and page to page when you type depends on the settings of the flow tags for the document you're working on. This topic forms the subject of Chapter 7. The preceding description applies to a document with a single, connected flow, which is the default when you create a new document.

Navigating in Text

You can move the insertion point to any point on the current page by clicking with the left mouse button at the desired location. In addition, you can navigate through your document using the key combinations in Table 3.1.

Several of these key combinations have been changed from Frame-Maker 3.0.

Table 3.1 FrameMaker keyboard shortcuts

To go to	Press
Next character	**Right Arrow**
Previous character	**Left Arrow**
Beginning of word	**Ctrl+Left Arrow**
End of word	**Ctrl+Right Arrow**

To go to	Press
Beginning of next word	**Esc b w**
Beginning of line	**Home**
End of line	**End**
Previous line	**Up Arrow**
Next line	**Down Arrow**
Beginning of sentence	**Ctrl+Home**
End of sentence	**Ctrl+End**
Beginning of next sentence	**Esc b p**
Beginning of paragraph	**Ctrl+Up Arrow**
End of paragraph	**Ctrl+Down Arrow**
Top of column	**Ctrl+Page Up**
Bottom of column	**Ctrl+Page Down**
Beginning of flow	**Shift+Alt+Page Up**
End of flow	**Shift+Alt+Page Down**

Typing Special Characters

Our PC keyboards are descended from the standard typewriter keyboard. They have evolved to include function keys, cursor-control keys, and separate numeric keypads, but as far as the keys that type characters are concerned, they are not much different from their ancestors. Unfortunately, this means that the PC keyboard doesn't include keys for most of the special characters required for proper typesetting of ordinary text, much less the special characters required for the various technical and scientific disciplines.

Many special characters are included in the Symbol and Zapf Dingbats fonts that are standard with most PostScript printers or in the similar TrueType fonts that are included in Windows 3.1. Additional character sets for specific disciplines, sometimes referred to as *pi fonts*, are available from various type vendors. To type characters from a special font, select the desired font by opening the Format menu and selecting **Font**, then type the appropriate keystrokes or ANSI codes. (To type a character's ANSI code, hold the **Alt** key and type the code on the numeric keypad; be sure to type the leading zero that is part of the code.) Alternately, you can apply a character format (see Chapter 5) to apply a different font to selected characters.

Even a conventional text font has a great many more characters than are found on a conventional keyboard. To access the special characters that are part of most standard text fonts, you can use a keyboard shortcut (in some cases, more than one) that is specific to FrameMaker, or you can type the character's ANSI code, by holding the **Alt** key and typing the code number on the numeric keypad. Occasionally, you may have to type a special character in a dialog box, as, for example, when performing a search or replace. The ANSI code will work in many instances, but in some cases you must type a symbolic code or a hexadecimal code prefaced by **\x** (a convention borrowed from the C programming language). Some of the most common special characters and their codes and keyboard shortcuts are shown in Table 3.2. For a complete listing, consult Appendix 1.

Table 3.2   FrameMaker special character keyboard shortcuts and ANSI codes

Character/Name	Keyboard Shortcut(s)	ANSI Code	Hex Code	Symbolic Code
• bullet	Ctrl+b or Ctrl+q %	0149	—	\b
– En dash	Ctrl+q Shift+p	0150	\xd0	\=
— Em dash	Ctrl+q Shift+q	0151	\xd1	\m
discretionary hyphen	Ctrl+hyphen	—	\x04	\-
Suppress hyphenation	Esc n s	—	\x05	_
nonbreaking hyphen	Esc hyphen h	—	\x15	\+
line break	Ctrl+Alt+Enter or Shift+Enter	—	\x09	\r
Numeric space	Esc space 1	—	\x10	\s#
Nonbreaking space	Ctrl+space or Esc space h	—	\x11	\space
Thin space	Esc space t	—	\x12	\st
En space	Esc space n	—	\x13	\sn
Em space	Esc space m	—	\x14	\sm
… Ellipsis	Ctrl+q Shift+i	0133	\xc9	\e
† Dagger	Ctrl+q space	0134	\xa0	\d
‡ Double dagger	Ctrl+q `	0135	\xe0	\D

Character/Name	Keyboard Shortcut(s)	ANSI Code	Hex Code	Symbolic Code
'Single-quote	**Ctrl+q Shift+t**	0145	\xd4	\"
"Double-quote left	**Ctrl+Alt+`** or **Ctrl+q Shift+r**	0147	\xd2	\`
" Double-quote right	**Ctrl+Alt+'** or **Ctrl+q Shift+s**	0148	\xd3	\'

N O T E

You can avoid the necessity of typing keyboard shortcuts or special codes for quotations marks by turning on the **Smart Quotes** feature, described later.

N O T E

When in doubt, you can find the keymapping and ANSI codes for the characters in all of the fonts installed on your system via the Windows 3.1 Character Map accessory. Open this accessory, select the font of interest, move the mouse pointer to any character, and press and hold the left mouse button. The keystroke(s) for the selected character will appear in the lower right corner of the Character Map window. You can also use the Character Map accessory to copy characters from a selected font to the Windows clipboard and then paste them into a document in FrameMaker or another Windows application.

Smart Quotes and Smart Spaces

Two settings in the Document Properties dialog box (accessed via the **Document** option on the Format menu) affect the way you type quotation marks and spaces. If you check **Smart Quotes**, FrameMaker automatically creates true left or right quotation marks (single or double), as appropriate, when you press the " or ' key. This saves you the trouble of using the rather awkward keyboard shortcuts. Of course, the font you're using must *have* true left and right quotes for this to work. You can still type straight single or double quotes if you want them, for example to represent feet and inches or minutes and seconds, by typing **Ctrl+'** and **Esc "**.

If you check **Smart Spaces**, FrameMaker will allow you to type only a single space between words or sentences (this is the convention in typeset proportionally spaced text). This is handy if you are unable to cure yourself of the old typewriter habit of typing two spaces after a period. (The **Smart Spaces** setting does not affect non-breaking spaces or fixed-width spaces.)

Unfortunately, the **Smart Quotes** and **Smart Spaces** settings do not work on text that is being imported into FrameMaker, a rather serious omission, considering that Ventura and PageMaker have had automatic quote conversion when importing text for years. The omission is mitigated to some extent by the ability to convert quotes and delete redundant spaces when spell checking text (see Chapter 11).

Controlling Line Breaks

Normally, FrameMaker automatically breaks lines as you type or when you import text and flow it into text columns. How lines break will be determined by the alignment, hyphenation, word spacing, and other aspects of text formatting, which will be covered in Chapter 5. However, there are two additional ways of controlling line breaks that you need to be aware of:

1. You can force a line break anywhere in text by typing **Shift+Enter**. Use this option to start a new line without starting a new paragraph. If you force a line break in justified text, the line ending with the break will not be justified.

2. You can limit the selection of characters after which a line break is allowed. To do this, open the Format menu and select **Document (Esc o d)** to display the Document Properties dialog box (see Figure 3.1). In the center of the dialog box is a text box labeled "Allow Line Breaks After." Initially this box shows the characters "/", "-", "\=" (en dash), and "\m" (em dash). This means that a pair of words connected by a forward slash, hyphen, en dash, or em dash can be broken after that character if it falls near the end of a line. You can add to or delete from this list to modify the set of characters after which line breaks can occur. For example, if you wanted such combinations as "and/or" and "125/64" kept together, you would delete the "/" from the list. If you were writing a book or article about programming, in which you used many variable names that included the underscore character ("_") and you wanted to allow such combinations to be broken, you would add the "_" to the list.

Hyphenation

FrameMaker can automatically hyphenate your text as required, using its spell checker dictionaries and a collection of rules. Automatic hyphenation is turned on and hyphenation characteristics are selected as part of a Paragraph Format, and so will be covered in detail in Chapter 5. In addition to automatic hyphenation, there are three special characters that you can type to affect hyphenation:

Figure 3.1 Document Properties dialog box

```
┌─────────────────────────────────────────────────┐
│              Document Properties                  │
│ Numbering:                                        │
│   1st Page #: │1    │   Page # Style: │Numeric  (4)│▼│
│   ☐ Restart Paragraph Numbering                   │
│ Text:                                             │
│   ☒ Smart Quotes       ☒ Smart Spaces             │
│   Allow Line Breaks After:  │/ - \= \m          │  │
│   Before Saving & Printing: │Delete Empty Pages │▼│
│            Superscript:  Subscript:  Small Caps:  │
│   Size:    │65.0%│      │65.0%│     │80.0%│       │
│   Offset:  │40.0%│      │25.0%│                   │
│                                                   │
│        [ Apply ]   [ Cancel ]   [ Help ]          │
└─────────────────────────────────────────────────┘
```

■ **Non-breaking hyphen (Esc hyphen h)**—this character ties together a hyphenated word so that the two parts do not split across a line break.

■ **Discretionary hyphen (Ctrl+hyphen)**—adds a hyphenation point to a word to override the hyphenation points supplied by FrameMaker's dictionaries. The word will only be hyphenated if automatic hyphenation is on and the word is positioned so as to fall across a line break.

■ **Suppress hyphenation (Esc n s)**—place this character immediately before a word to prevent FrameMaker from hyphenating the word.

Em Dashes, En Dashes, and Other Typographic Niceties—If you have come to the desktop publishing world from some other discipline and haven't picked up any training in the traditions and conventions of typography along the way, you may be confused about when to use some of the special characters that FrameMaker places at your disposal. In particular, the proper use of the hyphen and the various dashes seem to engender confusion in typographic tyros.

The hyphen is used to separate the syllables of a word that breaks at the end of a line (performed automatically by FrameMaker), to create compound adjectives, or to create other types of hyphenated compound words.

The em dash (—), so named because it is one *em* in width, is a punctuation mark used to mark a separation or break in text.

(The *em* is a horizontal unit of typographic measure equal to the height in points of the font to which it belongs. It is so named because it was once the custom in metal typography to cast a capital *M* on a square body; hence the width of the *M* was equal to the height of the font.) Strunk and White say that the dash is "stronger than a comma, less formal than a colon, and more relaxed than parentheses" (William Strunk, Jr., and E.B. White. *The Elements of Style,* Third Edition, New York, MacMillan Publishing Co., Inc., 1979). On a typewriter, two hyphens (--) are used to represent an em dash. One of the surest signs of a beginning desktop publisher is the use of a double hyphen in typeset text where an em dash is required. If you are using a monospaced typewriter font such as Courier or Letter Gothic, the double hyphen may be acceptable, but in any proportionally spaced font, use an em dash wherever a dash is used as punctuation in a sentence. The em dash is sometimes set with no spaces between it and adjoining words—like this, and it is sometimes set off with thin spaces — like this. Which you should use is a matter of style, but be consistent.

The en dash (–), which is one half the width of the em dash, is used in place of the word "to" in a range of numbers, for example, 1975–1982, pages 23–27, or 0.5–1.5 volts. It is also sometimes used in figure and page numbering schemes, such as page 3–5 (meaning Chapter 3, page 5) or Figure 3–12 (meaning Chapter 3, Figure 12).

The minus sign (−) is different from all of the above. A true minus sign can be found in the PostScript symbol font, where it maps to the hyphen key.

Another problem that may reveal a novice is the use of three periods in place of an ellipsis (…). This works on a typewriter or in a monospaced font, but not in proportionally spaced type. Three periods may be spaced differently depending on the justification of the line they're in, and may even get separated across a line break. Be sure to use a true ellipsis wherever required.

Several Kinds of Spaces

Among the special characters listed above, you may have noticed several kinds of spaces in addition to the standard space that is produced by pressing the space bar. A *nonbreaking space* is used to tie two or more words together so that they both appear on the same side of a line or page break. The nonbreaking space is not fixed in size; it may shrink, or expand, depending on the requirements imposed by justification and word spacing. The other special spaces, although they are also nonbreaking, are fixed in size. The largest, the *em space*, is equal in width to the height of the font to which it belongs. The *en space* is half the width of the em space, and the thin space is one-twelfth the width of the em space. The *thin space* is typically used between a figure and a unit of measurement, for example 250 mA or 500 kHz. Some typesetters place thin spaces between em dashes and surrounding characters. The final type, the *numeric space*, is the width of the zero in the selected font (figures or numerals are normally monospaced, even though the remainder of the font is proportionally spaced, so, in most cases, the numeric space is the same width as any of the numerals in the font). Numeric spaces can be used as an alternative to tabs for aligning figures.

Formatting as You Type

You can format text as you type, by *tagging* it with paragraph and character formats, or you can leave formatting for later. Once you have applied a format tag to a paragraph, all the subsequent paragraphs you start by pressing the **Enter** key inherit that format. When you start typing in a new document, your text receives the default Body paragraph tag. For detailed information on creating and using paragraph formats, consult Chapter 5.

You can also perform some text formatting with the tools on the Formatting Bar (see Figure 3.2). If the Formatting Bar is not visible on your FrameMaker screen, open the View menu and select it. The tools on the Formatting Bar can be used to set paragraph alignment, line spacing, and tab stops.

Figure 3.2 Formatting Bar

It is best to use the Formatting Bar only for occasional one-of-a-kind paragraphs. In order to maintain consistency, it is better, in most cases, to create and use paragraph and character formats to control the appearance of your type.

N O T E

Aligning Text

The left-most tool on the Formatting Bar is the Alignment tool. To use this tool, place an insertion point in a paragraph or select a group of contiguous paragraphs, and click on the tool. A small pop-up menu will appear below the tool. Select one of the four alignment options from the menu: **Left**, **Center**, **Right**, or **Justify**.

Setting Line Spacing

The next tool sets line spacing (vertical spacing between lines). To use this tool, place an insertion point in a paragraph or select a group of contiguous paragraphs, and click on the tool. A small pop-up menu will appear below the tool. Select from among the following options: **Single**, **1.5**, **Double**, **Custom**, and **Space Between**. The first three options set the paragraph spacing to single-spaced, one-and-one-half spaced, or double-spaced, based on the line height specified in the paragraph format. Selecting the **Custom** option opens the dialog box in Figure 3.3, which shows you the point sizes for the other options and allows you to enter the point size for a custom line spacing. The **Fixed Line Spacing** check box, when checked, selects a fixed line height, measured from baseline to baseline. If the box is unchecked, the line height will vary, based on the height of the tallest characters in the line. Select **Space Between** to set the spacing between two or more paragraphs (two or more paragraphs must be selected in order to use this option). The **Space Between** option opens a dialog box similar to the Custom dialog box, from which you can select no space, one line, two lines, or enter a custom spacing in points.

Figure 3.3 Custom line-spacing dialog box

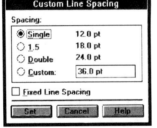

Setting Tab Stops

Before you can set tab stops, the ruler must be displayed at the top of the document Window—if it isn't, open the View menu and select **Rulers**. Click an insertion point in a paragraph, and the tab stops for that paragraph will appear below the top ruler (see Figure 3.4). To set a tab, select one of the four tab buttons on the Formatting Bar (left, center, right, or decimal), then move the mouse pointer just below the top ruler, to the point where it turns into a black arrow. Click and release the left mouse button to place a tab stop. The tab stop you place will affect only the paragraph where you have placed the insertion point. You can also drag the tab stop to a new position with the mouse. If you have **Snap** selected on the Graphics menu, you will be able to place tab stops only at the ruler ticks. To delete a tab stop, drag it down from the ruler and release the mouse button.

Figure 3.4 Top ruler, showing tab stops

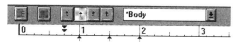

Editing Text

Selecting Text

As with most Windows word processing and page composition applications, you can select a block of text in FrameMaker by pressing the left mouse button and dragging to highlight the desired block, then releasing the button. In addition, you can use the mouse and keyboard actions in Table 3.3 to select specific portions of the text.

Table 3.3 Mouse and keyboard actions for selecting text

To...	Use this action
Select a block	Left click at the beginning of the block, and right click or **Shift**+click at the end of the block.
Select a word	Double-click on it.
Select a paragraph	Triple-click on it.
Add to a block	Right-click or **Shift**+click a new beginning or end for the block.
Remove text from a block	Right-click or **Shift**+click a new beginning or end for the block.
Select all text in a flow	Click in a text column and choose **Select All in Flow** from the Edit menu (keyboard shortcut: **Control+A**).
Deselect a block	Left click outside the block.

Cutting and Copying

Once you have selected a block of text, you can cut or copy it to the clipboard using the **Cut** or **Copy** command on the Edit menu. The keyboard shortcuts for these commands are **Ctrl+X** and **Ctrl+C** respectively. You can also delete a selected block of text by pressing the **Delete** or **Backspace** key, or selecting **Clear** from the Edit menu (**Esc e b**).

Deleting text does not copy the text to the clipboard, but you can recover the deleted text by immediately selecting **Undo** from the Edit menu or pressing **Control+Z**.

Pasting

Once a block of text has been cut or copied to the clipboard, you can paste it anywhere in your document, in another FrameMaker document (if you have more than one open), or even in another Windows application. The pasted text can be inserted into existing text, or it can overwrite an existing text block. To insert the text, click an insertion point where you want to place the text. To overwrite a block of text, select the block using one of the methods described above. To paste the text, select **Paste** from the Edit menu or press **Control+V**.

The **Cut**, **Copy**, and **Paste** functions can all be performed via buttons on the Quick Access Bar.

When you cut or copy text to the clipboard, it remains there until you perform another cut or copy. Hence, you can easily paste multiple copies of a block at different locations in a document.

When you cut or copy a full paragraph with its paragraph mark (¶) or a portion of a paragraph that includes the mark, the paragraph format information travels with the paragraph. When you paste such a block of text, its original format is retained. If you cut or copy a block of text that does not include a paragraph mark, it takes on the format of the location where it is pasted.

Quick-Copying Text

You can copy text from one location on the screen to another without using the clipboard. Both the text to be copied and the destination must be on the screen at the same time, although they can be in separate documents. The paragraph format is not copied with the text. To quick-copy text:

1. Place the insertion point at the destination.

2. Press and hold the **Alt** key and select the text to copy.

3. Release the **Alt** key.

Finding and Changing Text Strings

FrameMaker has extremely sophisticated facilities for finding and changing text (or virtually any other kind of item you are likely to find in a FrameMaker document). In fact, the **Find and Change** feature is so sophisticated that it requires its own chapter (Chapter 8).

SHORTCUT

Changing Capitalization—you can change the capitalization of a selected block of text via three buttons on the Quick Access Bar (see Figure 3.5). You can change the selected text to all lowercase, initial capitals (first letter of each word capitalized), or all caps.

Figure 3.5   Capitalization buttons on the Quick Access Bar

Importing Text

Although you can easily create text from scratch in FrameMaker, you can also import text files from many PC word processor and spreadsheet formats, and formats from other platforms as well. When you install FrameMaker on your system for the first time, you are asked to select the filters that the program will use to import text and graphics files. If you discover later that you need additional filters, you can install them by rerunning the FrameMaker setup program and checking only **Filters** in the Setup Options dialog box.

N O T E

If you need a filter that was not supplied with FrameMaker 4.0, check with the Frame Technology technical support department. The creation of filters is an ongoing process, and new filters may have been created since you obtained the program. If you have text in an obscure PC word processing format for which no FrameMaker filter is available, you may be able to use a third-party conversion utility, such as Software Bridge (Systems Compatibility Corp., 401 N. Wabash, Suite 600, Chicago, IL 60611, (312) 329-0700) to convert text to a more mainstream format, such as Microsoft Word or WordPerfect, before importing it into FrameMaker.

Also, a number of third-party vendors supply filters and conversion utilities for FrameMaker. A catalog of these products, *The Frame Connection Resource Guide*, is available to registered users from Frame Technology at no charge (call 1-800-U4FRAME). Be forewarned that some of these third-party filters are intended for large documentation shops and publishing operations that have hundreds of thousands of pages to be converted from older mainframe programs to FrameMaker on UNIX systems, and are priced accordingly; however, some of these software vendors also operate service bureaus that convert smaller documents at reasonable prices. Fortunately, most Windows users are unlikely to be confronted with such a daunting and costly task. If you have the necessary programming skills, Frame can provide you with C libraries that will help you write your own filters that will work on all FrameMaker-supported platforms.

Assuming that you have the necessary filters, importing text into FrameMaker is simple:

1. Open the File menu and select **Import**, then select **File** from the submenu (**Esc f i f**).

2. Place an insertion point in the document where you want to place the imported text.

3. Open the File menu and select **Import**.

4. Select the file you want to import from the list box. If FrameMaker recognizes the type of the file, it will import it automatically.

5. If FrameMaker doesn't recognize the file type, it will display the Unknown File Type dialog box (Figure 3.6). Pick the type of file you want to from the list of filters, then click on **Convert**.

Figure 3.6 Unknown File Type dialog box

If you're used to importing text files into other PC/Windows desktop publishing programs, you may find the way FrameMaker handles imported text a bit odd. When you import a text file from, for example, Word or WordPerfect, into a Frame-Maker template, you might expect FrameMaker to automatically flow the text into the template columns, as would happen in PageMaker or Ventura. But no, this is not what happens. FrameMaker starts a new page and places the imported text on that page, retaining whatever page format you gave it in your word processor. Hence, if you typed a document in Word as a doubled-spaced manuscript in 12-point courier with one-inch left and right margins, and import it into a FrameMaker document, that is exactly what you will get. To pour the text into the columns of your template, click an insertion point in your text, then open the Edit menu and select **Select All In Flow** (**Ctrl+A**), then **Cut** the text, place the insertion point in the template column, and **Paste** the text. Alternately, you can **Open** your word processor document and then import the page layout (and any other characteristics you want) from the template using the **Import>Formats** option on the File menu.

CHAPTER 4

Creating a Layout

In publication design, the term *layout* describes the placement of the various elements on the pages of a publication. Designing an appropriate layout for a publication is a nontrivial task, one best performed by a professional, or at least by someone with a bit of training and a good visual sense. Unfortunately, one of the downsides of the desktop revolution is that almost anyone may have the tools to produce a publication and may be called upon to do so, regardless of their talent or training (or lack thereof). If you find yourself needing to design the layout for a publication, without having first acquired either formal training or experience in this area, you may find some of the following suggestions helpful:

- The purpose of the publication design is to present the editorial matter (content) of the publication to the reader. It is *not* to show the reader how clever, creative, or original the designer is. Generally, the simpler the design that will achieve a particular goal, the better. A clean, uncluttered design is best.

- The design of the publication should reflect its content: Serious, formal publications need classic designs and typography; high-tech publications need a high-tech look; pop-culture publications should reflect (or presage) the latest trends in design and typography. If the form and the content clash, cognitive dissonance will result.

- Use a grid. The best-looking publications use a grid to align the various elements on the page. This results in clean, consistent, horizontal and vertical lines throughout the publication. (But don't be a "grid slave"— feel free to break the grid occasionally when you have an element, such as a large graphic, that won't conform to the grid, or when you want to draw the reader's attention to a particular element on the page.)

■   Be consistent. FrameMaker is a great help here.

■   If possible, become thoroughly familiar with the content of your publication before attempting to create a layout. Design all your master pages
before you start working with your copy. You still may run into tight spots
that require you to make modifications in your design, but if you have
designed your masters well, they will work for most pages without drastic
modifications.

■   The most difficult publications to lay out are those that use many figures,
tables, photographs, and other artwork and require that the textual references to the art and the art itself be on the same page (or at least the
same two-page spread). This is doubly difficult if you have no control over
the sizes and shapes of the artwork. The best approach in this case is to
create a flexible grid that can accommodate elements of different sizes. A
"three-on-two" format (the page divided into three columns, with two
combined into a single text column and the third reserved as an extra-
wide margin) can be useful in such situations. Depending on the requirements of individual pages, the margin can be left blank; small pieces of
artwork can be placed in the margin; artwork can be placed in the text
column with captions in the margin; or artwork can occupy the text column *and* the margin, with captions above or below.

■   Make ample use of white space, both in your page margins and the line
spacing of your text. The way the publication will be used should be taken
into account; for example, a normal-sized book that is to be held in the
hands and read in the conventional manner must have margins wide
enough to accommodate the reader's thumbs without covering the type.
A large format book that will be used on a table top can have narrower
margins. A book or other publication that is to be read through from
start to finish needs a typeface and line spacing that allow prolonged
reading without causing excessive eye fatigue. A catalog or directory can
get by with smaller, more condensed type and narrower columns.

There may be a desire on the part of management to keep printing costs
down by using smaller type and narrower columns to reduce page count,
but this, in most cases, is false economy. Your publication is going out into
the world to represent your company, your product, or your ideas (or
those of your clients). It will not serve this purpose well if it is cramped,
cluttered, and a torment to read.

■   Think in two-page spreads. Although FrameMaker treats documents on a
page-by-page basis, the readers are going to be looking at two-page
spreads, and the visual logic of the spreads will determine the way their

eyes move across the pages. Try to place artwork so that it aligns horizontally across the spread: Avoid the "checkerboard effect."

Use FrameMaker's **Facing Pages** scrolling option to view your two-page spreads frequently if your monitor isn't big enough to permit you to do all your work this way.

■ Don't think of your layout and your type specs as separate items. In particular, the width of your text columns and the size and style of your body type are directly related. If text lines are too short, sentences are broken up into small fragments and the reader has trouble maintaining continuity. If lines are too long, the reader has difficulty finding the beginning of the next line. Studies have shown that a good line length for most purposes is between 1.5 and 2.5 alphabets, or around 40–65 characters. You should therefore choose your body type size and style in conjunction with your text column width to achieve a result in this range. If you need to use a small text font in order to put a lot of information on a page, you should consider a two- or three-column format.

Using FrameMaker's Templates

The easiest way to create a layout for a new document is to use one that already exists, that is, one of FrameMaker's templates. The templates are sample documents, complete with body and master pages, and paragraph and character formats. FrameMaker comes with templates for letters, memos, Faxes, viewgraphs (overhead transparencies or slides), envelopes, business cards, outlines, reports, books, and newsletters. When you installed FrameMaker on your system, you were given the option of installing these templates. If you opted not to install the templates, you can always add them later, by rerunning the Setup program and checking only "Templates" in the Setup Options dialog box.

Assuming they are installed on your system, you will find the templates in a number of appropriately named subdirectories located under the \MAKER\TEMPLATE directory on the drive where FrameMaker is installed. To load one of the templates, select **New** on the File menu, use the Directory Selector box to go to the appropriate subdirectory, and double-click on the template you want to load.

If you're not sure which template you want, select the **Explore Standard Templates** button at the bottom of the dialog box. This button, new in FrameMaker 4.0, opens a hypertext document (like the FrameMaker help screens) that describes the purposes and features and displays thumbnail views of each of the templates. You can load any of the templates from the Explorer by selecting **Create** or **Show Sample**.

These two commands differ only in that the **Show Sample** loads a version of the template that contains some sample text, whereas **Create** loads a version that is relatively bare. After loading a template via the Explorer, you must select **Done** to clear the Explorer from the screen before you can work with the template.

The next step is to make whatever adjustments are necessary to adapt the template for your purposes. This may be as simple as importing a graphic file with your company logo to use on a letter or memo template, or it may involve making adjustments to the positions and size of the text columns, changes in paragraph formats, or the like. All techniques described in this and subsequent chapters for creating new documents are equally applicable to modifying templates.

Importing Layouts

A template is not just a set of blank page layouts; it includes paragraph, character, and table formats, variable definitions, cross-reference formats, reference pages, and other elements. If your primary concern is to create a usable document as quickly as possible, you may want to accept all of the baggage that comes with a FrameMaker template. Otherwise, there is no compelling reason to do so. If you just want to use the layouts (or any other feature) from a template, you can easily do so by importing them from the template into the document in which you want to use them.

1. Open the destination document (the one into which you want to import the layouts) and the template with the layouts you want to import.

2. Make the destination the active document.

3. Select the **Import>Formats** option from the File menu.

4. A dialog box like that in Figure 4.1 will appear. Check the aspects of the document you want to import, such as page layouts. Be sure to check *only* the appropriate characteristics; otherwise, you might drastically revise every aspect of your document in one fell swoop.

5. Open the list box that says "Current," meaning the document that's currently active, and select the document from which to import the formats (you can only select a document that's currently open).

6. Click the **Import** button to import the layouts from the source document into the destination document.

Figure 4.1 Import Formats dialog box

Import Formats

Import from Document: Current

Import and Update:

☒ Paragraph Formats   ☒ Reference Pages
☒ Character Formats   ☒ Variable Definitions
☒ Page Layouts   ☒ Cross-Reference Formats
☒ Table Formats   ☒ Conditional Text Settings
☒ Color Definitions   ☒ Math Definitions

While Updating, Remove:

☐ Manual Page Breaks   ☐ Other Format/Layout Overrides

Import [No Undo]   Cancel   Help

Of course, a template need not be one of those supplied with Frame-Maker. Any document that has layouts and formats you want to reuse can serve as a template, for example, another document that you created or one supplied by a client or an in-house art director or designer.

N O T E

Creating a Custom Document

For FrameMaker 3.0 Users: The commands pertaining to the creation and use of master pages, and to page layout in general, have been significantly changed in FrameMaker 4.0. Although the underlying concepts of master pages, body pages, template columns, background columns, flows, and the like remain essentially unchanged, the commands for manipulating these structures have undergone considerable reorganization and renaming. The Page menu has been removed, and the commands dealing with page layout have been redistributed among the Format, View, and Special menus. However, the changes are not simply a matter of renaming and reshuffling existing commands; there have been significant changes in the way the commands work, as will be described in the remainder of this chapter.

N O T E

The first step in creating a custom document is to design the basic blank page. Select **New** on the File menu and click the **Custom** button. This opens the Custom

Blank Paper dialog box (Figure 4.2). Use this dialog box to specify the size of the physical page size and the size and placement of the primary text column(s).

FrameMaker knows the dimensions of a number of common sheet sizes, including U.S. letter (8.5" × 11"), legal (8.5" × 14") and tabloid (11" × 17"), plus several metric sizes. If the sheet size you want to use is not present, select **Custom** and type the dimensions of the page you want to use in the Width and Height boxes. Frame-Maker will accept page dimensions of up to 216" × 216" (that's 18 feet square—don't ask me where to find an output device for such a monster page, or a monitor on which to view it). For example, the figure shows the settings for a 5.25" × 8.5" page, a common size for small hardware and software manuals, based on half of a standard 8.5" × 11" page in landscape orientation.

Figure 4.2 Custom Blank Paper dialog box

Custom Blank Paper	
Page Size: Custom ▼	Columns:
Width: 5.25"	Number: 1
Height: 8.5"	Gap: 0.25"
Column Margins:	Pagination:
Top: 1.0"	○ Single-Sided
Bottom: 1.0"	● Double-Sided
Inside: 0.5"	Right 1st Page ▼
Outside: 0.5"	Units:
	Inch ▼
Create	Cancel	Help	

N O T E There is no portrait/landscape orientation option in the Custom Blank Paper dialog box. All the standard paper types are assumed to be in portrait (tall) orientation. If you want to use a standard size in landscape (long) orientation, you must select a Custom size and type the long dimension in the Width box and the short dimension in the Height box. For example, to use a U.S. legal-sized sheet in landscape orientation, type Width = 14" and Height = 8.5".

Next, set pagination for a single- or double-sided document. (Moving through the controls in the dialog box with the **Tab** key will take you to the margin settings first, but you should set pagination first, because it affects the way you set margins.) Letters and memos are normally single-sided, as are some informal reports that will be stapled at the upper-left corner. Just about anything that is going to be bound will be a double-sided document. If you have selected a double-sided document, you can choose whether the first page will be a left page or a right page.

Next, set the column margins; these margins are the distances between the outer edges of the text column(s) and the edges of the physical page. The header and footer columns that FrameMaker automatically creates will fall outside the margins for the main text column(s), but there's no way to control their sizes or positions at this stage of the process. The margin settings for a single-sided document are labeled Top, Bottom, Left, and Right, whereas the settings for a double-sided document are Top, Bottom, Inside, and Outside. The settings for a double-sided document are necessarily bilaterally symmetrical; the two inside margins and the two outside margins are always the same. To create a document with an asymmetrical layout, you must do further work on the document's master pages, as described later in this chapter. If you're creating such a document, the best thing to do at this stage is to set the margins so that at least one of the pages is right.

Creating an Asymmetrical Layout

To create an asymmetrical layout on left and right master pages, you must either manipulate the columns on one of the pages with the **Object Properties** command on the Graphics menu, as described later in this chapter, or copy the columns from one page to the other using the **Copy** and **Paste** commands.

N O T E If you plan to use Side Heads (a new feature in FrameMaker 4.0), be sure to take them into account in specifying your margins. Although Side Heads appear to be outside the margins of the text columns, in fact the text columns are divided into two areas, one for regular text and the other for the side heads. Hence, you must define your columns to allow for both areas (see "Side Heads," under "Pagination Properties" in Chapter 5 for details).

The FrameMaker manual recommends making the inside margins of a double-sided document wider than the outside margins to allow "gutters" for binding. This is contrary to the traditional practice, at least for books. Of course, you should take your printing and binding method into account in specifying your margins, but you should also remember that double-sided documents are seen as two-page spreads, and hence the two inside margins combine into a single white space. For this reason, it is traditional to make inside margins *narrower* than outside margins in a symmetrical layout. It is also traditional to make bottom margins larger than top margins, in order to keep the text from seeming to "slide off" the page. Whether you decide to follow this last convention will depend, to some extent, on whether you are going to use headers or footers, where you intend to place the page numbers, and so forth.

An old formula for the relative widths of the margins for a book is 1.5:2:3:4 (inside:top:outside:bottom), but few designers rigorously adhere to such a formula today. Still, this is a good starting point for a classic book design. Most mass-circulation magazines today have hardly any margins at all. The same goes for mass-market paperback books. Most likely your output device (laser printer or image setter) will impose some minimal margin settings on your design. If you can afford to do so, be generous with your margins—give your text some room to breathe!

Next, specify the number of columns and the gap between them. You do not set the width of the columns directly. The space between the inside and outside (or left and right) margins less the gaps is divided evenly into the specified number of columns. You can also set the default unit of measure for the document. (This is the same setting that appears in the View Options dialog box. You can change the unit later in this dialog box.) Some users consider this global setting one of FrameMaker's shortcomings. As they rightly point out, some things are traditionally measured in points, some in picas, and still others in inches.

Select **Create** to open a new document based on the dimensions you have specified. The display will initially show the first body page (the only one that exists so far); if the document is double-sided, the first page will be a right or a left page, depending on the setting in the Pagination box. The document will also have at least one master page (two for a double-sided document) and one reference page, which you can examine by selecting the appropriate setting from the View menu. When you view the master pages, you will see that, in addition to the text column(s) you specified, they also have header and footer columns that are the same width as the main text column(s).

Working with Master Pages

What are Master Pages?

Every FrameMaker document, whether it is a custom document or is based on a template, has one or more master pages. Master pages determine the placement of text columns on their corresponding body pages and also contain what Frame terms *background* elements; that is, textual elements such as headers, footers, and page numbers, and graphic elements such as the arrows in the bottom and outside margins of this book, that appear on every body page based on the master.

Control and Freedom—the Best of Both Worlds

Although FrameMaker's master pages allow you to strictly control the layout of all the body pages in your document, you need not rigidly adhere to a predefined layout as your document grows and develops. When you create a new, custom document, FrameMaker automatically creates one or two master pages based on your column and margin specifications, depending on whether you specified a single- or double-sided document. As you type or import text, new pages are created and are automatically given the layout from the appropriate master page. However, you are not limited to the one or two master pages that the program initially creates; you can design new master pages and apply them to selected pages in your document at any time, mixing different column and margin formats, header and footer styles, and even different page orientations in the same document. You can have up to 100 different master pages in a single document (increased from 25 in FrameMaker 3.0). Although that number is likely to be more than adequate for all but the most elaborate projects, you can also modify the layouts of individual body pages without affecting the master pages on which they are based, and you can even design body pages from scratch, without reference to master pages. If you decide later that you want to use a modified or custom-designed body page as a master, you can easily copy the layout from the body page to a master page and then apply the layout of the new master page to other body pages. So, although it is obviously best to carefully consider the design of your document before you begin working and create all of your master pages as part of a unified design, you need never be bound by such a preconceived design, should unforeseen problems arise.

How Many Master Pages Do I Need?

When you enter the page specifications in the dialog box to start a new custom document, you automatically create one or two master pages with the margins and text columns that you specify, as described previously. You can view these master pages by opening your document, opening the View menu, and selecting **Master Pages**. When you view these pages, you will see that in addition to the text columns you defined, they contain predefined columns for headers and footers.

Left and right master pages many be sufficient for very simple documents, but most will require at least a few others. A newsletter will typically use a different design for the front page, with the banner and perhaps a contents box. The back page, too, might have a different design from the interior pages. A book or manual will typically use a different design for chapter openings. The title page, table of contents, other front matter, and index pages are all likely to use different layouts from the body pages. Study some well-designed publications of the type you're working on to get an idea of the number and variety of page layouts they require.

Creating a New Master Page

If you need more master pages than the basic one or two, you must create them. There is more than one way to do this. The most direct is to first switch the View to **Master Pages** and then select **Add Master Pages** on the Special menu (this is the short way to get to this command; you will also find it under the name **New Master Page**, under the Basic heading on the Layout Palette (select Format>**Pages**>**Layout Commands**). This command displays the dialog box in Figure 4.3. Type a name for the new master page, and select whether it will use the layout from an existing master page or be blank. If your new master is to be only a slight variation of an existing master page, it is obviously easier to base the new layout on that of an existing page, then make the necessary changes. If what you want is a drastic departure from the norm, you will want to start from a blank page. Click on the **Add** button to create and display the new master page.

Figure 4.3 Add Master Page dialog box

Adding Text Columns

If you created a blank master page, you will need to add some text columns. There are two ways to do this:

The techniques described here for adding and adjusting text columns on master pages can also be used to perform the same operations directly on body pages.

N O T E

1. Copy columns from another master page or body page and paste them on the new master. Switch to the source page for the element you want to copy. **Ctrl**+click on a column to select it (**Ctrl**+**Shift**+click to copy multiple objects) and select **Copy** from the Edit menu. Switch to the page where you want to paste the column and select **Paste** from the Edit menu. The objects you selected will be placed on the destination page in the same position they had on the source page. This technique can be used on tagged columns, untagged columns (for example, header and footer columns) and graphics.

2. Draw text columns on the blank page with the Text Column tool from the Tools Palette (the icon for this tool looks like a text page). Position the tool where you want to place one corner of the column, then drag with the mouse to the opposite corner and release the button. When you release the button, the Add New Text Columns dialog box appears. Use this dialog box to select the type of column you want to create: Template (for normal text) or Background (for headers, footers, or other background elements). If you specify a Template column, you can also select a flow tag, and choose whether to autoconnect the column to others with the same tag. (The default settings of flow tag A and autoconnect on will work for most publications—see Chapter 7 for more on flows.) Select **Add** to place the column or **Cancel** to abort the operation.

Adjusting Columns

Drawing is not a very precise way of placing and sizing a column, so once you have put the columns you want on the page, you will probably need to make some adjustments. You may also need to make adjustments if you copied the layout from an existing master page. There are three ways to adjust the position and size of a column:

1. The easiest and most precise way of positioning and sizing a column is to use the **Object Properties** option from the Graphics menu. This command displays the Object Properties dialog box (Figure 4.4). Type the values for the dimensions of the column and/or the offset of the upper-left corner of the column from the upper left corner of the page in the **Unrotated Size** and/or **Offset From** boxes. The Object Properties dialog box also gives you another opportunity to change the flow tag and connection. You can even rotate the column by a specified number of degrees. The baselines for text typed in the corresponding columns on body pages will be angled to match the column. (Not something you would want to do everyday, but a stunning bit of programming virtuosity.) When you have made the necessary adjustments, click **Set** to apply them. Click **Cancel** to exit the dialog box without changing the column.

Figure 4.4 The Object Properties dialog box (showing properties for a text column)

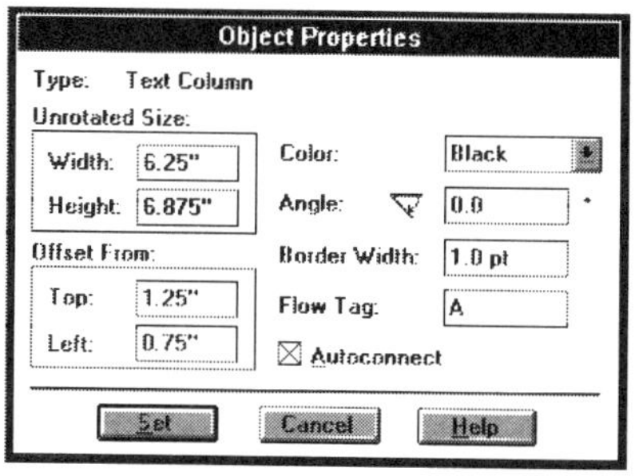

2. You can also resize (but not reposition) a column with the **Scale** command, also located on the Graphics menu. You can either rescale the column (change both dimensions) by specifying a scale factor, or you can type precise horizontal and vertical dimensions for the column (the more practical technique in most situations).

3. The most difficult way to reposition and/or resize a column, in my opinion, is to drag or stretch it using the mouse. Nevertheless, it is an option. To reposition a column with the mouse, **Ctrl**+click inside the column borders to select the column, then press and hold the left mouse button and drag the column to its new position. As you drag the column to its new position, the X and Y coordinates of its upper-left corner appear on the status bar in the lower-left corner of the Document Window. Use these coordinates to accurately position the upper-left corner of the column. To adjust the size of the column, move the selection tool outside the column borders and point to one of the column handles (the tool will change to a black arrowhead). Click and drag the handle to resize the column. As you drag, the width and height of the column will be displayed in the status bar. Use this information to accurately resize the column.

Turning the snap grid on with an appropriate grid interval will make it much easier to position the columns at the desired location.

N O T E

Two Kinds of Text Columns

There are two kinds of text columns that can appear on master pages: tagged (template) columns and untagged (background) columns. Tagged columns on master pages serve as templates for text columns on body pages. They are called tagged columns because they are assigned flow tags that control how text flows from column to column and page to page. Background columns are used for text elements that will appear on every body page that uses the master page, such as headers, footers, and page numbers.

You can also have untagged text columns on body pages. In such cases, the columns do not contain background—the text that is typed in them appears on the body page as you type it, but it is not part of any text flow. You can use untagged text columns for elements such as

N O T E drop quotes or captions.

Tagged Columns

You can type in a tagged column on a master page (for example, to add a comment about how the master page is to be used or who designed it), but the text you type will *not* appear on body pages based on that master page. Text that is to appear in the document must be typed or imported into the corresponding text columns on body pages. Text that is typed or imported into tagged columns on body pages becomes part of a flow and automatically flows from column to column and page to page throughout a document, using other connected columns that have the same flow tag. Whenever the insertion point is in a tagged text column, whether on a master page or a body page, the flow tag for the column will appear in the status area at the lower-left corner of the document window.

Many kinds of documents, including book or manual chapters, letters, memos, and reports have a single flow—text starts at the beginning of the document and flows continuously to the end. When you create a new custom document, FrameMaker assumes you want a continuous flow and gives the text columns on your left and right master pages the same default flow tag, "A." When you draw text columns on a custom master page, you specify a tag in the Add New Text Column dialog box. Other kinds of documents, such as newsletters and magazines, may have many separate, discontinuous flows, which may skip over adjacent columns or pages. For information on how to set up documents with these kinds of complex flows, consult Chapter 7.

Background Columns

Background columns exist only on master pages. They do not have flow tags and hence the text that appears in them is not part of a flow. Text is typed in background columns directly on the master pages, and appears as part of the background on all body pages based on those master pages. If you later update the background text on the master pages, the corresponding text on the body pages changes automatically.

When you start a new custom document, FrameMaker automatically creates background frames for headers and footers above and below the text columns you specify. If you are not satisfied with the size or position of these frames, you can resize and/or reposition them using any of the techniques described earlier in this chapter. Text in background columns can be formatted directly, using the commands on the Format menu or the Formatting Bar or by applying character and paragraph formats from the format catalogs (see Chapter 5).

Creating Headers or Footers

As mentioned previously, FrameMaker automatically creates untagged header and footer columns on the document's master pages. Once the header and footer have been correctly positioned and sized, you can create headers and/or footers in one of two ways:

1. You can type the text of the header or footer directly in the column. Use this method if the header or footer will be the same on each left or right page and will not change over the life of the document.

2. If you want your headers or footers to change from page to page to echo headings or other document features, or to include page numbers, the total page count, the current date or time, the file name of the document, or a number of other special items, you need to include one or more *variables* in your headers or footers. A variable is a symbolic place holder that is replaced by appropriate text, depending on the variable's definition. The most common variable used in headers or footers is the Current Page Number variable, represented by the # symbol. When this variable is placed in a header or footer column (or any untagged column) on a master page, the actual page number appears at the corresponding location on body pages based on the master page.

FrameMaker 4.0 provides a simple method for placing three of the most common system variables in headers or footers:

1. Click an insertion point in a header or footer column on a master page.

2. Open the Format menu and select **Headers & Footers**.

3. Select one of the three options from the submenu: **Insert Page #**, **Insert Page Count**, or **Insert Current Date**. The fourth option, **Insert Other**, opens the Variable dialog box, where you can access all the available variables or create new ones. Consult Chapter 9 for detailed information on creating and using variables, including the special Running Header/Footer variables.

Regardless of whether your headers and footers use variables, you can control the appearance of header and footer text by applying character formats and paragraph formats. Tabs can be used to position the various elements in a header or footer. Consult Chapter 5 for information on creating and using paragraph and character formats, including the placement of tab stops.

Page Numbering Style

The page numbering style for a document is set in the Document Properties dialog box, accessed via the **Document** option on the Format menu. You can select one of five numbering styles: Numeric (Arabic figures, the default), upper- and lowercase Roman numerals, and upper- and lowercase alphabetic characters. You can also specify the starting page number for the document. These settings are global for the document; that is, you can't restart the page numbering or change the numbering style within a document file. If you want to use different numbering styles or reset the numbering within a publication (for example, to use lowercase Roman numerals in the front matter and then restart with Arabic figures in the first chapter, or to have the numbering restart with each chapter), you must build a multifile book, as described in Chapter 18.

Other Background Elements

Master page backgrounds are not limited to text elements such as headers and footers. Backgrounds can also include graphic elements such as rules above, below, or between text columns, a company logo on a letterhead or memo, or a banner on the front page of a newsletter. Drawing or importing these elements on a master page is no different from performing the same operations on body pages. Consult Chapter 12 for information on drawing and editing graphics with the tools on FrameMaker's Tools Palette. Consult Chapter 13 for information on importing graphics created with other programs.

Applying a Custom Master Page

When you create a new master page, FrameMaker does not automatically use it. FrameMaker alternately applies its left and right master pages to new pages as they are created. If you want it to do anything else, you will have to tell it explicitly which master pages to use with which body pages. To do this, select **Master Page Usage** from the Page submenu of the Format menu (the same command is available on the Layout Palette). This opens the Master Page Usage dialog box (Figure 4.5). Use the upper portion of the dialog box to select the master page to use: Select either the **Normal Page Layout** (the left and right master pages, as used by default) or a **Custom Master Page** that you select from the pop-up menu.

Figure 4.5 Master Page Usage dialog box

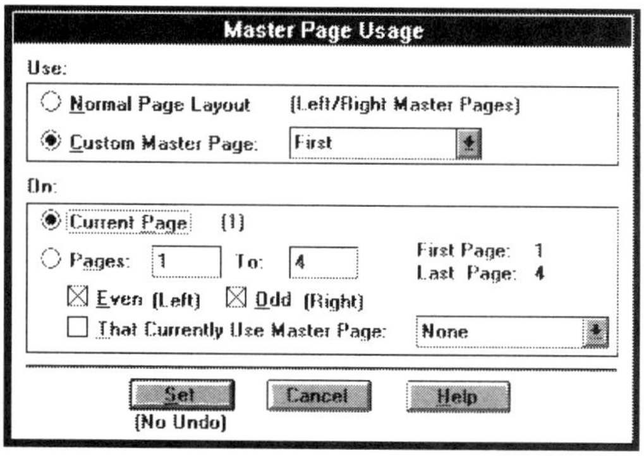

Use the lower portion of the dialog box to select the body pages to which to apply the master page. You can apply the master page to:

- The current page.

- A range of pages (by checking the appropriate check boxes, you can apply it to either odd pages, even pages, or all pages within the specified range).

- To all pages currently using another master page, which you select from a pop-up menu.

Select **Set** to apply the selected master page to the selected body pages. There is no undo for this operation, so it's a good idea to save your work beforehand, so you can revert to the saved version if the results are unsatisfactory.

When you apply a master page to body pages, FrameMaker checks the body pages for tagged columns with flows that match those on the master page; wherever it finds them, it replaces the tagged columns on the body pages with the corresponding ones on the master page. In so doing, it maintains existing connections between columns. If you are working on a document with a single, continuous flow, and you have set up the tagged columns on your master page correctly (that is, in most cases, with flow tag A and autoconnect on), then applying a new master page to body pages is straightforward and trouble-free. However, in a multi-flow document, problems may result. If the body page(s) to which you are applying the master page have tagged columns with text flows that are not present on the master page, FrameMaker will warn you that overlapping columns may result and ask you for your permission to proceed. If you go ahead, and overlapping columns do result, it may take a bit of manual tinkering to restore your pages to a reasonable state of order. It is better, in a complex, multi-flow document, to avoid this situation by using the methods described in Chapter 7.

Modifying the Layouts of Body Pages

All of the techniques described above for creating and modifying layouts on master pages, except for those dealing with headers and footers and other background elements, can also be used on body pages. You can add, delete, resize, or rearrange tagged and untagged columns, and you can also split or merge columns, as described later in this chapter. When you perform any of these operations on a body page, you create a *layout override;* that is, the layout of the body page no longer matches that of the master page on which it is based. This is not necessarily a problem; it is just a situation you need to be aware of. Whenever you switch the view from master pages to body pages, or perform certain operations involving layout, FrameMaker will remind you that some of your body pages have layout overrides and ask whether you want to retain or remove the overrides. As long as you instruct it to retain the overrides, your body page layout will not be changed.

Transferring a Body-Page Layout to a Master Page

If you want to use a layout created on a body page on other body pages, or if you just get tired of seeing the override message, you can use the **Update Page Layouts** command in the Basic group on the Layout Palette to apply the layout to a master page and to other body pages based on that master page. If you want to apply the layout selectively, it is best to create a new, blank, custom master page, as described earlier, and apply the modified layout to that master. You can then apply the new custom master page to other body pages as needed with the **Master Page Usage** command.

Splitting Columns

You can split any tagged or untagged column either horizontally or vertically using the **Split Current Column** option on the Layout Palette. This option can be used either on master pages or body pages, but because of the way it works, it is much more practical to use on body pages. There are three options for splitting a column:

- **Below Selection**—split the column vertically, with the division occurring between the line with the insertion point and the following line.

- **Right of Selection**—split the column horizontally at the insertion point.

- **Into Lines**—split the column vertically into many separate columns, one for each line of text. (This options is used mainly for creating runarounds for irregularly shaped graphics.

Splitting a column doesn't create any gutters between the new columns—they share a common boundary at the split point. If you want to create space between the new columns, resize or reposition the columns using one of the techniques described earlier in this chapter.

Because the insertion point on a master page can only be placed at the end-of-flow marker, which normally resides at the top of the first column in the flow, it is difficult to use this option on a master page. If you need to use split columns on a master page, the easiest method is to perform the operation on a body page, then copy the layout to the master page using the **Update Page Layouts** option in the Basic group on the Layout Palette (described earlier). (You could copy a block of text onto a master page in order to enable you to place the insertion point where you want to make the split, but that's a really roundabout way of doing things.)

Merging Columns

You can either split columns or merge selected vertical columns with the **Replace Columns** option, under Basic on the Layout Palette:

1. Select the columns you want to modify. **Shift**+click to select the first column, the **Ctrl**+**Shift**+click to select any subsequent columns.

2. Open the Layout Palette (Format>**Pages**>**Layout**) and select **Basic**; select **Replace Columns** on the submenu. The dialog box in Figure 4.6 will appear.

3. Type the values for the number of columns and the gap(s) between them. The value you type determines whether columns will be split or merged. For example, if you have selected one column and typed a value of two, the existing column will be split. If you selected two columns and type a value of one, you will merge the existing columns. The values for margins refer to the outer dimensions of the block of selected columns. If you want the new columns to occupy the same total space as the old ones, don't change these figures.

4. Select **Replace** to replace the existing columns with the new ones you have defined. (There is no undo for this operation).

Figure 4.6   Replace Columns dialog box

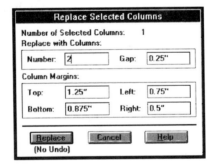

You cannot use the **Replace Columns** option to rejoin a column that has been split vertical by the **Split Current Column**>**Below Selection** option. If you want do this, you can either delete one of the split columns and resize the other or reapply the master page that had the original template column(s) with the **Master Page Usage** option.

N O T E

Creating a Body Page without a Master Page

Occasionally, you may want to create a body page that is not based on any master page. For example, you might want to make a page that has no headers or footers or other background elements. Of course, you could accomplish this by creating a custom master page without the background elements (the preferred method if you're going to use the layout more than once). To "disconnect" a body page from its master page, select **Master Page Usage** from the Page Format submenu or the Layout Palette, and set the usage for the selected page(s) to "None." Whatever modifications you make on the selected body pages thereafter will not be identified as layout overrides, since there is nothing to override. If you decide later that you want to transfer the layout you have created on the body page to a master page, you can do so with the **Update Page Layouts** option on the Layout Palette.

Changing the Layout of an Entire Document

To change the layout of *all* the pages in a document except those based on custom master pages, select **Normal Page Layout** from the Pages submenu of the Format menu or select the identical command from the Layout Palette. This command opens the Normal Page Layout dialog box (Figure 4.7), which is identical in structure and function to the Custom Blank Paper dialog box, described earlier in this chapter. Like the Custom Blank Paper dialog box, this dialog box can be used only to set up basic text columns and margins; it won't create asymmetrical layouts or control the position of header or footer columns. Also, like the Custom Blank Paper dialog box, it affects both the left and right master pages in a double-sided document, and all of the body pages based on those master pages. Hence, you should use this command only when you want to change a whole document, not just a few pages. You can restore normal page layout to selected pages with the **Master Page Usage** option.

If you attempt to use this command in a document with body pages with layouts that have been modified and no longer match their underlying master page, or with master pages that have complex layouts, FrameMaker will warn you that this may result in overlapping columns. Don't be overly alarmed by this; if you go ahead with the command it will only open the dialog box at this stage. When you select **Set** to apply the new margin and column values, the program will warn you again that your document has layout overrides and give you the option of keeping or removing the overrides.

Figure 4.7   Normal Page Layout dialog box

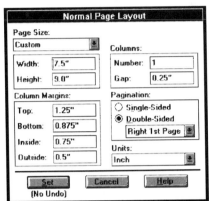

You cannot use the **Normal Page Layout** option in a document that contains rotated body or master pages.

N O T E

If you use the **Normal Page Layout** option on a document with asymmetrical left and right master pages, it will make your layout symmetrical.

WARNING

Deleting Pages

You can delete pages of any kind (body, master, or reference) with the **Delete Pages** command on the Special menu. If the active page is a body page, you will be asked to specify a range of pages to delete. Whichever type of page you delete, the delete pages operation is not undoable—the deleted pages and their contents will be permanently removed from the document. FrameMaker will warn you of this and prompt you for permission to proceed. You should make a habit of saving your document immediately before deleting pages so you can revert to the saved version if you make a mistake.

N O T E

You can instruct FrameMaker to automatically delete empty pages before printing or saving a document, or to add extra pages if necessary to make the page count odd or even, via the **Before Saving & Printing** option in the Document Properties dialog box.

You cannot delete a master page that is currently applied to body pages. You must first change the Master Page Usage so that no body pages use that master page. You can never delete left and right master pages from a document.

N O T E

Adding Disconnected Pages

Normally, FrameMaker automatically creates new pages based on the left and right master pages as needed when you type, import, or reformat text. Hence, in a single-flow document, where one stream of text flows continuously from beginning to end, you should never need to manually create new pages. However, in a multi-flow document, such as a magazine or newsletter, where different articles and stories jump from column to column and page to page, you will probably want to create new pages and connect columns manually. You create these *disconnected pages* (so called because their template columns are not automatically connected to others with the same flow tag) with the **Add Disconnected Pages** command on the Special menu. (For a detailed explanation of this command and of managing multi-flow documents, see Chapter 7).

Rotating a Page

Unlike most desktop publishing applications, FrameMaker can mix portrait- and landscape-oriented pages in a single document. This can be useful if you need to include extra-wide tables or figures in a normal, portrait-oriented publication. The **Rotate Page** command on the Layout Palette works on either master or body pages. There are three options for this command: **Clockwise**, **Counterclockwise**, (by 90° in either case) and **Unrotate**. When you rotate a page, the orientation of text in columns that were on the page prior to rotation rotates with the page. New text columns that are added to the page *after it has been rotated* are oriented horizontally relative to your screen and the new horizontal axis of the page. For example, if you rotate a page with a standard text column, such as that in Figure 4.8, the baselines of the text in the column will be vertical. If you then add a new column to the page and type text in the column, the baselines of the new text will be horizontal, at right angles to the old. You can type in the rotated columns, provided your brain can cope with typing on vertical baselines. If it can't, unrotate the column, type your text, and rotate it again.

In addition to rotating a whole page, you can rotate individual text columns (or any other selectable graphic object) with the rotation buttons on the Quick Access Bar, by changing the rotation setting in the Object Properties dialog box, or by **Alt**+dragging one of its handles.

N O T E

Whereas whole pages can only be rotated by 90°, selected columns can be rotated in fractions of a degree. Consult Chapter 12 for detailed information on rotating and other object manipulation techniques.

Figure 4.8 Text orientation on a rotated page

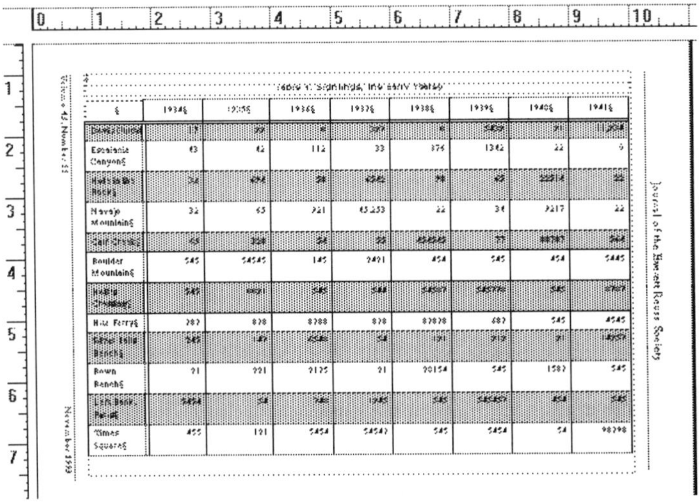

Creating and Editing Reference Pages

Reference pages are storage spaces for graphics, such as rules and icons, and for other frequently used elements. Every FrameMaker document, even an empty custom document, has at least one reference page. To view the reference pages in a document, open the View menu and select **Reference Pages**. A typical reference page, such as that in Figure 4.9, contains *reference frames* with rules to be used with various headings and as separators for footnotes. You can attach a reference frame to a heading or other paragraph using the **Frame Above ¶/Below ¶** options in the Paragraph Designer, as described in Chapter 5. Separators are automatically added to footnotes, as explained in Chapter 19.

Adding a New Reference Page

If you need more storage space in a document, you can add more reference pages. A document can have up to 100 reference pages, more than enough for any conceivable purpose. Use the following steps to create a new reference page:

1. Select **Reference Pages** on the View menu.

2. Open the Special menu and select **Add Reference Page**.

3. In the dialog box that appears, type a name for the new reference page.

4. Select **Add** to create the new reference page.

Figure 4.9   A typical reference page

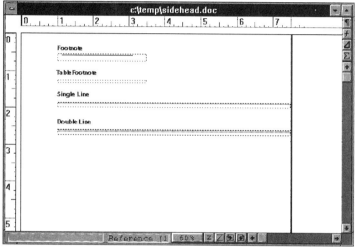

Creating a Reference Frame

A reference frame is an unanchored frame on a reference page. It can include rules or other graphic elements, or it can be an empty frame that is used as a spacer. Use the following steps to create a reference frame:

1. Draw the frame on the reference page using the Frame tool on the Tools Palette (see Chapter 12 for more information on using this and other drawing tools). Any frame you draw on a reference page is automatically a reference frame.

2. When you finish drawing the frame, a dialog box appears for you to enter a name for the frame. Give the frame a name that you will recognize later when you see it on the menu in the Paragraph Designer.

3. Adjust the size of the frame, if necessary, using the **Object Properties** option on the Graphics menu.

4. Use the other drawing tools to draw any rules or other graphic elements you want to include in the frame. You can also import a graphic created with

another program into the frame using the **Import>Files** option on the File menu.

5. (Optional) Use the Text Line tool to type the frame's name above it on the reference page. This name is solely for your convenience in identifying the frame if you want to edit it later. It need not be the same name that you typed earlier in the dialog box, though it's hard to think of a logical reason why it shouldn't be. You can also see the name of a reference frame in the status area at the bottom of the document window when the frame is selected.

To change the name of a reference frame, select the frame and click on its name in the status bar or use the **Object Properties** command on the Graphics menu.

N O T E

In addition to reference frames, reference pages can include graphics (either created with FrameMaker's drawing tools or imported) in anchored frames or placed directly on the page. They can also include tagged or untagged text columns. Such objects cannot be attached to paragraphs with the **Frame Above ¶/Below ¶** options, but they can be copied from the reference pages and pasted on body pages.

Deleting a Reference Page

You can delete any reference page by making it the current page and selecting **Delete Page "Name"** on the special menu, where **"Name"** is the name of the page to be deleted. This action is not undoable. Any graphics imported by reference onto body pages from the reference page will disappear when you delete the page. Paragraph formats that have **Frame Above ¶/Below ¶** settings using graphics from the deleted page will have this item set to "As Is."

CHAPTER 5

Formatting Text

Introduction

In FrameMaker, the appearance of text is controlled by applying formats. This process is also known as *tagging* text. There are two types of text formats in Frame-Maker; paragraph formats and character formats. Paragraph formats affect whole paragraphs, meaning any block or line of text that is terminated with a carriage return (¶). Character formats are applied to smaller blocks of text within paragraphs, for example, individual words, phrases, titles, or the like, or to text lines created with the text tool on the Tools Palette (see Chapter 12). FrameMaker stores both types of formats in *catalogs*, which can be accessed via the paragraph format (¶) and character format (*f*) buttons on the right border of the document window, as well as by other methods to be described in this chapter.

Every FrameMaker document has some formats in its catalogs, even an empty document that you have just created using the **New** command on the File menu. Documents that are based on FrameMaker templates inherit format catalogs from their templates, and even custom documents begin life with a modest selection of paragraph and character formats. You can build up the catalog for a document by creating formats one by one, as the need arises, or you can import complete catalogs of paragraph and character formats from another document, as described later in this chapter.

Formats make it easy to achieve a consistent appearance throughout a complex document or family of documents. By grouping together different characteristics, such as typeface, point size, line spacing, alignment, word spacing, and many more, paragraph formats allow you to determine all the essential properties of a paragraph or group of paragraphs with the single action of applying the appropriate paragraph tag. There's no chance of making an error or forgetting one of your paragraph's properties (did I set that last paragraph 10 on 12 or 10 on 11?... and was the letter spacing loose or normal?); all paragraphs tagged with the same format will have the same properties. And if you decide later to change the format, all the tagged paragraphs can be updated with a single action.

Paragraph Formats

After the design of the basic page layouts, as embodied in the document's master pages, the most important elements of the design will be found in the paragraph formats (what traditional publication designers and typesetters would call the type specs). In FrameMaker, any line or block of text that is terminated with a carriage return is considered a paragraph. Paragraph formats control such text properties as the default font, line spacing, word spacing, alignment, indentation, tab stops, space between paragraphs, and many others that will be described in detail in this chapter.

Applying Paragraph Formats

Applying a format to a paragraph is simple:

1. Open the Paragraph Format Catalog by clicking the ¶ button, pressing **Ctrl+1**, or selecting **Paragraphs>Catalog** from the Format menu.

2. Place the insertion point anywhere in the paragraph you want to format by clicking in it with the mouse. If you want to apply the same format to several successive paragraphs, drag with the mouse or click in the first paragraph, then press and hold **Shift** and click in the last paragraph. (Unfortunately, there is no way to select nonconsecutive paragraphs in FrameMaker.)

3. Click on the name of the format you want to apply in the catalog. The text in the selected paragraph(s) will change as required by the new format and the name of the new format tag will appear in the status area at the lower-left corner of the document window.

In addition to the Paragraph Format Catalog, you can also select paragraph formats from the pop-up menu on the Formatting Bar, or from the submenu under the Format menu. Except for opening the catalog window, this process works exactly as described previously.

SHORTCUT

For users who prefer command-line style operations to mousing around on the screen, there is an alternate method for applying paragraph formats:

1. Place the insertion point in a paragraph or select a group of paragraphs, as described previously.

2. Press **F9**; a ¶ will appear in the tag area at the lower left corner of the Document Window.

3. Begin typing the name of the tag you want to apply. You probably won't need to type the full name, just enough letters to identify the unique format name. When you have done so, the full name will appear in the tag area.

4. Press **Enter** to apply the format.

You can also apply a paragraph format from within the Paragraph Designer:

1. Click an insertion point in the paragraph, or select a group of contiguous paragraphs.

2. Select the desired format from the pop-up menu at the upper-left corner of the designer.

3. Click the **Apply** button.

Designing Paragraph Formats

Although applying paragraph formats is simple and quick, designing effective formats takes time and knowledge—knowledge both of how FrameMaker works and of the craft of typography.

Before undertaking a new project, it's good practice to make a list of all the possible paragraph formats your project will require. If you are working on a novel or a book of short stories, for example, the number of formats you need will be modest—body text, chapter titles, headers or footers, front matter, and perhaps a few others. If, on the other hand, you are designing a scientific textbook or a technical manual or journal, you many require dozens of formats: several levels of headings, bulleted and numbered lists, footnotes, tables, figure, table, and photo captions, quotes and extracted material... the list could go on and on. Magazines, newsletters, brochures, catalogs—each type of publication will require a particular set of paragraph formats. The job of the designer is to choose a format for each element so that they work together as a coherent, logical whole and convey a visual message that is consistent with the editorial content of the publication.

The Paragraph Designer

You create or edit paragraph formats in the Paragraph Designer (Figure 5.1). (The Paragraph Designer was called the Paragraph Format Window in previous versions of FrameMaker. This window has not just been renamed, but has been significantly redesigned and has several new features, as will be explained shortly.) To open the designer, open the Format menu and select **Paragraphs**, then select **Designer** from the submenu (or use the keyboard shortcut **Ctrl+M**). If a block of text is currently selected, or if there is an insertion point in a paragraph, the designer will display the format for that block or paragraph. If the selection includes two or more paragraphs with different formats, many of the settings in the window will be blank or set to "As Is." You can leave the designer open and move to different locations in the document, and the settings in the designer will change to reflect the current location of the insertion point.

Figure 5.1   The Paragraph Designer

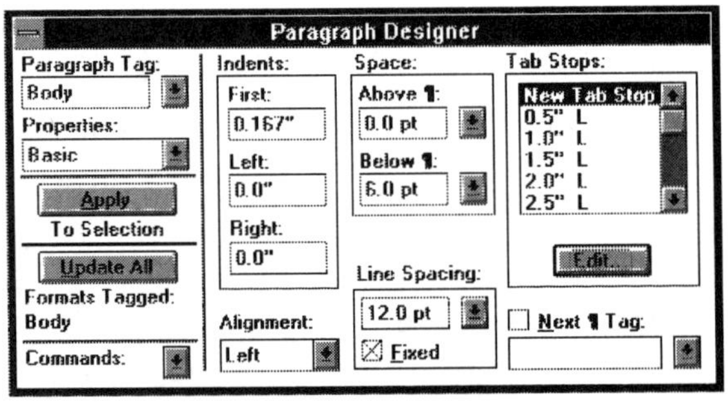

There is more to the Paragraph Designer than initially meets the eye. The designer has six different groups of related paragraph characteristics, which FrameMaker terms *properties*. You access these groups via the Properties list box, in the left-hand column of the designer. Opening this box reveals a list of the six groups: Basic, Default Font, Pagination, Numbering, Advanced, and Table Cell. (Pagination is a new addition in FrameMaker 4.0. The Tabs group that existed in previous versions has been eliminated and its functions incorporated in the Basic group.) Every paragraph will need settings for Basic and Default Font properties. The Advanced properties, which control hyphenation and word spacing, among other factors, are important for achieving legible, professional-looking text. The Pagination properties are mainly concerned with the formats of Side Heads and Run-In Heads, new features of FrameMaker 4.0. Numbering properties are used only in paragraphs with automatic numbering. Table Cell properties are used only for tables, and hence will be discussed in detail in Chapter 20.

Applying and Storing New or Modified Formats

Below the Paragraph Tags and Properties list boxes on the left side of the Paragraph Designer are the controls you use to apply or store new or modified paragraph formats: the **Apply** button, the **Update All** button, and the Command pop-up menu. These controls remain in view whenever the designer is open, whereas the rest of the designer changes when you select different properties groups.

N O T E

This section of the Paragraph Designer and the corresponding section of the Character Designer differ significantly from the comparable sections in FrameMaker 3.0. Although I cannot really agree that Frame has managed to simplify the operations performed by these controls, they have, at least, reduced the danger of accidentally updating all paragraphs or storing a format in the catalog when all you want to do is apply a modified format to a selection.

The processes of editing a group and of applying it to a selection or storing it in the catalog are distinct; you can make as many changes as you like in a property group, but no changes will occur in your document until you apply it. Applying the group changes the selection, but does not affect the formats in the catalog. Storing the edited group in the catalog is a separate operation, involving one of the options on the Commands menu. There are many options for applying or storing formats (perhaps *too* many—the wealth of options can be a bit confusing). Among the things you can do with an edited properties group are the following:

- Apply it to selected paragraphs.
- Apply it to all of the paragraphs with a particular format tag.
- Apply it to all paragraphs with tags that are included in the selection *and* update the corresponding formats in the catalog.
- Store it in the format catalog under a new or existing format name.
- Apply it to all of the paragraphs in the current document *and* replace all of the formats currently in the catalog.

Applying the Properties from a Group to a Selection

For safety's sake, it is always a good idea to apply a new or modified format to one or more selected paragraphs to be sure it works satisfactorily before applying it to all of the paragraphs with a particular tag or storing it in the catalog. Use the following procedure:

1. Click an insertion point in a paragraph, or select a group of consecutive paragraphs.
2. Make whatever changes you want in the properties group.
3. Click the **Apply** button.

NOTE

It is important to perform the steps in the order specified above. If you click an insertion point in a new paragraph *after* editing the properties, the properties will revert to those of the selected paragraph.

NOTE

If, after editing one group of properties, you select a different group of properties without first applying your changes, a dialog box like that in Figure 5.2 will appear, asking whether you want to apply your changes from the first group of properties before going to the second group, and offering you the choices of **Apply Changes**, **Update All**, **Don't Apply**, or **Cancel** (return to the first group of properties). Use **Apply Changes** to apply the properties to the selected paragraph(s). Use **Update All** to apply the changes to all the paragraphs with the specified tag. If you choose **Don't Apply**, the changes you made in the first group of properties will be lost.

Figure 5.2 Apply Changes prompt box

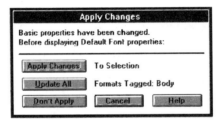

Updating All Paragraphs with a Given Tag

Use this procedure to change the format of *all* the paragraphs in a document with a particular format tag *and* store the edited format in the catalog.

1. Click an insertion point in a paragraph with the tag you wish to update.

2. Make whatever changes you want in the properties group.

3. Confirm that the correct tag name appears below the **Update All** button, then click the button to execute the update.

4. If some of the tagged paragraphs contain format overrides, a dialog box will appear to warn you of that fact, and offer you the options of retaining or removing the overrides or canceling the operation

N O T E Format Overrides are modifications to the paragraph format that have not been stored in the catalog. They may be the result of changes made via the Formatting Bar, via the text editing buttons on the Quick Access Bar, by applying a Character Format (described later in this chapter) or by applying an edited group of properties but not saving it in the catalog. Paragraphs with format overrides are identified by an asterisk (*) in front of the tag name in the status bar and on the Formatting Bar.

Replacing All Occurrences of One Tag with a Different Tag

1. Click an insertion point in a paragraph with the tag with which you wish to replace another tag.

2. Make whatever changes you want in the properties group.

3. Open the Command pop-up menu and select **Global Update Options**.

4. In the dialog box, select the **All Tagged** radio button. Open the pop-up menu next to the radio button and select the name of the tag you want to replace.

5. Click the **Update** button to perform the operation. (This command does not affect the formats stored in the catalog.)

Applying Properties to All Tags that Match Those in the Selection

1. Select two or more consecutive paragraphs with the formats you wish to modify. Keep in mind that this operation will modify *all* paragraphs *anywhere* in the document that have the same tags as those you selected, *not just the selected paragraphs.*

2. Make whatever changes you want in the properties group.

3. Open the Command pop-up menu and select **Global Update Options**.

4. In the dialog box that appears (Figure 5.3), select the **All Matching Tags in Selection** radio button. You can choose to update the specified paragraphs either with just the properties in the currently displayed group, or with *all* the properties of the selected format.

Figure 5.3 Global Update Options dialog box

Global Update Options

Use Properties in the Paragraph Designer:

○ All Properties
● Basic Properties Only

Update Paragraph Formats:

○ All Paragraphs and Catalog Entries
○ All Matching Tags in Selection
● All Tagged: Body ▼

[Update]   [Cancel]   [Help]

5. Click the **Update** button to apply the format. This operation modifies not just the paragraphs in the document with the selected tags, but also those tags in the format catalog.

Storing a New Format in the Catalog

1. Make whatever changes you want in the properties group.

2. Select **New Format** from the pop-up Command menu.

3. A dialog box like that in Figure 5.4 will appear. Type the name for the new format in the text box and check the **Store in Catalog** check box. (If you want to apply the new format to the selection at the same time, check that check box also.)

Figure 5.4 New Format dialog box

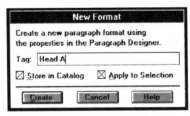

New Format

Create a new paragraph format using the properties in the Paragraph Designer.

Tag: Head A

☒ Store in Catalog   ☒ Apply to Selection

[Create]   [Cancel]   [Help]

4. Click **Create** to store the new format in the catalog.

5. An alternate way to store a new format is to type a new format name in the text box at the upper left corner of the designer, then click **Apply**. The dialog box in Figure 5.4 will appear. Proceed as described previously in steps 3 and 4.

Updating an Existing Format

1. Place the insertion point in a paragraph with the format you wish to modify.

2. Make whatever changes you want in the properties group.

3. Open the Command pop-up menu and select **Global Update Options**.

4. In the dialog box that appears (Figure 5.3), select the **All Tagged:** radio button. Check to be sure the format name in the text box next to the radio button is the one you want to modify. You can choose to update the format either with just the properties in the currently displayed group, or with *all* the properties of the selected format.

5. Click the **Update** button to apply the format. This operation will update all the paragraphs in the document with the specified tag and will also update that format in the catalog.

Applying a Format to *All* Paragraphs in a Document and *All* Entries in the Format Catalog

1. Place the insertion point in a paragraph with the format you wish to apply.

2. Edit the properties if necessary.

3. Open the Command pop-up menu and select **Global Update Options**.

4. In the dialog box that appears (Figure 5.3), select the **All Paragraphs and Catalog Entries** radio button. You can choose to update the paragraphs either with just the properties in the currently displayed group, or with *all* the properties of the selected format.

5. Click the **Update** button to apply the format.

6. This operation cannot be undone. A dialog box will appear and offer you three options: select **Yes** to update all paragraphs and catalog entries. Select **No** to update the formatting of all paragraphs without changing their tag names. Select **Cancel** to return to the designer without updating the paragraphs or catalog.

Deleting a Format from the Catalog

1. Select **Delete Format** from the pop-up Command menu.

2. Select the format you wish to delete from the list box in the dialog box that appears.

3. Click the **Delete** button to delete the format.

When you delete a format from the catalog, paragraphs already tagged with that format do not change. The format name simply disappears from the catalog window and from other menus where it would normally appear. You can restore a deleted format to the catalog by selecting an existing paragraph with the format and storing the format to the catalog as a new format, or by copying the format from another document.

Restoring the Designer to its Previous Condition

If you have made some changes to a properties group but have not yet applied them to a paragraph, you can restore the properties to those of the selected paragraph by opening the Command menu and selecting the **Reset Window From Selection** command. If you have edited a group of properties and applied it to a paragraph with unsatisfactory results, you can easily restore the paragraph to its previous state, provided you have at least one unmodified paragraph of the type you are working on. (This is one reason you should make a habit of testing a new format on a single paragraph before applying it to all of the formats with the same tag or storing it in the catalog.)

1. Click an insertion point in an unmodified paragraph of the appropriate type.

2. Open the Edit menu and select **Copy Special**>**Paragraph Format**.

3. Click an insertion point in the paragraph you want to restore.

4. Open the Edit menu and select **Paste** or press **Ctrl+V**.

This method can also be used to copy a format between documents.

Modifying a Few Paragraph Properties While Leaving the Rest Unchanged

Occasionally, you might want to modify only one or two properties of a group of paragraphs with different formats, while leaving all the other properties as they are. For example, you might want to change the font family of your body paragraphs and related items, such as bulleted and numbered lists, extracts, and figure captions, from Times Roman to Adobe Caslon, leaving all the other paragraph properties unchanged. To do this, set the options in the designer to As Is by selecting **Set Window to As Is** from the Command pop-up menu. This will reset *all* the properties groups to As Is; optional settings will be blank, settings which must have a value will display As Is, and check boxes will be shaded gray. Now you can edit the **Font Family** setting in the Default Font group and apply only this property to the paragraphs you choose. Unfortunately, there is no really simple way to apply such a format change to a large group of paragraphs with different tags. If examples of all the different formats exist in one contiguous block that doesn't include any paragraph formats you don't want changed, the process is simple: just use the **All Matching Tags in Selection** settings in the Global Updates dialog box. Otherwise, you may have to repeat the process for several different groups.

Basic Paragraph Properties

The Basic Properties group (Figure 5.5) is concerned with indents, alignment, line spacing, and tabs. These settings are, for the most part, simple and straightforward.

Figure 5.5 The Basic Properties Group in the Paragraph Designer

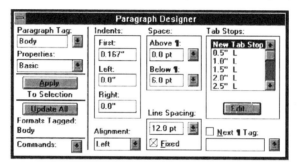

Indents

There are three types of indents you can set: First, Left, and Right. Except in the special case of side heads (in the Pagination group, described later), all three are relative to the borders of the text column. The values for these three settings are displayed in the unit selected in the View Options dialog box (see Chapter 2), but remember, you can type new values in whatever units you prefer and FrameMaker will perform the conversion if required.

The indent settings in FrameMaker differ slightly from some other desktop publishing applications with which you may be familiar, in that the first line indent is relative to the column edge, rather than to the left indent. Hence, to produce a hanging indent in FrameMaker, you would use a positive left indent and a zero first-line indent, rather than a negative first-line indent. For example, to set a one pica hanging indent, specify a first indent of 0 and a left indent of 1pica.

You can also change the indents for the current or selected paragraph(s) by dragging the arrowheads that appear on the top ruler in the document window. (You can do this whether or not the Paragraph Designer is open.) The upper black arrowhead on the left is the first indent, the lower one is the left indent, and the hollow arrowhead on the right is the right indent. If the **Snap Grid** option in the View Options dialog box is checked, you will only be able to drag the arrowheads to locations that match the ruler ticks. Changes made this way take effect immediately, without your having to select the **Apply** button if the dialog box is open. You can apply a set of indents created this way to other tagged paragraphs or save it in the catalog via the Global Update feature.

Space

There are two settings for this parameter: **Above** and **Below**. These settings control the vertical space between paragraphs. The space between consecutive paragraphs is always the larger of the space below the first paragraph and the space above the second. For example, if the first paragraph has a space below of 6 points and the second paragraph has a space above setting of 12 points, the space between paragraphs will be 12 points. The Above setting is not used when a paragraph occurs at the top of a page or column.

Line Spacing

This property replaces the one called Leading in FrameMaker 3.0. By default, FrameMaker uses a line spacing that is 120% of the default font height. You can specify a different line spacing in points by typing a new value in the box, or you can select multiples of 1.5 times or double the specified line spacing from the drop-down list box.

If the **Fixed** check box is checked, the line spacing will not change if there are over-sized characters in some lines of the paragraph. If the box is not checked, the line spacing will expand if necessary to accommodate taller characters.

Alignment

There is nothing novel in the alignment options offered by FrameMaker: **As Is**, **Left**, **Center**, **Right**, and **Justified**. **As Is** means leave the alignment of the paragraphs unchanged—handy when you're changing some other aspect of the format of two or more paragraphs with different alignments. The other options are familiar and self-explanatory to every desktop publishing or word processing software user.

Tab Stops

Use the Tab Stops section of the Basic Properties to set tab stops in the paragraphs that require them. All tab stops in FrameMaker have two properties: position (measured from the left edge of the text column) and alignment. FrameMaker uses the same four standard types of tab stop alignments found in most word processing and desktop publishing applications: left, right, center, and decimal. In addition, a tab can have a leader character (a character that fills the space created by the tab—used mainly in indices, tables of contents, and other tables). The alignment character for decimal tabs can also be changed; that is, it need not necessarily be a decimal point.

N O T E Tab stop positions in FrameMaker are absolute. That is, when you press the tab key, the *nth* press of the **Tab** key moves the insertion point to the *nth* tab position. Thus, if the position of the insertion point is between the third and fourth tab stops in a paragraph, and there are no other tabs in the line, you will have to press the tab key four times to move to the fourth tab position.

To edit an existing tab stop or create a new tab stop using the designer, select **New Tab Stop** or the position of an existing tab stop form the list box in the designer, then click **Edit**. This opens the Edit Tab Stop dialog box (Figure 5.6—you can also open this dialog box without opening the designer, by double-clicking a tab stop on the top ruler). The current position of the selected tab stop is shown at the top of the dialog box (if you selected **New Tab Stop,** this space will be blank). Below the current position is a box labeled New Position. Type a value here if you are creating a new tab stop or changing the position of an existing tab stop. Both the current position and new position are expressed in the display units you selected for the document, but don't forget you can type a value in any of the units supported by FrameMaker and the program will translate as necessary.

In addition to setting the position of the tab, you can also select the alignment (Left, Center, Right, or Decimal) with the radio buttons on the left side of the dialog box. If you select a Decimal tab, you must type an alignment character in the Align On box. A decimal point (.) will be appropriate for most uses, but you could use a comma if you are working with European currencies. Use the buttons on the right side of the dialog box to select a leader character. You can select among FrameMaker's predefined leaders or select **Custom** and type one or more characters in the adjacent text box. Some of the more obvious possibilities are the em dash (type \m in the box), the asterisk, or the underscore. Although it is not obvious why you would want to do so, you can use a different leader character for each of the tab stops in a paragraph.

It is now easy to create a series of evenly spaced tab stops in FrameMaker. Just check the **Create Every** check box and type a spacing value in the adjacent text box. Before you do this, you will probably want to clear any existing tab stops from the paragraph by selecting the **Delete All** button at the bottom of the dialog box. You can also delete the single selected tab stop by selecting the **Delete** button.

To save the new tab stops you have created, exit the dialog box by selecting **Continue**. To abandon your changes, select **Cancel**. As with all the properties in the Paragraph Designer, you must apply your edited tab stops to see their effect.

Figure 5.6 The Edit Tab Stops dialog box

Edit Tab Stop

Current Position: 1.5"
New Position: [1.5"]

Alignment: Leader:

◉ Left   ○ None
○ Center   ○ ......
                              ○ . . . .
○ Right   ○ . . . .
○ Decimal   ◉ . . . .
   Align On: [ ]   ○ Custom: [   ]

□ Repeat Every: [0.5"]

[Continue]   [Cancel]
[Delete] [Delete All] [Help]

After you apply an edited tab stop, the selection in the Tab Stops list box will always change to **New Tab Stop**. If you fail to notice this, you may waste some time opening and closing the Edit Tab Stop dialog box when you want to re-edit the same tab stop.

You can also use the ruler and Formatting Bar in conjunction with the designer. You can drag tab stops to new locations, delete tab stops by dragging them off the ruler, or add new tab stops using the buttons on the Formatting Bar. Whatever changes you make will be reflected in the Tab Stops list box in the designer, and can be stored or applied using the various **Update** and **Apply** options described earlier in the chapter.

If **Snap** is on when you drag tabs to new positions, you will be able to position the tab stops only at ruler ticks. However, when you type tab positions in the Edit Tab Stop dialog box, you can place tab stops anywhere, regardless of the Snap setting.

FrameMaker's sophisticated table editor, described in Chapter 20, largely eliminates the need for complex tab settings.

Next ¶ Tag

Normally, when typing text in FrameMaker, when you press the **Enter** key to end a paragraph, the next paragraph will automatically inherit the format of the preceding paragraph. In some cases, this is convenient—for example, when typing consecutive paragraphs of body text. In other cases, it isn't—for example, a particular type of heading or subheading will virtually never be followed by another heading or subheading of the same kind. The **Next ¶ Tag** option allows you to specify a different paragraph type to be started when you press **Enter** at the end of the specified paragraph. For example, you might choose to make the paragraph after a heading or subheading a body paragraph.

The **Next ¶ Tag** setting has no effect when tagging previously typed or imported text. It works only when you type new text.

N O T E

Default Font Properties

The next group in the Paragraph Designer selects the Default Font for the paragraph (see Figure 5.7). This font will be used for all text in the paragraph unless it is overridden by a character format (described later in this chapter).

Figure 5.7 The Default Font Properties group in the Paragraph Designer

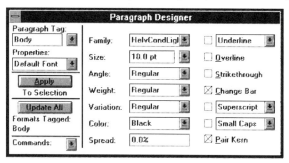

All the controls in the Default Font group are duplicated in the Character Designer (described later in this chapter) and can be applied to individual characters, words, and phrases via Character Formats.

N O T E

Font Family

The Font Family menu displays all the font families you have currently installed under Windows. This includes both type 1 PostScript fonts installed via Adobe Type Manager and TrueType fonts supplied with Windows or installed from the Windows Control Panel if both of these options are active.

WARNING

If you are producing final output on an in-house laser printer, its okay to freely mix TrueType and PostScript Type 1 fonts as you choose. However, if you're sending files to a service bureau for final output, you may need to limit yourself to Type 1 fonts, since most imagesetters have only Post-Script rasterizers. To save yourself some grief, consult your service bureau at the beginning of the design process on what fonts they support.

Size

Use this box to specify the font size in points. You can either open a pop-up menu and select from a list of the most common sizes or type a value between 2 and 400 in the box (fractional point sizes are supported). (See Chapter 6 for an explanation of point sizes and other typographic measurements.)

Below the Size box are three list boxes from which you select variations within the selected font family: **Angle**, **Weight**, and **Variation**. The options you see in these boxes will depend on the font family you have selected. Angle is usually limited to two choices, Regular and Italic, or Regular and Oblique. Italic and Oblique both mean the same thing in this context: type that slants to the right. The term italic seems to be used more often in reference to serif typefaces whereas oblique is used more frequently in reference to sans serif typefaces. However, there is no uniformity in this matter; the choice of the term seems to be at the whim of the type designer or vendor. Backslanted (left-leaning) type exists, but is extremely uncommon. Some decorative or display typefaces will have only a single (regular) slant.

Weight

Weight specifies variation in the thickness of the letter forms, the most common being regular (or medium) and bold. Some font families, however, include a greater variety of weights, including light, regular, demi- or semi-bold, bold, and extra-bold or black. As with slant, there are a variety of different terms for describing type weights and little uniformity in their use.

Variation

This option might more appropriately be called width, as it deals with type variations such as narrow, condensed, regular, semi-extended, and extended. Because of the way Windows groups type into families, in most cases you won't find any variations here except Regular and As Is. For example, if you have Helvetica, Helvetica Narrow, Helvetica Condensed, and Helvetica Extended installed on your system, these four typefaces would appear as four different families on the Font Family menu, rather than as a single family called Helvetica with four different width variations.

Color

Use this option to select one of eight predefined spot colors, or any new colors you have defined, from a pop-up menu. Obviously, this option is useful only if you are designing a document for a multicolor print job.

Spread

The final option in the Default Font Properties group is an important one, although it might escape your notice, hiding here under an obscure and unrevealing name. Spread controls what traditional typesetters call letter spacing (the spacing between characters within a word) as distinct from word spacing (the spacing between words). Letter spacing differs from pair kerning (another Default Font property, described later in this section) in that it affects all characters in a word, not just selected pairs. Some other Windows desktop publishing applications use the term *tracking* to designate this property.

The method FrameMaker uses to describe the amount of letter spacing is also unconventional. Normally, letter spacing is specified by general terms such as very loose, loose, normal, tight, and very tight, or more precisely, as fractions of an em to be added or subtracted. FrameMaker specifies letter spacing as a percentage, with zero percent representing normal (no space added or subtracted between characters). A positive value represents looser spacing; a negative value represents tighter spacing. Figure 5.8 shows a paragraph set with several different letter spacings.

Attribute Settings

On the right side of the Default Font group are seven check boxes for selecting additional variations on the default font: **Underline**, **Overline**, **Strikethrough**, **Change Bar**, **Superscript/Subscript**, **Capitalization**, and **Pair Kern**. These options, previously grouped together under the heading of Style, have undergone some additions and modifications in FrameMaker 4.0. Most of these options are straightforward, and are familiar to experienced Windows word processing and desktop publishing software users. Their effects are shown in Figure 5.9.

N O T E

Some of these options are more appropriately applied in Character Formats. (Can you think of a situation in which you would want to set a whole paragraph of superscript, subscript, or overline?)

Underline has been changed from previous FrameMaker versions and now offers three choices via a drop-down list box: **Underline** (single), **Double Underline**, and **Numeric Underline**. **Numeric Underline** differs from normal underline in that the offset and thickness of the line is constant. With the normal underline, the thickness of the line will vary with the size and weight of the underlined type. The thickness and offset of the **Double Underline** are also fixed.

Figure 5.8 Several paragraphs with different letter spacing ("spread") settings

Spread -5%

Congress shall make no law respecting an establishment of religion, or restricting a free exercise thereof; or abridging the freedom of speech, or of the press; or the right of the people peaceably to assemble, and to petition the Government for the redress of grievances.

Spread -2%

Congress shall make no law respecting an establishment of religion, or restricting a free exercise thereof; or abridging the freedom of speech, or of the press; or the right of the people peaceably to assemble, and to petition the Government for the redress of grievances.

Spread -1%

Congress shall make no law respecting an establishment of religion, or restricting a free exercise thereof; or abridging the freedom of speech, or of the press; or the right of the people peaceably to assemble, and to petition the Government for the redress of grievances.

Spread 0%

Congress shall make no law respecting an establishment of religion, or restricting a free exercise thereof; or abridging the freedom of speech, or of the press; or the right of the people peaceably to assemble, and to petition the Government for the redress of grievances.

Spread 1%

Congress shall make no law respecting an establishment of religion, or restricting a free exercise thereof; or abridging the freedom of speech, or of the press; or the right of the people peaceably to assemble, and to petition the Government for the redress of grievances.

Spread 5%

Congress shall make no law respecting an establishment of religion, or restricting a free exercise thereof; or abridging the freedom of speech, or of the press; or the right of the people peaceably to assemble, and to petition the Government for the redress of grievances

NOTE FrameMaker does not provide the controls for customizing the thickness and offset of underlines found in some other Windows desktop publishing programs.

The **Change Bars** option is specific to FrameMaker and is not really a typeset option at all. Change Bars are vertical bars that appear in the margin next to text that has been edited, as in Figure 5.10. This option is particularly useful when several people have to work together on a document. Change Bars can be turned on for specific types of paragraphs via the check box in the Paragraph Designer or an analogous check box in the Character Designer (described later in this chapter) or they can be turned on globally for the entire document by selecting the **Change Bars** option on the Format menu and checking the **Automatic Change Bars** box in the Change Bars dialog box (Figure 5.11). The other settings in the dialog box control the position and appearance of the bars and allow you to clear all the change bars in a document.

F i g u r e   5 . 9   The effects of the attribute settings in the Default Font group

Under**line**

Numeric **Underline**

Double Underline

Overline

~~Strikethrough~~

Super^{script}

Sub$_{\text{script}}$

Small Caps

F i g u r e   5 . 1 0   A document with change bars

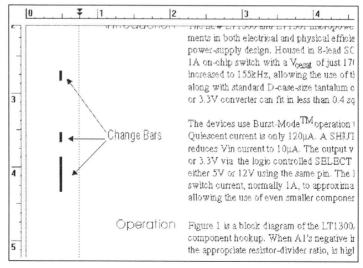

Figure 5.11 The Change Bars dialog box

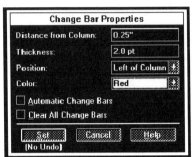

The settings in the Change Bars dialog box will allow you to position change bars beyond the margins of your physical page. It may also fail to display the change bars at some screen magnifications if you make the bars too thin. If you are going to use change bars, it is up to you to **NOTE** select settings that work in your document and on your screen.

Superscript/Subscript, which were two separate check boxes in FrameMaker 3.0, have been combined into a single drop-down list box. You can now set the offset and size of superscripted and subscripted characters in the Document Properties dialog box (select **Document** from the Format menu). Unfortunately, these settings are global for the document, which is really not satisfactory. Fine typography requires that superscript and subscript sizes and positions be selected in relation to the font in which they are used. Factors such as x-height, cap height, and ascender and descender heights should be taken into consideration. If you need superscripts and subscripts in your documents, it is probably best to set the size and offset for the text format in which you use them most frequently, for example, body text or figure captions. If these settings are not satisfactory for other text formats, you will have to shift them manually with the Control and arrow keys.

Capitalization is a new option in FrameMaker 4.0. There are three options in this drop-down list box: **Small Caps**, **Lowercase**, and **Uppercase**. **Lowercase** and **Uppercase** are straightforward, if not terribly useful: they set all of the text in the selection to either lowercase or uppercase. The **Uppercase** setting may occasionally be useful for headings, i.e., when you want to change a group of headings that were typed caps/lowercase to all caps.

The **Small Caps** setting requires some additional explanation. This setting formats regular caps/lowercase type as full-size caps/reduced caps. The height of the reduced caps is set, as a percentage of the normal cap height, in the Document Properties dialog box (Format>**Document**). This feature might better be called simulated small caps or reduced caps; the result is not the same as true small capitals.

The last check box, **Pair Kern**, adjusts the spacing of certain pairs of characters so that their bodies overlap. Which pairs of characters are adjusted depends on the design of the font and is based on kerning tables that are part of the font files. Some character pairs that are normally kerned are shown in Figure 5.12. Good kerning is particularly important for large display type. You can also apply pair kerning to selected pairs of characters via the Character Designer, described later in this chapter.

Figure 5.12 Kerned vs. unkerned character pairs

Not Kerned	**Kerned**
AT AY AV AW Ay Av Aw A' FA F. F, TO	AT AY AV AW Ay Av Aw A' FA F. F, TO
TA Ta Te To Ti Tr Tu Ty Tw Ts Tc T. T,	TA Ta Te To Ti Tr Tu Ty Tw Ts Tc T. T, T:
T: T; T- LT LY LV LW Ly L' PA P. P, VA	T; T- LT LY LV LW Ly L' PA P. P, VA Va
Va Ve Vi Vo Vr Vu Vy V. V, V: V; V- RT	Ve Vi Vo Vr Vu Vy V. V, V: V; V- RT RV
RV RW RY Ry ff WA Wa We Wo Wi Wr	RW RY Ry ff WA Wa We Wo Wi Wr
Wu Wy W. W, W: W; W- YA Ya Ye Yo	Wu Wy W. W, W: W; W- YA Ya Ye Yo Yi
Yi Yp Yq Yu Yv Y. Y, Y: Y; Y r. r, r- y. y,	Yp Yq Yu Yv Y. Y, Y: Y; Y- r. r, r- y. y, v.
v. v, w. w,	v, w. w,

Manual Kerning and Shifting

In addition to using the **Pair Kern** option in the Default Font Properties group, you can manually shift the position of selected characters either horizontally or vertically by pressing and holding the **Alt** key and pressing one of the arrow keys on the numeric keypad. The increment which the characters are shifted depends on the screen magnification—the higher the magnification, the finer the movement. Unfortunately, there is no way to store the shift as part of a format. Hence, if you want to use the same shift consistently (for example, to do a manual superscript or subscript), you'll just have to remember how many keystrokes to use.

N O T E

You can also use the **Spread** option in the Character Designer to adjust the horizontal spacing of selected characters.

Pagination Properties

The Pagination Properties group (Figure 5.13) is new in FrameMaker 4.0. It combines three options that were parts of other groups in FrameMaker 3.0, **Start**, **Keep With**, and **Widow/Orphan Lines**, with controls for two types of heads that are new in FrameMaker 4.0: **Run-In Heads**, which appear as part of the first lines of other paragraphs, and **Side Heads**, which "hang" in the margin outside of text columns.

Figure 5.13   The Pagination Properties group in the Paragraph Designer

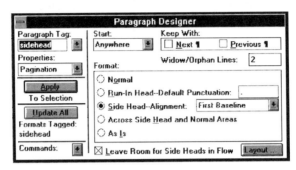

Start

This option can be used to restrict the placement of certain types of paragraphs. The options are **As Is, Anywhere, Top of Column, Top of Page, Top of Left Page**, and **Top of Right Page**. For example, you would probably allow body paragraphs to start at any location on the page where the text flow happens to put them, but you might want to restrict the placement of your highest level of heading to the top of the column or the top of the page. If you want each new chapter of a publication to start on a right-hand page, you could format your chapter titles or chapter numbers to start at the top of the right page.

Keep With

This option also affects the placement of paragraphs on the page by allowing you to force two consecutive paragraphs to stay on the same page or move to the next page together. The options are **Next ¶**, meaning keep the tagged paragraph on the same page as the following paragraph, and **Previous ¶**, meaning keep the tagged paragraph on the same page as the previous paragraph. For example, you would not want a subhead to appear at the bottom of a column or page, so you would format your subheads keep with **Next ¶**. This way, a subhead that would otherwise appear at the bottom of a column or page would be forced to the top of the next column or page in order to stay with the body paragraph to which it refers.

Widow/Orphan Lines

The term *widow* has two different meanings in typography. Traditionally, it meant a single word or hyphenated syllable forming the last line of a paragraph. In FrameMaker and other desktop publishing applications, a widow is the first line of a new paragraph that occurs at the bottom of a text column, with the remainder of the paragraph occurring at the top of the next column or page. An orphan is the last line of a paragraph occurring at the top of a text column. The **Widow/ Orphan Lines** value in the paragraph format specifies the minimum number of lines from the paragraph that must be kept together at the top or bottom of a text column. Be aware that, in multiple column formats, a widow/orphan setting greater than one may make it difficult to achieve even columns at the bottom of the page. However, you may be able to compensate for this with the **Feathering** feature (see Chapter 7).

Run-In Heads

A run-in head is a head that appears as part or all of the first line of a text paragraph, such as that in Figure 5.14. It is distinguished from the rest of the paragraph by having a different character format, for example a different type family, weight, or angle. In FrameMaker 3.0, you could create the appearance of a run-in head by applying a different character format, but the run-in head remained part of the text paragraph, and hence could not be included in a table of contents or other generated list, used as the target of a cross-reference, or mirrored in a header or footer. Nor was it easy to transform freestanding heads to run-in heads or vice versa. Either operation required considerable manual editing. FrameMaker 4.0 corrects this shortcoming.

Figure 5.14 A Run-in head

> **Article V**—The Congress, whenever two thirds of both houses shall deem it necessary, shall propose Amendments to this constitution, or, on application of the Legislatures of two thirds of the several States, shall call a Convention for proposing Amendmendments, which, in either case, shall be valid to all Intents and Purposes as part of this Constitution, when ratified by the

To transform another paragraph, such as a freestanding head, to a run-in head, click an insertion point in the paragraph, then select the **Run-In Head** radio button. You may optionally specify a space and/or punctuation mark to separate the run-in head from the rest of the paragraph by typing it in the adjacent text box. If you want to use a special character, type its symbolic code (for example, \m for an em dash). Apply the run-in head properties to the selection like any other paragraph properties and the run-in head will move to the appropriate position in the following paragraph. If necessary, switch to the Default Font properties group to change the format of the run-in head to distinguish it from the text paragraph it runs into.

Side Heads

Side heads are headings that appear to hang in the margins, outside the text columns of a document. Actually the heads are *in* the text columns, but the columns have been divided into two areas, one for regular body paragraphs and another for the heads. Hence, side heads require a bit more planning than most other paragraph format options (though, of course, you should carefully plan *all* aspects of a publication design). You must design the text columns of your document (see Chapter 4) to allow room for both the regular text area and the heads. This entails making the text columns wider than normal, extending them into what would normally be the margins.

Having designed a page layout with text columns of appropriate dimensions, use the following procedure to create a Side Head format:

1. Place an insertion point in the text flow where you want to use the format. (Unlike other paragraph format properties, a side head format affects all of the text in the flow—all paragraphs that are *not* formatted as side heads are indented to make room for the heads.)

2. Select the **Layout** button in the lower-left corner of the designer. The dialog box in Figure 5.15 will appear.

Figure 5.15 Side Head Layout for Current Flow dialog box

3. Check the **Leave Room for Side Heads in Flow** box.

4. Specify the Width of the side head column and the Gap between the side head column and the regular text column. The sum of these spaces will be subtracted from the text column.

5. Select the position of the side heads from the pull-down list box. The options are **Left**, **Right**, **Inside**, and **Outside** (see Figure 5.16).

Figure 5.16 The four side head positions

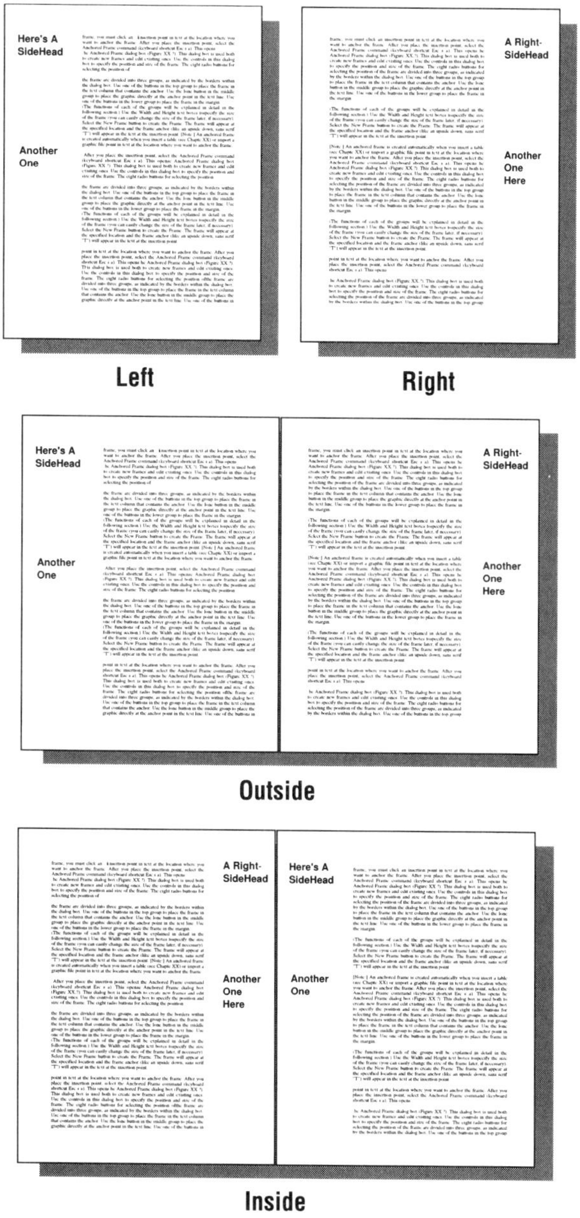

Left

Right

Outside

Inside

6. Select **Set** to apply the format to the flow. Any text paragraphs *not* tagged as side heads will move out of the area reserved for the heads.

Having prepared the columns for the heads, you can design the heads themselves:

1. Click an insertion point in a paragraph that you want to format as a side head.

2. Select the **Side Head** radio button.

3. Select one of the three alignment options: **First Baseline**, **Top Edge**, or **Last Baseline**. **First Baseline** aligns the first baseline of the body paragraph with the first baseline of the side head. **Top Edge** aligns the top edge of the first line of the body paragraph with the top edge of the first line of the side head. **Last Baseline** aligns the baseline of the first line of the body paragraph with the baseline of the *last* line of the side head. (For side heads with a single line, there is no difference between **First Baseline** and **Last Baseline** alignment.)

4. Apply the format to your selection and/or store it in the catalog.

5. Create whatever other properties your side heads require (for example, font family, weight, alignment, and so on), as you would for any other paragraph.

When you use a side head format, all indents and tab stops in non-side head paragraphs are measured from the edge of the normal text area, rather than from the edge of the larger text column.

N O T E

When you change the vertical alignment of side heads, the heads remain stationary and the body paragraphs are shifted up or down to make the alignment. Hence, choosing **Last Baseline** for multi-line side heads can result in significant extra space being inserted between body paragraphs.

N O T E

Positioning Heads Across the Full Page Width

There is one other head-formatting option in the Pagination Properties group, represented by the **Across Side Head and Normal Areas** radio button. Applying this option causes a head to occupy both the side-head column and the regular text column. You could use this setting for major, top-of-page headings or chapter titles in a publication that uses side heads for minor headings. Or you could use it in conjunction with various left indents to create staggered headings that begin in the margin and overlap the body text columns (Figure 5.17), a popular format in technical books and manuals at present.

Figure 5.17 Staggered headings (created with the "Across Side Head and Normal Areas" option)

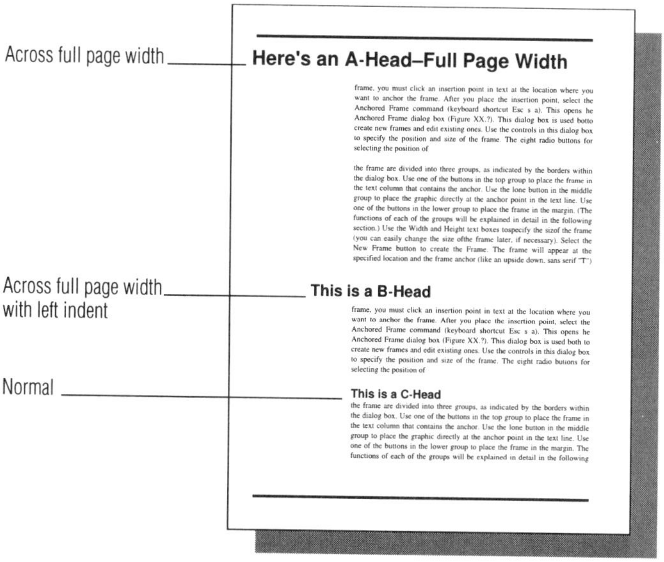

Numbering Properties

The fourth group in the Paragraph Designer is used to create autonumbered paragraphs. Autonumbering is a powerful feature of FrameMaker that allows you to create numbered series of paragraphs, such as steps in a process, series of equations, numbered headings, figure and table captions, or topics in an outline. When you add or delete items in an autonumbered series, FrameMaker automatically adjusts the numbering.

The principal action to be performed in the Numbering Properties group (see Figure 5.18) is the design of the autonumbering format for the selected paragraph type. An autonumbering format can include the following items (see Figure 5.19): A series label, one or more counters, text and punctuation (which can occur both before and after the counter), and special characters such as bullets or tabs. If you want the numbering to use a different typestyle than the default for the paragraph, you can include a character format.

To create a numbering format, turn autonumbering on by checking the check box. Next, select a counter from the building blocks displayed in the list box. You can type the building blocks in the text box below the autonumbering check box, or you can add building blocks to the format by clicking on them in the list box. The principal building blocks are described in Table 5.1.

Figure 5.18   The Numbering Properties group in the Paragraph Designer

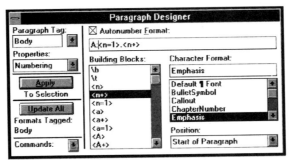

Figure 5.19   Anatomy of a numbering format

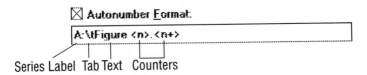

Series Label Tab Text Counters

Table 5.1   Numbering format building blocks

Code	Meaning	Example
n	Arabic numeral	1, 2, 3, ...
a	lowercase alphabet	a, b, c, ...
A	uppercase alphabet	A, B, C, ...
r	lowercase Roman numeral	i, ii, iii, ...
R	uppercase Roman numeral	I, II, III, ...

The counter portion of the format is placed between angle brackets (<>). Other items, such as text, punctuation, or tabs, are placed outside the brackets. The additional symbols + and = are used inside the brackets to control how the numbering is updated: + means update the counter by 1, and = means set the counter to the value that follows the = sign. For example, <n+> means use Arabic numerals and update the counter for each paragraph with the tag; <n=1> means use the number 1 for each paragraph with the tag. A numbering symbol without a + or = sign, such as <n>, means don't update the counter value (use the value from the previous numbered paragraph).

FrameMaker 4.0 includes two new symbols for controlling the counter: 〈 〉 means keep the counter value the same, but don't display it, and 〈 =0〉 means reset the counter to zero but don't display it. These symbols are useful as place holders in complex formats using multiple counters, as will be demonstrated shortly.

The easiest format to create is a simple numbered list. The only format code this requires is 〈n+〉. ; this means use Arabic numerals followed by a period and a space and increment the value with each new paragraph. We'll call this format "List Item." This produces a result such as that in Figure 5.20. You could use Roman numerals or alphabetic characters instead of Arabic numerals by substituting their codes for the n, but the basic principle remains the same. Suppose, however, that you want to create a second numbered list in the same document or chapter using the same format. If you just tag the paragraphs in the second list with the List Item format, the second list will pick up the numbering where the first list left off. You could create a different format for the second list, and for each subsequent list in the document, but fortunately, there is a more efficient approach. You need only create a new tag for the first item in the list (we'll call it, imaginatively, "First Item") with the code 〈n=1〉. . This format resets the number to one. Apply this format to the first item in each subsequent list and apply the List Item tag to all the remaining items in the list. You can create as many simple lists in a document as you wish, using only these two formats.

Figure 5.20   A simple autonumbered list

1. Open both the document with the format you want to copy (the source) and the document in which you want to use the copied format (the destination).

2. Click an insertion point in the source document paragraph (paragraph format) or select a text block (character format) with the format you want to copy.

3. Open the Edit Menu and select **Copy Special> Character Format** or **Copy Special>Paragraph Format**, as appropriate.

4. If you are copying a paragraph format, click an insertion point in the paragraph in the destination document where you want to apply the format; if you are copying a character format, highlight the block of text in the destination document to which you want to apply the format.

5. Open the Edit menu and select **Paste** to apply the format.

SHORTCUT

You can use the **Next ¶** setting in the Basic Properties group to ensure that a First Item paragraph is always followed by a List Item paragraph.

Using Series Labels

The formats described above will work well for a series of non-overlapping lists, such as the steps in a series of procedures to be performed in succession in a service manual or instructional book. However, it will not work for numbered lists that overlap. For this situation, you need to use a *series label*. A series label can be any printing character followed by a colon. If it is included, the series label must be the first item in the format. The purpose of the series label is to distinguish among different overlapping series in the same text flow. For example, you might want to number figures, tables, and photographs in the same chapter or publication, with the numbered items being freely interspersed in the layout, using formats such as Figure `<n+>`, Table `<n+>`, and Photo `<n+>`. If you don't use series labels, FrameMaker will simply update the counter once for each numbered item it finds, producing a single continuous series of numbers for figures, tables, and photos combined. However, if you use series labels, such as F:Figure `<n+>`, T:Table `<n+>`, and P:Photo `<n+>`, FrameMaker will distinguish among the three formats and maintain three separate numbered series.

A more complex task is to create the numbering formats for a standard outline. The codes for the first four levels of a standard outline are shown in Table 5.2. An outline must have formats for each level in the hierarchy, and the counters for each level must be updated only when appropriate. This means that FrameMaker must keep track of several different counters, updating the one that is currently displayed, while maintaining all the others. Here, the `< >` symbol is used to keep the counters for the higher levels from being updated while the lower level is updated and displayed. Hence, each level has one `< >` for each higher level. If the `< >` were not included, FrameMaker would assume that all the formats belonged to a single list, and the first three items would be I, B, and 3, rather than I, A, and 1.

Table 5.2 Numbering codes for a standard outline format

Code	Function	Example
`<R+>.`	First level	I.
`\t< ><A+>.`	Second level	A.
`\t\t< >< ><n+>.`	Third level	1.
`\t\t\t< >< >< ><a+>.`	Fourth level	a.

N O T E Placing the tab codes in a numeric format does not create the necessary tab stops. They must be created using the **Tab Stops** option in the Basic Properties group or the tab buttons on the Formatting Bar. You could also use different left indents rather than tabs to align the different levels of an outline.

A slightly different format is used for a legal or numeric outline, which attaches the number from the higher hierarchical level to its subtopics (for example, 1., 1.1., 1.1.1., and so on.) The codes for this format are shown in Table 5.3. This format is also used to number headings, figures, and tables in some technical publications. For additional examples of numbering formats, examine FrameMaker's outline templates.

Table 5.3 Formatting codes for a legal or numeric outline

Code	Function	Example
`<n+>.<n=0>`	First level	1.0
`<n>.<n+>`	Second level	1.1
`<n>.<n>.<n+>`	Third level	1.1.1
`<n>.<n>.<n>.<n+>`	Fourth level	1.1.1.1

Bulleted Lists

You can use an autonumbering format to create a bulleted list. You can also create bulleted items by manually typing the bullet character and a tab, but using an autonumbering format offers the advantages of being able to quickly change the bullet style or other aspects of the format, and to transform numbered lists or other formats into bulleted lists and vice versa.

This simplest method for creating a bulleted list is to define a paragraph tag with a numbering format that consists of just the bullet character code and the tab code (`\b\t`). To create a paragraph that "hangs" from the bullet, you must also use the Basic Properties group to set a first line indent of zero and a positive left indent. Set the first tab stop in the paragraph to the same position as the left indent. (Use this same procedure for numbered lists that hang.) If you are going to mix bulleted lists with body paragraphs that use a first-line indent, it is a good idea, design-wise, to use the same figure for the left indent of bullet paragraphs and the first-line indent of body paragraphs. In many cases, a one-em indent makes a good starting point. If you're using a side head format, (described earlier in this chapter) you can create bullet lists with bullets that hang in the left margin by making the bullet list items side heads with wide left indents.

If you don't want to use the predefined bullet character, you can substitute any other character that is available on your system. The Zapf Dingbats font offers many good choices, as do other decorative fonts. To use a character from one of these fonts as a bullet, you must create a Character Format (described later in this chapter) with the appropriate font and size. The format will appear in the Character Format list in the Numbering Properties group. Type the character you want to use as part of the numbering format, then select the Character Format from the list box. The selected character format will appear in the text box above the list. For example to use the shaded box character from the Zapf Dingbats font (❏), followed by a tab, type o\t in the numbering format box, then select the Zapf Dingbats character format.

Advanced Properties

Don't be put off by the name if you don't consider yourself an "advanced" user—this group of properties controls paragraph characteristics that are important to the overall appearance and legibility of body type, namely hyphenation and word spacing. It is essential to understand the effect of these characteristics and use them correctly to obtain consistent, professional results.

Hyphenation

FrameMaker uses a combination of dictionary-based and rule-based hyphenation. When it encounters a word that needs to be hyphenated, FrameMaker first looks up the word in the spell-checker dictionaries. If the word is listed in one of the dictionaries, FrameMaker uses one of the hyphenation points stored there. If the word is not listed, FrameMaker applies a series of rules to select a hyphenation point. You can also manually control hyphenation of selected words by inserting discretionary hyphens and nonbreaking hyphens while you type (see Chapter 3), by suppressing the hyphenation of selected words, or by altering the hyphenation points of words in the spell-checker dictionaries (see Chapter 11).

In the Automatic Hyphenation area of the Advanced Properties dialog box (Figure 5.21), you can set the following hyphenation properties, in addition to turning hyphenation on or off:

Figure 5.21   The Advanced Properties dialog box

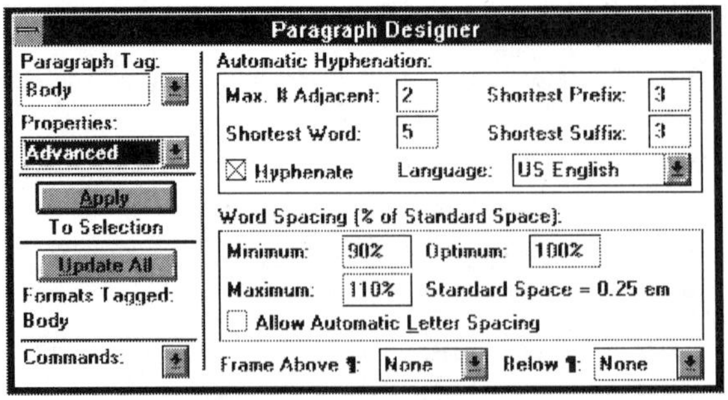

Max # Adjacent—selects the number of consecutive lines that can end in a hyphen. Fewer hyphenated lines make body text easier to read, but may result in more loose lines in justified text or a more ragged edge in left-, right-, or center-aligned text. The narrower the column for a given type size, the more consecutive hyphens will be needed to avoid loose or ragged lines. For reasonably sized columns of body type, a maximum of two consecutive hyphens is a good rule of thumb.

 You may be used to a program, such as PageMaker or Ventura, that can automatically flag loose lines. FrameMaker does not offer this feature, so you will have to keep an eye open for them. Look for lines that stand out visually from the flow of body text because of excessive white **N O T E** space between words.

Shortest Word—designates the shortest word length that can be hyphenated. The higher the value, the fewer the words that may be hyphenated and hence the greater the possibility of loose or ragged lines.

Shortest Prefix/Shortest Suffix—these two settings control the length of the shortest syllable that can occur before and after a hyphen. As with the **Shortest Word** option, increasing the value of either of these settings will tend to reduce the number of hyphens and increase the likelihood of loose lines or excessively ragged line ends.

Language

This selection determines which dictionary FrameMaker uses to look up hyphenation points. If you create documents that mix different languages and have the appropriate foreign language dictionaries installed, you can select the appropriate language to use in hyphenating any given paragraph. The Language setting is also used by the spelling-checker for selecting the appropriate dictionaries when checking multilingual documents.

Word Spacing

Word spacing, not surprisingly, is the space between consecutive words (here FrameMaker has retained the conventional term). There are three settings here which, in conjunction with the letter spacing (Spread) and hyphenation settings, have a considerable effect on the spacing and overall appearance of paragraphs, especially body text. The three settings—**Minimum**, **Maximum**, and **Optimum**—are expressed as percentages of the standard spacing for the default font, which also appears in the dialog box. The latter figure is a feature of the font and cannot be easily altered by the user.

FrameMaker uses the **Minimum**, **Maximum**, and **Optimum** values in adjusting the spaces between words in each line. The greater the range of values you give it, the more flexibility it will have. How this is manifest depends on the type of alignment you have selected for the paragraph. In left-, right-, and center-aligned paragraphs, a wider range results in less ragged line ends, whereas in justified paragraphs a wider range results in tighter spacing and fewer loose lines (see Figure 5.22). An additional setting, **Allow Automatic Letter Spacing**, affects only justified paragraphs. When on, this setting allows FrameMaker to adjust the spacing between characters in order to keep the spaces between words within the limits specified by the **Minimum** and **Maximum** settings.

F i g u r e   5 . 2 2   A paragraph set with several different word spacings

Justified—50/100/150

The right of the people to be secure in their persons, houses, papers, and effects, against unreasonable searches and seizures, shall not be violated, and no Warrants shall issue, but upon probable cause, supported by oath or affirmation, and particularly describing the place to be searched and the persons or objects to be siezed.

Justified—100/100/100

The right of the people to be secure in their persons, houses, papers, and effects, against unreasonable searches and seizures, shall not be violated, and no Warrants shall issue, but upon probable cause, supported by oath or affirmation, and particularly describing the place to be searched and the persons or objects to be siezed.

Left Aligned—50/100/150

The right of the people to be secure in their persons, houses, papers, and effects, against unreasonable searches and seizures, shall not be violated, and no Warrants shall issue, but upon probable cause, supported by oath or affirmation, and particularly describing the place to be searched and the persons or objects to be siezed.

Left Aligned—100/100/100

The right of the people to be secure in their persons, houses, papers, and effects, against unreasonable searches and seizures, shall not be violated, and no Warrants shall issue, but upon probable cause, supported by oath or affirmation, and particularly describing the place to be searched and the persons or objects to be siezed.

Frame Above ¶/Below ¶

This option is used to attach reference frames to selected paragraphs. Reference frames contain frequently used graphic or textual elements, such as rules, icons, ornaments, or special headings, that are stored on reference pages. The available reference frames for the document can be selected from pop-up menus and attached either above or below the selected paragraphs. For information on creating reference frames, see Chapter 4.

Table Cell Properties

The final group in the Paragraph Designer, Table Cell Properties, applies only to tables, and will therefore be reserved for Chapter 20.

Character Formats

Character formats behave similarly to paragraph formats, except that they are applied to individual characters, words, or phrases, rather than to entire paragraphs. The most obvious uses of character formats are to emphasize selected words with type variations such as boldface or italics and to apply attributes such as superscript, subscript, or underline. You can also use a character format to apply a special font such as Symbol, Zapf Dingbats, or a decorative or technical Pi font.

The Character Designer

The Character Designer (Figure 5.23) has also been renamed and redesigned in FrameMaker 4.0. It is much simpler than the Paragraph Designer, consisting of only one group. In fact, the Character Designer is identical to the Default Font group in the Paragraph Designer, and all of the options perform in exactly the same manner as described above, so we won't duplicate that information here. Similarly, the Apply and Update All buttons and the Command menu work the same way as those in the Paragraph Designer.

Figure 5.23 The Character Designer

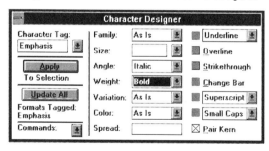

Creating Flexible Character Formats

If you want a character format to change only one or two aspects of the text that it is applied to (as is usually the case), set the Character Designer to As Is using the option on the Command menu, then set only the characteristics you want the format to change. This way, you won't have to revise your character formats whenever you change some property of the paragraphs they reside in. It will also allow you to use your character formats on a variety of different types of paragraphs, rather than having to create lots of different formats for use in special cases.

Suppose, for example, that your body text font is 11-point Times Roman. If you wanted to use boldface for emphasis, it would seem logical to define the Emphasis character format as 11-point Times bold. This would be okay, provided you intend to use the format only in body paragraphs and you never decide to change the family or size of your body type. But suppose you decide later to change your body type to 12-point Adobe Garamond. When you apply the new paragraph format to your body paragraphs, you will be asked whether to remove or retain overrides. Since you don't want to lose your emphasized characters and other character formats, you choose to retain your overrides. The result is that you now have body text in 12-point Adobe Garamond regular, with emphases in 11-point Times bold. Not what you want. Now you have to go back and redefine your Emphasis format as 12-point Adobe Garamond bold (you can't change it to As Is at this point, because that would just cause it to remain 11-point Times). And you will have to re-edit the format (and any others you defined along the same lines) *every time* you change the Body paragraph format.

If you use the As Is setting when you first create the Emphasis format, then all the other characteristics of the emphasized characters will change appropriately when you change the Body paragraph format. This works even when the font family uses a different name for boldface, though, of course, it will not work if you don't have a boldface version of the font installed on your system. Use the same technique for any other character format you use to apply a single variation, such as subscript, superscript, italic, small caps, or the like, and you'll spend far less time fooling with character formats. This not only allows you to change paragraphs that have character format overrides and have the formatted characters change appropriately, it also allows you to use the same character formats in paragraphs with different typefaces or sizes.

N O T E

Using a character format to select a non-text font, such as Symbol or Zapf Dingbats, is a bit tricky if the characters to which you are applying the format have ANSI codes higher than 0126 (see Appendix 1 for a complete listing of characters and their ANSI codes). If you type the character(s) first and then apply the format, the wrong characters will appear and frustration will likely ensue. To get the right characters, you must apply the character format at the insertion point first, and then type the ANSI codes.

NOTE If you select all the text in a paragraph, *including the paragraph mark (¶) at the end* and apply a character format, you will change the Default Font properties of the paragraph format to match those of the of the character format. To change the character format of an entire paragraph *without* changing the paragraph format, select all the characters in the paragraph *except the paragraph mark.*

Using Formats from Other Documents

In addition to using the formats that you have created in a particular document or inherited from one of FrameMaker's templates, you can borrow a few formats or even a whole catalog from another FrameMaker document. This applies equally to Paragraph Formats and Character Formats.

If you want to use only a few formats from another document, the easiest approach is to copy the format from one document and paste it in the other:

1. Open both the document with the format you want to copy (the source) and the document in which you want to use the copied format (the destination).

2. Click an insertion point in the source document paragraph (paragraph format) or select a text block (character format) with the format you want to copy.

3. Open the Edit Menu and select **Copy Special>Character Format** or **Copy Special>Paragraph Format**, as appropriate.

4. If you are copying a paragraph format, click an insertion point in the paragraph in the destination document where you want to apply the format; if you are copying a character format, highlight the block of text in the destination document to which you want to apply the format.

5. Open the Edit menu and select **Paste** to apply the format.

NOTE Copying a single paragraph or character format into a document doesn't automatically add that format to the catalog in the destination document. If you want to add the new format to the catalog, you must open the Paragraph Designer or Character Designer, as appropriate, and follow the procedure described earlier in this chapter for storing a new format in the catalog.

You can also import all the Paragraph and/or Character formats from another document or template, along with many other characteristics:

1. Select the **Import>Formats** option from the File menu.

2. A dialog box like that in Figure 5.24 will appear. Check the aspects of the document you want to import, that is, paragraph formats and/or character formats. Be sure to check *only* the appropriate characteristics; otherwise, you might drastically revise every aspect of your document in one fell swoop.

Figure 5.24   The Import Formats dialog box

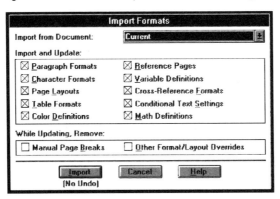

3. Open the list box that says "Current," meaning the document that's currently active, and select the document from which to import the formats (you can only select a document that's currently open).

4. Click the **Import** button to import the selected formats from the source document into the catalog(s) of the destination document, where they will be added to the existing formats.

N O T E The formats from the source catalog will replace formats in the destination catalog with the same name. If you're not careful, this might cause unforeseen results where formats of the same name exist in both catalogs. Since the operation of importing the formats is not undoable, it's a good idea to save your document immediately before performing this operation, so you can revert to the saved version if something goes awry.

Formatting Characters on the Fly

In addition to creating and applying character and paragraph formats, Frame-Maker allows you to perform limited text formatting using three commands on the Format menu: **Font**, **Size**, and **Style**. The **Style** option duplicates several of the choices found in the Character Designer and the Default Font Properties group in the Paragraph Designer: **Plain**, **Bold**, **Italic**, **Underline**, **Double Underline**, **Strikethrough**, **Overline**, **Change Bar**, **Superscript**, and **Subscript**. To use these commands, a block of text must be highlighted.

Six of the buttons in the Text Editing group on the Quick Access Bar affect text formatting:

P   Plain text (the default font for the paragraph)

B   Bold text

U   Underlined text

I   Italic text

A   Increase type size by one point

A   Decrease type size by one point

You can also set paragraph alignment, tab stops, and line spacing with the buttons on the Formatting Bar.

Use these formatting methods for occasional, one-of-a-kind format changes. In most cases, it is preferable to use paragraph and character formats, as they ensure consistency throughout a document or family of documents and make it easy to change all occurrences of a particular format.

CHAPTER 6

Typographic Tips and Techniques

As mentioned in the introduction to this book, the aesthetic traditions of typography in the West have evolved over the course of the last 500 years (much longer if we consider the work of the scribes and stone carvers who first developed the letter forms that we now take for granted). We see the results of these typographic traditions daily in our books, magazines, and newspapers (and even on our computer screens), but most of us are blissfully unaware of the choices a designer makes in specifying type for a particular publication. For the average reader, this ignorance is not a problem—either a publication is easy to read and to navigate, or it is not. How it came to be that way is not the reader's concern. However, when one sits down at a computer equipped with a program like FrameMaker, bristling with typographic controls, and attempts to produce an attractive publication, these matters take on a new importance. It is all well and good to know which buttons to push in FrameMaker to achieve a given typographic effect (and to teach you this is, of course, the primary object of this book), but such knowledge is of limited utility if one doesn't know when or where it is appropriate (or inappropriate) to use these devices.

It is beyond the scope of this book (and perhaps beyond the skills of the author) to provide a thorough course in the aesthetics of typography, but I hope the following tips and suggestions will at least make the reader aware of what some of the issues are in choosing and setting type and provide some useful rules of thumb for making such decisions. I hope also that at least some readers will not be content with the information presented here, but will be stimulated to further study of this fascinating field.

Users of FrameMaker and other desktop programs have one advantage that traditional designers lacked: the ability to experiment with the different parameters that affect the appearance of type and see the results almost instantaneously. If you're in doubt about the effect a particular setting will have, try it, print a page, and compare. It will cost you nothing but a bit of paper and toner—a far cry from the costs of experimentation with traditional metal or photo typesetting methods!

Typefaces, Families, and Fonts

Traditionally, typesetters and designers use the term *typeface* to refer to a particular type style. For example, Times Roman, Times bold, Times italic, and Times bold italic are four different, but related, typefaces. These, and whatever other versions of Times are available from a particular type vendor, constitute a family. Some typefaces have large families and others are virtual orphans. By contrast, the term *font* traditionally meant a particular typeface in a particular point size, for example, 12-point Times italic or 14-point Helvetica bold. In the desktop computer realm, font has usurped the traditional meaning of typeface. This makes a certain amount of sense, because when one purchases a font for desktop computer use, one is purchasing an outline from which software can generate a virtually unlimited range of point sizes. Hence individual fonts of fixed size, in the traditional sense, don't exist on desktop computers. In any case, the term font, on the menus of FrameMaker and elsewhere in the PC/Windows environment, means what typeface traditionally meant, and is so used in this book. Just be careful how you talk around traditional typesetters and designers if you don't want a lecture.

Body Type vs. Display Type

There are basically two kinds of type in a typical publication: body type and display type. Body type is the type that is used to set the body text in a publication, that is, the type that conveys most of the subject matter. Certain other elements in a publication will most likely use the same type family as the body type, for example, bulleted lists, numbered lists, quoted material (extracts), figure and table captions, and footnotes. They will be distinguished from the basic body type by differences in size, weight, width, angle, placement, or the like. For example, extracts (paragraphs of material quoted from another source) are normally distinguished from body type by being indented from both the left and right margins of the text column. They may also be set in a size one or two points smaller than the body text, with a corresponding reduction in line spacing, and/or set in italic type.

Display type includes chapter titles and numbers, headings and subheadings, display quotes, headers and footers, and the like. Display type needs to call attention to itself by contrasting with body type. There are many ways that this can be accomplished:

- A different type family (for example, it is a common practice to use a serif face for body type and a sans serif face for display type)

- A different (usually larger) size

- A different weight or width (for example, boldface or extended)

- A different color

- Different letter spacing (usually looser than body type)

- An unusual position, (for example, set full-page width in a multi-column page format, or "outdented" into or hanging in the margin)

- By graphic emphasis, such as the use of rules, icons, or other attention-getting devices

There are many approaches to the design of display type. The *Chicago Manual of Style* (The University of Chicago Press, Thirteenth Edition, 1982), for example, recommends that the same type family and size be used for headings and body type, with the headings being distinguished by being set in caps/small caps, all small caps, italics, or the like. This is a very conservative practice. It is much more common these days to use a contrasting type family for display type, as is done in this book. Still, it is a good idea to keep the number of different type families in a publication to a minimum in order to achieve a unified appearance. There are few publications that need more than two type families, one for body text and one for display, ignoring the occasional use of special fonts for technical and scientific characters and of decorative fonts such as Zapf Dingbats.

In complex publications, display type needs to reflect the hierarchical organization of the publication, by placing the greatest emphasis on the most important items. For example, if the publication uses three levels of headings, the most important (highest) level should be the largest, the heaviest, or the most contrasting in whatever element you have selected. Less important headings should be smaller, lighter, or less conspicuously positioned than the more important ones. The reader should be able to tell at a glance the relative importance of a heading and should be able to find the beginning of a section or topic easily based on headings.

Measuring Type

The height of type is traditionally measured in points, where 1 point = .01384" or approximately 1/72 of an inch. FrameMaker, like most other desktop publishing programs, uses PostScript points, which are exactly 1/72 of an inch, or approximately 0.01388". The difference between the traditional point and the PostScript point is thus only 0.0000488", or about 5/100,000 of an inch. This does not seem to be a quantity worth getting upset about, but some traditional typographers and designers do. Just try telling some of these people that a point is 1/72 of an inch and you'll find out what I mean.

The width of lines of type and other measurements such as indents and offsets on a page are traditionally measured in picas, where 1 pica = 12 points. Hence, in FrameMaker and other PostScript-oriented desktop publishing applications, there are exactly six picas to the inch. This is the American and English practice; a slightly different system, using Didot points and Ciceros, is used in continental Europe. Another common unit of measure is the em, which is a horizontal measure equivalent to the height of the type in points. Hence, whereas the point and the pica are fixed measures, the em varies in size with the height of the type.

This is all clear and comprehensible enough, but unfortunately, when we use points to specify the height of type on our computers, we are not measuring anything that can be seen. The novice may naively assume that the height of a font in points measures some visible property of the characters, such as the distance from the bottom of the lowest descender to top of the highest ascender or cap, but this is not the case, as can be seen from a comparison of several different type styles set at the same point size, as in Figure 6.1. What is actually being measured is the height of the *body* of the character. This term derives from the days when type was cast from lead—the body was the slug of lead on which the character was cast. However, the percentage of the height of the slug that was occupied by the actual letter forms varied considerably among different typefaces, so that letter forms from different typefaces that were the same point size often differed considerably in height.

Figure 6.1   Several typefaces set at the same point size (note the difference in actual character heights)

Hamburgefons	**Hamburgefons**	Hamburgefons	**Hamburgefons**
(Avant Garde)	(Helvetica Condensed)	(Gill Sans)	(Franklin Gothic)
Hamburgefons	Hamburgefons	Hamburgefons	Hamburgefons
(Times Roman)	(Palatino)	(Weiss)	(Garamond)

For reasons beyond my comprehension, this practice was carried over from lead type to photo typesetting, and thence to digital type. Thus, we have a system of measurement based on something that no longer exists. As a consequence, it is impossible to accurately measure an example of an unknown typeface. One cannot tell, for example, whether one is looking at 14-point type that is set "solid" (i.e., with no additional line spacing) or 12-point type set with two points of additional spacing.

The only way to find out for sure is to consult a type specimen book or to reproduce the desired effect by trial and error. Perhaps someday this system will be
reformed and the measurement of type will be based on the dimensions of the
actual characters, rather than on nonexistent pieces of lead. I expect this to happen right after the ambiguities of English spelling are corrected.

X-Height

Another important concept in understanding the proper formatting of type is a
measure known as the *x-height*. The x-height of a typeface is the height of the portion of the lowercase characters above the baseline, not counting the ascenders.
Typefaces with larger x-heights, such as Avant Garde or Bookman, appear larger
than typefaces with smaller x-heights such as Times Roman, even when the overall
heights of the letter forms are the same. It is important to consider the x-height of
a typeface when setting line spacing. Typefaces with taller x-heights need more vertical space in order not to appear crowded.

Choosing a Typeface

Among the most important decisions in designing any publication will be the selection of the typeface and size for body text. If your publication is intended for
extended reading, the body should probably be set in a serif typeface. Studies have
shown that, in general, serif types are easier to read than sans serif faces. Sans serif
faces are all right for fairly short publications, or for publications meant to be
browsed rather than read straight through. Although we now have hundreds of digital typefaces to choose from, as opposed to the dozen or two that a traditional typesetter might have had available, it is still hard to go wrong by choosing a classic serif
face such as one of the varieties of Caslon, Baskerville, Garamond, or even the ubiquitous Times Roman. (This book is set in Baskerville).

What size you choose for your body text and how much line spacing you give it will
depend, in part, on how much text you have to set and how much space is available
to fit it in. The traditional method of determining the proper type size for a publication involved getting an accurate character count of the manuscript (assuming a
complete manuscript existed when you designed your type specs!) and then looking up the typeface in a sample book to see how many characters per pica it aver-
aged. This, in combination with the text column size of the publication, would
yield an approximation of how many pages the publication would require for a
given type size and line spacing. (Of course, the amount of display type and artwork complicates matters.) If you have access to type specimen books (or are willing to make your own in FrameMaker) and have the luxury of starting work with a
completed manuscript, you can use the traditional method. Much desktop work,
however, is too ad hoc for this, and the best way to judge the amount of space

required by a given project in a given typeface may be simply to create your basic page layout and apply it to your text and see how many pages result. Then you can easily adjust the size and line spacing of your body paragraph format and observe the results. Whatever the constraints imposed by the amount of material, you should probably avoid type smaller than nine points in a standard text face for publications intended for extended reading.

You have a great deal more freedom in selecting display type, so much so that I am not going to attempt to offer advice on this matter. The choice of the proper display type depends on the purpose of your publication and the kind of impression you wish to make on the reader. I will only reiterate that you should, in most cases, try to keep the number of type families to a minimum—one family for display type and one for body text should be enough in most situations.

Indents and Spacing

It is traditional to use either a first-line indent or extra spacing, or both, to indicate the beginnings of paragraphs. A typical first-line indent is one em. FrameMaker doesn't offer an em as a measurement for specifying indents, but you can achieve the same result by specifying an indent equal to the height of your font in points. Many contemporary designers omit the first-line indent in paragraphs immediately following a heading or subhead, considering that the heading alone is more than sufficient to indicate the beginning of a new paragraph. Based on an informal survey, most contemporary books and magazines do not use extra line spacing between paragraphs. This is a good practice, in that it helps avoid widow/orphan problems (see later). Extra spacing between paragraphs seems to be more common in manuals and other technical publications. If you're going to add space between paragraphs, half a line of extra space (for example, six points if your body text is set with 12-point spacing) is probably sufficient in most cases. The only obvious exception to this is in multi-column publications, where using a half space between paragraphs forces the baselines of adjacent columns out of alignment. In such a case, you should use either a full space or none.

In setting the spaces above and below body paragraphs, it is important to consider the effect on headings. If you want headings to "rest" on the paragraphs to which they refer, rather than "floating" in space above them (generally a good practice, in my opinion), use a Space Below setting if you want to create space between body paragraphs. That way, you won't have to create separate formats for body paragraphs with and without headings.

How Much Line Spacing to Use

By default, FrameMaker uses a line spacing of 120% of the default font height. This is not a bad rule of thumb for body type, but it should not be rigidly adhered to. Both the characteristics of the font being set and the context in which it appears should be taken into consideration in selecting line spacing. Remember, the height of a font in points is the height of the *body* on which the type was traditionally cast, not the height of the actual characters. There is considerable variation among typefaces in the percentage of the body height occupied by the letter forms. Typefaces with letter forms that occupy more of the body height will need more line spacing to be legible, whereas typefaces that have built-in white space may look all right with little or no added line spacing. Line length is another factor to consider. Long text lines can make it difficult for the eye to move quickly from the end of one line to the beginning of the next. Using more line spacing can help compensate for this effect. The line spacing for titles, headings, and other large display elements that occupy two or more lines needs particular attention—FrameMaker's 120% default line spacing is often far too loose for these items. You may want to use only one or two points of added space for these, or even set them solid (no added space) if the text is such that ascenders and descenders don't collide. Of course, very loose spacings of display type can also work, especially with such devices as side heads. It all depends on the overall page design.

Using non-fixed line spacing, one of FrameMaker's line spacing options, should probably be avoided, at least in body type. Non-fixed spacing may produce irregularly spaced lines, which can look clumsy and unprofessional. If you must use fonts of different heights in a block of body text, it is probably better to choose a larger line spacing for the whole block of text, rather than using irregular line spacing, although, of course, the effect must be judged in context.

Letter Spacing (Spread)

Use this option with caution at least in body text; small changes can produce significant results, both in the amount of space a block of text occupies and in its appearance and readability. You can use small negative settings to tighten lines and get rid or a widow or a loose line, or to eliminate a situation where the same word is hyphenated on two successive lines, but you should probably avoid settings tighter than about -2.0%, depending on the typeface. All else being equal, tighter letter spacing will make a block of text look darker and looser spacing will make it look lighter.

Letter spacing should not be viewed in isolation. For the best results letter spacing needs to be selected in conjunction with line spacing and word spacing to create attractive, readable type. Although you can use tighter letter spacing (and word spacing) to fit a block of text in a particular fixed space, there are limits to how far you can go with this approach before producing ugly, crushed, illegible type. It is preferable to edit the text to fit the space (if you have the authority) rather than to pack it in with overly tight spacing. If you have a large project that requires setting a lot of text in a small space, it is better to select a condensed font that was designed to be set tight than to use a conventional-width font with tight letter spacing.

About the only situation where you might want to use looser line spacing in body text would be in justified text in a narrow column, such as a runaround for a graphic. A situation like this can sometimes create excessive space between words, and you might want to increase letter spacing in order to reduce the word spacing. You have more leeway in spacing display type. For example, setting type very loosely is a common practice in headings and titles, as shown in Figure 6.2.

Figure 6.2   A heading set with loose letter spacing

POSITIVE   LETTER   SPACING

Letter spacing should not be viewed in isolation. For the best results letter spacing needs to be selected in conjunction with line spacing and word spacing to achieve attractive, readable type. Although you can use tighter letter spacing (and word spacing) to fit a block of text in a particular fixed space, there are limits to how far you can go with this approach before producing ugly, crushed, illegible type. It is preferable to edit the text to fit the space (if you have the authority) rather than to pack it in with overly tight spacing. If you have a large project that requires setting a lot of text in a small space, it is better to select a condensed font that was designed to be set tight than to use a conventional-width font with tight letter spacing.

About the only situation where you might want to use looser line spacing in body text would

---

Small Caps

FrameMaker 4.0 offers what it calls small caps in the Default Font group of the Paragraph Designer, but, as mentioned previously, these are not true small caps. In traditional metal typography, small caps were a separate part of the font, distinct in both design and size from full-sized caps. Figure 6.3 shows the difference. The Times Roman small caps in the figure are equal in height to the x-height of the lowercase characters of the same point size, and they also have a stroke width that matches the lowercase characters. The reduced caps, in contrast, have considerably thinner strokes and, consequently, a narrower set width than the true small caps or the lowercase. As a result, the reduced caps will look weak when combined with normal lowercase type.

Figure 6.3 True small caps vs. reduced caps

ABCDEabcde	ABCDEFHGIJ	ABCDEFGHIJ
Times Roman clc (caps lower case)	Times Roman small caps (same height as lc Times Roman)	Times Roman caps reduced to size of small caps

True small caps are now available for many popular typefaces. You may be able to get away with using reduced caps occasionally, especially in display type, but if you want to use small caps in body paragraphs as a regular part of your typographic repertory, you would be well advised to get the real thing for your most frequently used typefaces. Consult your font vendors for information. If you install true small caps on your system, they will appear as a separate font family in the Paragraph and Character Designers and in the Font Family pop-up menu. Be sure to select them this way, rather than via the **Small Caps** option in the Paragraph or Character Designer.

Small capitals are typically used in display type—they are well suited for minor headings in publications that use several levels of headings, as they are distinctive without being overly obtrusive. Another use for small caps is for setting acronyms and initials, which are normally set in all caps, as well as for abbreviations such as A.D./B.C. and A.M./P.M. Compare the two examples in Figure 6.4. The left column sets acronyms in full-sized caps and the right column uses small caps. The acronyms set in small caps are much less obtrusive than those in full-sized caps and blend more smoothly with the rest of the text. Additionally, the paragraph occupies less space because the small caps have a narrower set width.

The right column also uses "old-style" or non-lining figures (numerals). Old-style figures are a natural complement to small caps. Like small caps, they blend unobtrusively with lowercase text. Unlike "modern" or lining figures, the tops of most old-style figures match the x-height of the font; 6 and 8 have ascenders, 3, 4, 5, 7, and 9 have descenders, and 0, 1, and 2 have neither. Adobe packages small caps and old-style figures together for many popular serif fonts, so if you have true small caps for a given typeface, you probably have old-style figures as well.

Figure 6.4 Small caps vs. full-sized caps

—Features 250MB SCSI or IDE HD, VRAM SVGA adapter and monitor, 5 EISA and 2 VESA expansion slots, and 4MB RAM (upgradable to 16MB).	—Features 250MB SCSI or IDE HD, VRAM SVGA adapter and monitor, 5 EISA and 2 VESA expansion slots, and 4MB RAM (upgradable to 16MB).

Widows and Orphans

The term "widow" has two different meanings in typography. Traditionally, it meant a single word or hyphenated syllable forming the last line of a paragraph. In Frame-Maker and other desktop publishing applications, a widow is the first line of a new paragraph that occurs at the bottom of a text column, with the remainder of the paragraph occurring at the top of the next column or page. An orphan is the last line of a paragraph occurring at the top of a text column. How serious a design sin is allowing widows and orphans? It depends. Although some writers roundly condemn all widows and orphans, one sees numerous examples in general-interest magazines and daily newspapers (not that these are necessarily paragons of good design). My preference is to avoid widows and orphans in cases where extra space is inserted between paragraphs. In these cases, the widow or orphan, separated from the rest of the text by white space, just draws too much attention to itself. However, if the spacing between paragraphs is the same as the line spacing within the paragraphs, widows and orphans are quite inconspicuous, and I cannot see that they do any harm…that is, unless an orphan is also a widow in the older sense, i.e., a single word or syllable forming the last line of the paragraph. In this case, it's probably best to edit the text, if you have editorial authority, or tighten the letter spacing in the preceding line, to draw the stray word up into the previous line.

Word Spacing

Word spacing is another important factor in producing clean, legible type. This is another characteristic that should not be viewed in isolation; it interacts closely with hyphenation, letter spacing (spread), and line length. The goal in selecting word spacing is to achieve relatively uniform spacing in all the lines of a paragraph, without producing loose lines (in justified type) or excessively ragged line ends (in left-aligned type). If word spacing is too tight, words tend to run together, making reading difficult. If spacing is too loose, "rivers" of white space appear, meandering through the text columns and distracting the reader from the type. Both undesirable extremes should be avoided.

The narrower the column width, the more difficult it can be to achieve good word spacing in justified type. In a narrow runaround next to a graphic, there might be only two or three words; in a situation like this, FrameMaker has no choice but to justify the line by expanding the one or two spaces between the words. If you turn on the **Allow Automatic Letterspacing** option, the program can increase the letter spacing in problem lines, thereby reducing the excessive word spacing. Designers differ as to whether this is a good idea, but you might want to try it in paragraphs with word spacing problems.

Hyphenation is another important factor in the word spacing equation. Allowing hyphenation will help FrameMaker maintain even word spacing. In narrow columns of justified type, some hyphenation will be necessary to achieve good word spacing. In left-aligned type, hyphenation can also be used to control the shape of the ragged edge. On the other hand, too much hyphenation can also be a problem—generally, you should not allow hyphens in more than two successive lines, although in very narrow columns, it may be necessary to violate this rule to achieve good word spacing. In problem areas, you may need to use discretionary hyphens and/or to suppress hyphenation of certain words to achieve satisfactory results. (Consider yourself lucky if you can find time for such niceties.)

Generally, letter spacing and word spacing should be consistent; that is, tight word spacing should be used with tight letter spacing and loose word spacing with loose letter spacing, although, as mentioned previously, in some situations looser letter spacing can help overcome bad word spacing in narrow lines. Condensed fonts generally require less word spacing than extended fonts. This is, to some extent, built into the font files—observe the different Standard Word Spacing values for the different fonts installed on your system in the Advanced Properties group in the Paragraph Designer. The legibility of small type may be improved by increased word spacing.

CHAPTER 7

Managing Text Flows

What Is a Text Flow?

Every FrameMaker document has one or more text flows. A text flow is a stream of text that flows in a controlled manner through the columns and pages of a document. A text flow is identified by a flow tag. When you click an insertion point in a text column, the flow tag for that column appears in the status area at the lower-left corner of the document window, as in Figure 7.1. Flow tags and their associated settings determine how text flows from column to column and page to page. In addition, flow tags can optionally control the alignment of text across columns in multi-column formats (synchronization) or space text vertically so that it fills columns to the bottom of the page (feathering).

Figure 7.1   A flow tag in the status area

Many types of documents, such as books, manuals, and reports, use only a single text flow, which runs continuously from the beginning to the end. Others, such as newsletters, magazines, and journals, may have many discontinuous text flows, which skip over columns or pages. Creating a document with a continuous text flow is easy. When you start a new document based on the predefined landscape or portrait page or on a custom blank page, FrameMaker automatically assigns the text columns on the master pages a flow tag of A and turns their autoconnect settings to "on." FrameMaker templates intended for documents with continuous text flows, such as book chapters, reports, letters, and memos, are set up the same way. When a document is set up with one text flow and autoconnect is on, text will automatically flow from column to column and from page to page. As you add new text to the document, new pages are automatically created as needed, based on the left and right master pages. Text columns on body pages inherit the flow tags of the template columns on their corresponding master pages. For this kind of document, you really never have to worry about flows, although you may still want to use the **Synchronization** or **Feathering** options, described later in this chapter, when you work in a multi-column format.

Creating documents with multiple and/or discontinuous flows requires more effort and planning. The process of creating such documents forms the principal subject of this chapter.

Assigning Flow Tags

Flow tags can be assigned to text columns either on master pages or on body pages. Columns on body pages automatically inherit the flow tags of the template columns on the master pages on which they are based. Columns on body pages can be assigned new flow tags, and those changes can be transferred to master pages, as described in Chapter 4. When you have a set of flows that is the same on most or all pages, it is usually best to assign your flow tags on master pages and use the auto-connect setting to create new pages. In a document such as a newsletter or magazine, where text flows may skip columns or pages, it is usually preferable to use the master pages to create the basic column layout, but to manage the flow from column to column directly on the body pages.

Whether you're working on a master page or a body page, the process of assigning a flow tag is the same:

1. Click an insertion point in the column to which you want to assign the tag.

2. Open the Format menu and select **Flow**. The Flow Properties dialog box (Figure 7.2) will appear.

3. Type a name for the flow tag. The convention in FrameMaker is to use uppercase letters for flow tags, but this is not mandatory. You should, however, keep flow tag names fairly short, so there will be room for both the flow tag and paragraph tag names in the status area.

4. Check or uncheck the Autoconnect check box. The autoconnect setting determines whether FrameMaker will automatically create a new page when the text in the tagged column expands beyond the space on the current page. Do not confuse this with the process of connecting columns, which will be described later in this chapter.

Figure 7.2   The Flow Properties dialog box

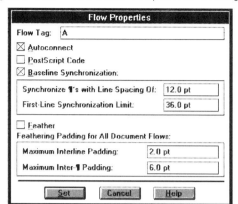

5. You might also want to turn on the **Baseline Synchronization** or **Feathering** option. These features will be described later in this chapter, as will the **Post-Script Code** option.

6. Select **Set** to assign the tag.

When you start a new document, all the columns on the page will initially have the same flow tag. Before you can assign a different tag to a single column, you must disconnect that column from the others using the **Disconnect Current Column** command on the Layout Palette. This process will be explained in detail later in this chapter.

If you attempt to give a column a flow tag that is already used by another column on the same page, FrameMaker will notify you that the tag name is already in use and instruct you to use a different name or to connect the column to the other column that already uses the tag name. Do the former if you want to create a different, independent flow; do the latter if you want text to flow from the column that already has the tag name to the other (or vice versa). The process of connecting columns will be explained later in this chapter.

Creating a Document with Parallel Flows

One situation where it is desirable to use flow tags with autoconnect on master pages is in creating a document with two or more flows that run in parallel columns throughout a document, such as a parallel translation or a cue sheet for a film or play. To create such a system of parallel flows, use the following procedure (see Figure 7.3 for an illustration of the steps):

Figure 7.3 Creating parallel flows

1. Three connected columns, one flow

2. Disconnect center column from left and right

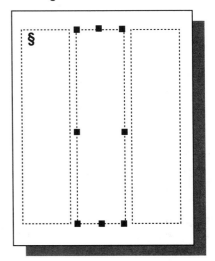

3. Three disconnected columns with separate, untagged flows

4. Assign a new flow tag to each column

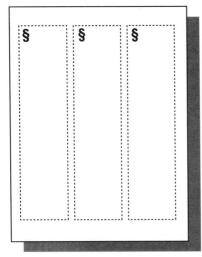

1. Create the basic page layout, as described in Chapter 4. Make whatever adjustments are necessary to your column sizes and positions.

2. Initially, all the columns on the master page(s) will be connected and have the same flow tag. (This is shown by the fact that only the first column has an end-of-flow symbol.) Before you attempt to change the flows of the second and third columns, they must be disconnected:

   a. **Ctrl**+click on the center column to select it. Only the center column should be selected.

   b. Open the Layout Palette (Format>**Pages**>**Layout Commands**) and select **Disconnect Current Column**. From the submenu, select **From Both**. (If you were performing this operation on a page with two columns, you could select the left column and disconnect it **From Next** or select the right column and disconnect it **From Previous** with the same results).

   c. The three columns on the page are now disconnected, as is evident from the fact that each has its own End of Flow symbol (§). Each is a separate, untagged flow. Now you can assign a separate flow tag to each column:

3. Click an insertion point in the first column and select **Flow** from the Format menu.

4. Type a flow tag and check the **Autoconnect** box.

5. Select **Set** to assign the tag.

6. Repeat the preceding three steps for the other columns.

7. If you are working on a double-sided document, you will have to repeat this process for the other master page. If the column layout for the left and right master pages is the same, it will be quicker to copy the columns and paste them on the other master page.

Unfortunately, FrameMaker will not automatically create parallel flows on facing pages (the conventional format for parallel translations). In order for FrameMaker to properly apply left and right master pages to new pages as they are created, the same set of flows must exist on both the left and right masters. When this is not the case, FrameMaker will automatically create a new page based on the same master and using the same flow tag as the previous page when the flow reaches the bottom of the page. If you want to create a document with parallel flows on facing pages, you must turn off autoconnect for your flows and manually add disconnected pages and connect them as needed, as described later in this chapter.

Setting Up Newsletter Pages

When you work with a multi-column format with several independent flows, such as a newsletter, it is best to set up the basic layout on master pages, but to manage the flow of text on body pages. When you set up master pages as described in this section, the master pages control the placement of text columns on the body pages, but do not control text flow from page to page. New pages *will not* be automatically created when the text flow reaches the bottom of the last column on a page; you will have to create new pages manually.

1. Create the basic column layout, as described in Chapter 4.

2. Once the empty document has been created, set the view to Master Pages.

3. Click an insertion point in the first column on the first master page.

4. Select **Flow** from the Format menu.

5. In the Flow Properties dialog box, uncheck the **Autoconnect** check box.

6. Repeat steps 3–5 for each master page in the document.

All the columns on all the master pages will have the default flow tag, A, and the columns on a given page will be connected to one another, but not to columns on other pages. You will create new pages and connect columns manually, as described later. If you don't want the columns on the same page to be connected automatically, disconnect the columns on the master pages from one another.

Adding Disconnected Pages

If you are creating a document based on master pages that are not autoconnected, FrameMaker will not automatically add a new page when the flow reaches the end of the current page. Instead, it will display a solid line at the bottom of the last text column on the page to indicate that the text has overflowed the column (see Figure 7.4). (You must have **Borders** selected on the View menu for the line to be visible.) The overflowing text is not lost; it is simply hidden until the overflowing column is connected to another column where the flow can continue. To continue the flow, you must manually add a disconnected page (so called because its text columns are not automatically connected to those on preceding pages). Use the following procedure:

1. Open the Special menu and select **Add Disconnected Pages**. The Add Disconnected Pages dialog box (Figure 7.5) appears.

Figure 7.4 An overflowing text column

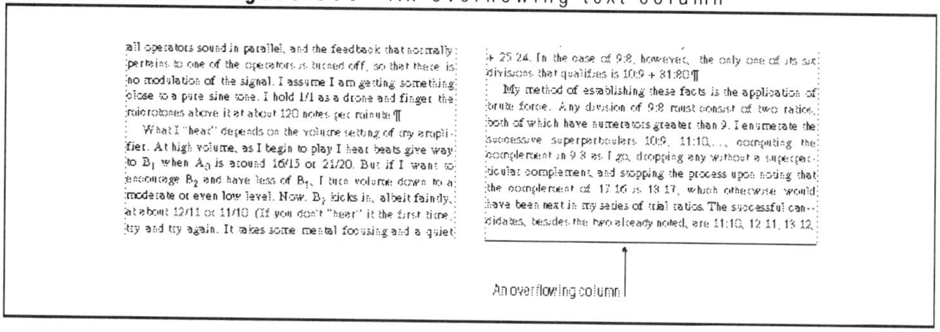

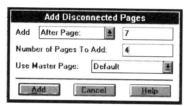

Figure 7.5 Add Disconnected Pages dialog box

2. Specify the location where you want to add the page(s). By default, the dialog box is set to add pages after the current page number, which is what you usually want to do, but you can opt to add the pages before or after any page in the document.

3. Specify the number of pages to add.

4. Specify the master page(s) to use for the new page(s); you can select any individual master page, none, or "Default," which means use the left and right master pages alternately, as appropriate.

5. To add the specified pages, select **Add**. At this point FrameMaker displays a rather hysterical prompt box, saying that you normally type into existing pages and new pages are added automatically. Ignore this unnecessary message and select **OK**.

6. Once the disconnected pages have been added, you must manually connect the overflowed column on the preceding page to a column or columns on the new page(s) in order to continue the flow (see Connecting and Disconnecting columns, next.)

Connecting and Disconnecting Columns

When you work with disconnected pages, you control the flow of text from page to page and column to column by manually connecting and disconnecting columns. When you work this way, it is not mandatory that different stories or articles have different flow tags, or, indeed, that they have any flow tags at all. The only thing that matters is which columns are connected and the order in which you connect them. You can assign different flow tags to different articles as an aid in keeping track of them, but you may find this a nuisance if you use the **Synchronization** or **Feathering** options, which must be turned on or off separately for each flow.

Connecting Columns

The basic process of connecting columns is simple:

1. Select the first of the two columns you want to connect (**Ctrl**+click in the column). The order in which you select the columns determines the direction in which text flows.

2. Select the second column (**Ctrl+Shift**+click in the column). If the second column is on a different page, the first column will appear to be deselected, but FrameMaker remembers the selection.

3. If the Layout Palette is not already on the screen, open it by selecting **Pages** on the Format menu and selecting **Layout Commands** from the submenu.

4. Select **Basic** from the Layout Palette and select **Connect Columns** from the submenu.

5. If the columns you selected are not already connected and connecting them will not create a circular flow, FrameMaker makes the connection.

If the first of the connected columns has overflowing text, the text will flow into the next column when the connection is made. If one of the two columns has a flow tag and the other does not, both columns will have the flow tag after they are connected. If both columns have flow tags, the tag from the first column will be applied to both.

It may or may not be necessary to connect columns that appear on the same disconnected page. It depends on the template columns on the master page on which the disconnected page is based. If the columns on the master page have the same flow tag, the columns on the body page will be connected; if the columns on the master page are disconnected and have different flows, the columns on the body page will also be disconnected, and you will need to connect them, as described previously, if you want the text to flow from column to column.

Disconnecting Columns

You disconnect columns on body pages when you want to start a new story or article at a particular location on a page, or to jump the continuation of a story to a different column or page. To disconnect a column:

1. **Ctrl**+click in the column to select it. (Only one column can be selected when you perform this operation.)

2. If the Layout Palette is not already on the screen, open it by selecting **Pages** on the Format menu and selecting **Layout Commands** from the submenu.

3. From the Layout Palette, select **Disconnect Current Column**.

4. Select one of the three options from submenu: **From Previous**, **From Next**, or **From Both**.

What happens to flow tags when you disconnect columns depends on their respective positions. If you disconnect columns that are on different pages, the disconnected columns retain whatever flow tags they had previously. If you disconnect columns that are on the same page, the disconnected columns have separate, untagged flows. I cannot discern the logic behind this behavior, but it doesn't really matter much. As mentioned previously, what matters in managing text flows in a complex, multi-flow document is which columns are connected and in what order.

Another non-intuitive aspect of the behavior of disconnected columns is that disconnecting columns doesn't affect any text already in the columns when they are disconnected. For example, if you have two connected columns on a page that both contain text that is part of a flow, and you disconnect the columns, the text stays right where it was. If you want to place another story in the second column, you must first cut the current text and paste it elsewhere (for example, at the bottom of the first column, where it will become overflow). However, if you disconnect a pair of columns *before* typing or placing text in them and then add text to the first column, the text flow will stop at the bottom of the column and become overflow or jump to the next connected column, if one exists.

Skipping Columns

You can make a text flow jump over one or more adjacent columns in the middle of a flow by selecting and connecting two non-adjacent columns. The process of selecting and connecting the columns is exactly as described previously. In this case, the text that was in the skipped columns moves and the columns are left empty. The skipped columns become an untagged, disconnected flow, just as if you had disconnected them from both surrounding columns.

FrameMaker will only allow you to disconnect a column from columns to which it is connected. For example, the last column in a flow can only be disconnected From Previous, whereas the first column can only be disconnected From Next. This may seem self-evident, but there is no easy way to tell visually which column is connected to which, so you may find yourself trying to disconnect columns that are not connected and getting a rude error message as a result.

Splitting Columns

As described in Chapter 4, FrameMaker can split text columns either horizontally or vertically. This can be used either to modify page layouts, or, in conjunction with the commands described earlier for connecting and disconnecting columns, to control text flow. (Actually, the distinction between these two uses is rather artificial—when you're splitting, connecting, and disconnecting columns on a page, you're most likely concerned with both the page layout and the text flow.) The process of splitting a column is simple. Place the insertion point at the location in the column where you want to make the split, select **Split Current Column** from the Layout Palette, and select one of the three options from the submenu: **Below Selection**, **Right of Selection**, or **Into Lines**. **Below Selection**, which splits the column vertically, is the most useful option in a normal multi-column layout. Use **Into Lines** when you want to wrap text around an irregularly shaped graphic.

Splitting columns does not, by itself, disconnect the columns. Text will continue to flow through the columns just as it did before they were split.

Some Uses for Split Columns

Placing a Sidebar

Suppose you are working on a three-column newsletter page, as in Figure 7.6, and you want to interrupt the flow of the text to put a sidebar in the upper portion of the right column. To do this, use the following procedure:

1. Split the right column vertically at the point where you want the sidebar to end.

2. Adjust the two new columns via the Object Properties dialog box or by dragging with the mouse to add some vertical space between the columns.

3. Connect the middle column to the lower section of the right column to make the text flow around the upper section of the column. The upper section of the column is now a separate, untagged flow.

4. Type or paste the sidebar text in the upper section of the right column.

Figure 7.6 Placing a sidebar

1. Split column

2. Adjust split columns

3. Connect Columns

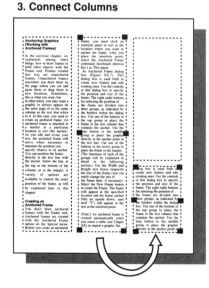

4. Place sidebar

Dividing a Page Vertically

Another useful technique is to divide a page vertically, in order to place one story on the top and the other on the bottom (see Figure 7.7). In the example, we will assume that all three columns initially contain the story that we want to place on the upper section of the page.

Figure 7.7 Splitting a page vertically

1. Split columns

2. Adjust split columns

3. Connect upper & lower flows

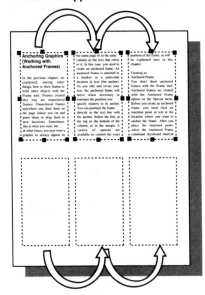

4. Place new story in lower flow

1. Split each of the columns vertically at the same position.

2. Adjust the columns via the Object Properties dialog box or by dragging with the mouse to add some vertical space between the columns.

3. Connect the top left column to the top center column, connect the top center column to the top right column, and connect the top right column to a column on another page. (Remember, the order in which you connect the columns is important—it determines the direction of the text flow.) The text will re-flow, leaving the bottom columns empty.

4. Now, you must connect the lower columns, which are each separate, disconnected flows. Connect them in the proper order—left to center, center to right.

5. Type or paste the text for the second article in the lower columns. The text will flow from column to column, as appropriate.

Placing a Multi-Column Headline

Placing a headline that spans multiple columns (see Figure 7.8) also requires manipulating columns (Ventura users will marvel at the complexity of this process). There are two ways to do this:

■ You can shrink the main text columns and draw a new column for the headline a the top of the page, then connect the headline column to the first text column, or

■ You can split the first text column vertically and stretch it horizontally to accommodate the headline, shrinking the other text columns to make room for it.

Placing a Pull Quote

Yet another situation where you need to split columns is to place a pull quote or drop quote (the same techniques will work for any kind of text box that is not part of a flow). If you want to place the pull quote in a single column width space, the procedure is easy. Just split the original text column above and below where you want to place the pull quote, then connect the sections of the column above and below the one in which you wish to place the quote to jump the text over the center section; this creates a disconnected, untagged flow in which you can place the quote. Adjust the columns as needed, then type or paste the text for the quote. Apply an appropriate paragraph format to the quote.

Figure 7.8   Placing a multi-column headline

1. Before adding head

2. Shorten body text columns

3. Draw text column for head

4. Connect new column to first body column & format head

If you want to place a pull quote that straddles two or more columns, the process is similar, but more elaborate. Assuming that the quote is to straddle two columns, as in Figure 7.9, you should first split both columns into three sections, as shown in the figure. Next, shrink the two sections adjacent to the space where you want to place the quote. It is not necessary to change the column connections—the text will continue to flow as before. Draw a column for the quote in the space you have created. The column you have drawn will be an untagged, disconnected flow. Type or paste the text of the quote in the column and apply an appropriate format.

Figure 7.9 Placing a pull quote across two columns

1. Split columns horizontally

2. Shrink middle sections of split columns

3. Draw a new text column in the gap

4. Type or paste the quote in the column

Tracking Text Flows

When you have a publication that has many text flows that jump around from column to column or page to page, it's easy to lose track of where some of your flows go. You can highlight all the text in a flow by clicking an insertion point anywhere in the flow and using the **Select All in Flow** command on the Edit menu (keyboard shortcut **Ctrl+A**). To track the flow, you can either page through the document or set the scaling to a very small page size to see several pages at one time.

FrameMaker recommends the above technique for keeping track of flows in a complex, multi-flow document such as a newsletter or magazine, but there is another possibility: using color. Click in a given flow and select all the text in the flow, then use the Character Designer to apply a color to all the text in the flow. (Select a color from the pull-down menu, then select the **Apply** button.) Repeat this action for each of the flows you want to track, using a different color for each flow. Again, you can either page through the document or zoom out to view multiple pages. When you're satisfied that all your text is where it belongs, you can use the designer to change the text back to black (or to whatever color you prefer).

Text Flows on Master Pages

If a column on a master page is to act as a template for body pages, it *must* have a flow tag. A column on a master page that lacks a flow tag is assumed to be a background column. When you draw a column on a master page, the Add New Text Columns dialog box appears, in which you specify whether the column is a background or template column. If you are creating a template column, use this dialog box to specify the flow tag and autoconnect setting.

If you disconnect columns on a master page, the disconnected columns become untagged flows, just as they do on body pages. When you do this, FrameMaker doesn't warn you that you have changed these columns from template to background columns. You won't find out until you try to create a new body page based on the master page. Then FrameMaker will warn you that you're about to create a page with no text columns. If you disconnect columns on a master page and you want them to act as template columns, be sure to give each of the columns a flow tag, as described at the beginning of this chapter.

Synchronization and Feathering

These two features don't affect how text flows from column to column and page to page, but rather how the text lines within a given column are aligned and spaced.

However, FrameMaker has placed these options in the Flow Properties dialog box and made them act on all the text in a flow, so they form part of this chapter. Put simply, synchronization causes the baselines of text in different columns to align on a common, invisible grid. Feathering causes text lines in a column to be vertically spaced so that the available text fills the column to the bottom. (Some desktop publishing applications use the term *vertical justification* to describe this effect.) Thus, synchronization is only useful in multiple-column formats, whereas feathering can be used on any page format.

Baseline Synchronization

In a multiple-column document, it can be quite a chore to keep the baselines of body paragraphs aligned across two or three columns (so much so that many people don't seem to bother with it). Opinions differ on the importance of aligning text across columns; I much prefer the clean horizontal lines that result from keeping the baselines of body paragraphs aligned. If your columns are solid text, and you don't add extra line spacing between paragraphs, the baselines will all be aligned, but as soon as you start adding headings, tables, figures, and other elements, the baselines start to go out of alignment. You can avoid this problem to some extent by picking type sizes and line spacings for headings that are multiples of body text line spacing, but sooner or later, something will come along and mess up the grid. In some programs, your only option is to manually add space between paragraphs and above or below tables and figures. In FrameMaker, you can use Baseline Synchronization.

Baseline synchronization creates an invisible grid and aligns baselines of body paragraphs to the grid. There are two important settings for baseline synchronization:

- **Synchronize ¶'s with Line Spacing Of**—this setting establishes the grid to which lines will be synchronized. You should set this to the line spacing of your body paragraphs.

- **First-Line Synchronization Limit**—when a heading that is taller that the synchronization grid appears at the top of a column, as often happens, it has the potential to spoil the synchronization for the whole column. FrameMaker deals with this by placing the baseline of the heading on the grid and letting the tops of the characters extend above the border of the column. The First-Line Synchronization Limit is the maximum character height that FrameMaker will apply this treatment to. Obviously, if you are using synchronization, you should take the effect of first line synchronization into account in designing your headings.

You must set the line spacing for your body paragraph format to "Fixed" for synchronization to work properly.

N O T E

There is a separate synchronization grid for each column on a page. If all the columns on a page start at the same vertical position, then their grids, and, hence, the baselines of their body paragraphs, will be aligned; if the columns don't all start at the same vertical position (for example, some columns are shortened to make room for a graphic at the top of the page), the grids may not be aligned. To make sure that the text is aligned in such a situation, adjust the height of the shortened columns so that they start at a position that is lower than the full-height columns by an exact number of grid lines. For example, if your grid spacing is 12 points, your shorter columns should be shorter than the full-height columns by some whole-number multiple of 12 points.

If you have a format in which columns with different flows appear side by side on the page, you must turn on Synchronization with the same grid settings for all the flows to produce satisfactory results.

N O T E

Feathering

Feathering adds extra space between paragraphs and between lines in order to space text vertically so that it extends to the bottom of the columns. There are two settings for feathering:

- **Maximum Interline Padding**—the maximum amount of space that can be added between lines in feathering.

- **Maximum Inter-¶ Padding**—the maximum amount of space that can be added between paragraphs in feathering.

When FrameMaker feathers text, it first adds space between paragraphs. If it cannot move the last line of a column to the bottom of the page using the maximum inter-¶ padding, it then adds space between lines. If it still cannot feather the column to the bottom of the page without exceeding the maximum interline padding, FrameMaker will not feather the column.

N O T E

If both Synchronization and Feathering are turned on, Feathering takes precedence. However, the first lines of the columns on each page will always be synchronized.

Creating an Image with PostScript Code

PostScript code is ASCII text consisting of commands in the PostScript page description language. PostScript is a programming language that is output by FrameMaker and other desktop publishing, word processing, and drawing programs and is interpreted by laser printers and image setters to produce hard copy output. Although PostScript code is normally output by applications, a skilled programmer can create images by writing PostScript code directly with a text editor or modifying the code produced by an application. FrameMaker has a provision for placing such images in documents.

To import a PostScript code file into a FrameMaker document, draw a text column of an appropriate size for the image. Click an insertion point in the column, then import the file. Open the Flow Properties dialog box, uncheck the **Autoconnect** check box, and check the **PostScript Code** check box.

The PostScript image will not be displayed on the screen as it would be if you imported an EPS file, but the image will print when you print the document, assuming the code is correctly written and free of errors. If there is an error in the code, it may prevent the rest of the document from printing. The PostScript code will be displayed on the screen, but you will not be able to edit the code. To edit the code, you must uncheck the **PostScript Code** box in the Flow Properties dialog box. After you have finished editing the code, check the check box so that you can print the image.

Creating PostScript code is an arcane discipline that is beyond the scope of this book. For those who have some knowledge of PostScript programming, the PostScript code file BIGRGB.PS and the document SEFFECTS, located in the \MAKER\ SAMPLES\PSCRIPT directory, include examples of how PostScript code can be used in a FrameMaker document.

CHAPTER 8

Finding and Changing Items in a Document

Introduction

Every word processor has some kind of *search-and-replace* feature for finding a text string and replacing it with another text string. Early PC desktop publishing programs, which assumed that you would create text in a separate word processor, were rather deficient in this area (Ventura didn't add a search-and-replace feature until version 4.0 for Windows); at present, every major Windows desktop publishing application has a workable search-and-replace, at least for text.

FrameMaker's Find/Change feature is exceptional in that it searches not only for text strings, but for virtually *anything* that exists in a FrameMaker document and is associated with or influences text: character formats, paragraph formats, variables, cross-references, markers of all kinds, and so forth. (For a complete list, see "What You Can Find," later in this chapter.) About the only items you can't search for directly in FrameMaker are graphic images, although you can search for these indirectly by searching for anchored frames. The "change" side of FrameMaker's Find/Change feature is not quite as powerful and flexible as the "find" side (you can't just pick any item from the Find menu and then specify another item of the same or a different class from a comparable Change menu), but it includes a **Change by Pasting** option that will allow you to work around most of its apparent limitations.

Basic Find Procedure

Regardless of what you're looking for, the basic Find procedure is the same:

1. Select **Find/Change** from the Edit menu or use the keyboard shortcut **Ctrl+F**. This opens the Find/Change window (Figure 8.1). (As an alternative, press **Esc f i s** to open the Find/Change dialog box. The dialog box has all the same controls as the window, albeit in a slightly different arrangement, but because it is a dialog box rather than a window, you can't leave it open on the screen while you perform other operations.)

2. In the Find/Change window, open the Find list box and select the type of item you want to search for. Two of the items in the list, Character Format and Conditional Text, open additional dialog boxes; these items will be explained later in this chapter.

3. Depending on the item you have selected, you may or may not need to type a text string in the adjacent text box. In the most obvious case, searching for a text string, you would type the text to search for here. If you are searching for a character format or paragraph format tag, you would type the tag name. If you are searching for a cross-reference with a particular format or a particular variable, you would type the format or variable name, and so on. You can type up to 255 characters in the Find Text box. If you are searching for *any* cross-reference, *any* variable, *any* marker, or some similar broad class of items, you would leave the box blank. (Detailed procedures for searching for particular classes of items will be given later in this chapter.)

4. Check or uncheck each of the four check boxes, as appropriate to your search:

   ■ **Consider Case**—check this box for a case sensitive search (for example, you want to find "Windows," but not "windows" or "WINDOWS").

   ■ **Whole Word**—check this box if you want to find the specified text only as an independent word and not as a component of a larger word. For example, if you entered the word "range" and checked the box, FrameMaker would find "range," but not "strange," "arrange," or "ranger." If you unchecked the box, all the examples could be found.

   ■ **Use Wildcards**—check this box to enable FrameMaker to use wildcard characters in search strings. Most PC users are familiar with the DOS wildcard characters "*" (meaning any group of characters, including zero characters) and "?" (meaning any single character). FrameMaker uses these, plus several other UNIX-derived wildcards, to permit more flexible searches. FrameMaker's wildcards are explained later in this chapter under "Using Wildcards in Searches."

■ **Find Backward**—normally, FrameMaker searches from the insertion point toward the end of the document. Check this box to have it search from the insertion point toward the beginning of the document. (FrameMaker searches by flows rather than page by page, so in a multi-flow document, it may appear to jump around erratically.)

5. Select the **Find** button to begin the search. If the item is found, FrameMaker makes the document window the active window and highlights the item. If it is not found, FrameMaker displays a message to that effect.

N O T E

The Find procedure works on only one class of pages at a time. For example, if you begin your search with the view set to Body Pages, FrameMaker will search all the flows on the body pages in your document, but it will not search master pages or reference pages. If you want to search on these pages, you must change the view and perform separate searches. In addition to searching text *flows* on pages, Find/Change also finds instances of its search text string in *text lines* created with the text tool on the Tools Palette (see Chapter 12).

Figure 8.1 Find/Change dialog box

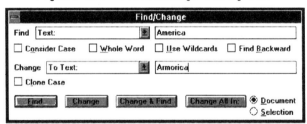

Stopping a Search

You can stop a search in progress at any time by pressing the **Esc** key.

What You Can Find

FrameMaker will search for the following items:

■ **Text**—the text that you type in the Find Text box.

- **Character Format**—search for text with a character format that you specify in a dialog box that appears (not the same as searching for a character format *tag*).

- **Paragraph Tag**—search for a paragraph with the tag name you enter in the Find Text box.

- **Character Tag**—search for text with the tag you enter in the Find Text box.

- **Any Marker**—search for an instance of any of FrameMaker's marker types.

- **Marker of Type**—search for any instance of a particular marker type that you specify in the Find Text box (for example, Index, Cross-Ref, Header/Footer $1, etc.).

- **Marker Text**—search for a marker with particular marker text that you specify in the Find Text box.

- **Any Cross-Reference**—search for any cross-reference, regardless of format (finds the *reference*, rather than the *source*; to find the source of a cross-reference, search for Marker of Type: Cross-Ref, or, if you know the text to search for, Marker Text.

- **Cross-Reference of Format**—searches for any cross-reference with the format name you specify in the Find Text box.

- **Unresolved Cross-Reference**—searches for any unresolved cross-references, that is, cross-references for which FrameMaker cannot find the source (see Chapter 10).

- **Any Variable**—searches for any variable.

- **Variable of Name**—searches for any instance of the variable with the name you specify in the Find Text box.

- **Anchored Frame**—searches for any anchored frame (an indirect way to search for graphics).

- **Footnote**—searches for any footnote. (Both the reference and the note are highlighted.)

- **Any Table**—searches for any table, regardless of its tag.

- **Table Tag**—searches for tables with the tag you specify in the Find Text box.

- **Conditional Text**—searches for visible conditional text with the condition tag you specify in the dialog box that appears.

- **Automatic Hyphen**—searches for any hyphen placed in text by Frame-Maker.

- **Text & Character Formats on Clipboard**—searches for text that matches the contents of the clipboard in terms of text, capitalization, and character format.

Using Wildcards in Searches

Most DOS/Windows word processors support the use of the standard DOS wildcard characters "*" and "?" or their equivalents in search-and-replace operations. FrameMaker greatly enhances the flexibility of searches by supporting a more extensive set of wildcards derived from the UNIX environment, where it originated. The FrameMaker wildcard set is shown in Table 8.1.

T a b l e 8 . 1 FrameMaker Wildcard Characters

Character	Represents	Example
*	Any group of zero or more characters, excluding punctuation and spaces	g*d finds words such as good, god, guild, gild, gold, etc.
|	One or more spaces and punctuation at the end of a word	*out| finds out?, bout., flout, and rout, but not route, outrage, outline, etc.
?	Any single character except a space or punctuation mark	r??d finds words such as reed, read, road, raid, etc.
[ab]	Any one of the characters enclosed in the brackets	[fj]ade finds fade or jade, but not made
[^ab]	Any single character *except* those enclosed in the brackets	[^hm]are finds bare and tare but not hare or mare
[a-f]	Any single character in the range in brackets	[q-t]aid finds raid and said but not maid or laid
^	The beginning of a line	
$	The end of a line	

Although the wildcards are obviously useful in searching for text in a document, they are not limited to this use. You can use wildcards in searching character and paragraph format tags, variable names, cross-reference formats, or marker text—in short, anything in the Find list box that uses text for a label.

If you want to search for wildcard characters as ordinary characters in a search in which wildcards are used, precede those that you want interpreted as ordinary characters with a backslash (\). For example, g*d\? would find gold?, gild?, or the like.

Searching for Special Characters

To search for special characters, type their symbolic codes in the Find Text box. (See Table 3.2 in Chapter 3 for a list of the codes.) For example, to find an em dash surrounded by thin spaces, search for \st\m\st. There are three additional special characters that you can only use in searches:

\<	Start of word
\>	End of word
\f	End of flow

You can include these characters in a search string, but not in a replacement string.

Whenever it encounters a backslash in a search text string, FrameMaker assumes that it indicates a special character. Hence, if you want FrameMaker to search for a backslash, you must type two backslashes; for example, to find the string C:\MAKER, search for C:\\MAKER. Similarly, if you want to search for one of the symbolic codes as a text string, rather than as a special character, precede it with an extra backslash. That is, search for \m to find an em dash, but search for \\m to find \m.

Searching for a Character Format

To find text that has a particular character format but does not have a character format *tag* (for example, text that has been formatted using the Formatting Bar or the Quick Access Bar), select **Character Format** from the Find list box. This opens the Find Character Format dialog box (Figure 8.2). This dialog box closely resembles the Character Designer and the Default Font Properties group in the Paragraph Designer.

If you want to search for a complex format, and you already know where to find an example in your document, click an insertion point in a paragraph with the format *before* you select **Character Format** from the list box. The dialog box will be set to the properties of the text where you have placed the insertion point. If you just want to search for text with one or two properties, such as any italic text, regardless of its size or typeface, first set the dialog box to As Is by pressing **Shift+F8**, then select just those properties you want to search for. When the dialog box shows the format you want to search for, select **Set**, then proceed with the search as described previously.

Figure 8.2   Find Character Format dialog box

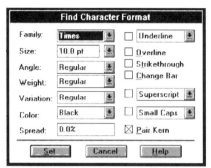

Searching for a Text String with a Particular Format

It might appear that you could search for a particular text string with a particular character format by selecting **Character Format,** as described previously, and then typing a text string in the Find Text box. Alas, this does not work. If you select **Character Format**, FrameMaker ignores any text in the Find Text box and searches for any instance of the character format. The way to find a particular text string with a particular character format is to use the **Text & Character Formats on Clipboard** option. To use this option, you must first cut or copy an instance of the string you want to find to the clipboard. If you don't know where to find at least one instance of the search string in your document, type one, apply any formatting required, and then cut it. FrameMaker will try to match the search string in terms of text, case, and character formatting.

The search string used in a search for Text & Character Formats on Clipboard is limited to 126 characters. There can be more than 126 characters *on* the clipboard but only the first 126 will be used in the search.

N O T E

Searching for Conditional Text

Conditional text is a unique FrameMaker feature that allows you to create multiple versions of a document from a single master version by tagging paragraphs with different condition tags and selectively hiding or revealing text with particular tags.

FrameMaker will search for text with (or without) a specified condition tag. First, text with the tag for which you wish to search must be made visible (see Chapter 22 for details.)

Once you have made your conditional text visible, select **Conditional Text** from the Find list. This opens the Find Conditional Text dialog box (Figure 8.3). Select the name of the condition tag on which you wish to base your search. If you want to search for text with the tag, use the arrow buttons to move the tag name to the In box. If you want to search for text without the tag, move the tag name to the Not In box. To search for all conditional text, move all the tag names to the As Is box. When you have selected the appropriate tag for your search, click the **Set** button, then proceed with the search as described previously.

Figure 8.3   Find Conditional Text dialog box

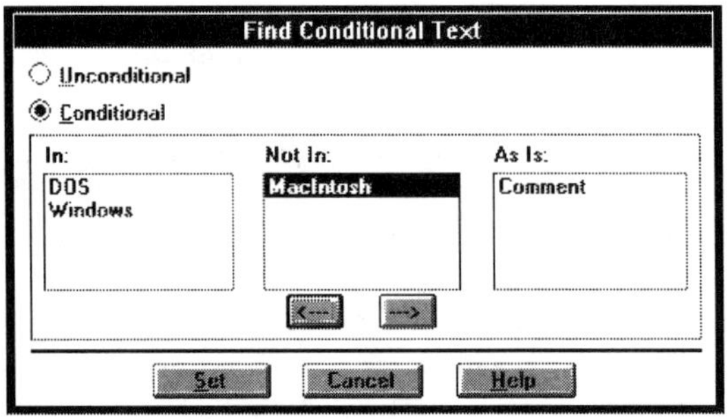

Basic Change Procedure

Once you have found what you are searching for, you can change it. Use the following steps:

1. Select what class of item you will use to replace the item you found. There are only three choices here, as opposed to the multitude of different items you can search for: Text, Character Format, and By Pasting. The last is a very powerful option and makes up, to a significant extent, for the limited number of choices available here.

2. If you are replacing something with text, type the replacement string in the Change Text box.

3. If you are replacing text with text, check or uncheck the Clone Case check box, as appropriate. This box causes the replacement text to take on the capitalization of the search text. For example, you could use this option to replace soap with soup and Soap with Soup.

4. Select one of the buttons at the bottom of the dialog box to make the change:

   ■ **Change**—change only the first instance that you have found.

   ■ **Change & Find**—change the first instance and search for the next.

   ■ **Change All In**—change all the occurrences of the search string in the document or in the selection, depending on the setting of the radio buttons.

What You Can Change To

You have only three options for the class type of items you can use to replace what you find:

   ■ **To Text**—replace what you found with the text in the Change Text box.

   ■ **To Character Format**—replace what you found with a character format that you type in a dialog box such as that in Figure 8.2 (*not* for replacing one character format *tag* with another).

   ■ **By Pasting**—replace what you found with the contents of the clipboard. (Use this for almost any kind of change that does not involve text or character formats, as explained in the following section.)

Changing By Pasting

This feature embodies most of the hidden power in FrameMaker's Find/Change feature: It enables you to replace anything you can find in a document with anything that you can cut or copy to the clipboard, including character and paragraph format tags, elaborately formatted text strings, graphics, equations, variables, cross-references—in short, almost anything that exists in a FrameMaker document *except markers.*

Changing Paragraph and Character Format Tags

The process of changing a character or paragraph format tag has three parts:

1. First, copy the paragraph or character format that you want to paste to the clipboard.

   a. For a paragraph format, place the insertion point in a paragraph with the format you wish to copy; for a character format, select a block of text with the format you wish to copy.

   b. From the Edit menu, select **Copy Special**; from the submenu, select **Paragraph Format** or **Character Format**, as appropriate.

2. Open the Find/Change window, as described earlier, select the item you want to search for, and start the search.

3. When you have found an instance of the item you're searching for, select **By Pasting** from the Change list box and make the change.

As a way of replacing one format tag with another, there is really nothing to recommend this method over the various options offered by the paragraph and character designers; its real utility lies in being able to replace *something else* with a paragraph or character format. For example, most copy editors prefer to work on unformatted copy: double-spaced, unjustified text, in an easily read typeface, with wide margins. In a manuscript intended for copy editing, headings, titles, and the like are typically identified with typed tags, such as <CT> (Chapter Title),<A-head>, and the like. Once the copy editing is finished, the production editor (who may also be the copy editor) has to manually delete the typed tags and apply the proper paragraph formats. In a large publication with complex formatting, this is a tedious and time-consuming process. The FrameMaker Find/Change feature can easily automate this process: Just search for each of the typed tags and replace it with the appropriate paragraph format tag, which you have previously copied to the clipboard.

Placing Text with Complex Formats

Just as you can use Find Text & Character Formats on Clipboard to search for text with complex character formatting, you can use Change By Pasting to replace what you find with formatted text. For example, you might want to search for the string 6.28RC and replace it with $2\pi RC$. The replacement string includes a character (π) from the symbol font, and hence cannot be typed directly in the Change Text box, which doesn't allow for formatting. Instead, type the replacement string anywhere in your document as 2pRC, select the "p" and apply the symbol font using the **Font** command on the Format menu, then cut the string to the clipboard. Search for 6.28RC as text and select Change By Pasting to place the replacement string.

Deleting the Search String

You can delete any class of item that FrameMaker finds, by selecting **Change To Text** and leaving the Change Text box empty. This is a good way to get rid of unwanted markers, which are hard to delete cleanly without also deleting surrounding text.

Working with Markers

Markers behave differently than other FrameMaker objects in that you can search for them, but you cannot automatically change or replace them. FrameMaker gives you three options in searching for markers:

- **Any Marker**—searches for the first marker of any type in the direction of the search. FrameMaker will show you the location of the marker in text, and you will see the T-shaped marker symbol if you have the **Text Symbols** option turned on, but you won't see any other information about the marker. To determine what kind of marker you have found and to read its marker text, open the Marker window and leave it open while you search.

- **Marker of Type**—searches for one 26 marker types:

Header/Footer 1$	Used in running headers and footers
Header/Footer 2$	Used in running headers and footers
Index	Used in generating indexes
Subject	Used in generating indexes
Author	Used in generating indexes
Glossary	
Equation	
Hypertext	Used for navigating in hypertext documents
Cross-Ref	
Conditional Text	
Types 11–25	

You can search for any of these types, and FrameMaker will locate the nearest instance in the search direction and highlight its location in the text. Again, you will need to have the Marker window open in order to see the marker text.

- **Marker Text**—searches for a marker by means of its associated text. This works even if the marker text is not visible in the text flow (as is often the case). If you are uncertain of the marker text, you can use wildcards, as described earlier in this chapter.

Changing a Marker

No matter how you find a marker, you cannot automatically change it, except by deleting it, as described previously. If you want to replace a marker of one type with a different type, or if you want to change the marker text, you must do so manually, using the Marker Window. You might expect that if you searched for marker text, then selected **Change To Text** and entered a string in the Change Text box, Frame-Maker would replace the marker text with the text you entered, but this does not work. Instead, it replaces the *marker*, rather than the *marker text*, with the text in the Change Text box.

CHAPTER 9

Using Variables in Place of Text

What is a Variable?

Variables are familiar to programmers, and we all remember them from algebra class, but what do variables have to do with publication design and production? In FrameMaker, a variable is a place holder for a text string that you expect to change in the future. FrameMaker recognizes two kinds of variables: *user variables* and *system variables*. A user variable is one that you create and update as needed. For example, in writing documentation for a forthcoming product that has not received its final name, you could create a variable and define it as the product's in-house code name and place the variable in your text wherever the name is to appear. When the final name is decided, you would just change the variable definition to the final name and FrameMaker would automatically update all occurrences of the variable to the proper name.

System variables are built into FrameMaker. They are similar to user variables, but their definitions are derived from the state of your computer system or of the document in which they are used and they are updated automatically by FrameMaker. System variables include the current date, the file name of the document, the current page number, and the page count of the document. There are also special system variables for creating running headers and footers that mirror headings, chapter titles, or other document features.

NOTE A related device in FrameMaker that also uses place holders for changeable text strings is the *cross-reference*. Cross-references differ from variables in that they refer to the location of text or other items elsewhere in the publication. Cross references are the subject of Chapter 10.

Anatomy of a Variable

Every variable consists of two parts: a name and a definition. The name is used by FrameMaker to keep track of the variable. With the exception of a few special system variables, to be described later, variable names do not appear on either body pages or master pages. The names are seen only in the dialog boxes you use to create, edit, and place the variables. The definition of a variable is the text string that FrameMaker displays in the document wherever the variable is placed in text. A variable definition can include any characters that you can type, including special characters, character formats, and, in the case of system variables, predefined *building blocks*, which will be described later in this chapter. With a few exceptions, both user variables and system variables can be placed anywhere in a document, either on body pages or master pages. The exceptions are the Current Page Number system variable (#), and the four Running Header/Footer system variables, which can be used only on master pages.

Placing a Variable in Text

The process of placing a variable is simple. It is the same regardless of whether you are placing a user or a system variable or whether you are placing it on a body page or a master page.

1. Click an insertion point in the text where you want to place the variable. (If you want the variable to replace an existing word, double-click to highlight the word.)

2. Open the Special menu and select **Variable**.

3. Select the name of the variable you want to insert from the scrolling list box in the Variable dialog box (see Figure 9.1).

4. Click the **Insert** button or press **Enter** to insert the variable.

Figure 9.1 Variable dialog box

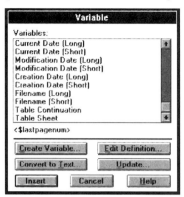

As an alternative, use this keyboard shortcut to place a variable in text:

SHORTCUT

1. Click an insertion point or highlight a word to replace.

2. Press **Ctrl+0**. "V:" will appear in the status area at the lower left corner of the document window to indicate that FrameMaker is ready for you to type a variable name.

3. Start to type the name. It is not necessary to type the full name; you need to type only enough letters to identify a unique name, and the full name will appear in the status area after the V:. For example, by default there is only one system variable starting with P (Page Count), so if you haven't defined any user variables starting with P, you would only need to type a P to specify the Page Count variable.

4. Press **Enter** to place the variable.

Replacing One Variable with Another

To replace one variable with another, double-click on the variable that you want to replace. This opens the Variable dialog box. Select the replacement from the list of variables, then select the **Replace** button. This works for either user or system variables and can replace one type with the other.

Converting Variables to Text

You can convert any user variable or any system variable except the Current Page Number and Running Header/Footer to text at any time after it is placed. When a variable is converted to text, it ceases to be a variable and becomes a part of the ordinary text of the document. This means that it can be edited directly on a body page or master page, but it can no longer be automatically updated by FrameMaker (in the case of system variables) or by the user (in the case of user variables).

To convert variables to text:

1. Open the Special menu and select **Variable**.

2. In the Variable dialog box, select **Convert to Text**. The dialog box in Figure 9.2 will appear.

3. Select one of the three radio buttons to determine which variables will be converted:

   ■ **Variables in the Current Selection**—converts all variables in the selected text (assumes a block of text has been selected in the document).

   ■ **Variables Named**—converts instances of the variable name highlighted in the list box.

   ■ **All Variables**.

4. Select **Convert** to make the conversion, or **Cancel** to exit the dialog box without converting any variables.

Figure 9.2   Convert Variables to Text dialog box

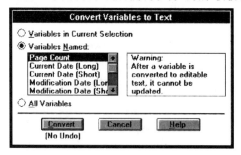

As the dialog box indicates, the conversion of variables to text is not undoable, so take great care in performing this operation. If you have any doubt whatever that you may want to update the variables at some point in the future, *don't convert them.* One situation where you might **N O T E**   want to convert a variable to text is a system variable used for the date in a letter or memo template. Once you have used the template to create a particular letter or memo, you would change the date variable to text to freeze the date. Then, if you had occasion to call up the letter or memo again, you could see the date when it was written, rather than the current date.

NOTE

The Current Page Number and Running Header/Footer variables cannot be converted to text.

User Variables

Some Uses for User Variables

Employ a user variable for any text string that you expect to change later, especially one that will be used many times in a document. One example already mentioned is the name of a product that is under development and has not been finalized. Another use for user variables is to save typing time when you have a lengthy title or phrase that must be typed in exactly the same form every time it appears. This is especially useful where a phrase always appears with special character formats. Suppose, for example, you are writing about a product called the **HyperPhaze 2000**™, and the corporate style guide requires that the name always be expressed in exactly that form, that is, in boldface, with the trademark symbol, and with the ridiculous capital letter in the middle that marketing people love so much. That requires a fair number of keystrokes and mouse movements, typing the characters and selectively applying boldface and symbol-font character formats to selected ranges. It's much easier to create a user variable and define it as `<Emphasis>HyperPhaze 2000\T` (\T is the code for the trademark symbol) and give it a short name like hp. Using the keyboard shortcut, this is reduced to **Ctrl+O** hp **Enter**. And you'll be all ready when the V.P. of marketing decides to change the name to HyperPhaze 2001.

I frequently need to type units of measure for various types of electronic parameters that combine a standard character with one from the symbol font, such as μA (microamperes), μF (microfarads), mΩ (milliohms), and the like. Typing these units in the normal way is relatively tedious; I must first type the two letters, then select the one that needs to be changed to the symbol font and apply an appropriate character format. It's much quicker to define user variables for each of these commonly used units and then type them using the **Ctrl+0** keyboard shortcut, described above. For example, assuming you have already defined a character format for the symbol font, you could create a user variable ma (for microamperes) and define it as `<symbol>m<Default ¶ Font>A`. Then, to place the symbol in text, you would type **Ctrl+0** ma **Enter**. This is much quicker than typing the text and then applying the character format because you don't have to take your hands off the keyboard to use the mouse to select the character or apply the format.

If you use the technique described above, be sure to give each of your variables a unique two-letter name that does not conflict with any of the predefined system variables.

N O T E

When Not to Use a User Variable

Don't use a user variable to refer to another location in a document, such as the page number that contains particular information, a chapter title or number, a figure or table title or number, or the like; for this purpose, use a *cross-reference* (consult Chapter 10 for a discussion of cross-references).

Creating a User Variable

To create a new user variable, use the following sequence:

1. Open the Special menu and select **Variable**.

2. In the dialog box that appears (Figure 9.1), select the **Create Variable** button.

3. The Edit User Variable dialog box (Figure 9.3) appears. Type the name of the variable and its definition in the respective text boxes. Remember, the name is what you will refer to when updating the variable or placing it in text; the definition is the string that will appear in text where you place the variable.

4. (Optional) Note the list of character formats on the right side of the dialog box. If you want your variable text to appear in a different font or with different attributes than the paragraphs in which you insert it, include a character format (or several, if necessary) in the variable. Place the insertion point in the definition where you want to place the format tag and select the desired tag from the list. Variable definitions are limited to 255 characters, including character formats.

Character format tags placed in a variable apply *only* to the text in the variable. Hence, although the <Default ¶ Font> tag appears in the list, you do not need to place this tag at the end of your variable to restore the default font and attributes. Use the <Default ¶ Font> tag only if you want to restore the default font *within* the variable after using another format.

N O T E

5. Select **Done** to exit the Edit User Variable dialog box and return to the main Variable dialog box.

6. Select **Done** again to exit the Variable dialog box or select **Insert** to place the newly created variable in your text at the insertion point.

Figure 9.3 Edit User Variable dialog box

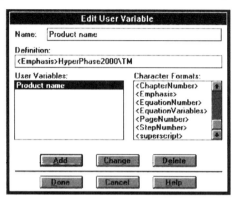

Editing a User Variable

The process of editing an existing user variable is largely the same as that of creating a new one:

1. (Optional) Click on any occurrence of the variable text in your document. (When you click on variable text on a page, you select the complete variable rather than placing an insertion point in the text.)

2. Open the Special menu and select **Variable**.

3. The Variable dialog box appears. If you selected a variable in your document, as in step 1, the variable name is highlighted in the list box. If you did not, select the name of the variable you want to edit from the list.

4. Select the **Edit Definition** button.

5. The Edit User Variable dialog box (Figure 9.3) appears. Edit the definition of the variable in the text box as required.

6. When you have finished editing the definition, select **Done**. This will update all occurrences of the variable in the document and return you to the main Variable dialog box, where you can perform additional operations on variables or select **Done** to return to the document window.

System Variables

The set of system variables provided by FrameMaker is fixed; you can neither create new system variables nor delete existing ones (a lot like matter and energy!), although you can change their definitions. Table 9.1 shows the complete set of system variables in FrameMaker 4.0 with their default definitions.

Table 9.1 FrameMaker 4.0 system variables

System Variable	Default Definition	Sample Display
Current Page #	`<$curpagenum>`	1
Page Count	`<$lastpagenum>`	256
Current Date (Long)	`<$monthname> <$daynum>, <$year>`	October 8, 1993
Current Date (Short)	`<$monthnum>/<$daynum>/<$shortyear>`	10/8/93
Modification Date (Long)	`<$monthname> <$daynum>, <$year>` `<$hour>:<$minute00> <$ampm>`	October 8, 1993 4:25 pm
Modification Date (Short)	`<$monthnum>/<$daynum>/<$shortyear>`	10/8/93
Creation Date (Long)	`<$monthname> <$daynum>, <$year>`	October 8, 1993
Creation Date (Short)	`<$monthnum>/<$daynum>/<$shortyear>`	10/8/93
File Name (Long)	`<$fullfilename>`	C:\MAKER\BOOK\CHAPTER1.DOC
File Name (Short)	`<$filename>`	CHAPTER1.DOC
Running H/F 1	`<$paratext[Title]>`	———
Running H/F 2	`<$paratext[Heading1]>`	———
Running H/F 3	`<$marker1>`	———
Running H/F 4	`<$marker2>`	———
Table Continuation	`(continued)`	Continued
Table Sheet	`(Sheet <$tablesheetnum> of` `<$tablesheetcount>)`	(Sheet 1 of 2)

(The appearance of Running Header/Footer variables depends upon the paragraph tags and/or markers you select; the use of these variables will be explained in detail later in this chapter.)

The system variables in the table consist primarily of pre-defined *building blocks*. Each text string enclosed in angle brackets (<>) and beginning with a dollar sign ($) is a building block. Some system variables, such as those for page numbers or file names, consist of a single building block, whereas others combine several building blocks with additional text and/or punctuation. The building blocks themselves are fixed, but you can change the selection or order of the building blocks making up a given system variable and combine them with additional text.

System variables are not limited to combinations of the building blocks used in the default definitions in Table 9.1; there are a variety of other building blocks available. The set of building blocks for date and time is particularly rich. Table 9.2 shows the complete set of variable building blocks, except those for running headers and footers, which will be described later in this chapter.

 FrameMaker assumes that any text in a variable definition beginning or ending with a < or > is a building block or character format. If you need to include a < or > in a variable definition, precede it with a backslash (\).

N O T E

Table 9.2 Variable building blocks

Page Number Building Blocks

Building Block	Example
<$curpagenum>	1
<$lastpagenum>	256

File Name Building Blocks

Building Block	Example
<$fullfilename>	c:\frame\book\chapter1.doc
<$filename>	chapter1.doc

Date/Time Building Blocks

Building Block	Example
<$second>	3, 30
<$second00>	03, 30
<$minute>	1, 15
<$minute00>	01, 15
<$hour>	1, 11
<$hour01>	01, 11
<$hour24>	01, 23

Building Block	Example
<$ampm>	am, pm
<$AMPM>	AM, PM
<$daynum>	1, 31
<$daynum01>	01, 31
<$dayname>	Monday
<$shortdayname>	Mon
<$monthnum>	1, 12
<$monthnum01>	01, 12
<$monthname>	January
<$shortmonthname>	Jan
<$year>	1993
<$shortyear>	93

N O T E When you place system variables on master pages, FrameMaker automatically updates them as needed. However, when you place system variables on body pages, FrameMaker updates them only when you open the document. If you need to update system variables on body pages while working on a document (for example, before printing), open the Variable dialog box and select **Update**. A prompt box will ask you to confirm that you want to update all system variables in the document.

Modifying System Variables

To modify a system variable:

1. Select **Variable** from the Special menu.

2. Select the name of the variable you want to modify from the list box and click on the **Edit Definition** button.

3. In the dialog box that appears, enter the new definition in the text box. You can add new building blocks either by typing them or by selecting them from the scrolling list box. Character format tags appear at the end of the list, and can also be included in the variable definition.

4. Click on **Edit** to accept your modified definition, or click on **Cancel** to restore the variable to its previous state. Either action returns you to the main Variable dialog box, where you can insert the modified variable, select another variable to modify, or return to the document window.

N O T E

The Current Page Number and Running Header/Footer variables appear in the list box only when the current page is a master page and the insertion point is in an untagged text column.

Some Sample Modifications

Some of the system variables lend themselves readily to modification; others do not. The Current Page Number variable, which, by default, consists simply of the number, can be modified in a variety of ways:

Definition	Result
`page <$currentpagenum>`	page 1
`page <$currentpagenum> of <$lastpagenum>`	page 1 of 256
`page 5\=<$currentpagenum>`	page 5–1
`<Emphasis>page <$currentpagenum>`	*page 1*

(The third example uses the code \= for an en dash. The fourth example uses the character format "Emphasis," which has been defined as bold italic.) The character format tag applies only to the text in the variable; hence it is not necessary to include the character format `<Default ¶ Font>` at the end of the variable to restore the normal text font and attributes. You would include this tag if you wanted to restore the normal font *within* the variable.)

N O T E

The same results as shown above could be obtained by placing the unmodified Current Page Number variable on a master page and adding the other text items around it.

A virtually unlimited number of different date and time formats can be created with the large selection of available building blocks provided. A few of the more common ones are shown in Table 9.3

Table 9.3 Common date and time formats

Style	Definition	Result
U. of Chicago Press	`<$daynum> <$monthname> <$year>`	4 July 1776
U.S. Army	`<$daynum> <$shortmonthname> <$shortyear>`	7 Dec 42

Style	Definition	Result
Conventional	<$monthname> <$daynum>, <$year>	October 8, 1950
24-hour time	<$hour24><$minute00>	0745
American time	<$hour>:<$minute> <AMPM>	7:45 PM
British time	<$hour>.<$minute> <ampm>	7.45 pm

N O T E FrameMaker uses the language setting of the current paragraph (see Chapter 5) to determine the language used in date and time system variables (for month names and am/pm designations). If you change the language of a paragraph that includes a date or time variable, FrameMaker automatically updates the language of the variable.

The File Name system variables do not lend themselves to or require modification.

Using the Running Header/Footer Variables

If you just want to create a simple header or footer that includes a publication or chapter title and a page number, you can do so by typing the header or footer text and the Current Page Number variable in an appropriately placed, untagged text column on a master page, as described in Chapter 4. However, if you want to create more complex running headers or footers that change from page to page to reflect the structure of the publication, you will need to use one or more of the Running Header/Footer system variables.

FrameMaker predefines four Running H/F system variables. Two of these variables refer to *paragraph tags* (the names of paragraph formats included in the document's Paragraph Format catalog), and two refer to *markers* that you place in your text to identify selected locations. These four variables, along with the Current Page Number variable, can be used *only* on master pages. They cannot be placed on body or reference pages.

Echoing Titles or Headings in Headers or Footers

When you want to include the complete text of a paragraph, such as a chapter title or a heading, or the number of an autonumbered paragraph in a header or footer, use a Running H/F variable that refers to a paragraph format tag. The two predefined variables that refer to paragraph tags are defined as follows:

Variable Name	Definition
Running H/F 1	`<$paratext[paratag]>`
Running H/F 2	`<$paratext[paratag]>`

In these definitions, *paratag* represents the name of the paragraph format tag to which the variable refers. When you work with these variables in the Variable dialog box, you will see the actual format name, rather than paratag. In many of Frame-Maker's templates, these two variables have been defined to refer to the paragraph formats [Title] and [Heading]. You can change the tag name to refer to the name of whatever type of paragraph you want to appear in the header or footer. Frame-Maker searches each page for an occurrence of the specified tag and places the text of that paragraph in the header or footer. If it does not find the tag on the current page, it searches backward through previous pages until it finds one.

It is a common practice in a multi-chapter publication, such as a book or manual, to have alternate footers on left and right pages, with the page numbers at the out-side edges of the respective pages. One footer might include the publication title, and the other might echo the chapter number and/or title. This is easily done with FrameMaker's Running H/F variables, as illustrated in Figure 9.4. In the figure, the left-page footer, which has the publication title, uses only the Current Page Num-ber variable; the publication title is entered as regular text. The right-page footer uses two Running H/F variables: one for the chapter number and the other for the chapter title. This was necessary because the chapter number and chapter title in this publication have different paragraph formats. Another common format is to have one header or footer echo the chapter title and the other echo the highest level of heading on the page on which it appears. This is also easily done using the Running H/F variables, as shown in Figure 9.5

Figure 9.4   Chapter title and number footers

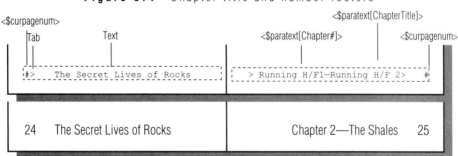

Figure 9.5 Chapter title and heading footers

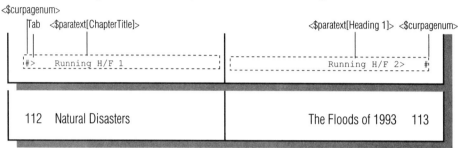

If you wish, you can include more than one paragraph tag in a variable definition using the `<$paratext[]>` building block. Enclose them all in the same pair of square brackets and separate them with commas, as in the following example:

`<$paratext[paratag1, paratag2, ..., paratagn>`

The `<$paratext>` building block indicates that the full text of the tagged paragraph will be included in the header or footer. This is useful when the tagged paragraph is a piece of display type, such as a chapter title, chapter number, table title, heading, or the like. Obviously, it would be neither possible or useful to refer to a body paragraph in a header or footer, though you can refer to a selected text string *within* a body paragraph using one of the Running H/F variables that refers to a marker, as explained later in this chapter.

Using the `<$paratext>` building block does not apply the *paragraph format* of the tagged paragraph to the header or footer. Control the format of the header or footer by defining and applying an appropriate paragraph format and/or by including a character format tag in the Running H/F variable definition. (Consult Chapter 5 for information on creating and applying paragraph and character formats.)

N O T E

Modifying the Running H/F Variables

Although the predefined Running H/F 1 and Running H/F 2 variables use the `<$paratext>` building block, they, like the other system variables, can be modified. There are three other building blocks that you can use to refer to paragraph tags:

Building Block	Explanation
`<$paranum[paratag]>`	Displays the complete numbering format, including any punctuation, text, or spaces, of an autonumbered paragraph with the tag name `[paratag]`.

`<$paranumonly[paratag]>`   Displays the paragraph number *only* of an autonumbered paragraph with the tag name [paratag].

`<$paratag[paratag]>`   Displays the tag name of a paragraph with the tag name [paratag].

For example, if your full autonumber format appeared in the document as Section 1.3 and you used the `<$paranum[paratag]>` building block in a Running H/F definition, then Section 1.3 would appear in the header or footer. However, if, in the same situation, you used `<$paranumonly[paratag]>` building block, only 1.3 would appear. The `<$paratag[paratag]>` building block is a bit of an oddity; it is intended mainly for debugging and auditing purposes, and doesn't really have any practical applications in production.

Using Running Headers/Footers to Create Dictionary-Style Reference Words

Reference books such as dictionaries, encyclopedias, and telephone directories commonly use *reference words* placed near tops of pages, above the outer text columns, to identify the first and last entries on each two-page spread. You can create dictionary-style reference words using FrameMaker's Running H/F variables. Define Running H/F variables for the left and right pages as `<$paratext[paratag]>` and `<$[+, paratag]>`, respectively. The + in the second definition causes this variable to display the *last* occurrence of the specified paragraph tag, rather than the first, as it normally does. Place the two variables in appropriately located untagged columns on left and right master pages for your document.

Because the `<$paratext[paratag]>` variable displays the full text of the paragraph with the specified tag, it is necessary to make your dictionary entries, article titles, or whatever items you want to refer to separate paragraphs from their definitions, opening paragraphs, or the like. In FrameMaker 3.0, this constrained you to place these elements on separate lines. However, by using the Run-In Heads option in FrameMaker 4.0 (see Chapter 5) you can create titles that run into the opening lines of body paragraphs while retaining separate identities as paragraphs. Hence, you can now design dictionaries, glossaries, and the like however you choose.

Using Other Text in a Header or Footer

When the text you want to appear in a header or footer is not a full paragraph or a paragraph autonumber, use a Running H/F variable that refers to a marker. For example, in a publication that uses few headings and subheadings, you might use a header or footer to describe the principal topic on each page. You could do this by placing a marker on each page and associating a sentence describing the topic with the marker, as described later.

FrameMaker predefines two Running H/F variables that refer to markers:

Variable	Definition
Running H/F 3	Header/Footer $1
Running H/F 4	Header/Footer $2

In order to use a marker in a running header or footer, you must place a marker at an appropriate location in the text. The marker can refer either to a text string that is part of the document, or to an independent text string that you type in the marker dialog box, as described later.

To place a marker for a running header or footer:

1. If you want the marker to refer to a text string in the document, highlight the text string. Otherwise, click an insertion point anywhere in the text columns on the page where you want the marker to appear.

2. Open the Special menu and select **Marker**. This opens the Marker window (Figure 9.6).

3. From the list box, select the marker named **Header/Footer $1** or **Header/ Footer $2**, as appropriate. (By default, H/F $1 is the marker for Running H/F 3 and H/F $2 is the marker for Running H/F 4.)

4. If you started by highlighting a text string on the page, that text string should appear in the Marker Text box at the bottom of the window. If so, you can click on the **New Marker** button to place the marker. Otherwise, type the text you want to associate with the marker in the text box, then click on the **New Marker** button.

5. Double-click on the menu box or press **Alt+F4** to close the Marker window.

Figure 9.6   *The Marker window*

Because Markers are created in a window, rather than in a dialog box, you can move freely back and forth between the document window and the marker window. For example, you can go back into the document window and highlight a different text string before creating a marker, or go to another page and create another marker, without having to close and reopen the window.

N O T E

As you can see by scrolling through the list box, FrameMaker uses markers for many other purposes than running headers and footers, including cross-references, index entries, hypertext, and conditional text. Each of these topics is the subject of a separate chapter in this book.

Referring to Condition Tags

Condition tags are used to identify *conditional text*. Conditional text is a unique FrameMaker feature that enables you to easily create multiple versions of a document by selectively hiding or showing certain paragraphs or graphics. Text that can be selectively shown or hidden is identified by a condition tag and is known as conditional text. Conditional text is the subject of Chapter 22.

There is no predefined Running H/F variable for showing a condition tag, but there is a building block for this purpose that you can use to define such a variable if needed. This building block has the form:

```
<$condtag[hitag,....,lotag,nomatch]>
```

You can redefine any of the four Running H/F variables with this building block to display a condition tag in a header or footer. You must replace the symbols *hitag*, *lotag*, and *nomatch* with the names of actual condition tags used in your document. You can type as many tags names as you like, separated by commas. Unlike the building blocks that refer to paragraph formats or markers, FrameMaker searches only the current page for condition tags. The last item in the list is the text shown if no condition tag is found on the current page. If you don't want to show any text when no tag is found, type a non-breaking space (**space**) at the end of the list of condition tags.

CHAPTER 10

Using Cross-References

What Is a Cross-Reference?

A cross-reference is a reference in the text of a publication directing the reader to other locations for information on related topics. This book, like almost any technical publication, contains many such references, such as "see Chapter 14 for a detailed discussion of…" or "use the keyboard shortcut, as described earlier in this chapter." Trying to maintain such references manually as a publication is edited and revised is a challenging, if not impossible task. FrameMaker's Cross-Reference feature makes the task relatively easy. You place a cross-reference in your text and identify its *source* (the location to which it refers), which can be in the same document or a different document. Each cross-reference has a *format*, which determines how the cross-reference will appear in text—for example, whether it will refer the reader to a page number, a chapter title, a heading, a table title, or some other landmark. FrameMaker comes with several predefined cross-reference formats, and you can create others as needed. You can include a character format in a cross-reference format if you want the cross-reference to appear in a different typestyle than the text in which it is placed.

Two Kinds of Cross-References

FrameMaker uses two types of cross-references: *paragraph* cross-references and *spot* cross-references. Use a paragraph cross-reference to refer to the page number on which a paragraph or section begins or when you want the reference to include the complete text of a paragraph, such as a chapter title, heading, table title, figure caption, or the like. Use a spot cross-reference to refer to a location within a section or paragraph. If the paragraph that you want to reference splits across a page break, a spot cross-reference will allow you to display the page number where the cross-reference marker is placed, rather than where the paragraph begins.

A cross-reference cannot be placed in a document that has not yet been saved to disk. If you attempt to insert a cross-reference in an unsaved document, FrameMaker will prompt you to save the document first.

N O T E

Using Paragraph Cross-References

To place a paragraph cross-reference, use the following steps:

1. Place the insertion point at the location where you want the reference to appear in your text.

2. Open the Special menu and select **Cross-Reference** or use the keyboard shortcut **Esc s c**. This opens the Cross-Reference dialog box (Figure 10.1).

3. At the top of the dialog box is a pull-down list box labeled Source Document, which initially displays "Current." The source document is the document containing the location to which you wish to refer (the source). If the location is in the same document where you are placing the reference, leave the setting as "Current." If you want to refer to a location in another document, open the box and select the document name. (The document you wish to refer to must already be open.)

4. On the left side of the dialog box is a list box labeled Source Type. This box displays a list of all the paragraph format tags in your document. Highlight the format tag for the type of paragraph to which you wish to refer, for example, a chapter title, heading, or table title.

5. On the right side of the dialog box is another list box labeled Reference Source. This box displays the first lines of the paragraphs with the tag that is highlighted in the Source Type box. Highlight the paragraph to which you want to refer.

6. Select a format for the cross-reference. Below the Source Type list box is a pull-down list box labeled Format. To the right of this box is an example of the currently selected format. Open the list box and select a format. (If none of the formats are to your liking, you can edit them or create new ones, as described later in this chapter. The section on creating and editing formats also explains the bracketed building blocks used in the formats.)

7. Select the **Insert** button to place the cross-reference. The text specified by the format will appear at the location where you placed the insertion point, and a marker symbol (like a large sans serif T) will appear in front of the source paragraph. (The marker symbol does not print, and will be visible only if you have selected **Text Symbols** on the View menu.)

Figure 10.1   Cross-Reference dialog box

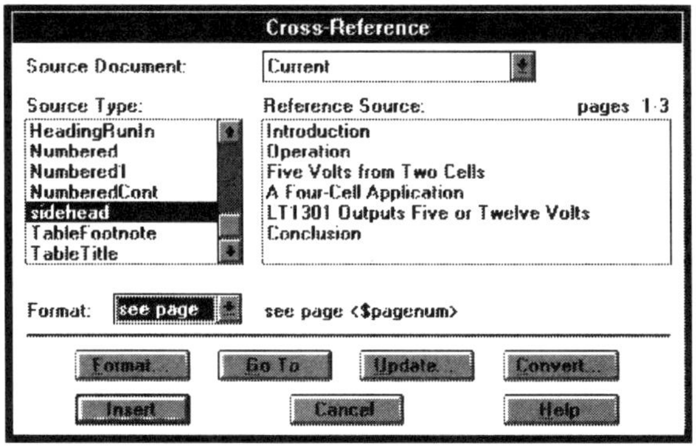

Using Spot Cross-References

Spot cross-references are similar to paragraph cross-references, but they refer to markers you place in text rather than to paragraph format tags. Hence, before you create a spot cross-reference, you must place a marker in your text at the location to which you want to refer:

1. Click an insertion point at the location where you wish to place the marker.

2. Open the Special menu and select **Marker** or use the keyboard shortcut **Esc s m**.

3. In the Marker window, open the Marker Type list box and select **Cross-Ref**.

4. Type your marker text in the text box provided for this purpose. The marker text is solely for the purpose of identifying the marker when you select it in the Cross-Reference dialog box—it does *not* appear in the cross-reference. The marker text can be up to 255 characters long, but it is obviously desirable to keep it short and succinct.

5. Click the **New Marker** button to place the marker. The Marker window stays open after you place the marker. You can place additional markers for other cross-references or other purposes, or you can close the window by double-clicking its control box.

N O T E If you are going to use many spot cross-reference markers, it is important to use marker text that will enable you to easily recognize and distinguish among your markers, not just today, but when it comes time to revise your document, six months or a year from now. This is doubly important if someone else may have to revise your documents.

Having placed your marker(s), you are ready to insert a spot cross-reference:

1. Place the insertion point at the exact location where you want the reference to appear in your text.

2. Open the Special menu and select **Cross-Reference**. This opens the Cross-Reference dialog box.

3. At the top of the dialog box is a pull-down list box labeled Source Document, which initially displays "Current." The source document is the document containing the location to which you wish to refer. If the location is in the same document where you are placing the reference, leave the setting as "Current." If you want to refer to a location in another document, open the box and select the document name. (The document you wish to refer to must already be open.)

4. On the left side of the dialog box is a list box labeled Source Type. At the top of the list, above the paragraph format tags for the publication, is the item Cross-Ref Markers. Highlight this item if it is not already highlighted.

5. On the right side of the dialog box is another list box labeled Reference Source. This box displays the first lines of the marker text for all the cross-reference markers in the source document. Highlight the text for the marker to which you want to refer.

6. Select a format for the cross-reference. Below the Source Type list box is a pull-down list box labeled Format. To the right of this box is an example of the currently selected format. Open the list box and select a format. (If none of the formats are to your liking, you can edit them or create new ones.)

7. Select the **Insert** button to place the cross-reference. The text specified by the format will appear at the location where you placed the insertion point, and a marker symbol will appear at the source.

Editing Cross-References

You can change almost any aspect of a cross-reference, using approximately the same procedure you used to create it. To modify a cross-reference, double-click on the reference in text. This will open the Cross-Reference dialog box. To change the source for the cross-reference, use the Source Document, Source Type, and Reference Source boxes to select the new source. If you want to change the format, select a new one from the Format box. When you have made the necessary changes, select the **Replace** button to replace the old reference with the edited version.

You can cut, copy, paste, and delete text containing cross-references just like any other text. The only thing you cannot do is edit the content or format of the cross-reference directly on body pages. If you want to change the content or appearance of a cross-reference, you must change the source, or edit the format, as described later in this chapter. You can also cut and paste text containing a cross-reference marker. The marker travels with the text, and, when you update the reference (see later in this chapter) the reference will refer to the new location. If you attempt to copy and paste a block of text containing a cross-reference marker, the marker will remain at the old location and a duplicate *will not* be placed with the pasted text. If you want a marker in the pasted text, you must place it manually, as described previously. The cross-reference will still point to the original marker. If you want it to point to the new location, you will have to edit it, as described previously.

Changing a Cross-Reference to Text

You can convert any paragraph or spot cross-reference to text at any time after it is placed. When a cross-reference is converted to text, it ceases to be a cross-reference and becomes a part of the ordinary text of the document. This means that it can be edited directly on a body page, but it can no longer be updated by FrameMaker.

To convert cross-references to text:

1. Select a cross-reference or a block of text containing multiple cross-references.

2. Open the Special menu and select **Cross-Reference** or use the keyboard shortcut **Esc s c**.

3. In the Cross-reference dialog box, select **Convert to Text**. The dialog box in Figure 10.2 will appear.

4. Select one of the three radio buttons to determine which cross-references will be converted:

   ■ **Cross-references in the Current Selection**—converts all cross-references in the selected text (assumes a block of text has been selected in the document).

   ■ **Cross-references Named:**—converts instances of the cross-reference name highlighted in the list box.

   ■ **All Cross-references**.

5. Select **Convert** to make the conversion, or **Cancel** to exit the dialog box without converting any cross-references.

Figure 10.2 Convert Cross-Reference to Text dialog box

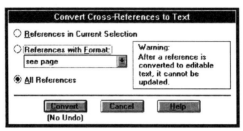

As the dialog box indicates, the conversion of cross-references to text is not undoable, so take great care in performing this operation. If you have any doubt whatever as to whether you may want to update the cross-references in the future, *don't convert them.*

N O T E

Understanding Cross-Reference Formats

Like numbering formats and system variables, cross-reference formats are assembled from predefined building blocks, combined with text and optional character formats. Depending on the formats you use, cross-references can be as simple as "page 3," or as elaborate as "see Section 4.37, "Grounding," in Chapter 4, Circuit-Board Layout Tips."

FrameMaker provides a number of predefined cross-reference formats in each FrameMaker template. The formats vary according to the purpose of the template. Table 10.1 shows the predefined formats you get when you select a blank sheet of paper to start a new document:

Table 10.1 Cross-reference formats

Name	Format	Example
Heading & Page	\'<$paratext>\' on page <$pagenum>	"Conclusions," on page 15
Page	page <$pagenum>	page 15
See Heading & Page	See \'<$paratext>\' on page <$pagenum>	See "Conclusions," on page 15

Table All	Table <$paranumonly>, \'<$paratext>,\' on page <$pagenum>	Table 1.5, "AC Parameters," on page 6
Table	Table <$paranumonly> on page <$pagenum>	Table 1.5 on page 6

(The \' symbols represent left and right double quotes.)

Each of the examples in the table is composed of a mixture of regular text and pre-defined building blocks. The building blocks are the elements enclosed in angle brackets (<>). FrameMaker includes a large selection of building blocks that can be combined in a virtually unlimited number of formats. The complete set of building blocks for cross-reference formats is shown in Table 10.2. Examine the Frame-Maker templates for additional examples of cross-reference formats.

N O T E

FrameMaker assumes that anything in a cross-reference format that is enclosed in angle brackets is a building block. If you want to include an angle bracket in a cross-reference format, precede it with a back-slash (for example, \< or \>).

You can also include a character format in a cross-reference, although none of the examples in the table do so. If you include a character format, it applies only to the characters that follow it in the cross-reference. Hence, it is not necessary to use the <Default ¶ Font> format at the end of the cross-reference to restore the normal font for the remainder of the paragraph where the cross-reference is located. Use the <Default ¶ Font> format only if you want to switch back to the default font within the cross-reference after using another format.

Table 10.2   Cross-reference building blocks

Building Block	**Explanation**
<$pagenum>	Page number of the source
<$paratext>	Complete text of the source paragraph, excluding its autonumber, if any
<$paratag>	Tag of the source paragraph
<$paranum>	Autonumber of the source paragraph, including any text or punctuation

Building Block	**Explanation**
`<$paranumonly>`	Counter(s) only from the autonumber format
`<$fullfilename>`	Full file spec of the source document
`<$filename>`	File name of the source document
`<$pagenum[paratag]>`	Page number of the preceding paragraph with the tag `[paratag]`
`<$paratext[paratag]>`	Text of the preceding paragraph with the tag `[paratag]`
`<$paratag[paratag]>`	Tag of the preceding paragraph with the tag `[paratag]`
`<$paranum[paratag]>`	Autonumber, including text and punctuation, of the preceding paragraph with the tag `[paratag]`
`<$paranumonly[paratag]>`	Counter(s) only from the autonumbering format of the preceding paragraph with the tag `[paratag]`

(In all the above examples the tag name `[paratag]` must be replaced with an actual paragraph format name in square brackets.)

The building blocks in the table that include the tag `[paratag]` are used to include a preceding heading, number, or title in a cross-reference. For example, you might want a cross-reference to refer to both the subheading and heading of the source, such as "see "Filter Capacitors," in Section 3.4.1, "Component Selection"." To create such a reference, use a format such as see `\'<$paratext>,\'` in `<$paranum[section head]>, \`<paratext[section head]>`. This is a paragraph cross-reference. The source for the cross-reference is the "Filter Capacitors" subhead. FrameMaker searches for the preceding paragraph with the "section head" format tag and includes the autonumber and text in the cross-reference.

Creating and Editing Cross-Reference Formats

1. Open the Special menu and select **Cross-Reference** or use the keyboard shortcut **Esc s c**.

2. In the Cross-Reference dialog box, click the **Format** button. The Edit Cross-Reference Format dialog box (Figure 10.3) opens.

3. If you want to create a new format, type a new name in the Name box at the top of the dialog box. If you want to edit an existing format, leave the name as it is.

4. Edit the definition in the Definition box. (The definition can be up to 255 characters long; the text in the box will scroll left or right with cursor movements.) Add building blocks to the definition by clicking an insertion point in the definition and selecting the building block from the list box. If you want to include a character format, the formats for your document will be found at the bottom of the list. They are added to the definition in the same way as the building blocks.

5. If you are creating a new format, select the **Add** button to add it to the list. If you are editing an existing format, select the **Change** button to replace the original format with the edited version.

6. Select the **Done** button to return to the main Cross-Reference dialog box. Here, you can either insert a cross-reference using your newly created format or select **Done** again to return to your document.

Figure 10.3 Edit Cross-Reference Format dialog box

Creating a Cross-Reference to a Range of Pages—FrameMaker does not provide a predefined cross-reference for a range of pages, such as "see pages 4–6," but you can create one using spot cross-references and two special formats:

1. Place cross-reference markers with appropriate text at the beginning and end of the text to which you want to refer.

2. Create two cross-reference formats, as described previously. (It is necessary to use two formats because FrameMaker won't allow you to refer to two different sources in one cross-reference.) Name the first one "see pages" and define it as see pages <$pagenum>; name the second one "thru pages" and define it as \=<pagenum>;   (\= is the code for an en dash).

3. Click the insertion point where you want to place the reference. Choose the marker at the beginning of the range as the source and use the "see pages" format.

4. Without changing the insertion point, place the second cross-reference. Select the marker at the end of the range as the source and use the "thru pages" format. The result will be a cross-reference such as "see pages $x-y$," where x and y are the pages where you placed the markers. This cross-reference can be updated as your document is revised and edited, like any other.

Importing Cross-References from Another Document

Like almost every other aspect of a FrameMaker document, you can import a set of cross-reference formats from one document into another:

1. Open both the document with the formats you want to copy (the source) and the document where you want to use the formats (the destination).

2. Make the destination the active document.

3. Open the File menu and select **Import**; select **Formats** from the submenu or use the keyboard shortcut **Esc f i o**.

4. In the Import Formats dialog box, open the Import from Document list box and select the source document.

5. Check the Cross-Reference Formats check box, along with the boxes for any other characteristics you want to import. Be careful to check only the boxes you want—importing formats is not undoable.

6. Select the **Import** button to import the formats. The formats from the source are merged into the list in the destination. If any of the formats in the source have names already used in the destination, the formats from the source replace those in the destination.

Updating Cross-References

When you first place cross-references in a document, the references are accurate as to page numbers, section numbers, headings, and the like. However, as you edit, revise, and repaginate your document, FrameMaker does *not* automatically update your cross-references, and they may become invalid. You must tell FrameMaker when you want the cross-references updated. You should do this whenever you complete a major update, repaginate your document, print a copy, or at any other time when you require your cross-references to be accurate. This is easily done:

1. Select **Cross-Reference** from the Special menu (keyboard shortcut **Esc s c**.

2. In the Cross-Reference dialog box, select **Update**. The Update Cross-References dialog box (Figure 10.4) opens.

3. Select one of the radio buttons to choose which cross-references to update.

   ■ **Internal Cross-References**—updates only those cross-references whose sources are in the current document.

   ■ **References to All Open Documents.**

   ■ **References to All Documents**—both documents that are open and documents on your disks.

   ■ **Unresolved References**—this option will be explained in the next section.

4. Select the **Update** button to update the references.

5. If FrameMaker successfully updates all the references of the selected type, it will return you to the main Cross-Reference dialog box. If it is unable to update one or more references, it will open the Unresolved Cross-References dialog box. Use the procedures in the next section to repair your unresolved cross-references.

Figure 10.4 Update Cross-References dialog box

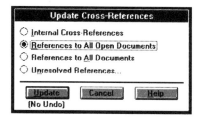

NOTE

FrameMaker will update all cross-references in the selected files *except* for cross-references in *hidden* conditional text. If you want to update cross-references in conditional text, be sure to un-hide your conditional text *before* updating the references.

Solving Problems with Unresolved Cross-References

When FrameMaker attempts to update your cross-references, but is unable to find the markers to which one or more of the references refer, the result is an unresolved cross-reference. Unresolved cross-references can occur for a number of reasons. If the marker was in the same document as the reference, you may have deleted the text containing the marker. If the marker was in another file, the file may have been moved, renamed, or deleted.

When FrameMaker detects unresolved cross-references during an update, it opens the dialog box in Figure 10.5. (You can open this dialog box at any time by selecting **Update** in the Cross-Reference dialog box and selecting the **Unresolved References** radio button in the Update Cross-References dialog box.) This dialog box displays the number of unresolved references found and the files in which the program expected to find their markers. You can use the file, directory, and drive selection boxes in the dialog box to tell FrameMaker to search in another file if you think the file with the reference has been moved or renamed. For example, if you have a reference in your document to a location in a file called INTRO.DOC, but you have since renamed that file CHAPTR01.DOC, you must instruct FrameMaker to look in the CHAPTR01.DOC file for the missing reference source. Select the name of the original file in the list box at the top of the dialog box. Next, select the name of the new file where you want FrameMaker to search for the marker from the drive, directory, and file lists, then select the **Update** button. FrameMaker searches the indicated file for the source of the reference, and, if it finds the source, removes the cross-reference from the list. Repeat the procedure for as many unresolved references to other files as your document contains.

SHORTCUT

Double-click on the name of the file you want FrameMaker to search for the marker to skip selecting the **Update** button.

If the missing marker was in the same file as the reference, you can't repair it in the Unresolved Cross-Reference dialog box. Instead, you must use the following technique:

1. Select **Find/Change** on the Edit menu.

2. In the Find/Change dialog box, set the Find box to **Unresolved Cross-Reference**, then select **Find**. This will highlight the location of the first unresolved cross-reference in your document, and will also display the marker text of the missing marker to which the reference formerly referred.

Figure 10.5 Update Unresolved Cross-References dialog box

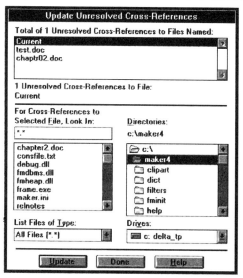

3. By changing the Find box to text, you can search for the text of the source, assuming there is a text string near the marker location that is the same as the marker text. If not, type whatever text string you think may lead to the marker location, then select **Find**.

4. Once you have found the proper location, what you do will depend on whether the unresolved cross-reference was a spot cross-reference or a paragraph cross-reference. If it was a spot cross-reference, place a new marker at the location, as described earlier in this chapter. If it was a paragraph cross-reference, just note the paragraph tag and content of the paragraph to which you wish to refer.

5. Return to the location of the unresolved cross-reference that you found in step 2. (Use the Find/Change operation again if necessary.) Double-click on the unresolved reference to open the Cross-Reference dialog box, and proceed as described earlier in this chapter to create a paragraph or spot cross-reference.

CHAPTER 11

Checking Spelling and Usage

Spell checking has long been a standard feature of stand-alone word processors; over the past couple of years, spelling checkers have become increasingly common in desktop publishing applications as well. FrameMaker's spelling checker is a powerful and flexible one, the equal of those in most stand-alone word processors and certainly superior to the rather perfunctory implementations in some competing Windows desktop publishing programs. FrameMaker 4.0 also includes an on-line thesaurus, the first implementation of this feature in a desktop publishing application.

FrameMaker's spelling checker looks for words that don't match any of the entries in its dictionaries. FrameMaker uses four different dictionaries to check any document:

- The main dictionary for the language in the paragraph that is being checked, with over 130,000 entries. If you have installed foreign-language dictionaries and have paragraphs tagged for different languages, Frame-Maker will use the appropriate dictionary for each paragraph (see Chapter 5 for information on language assignment).

- A site dictionary that includes common computer terms and may contain terms specific to your company.

- A personal dictionary that contains the accumulation of words that you have told FrameMaker to learn from previous documents.

- A document dictionary that contains words that you have told Frame-Maker to accept for the current document, but not to add to your personal dictionary.

N O T E

Frame has dictionaries available for most Western European languages. Contact Frame customer services at 1-800-U4FRAME for information on obtaining additional dictionaries.

In addition to looking for words that don't match its dictionary entries, the spelling checker can identify and correct many common typing errors, such as repeated words, inappropriate spaces before or after punctuation marks, straight quotes where true double quotes are required, and incorrect capitalization. You can speed up the spell checking process by telling FrameMaker to ignore various items that are otherwise likely to be flagged as misspelled words, such as Roman numerals, file names, and words containing numbers. See "Setting Spelling-Checker Options," later in this chapter, for information on selecting which typing errors the spelling checker will look for and which items it will ignore.

Checking the Spelling of a Document or Page

The basic spell-checking process is simple, and will be familiar to anyone who has used a Windows-based word processor:

1. Place the insertion point at the beginning of the document or page that you wish to check. FrameMaker begins checking at the insertion point.

2. Select **Spelling Checker** from the Edit menu, or use the keyboard shortcut **Esc e s**. The Spelling Checker window (Figure 11.1) appears.

Figure 11.1   The Spelling Checker window

3. Select the appropriate radio button to choose whether to check the whole document or the current page.

4. Click the **Start Checking** button to begin the spell checking process. When FrameMaker finds a word that doesn't have a match in the dictionaries or a

probable typing error, it displays it in the Word text box in the dialog box. To the left of the text box, it displays a message indicating the type of error it believes it has found (e.g., misspelling, double word, incorrect capitalization, or the like). In the Correction box, it displays what it considers the most likely correction; additional choices may be displayed in the scrolling text box below the Correction box.

5. At this point, you have several choices:

   a. If the item the program has found is incorrect *and* the replacement shown in the Correction box is correct, click the **Correct** button to replace the item with the correction.

   b. If the item the program has found is incorrect, but the replacement shown in the Correction box is also incorrect, you can scroll through the list box to find the correct replacement and click on it to replace the choice in the Correction box, or you can type the correct replacement directly in the box before clicking the **Correct** button.

   c. If the item the program has found is correct and you want to add it to your personal dictionary, click the **Learn** button.

   d. If the item the program has found is correct, but you don't want to add it to your personal dictionary (for example, it is a personal name or an obscure technical term that is specific to this particular document), click the **Allow in Document** button to add the word to the document dictionary. FrameMaker will accept other occurrences of the word in the current document, but not in other documents.

6. Once you have performed one of the preceding operations, FrameMaker will automatically proceed with the spell checking from the location of the last item it found. You can interrupt the spell checking process at any time by clicking an insertion point in the document window. The Spelling Checker window remains on the screen. You can edit the document and then resume checking spelling from the current insertion point by clicking the **Start Checking** button again.

7. The process continues until the program reaches the end of the page or document, at which point it displays the message **Spelling OK**.

N O T E   As it checks spelling, FrameMaker scrolls through the document in the document window, highlighting the words it flags. Depending on the size of your monitor and the current zoom setting, you may or may not see the flagged words in context, because they may be hidden behind the Spelling Checker window. If you have a big enough monitor and a graphics card with high enough resolution that you can display a full page at a legible size, with room left over to place the Spelling Checker window outside the page margins, it is a good idea to set up your screen this way while checking spelling, so that you can see the flagged items in context without having to keep moving the Spelling Checker window.

Checking a Word or Selection

The procedure for checking an individual word or a range of selected text is almost exactly like that described previously for checking a document or page: Select the word or range that you want to check, open the Spelling Checker window, and click on the **Start Checking** button while holding the **Ctrl** key. Proceed as described previously.

N O T E

FrameMaker, for reasons best known to its creators, will not check the spelling of subscripted or superscripted text or of other text that has been shifted vertically. Since subscript and superscript are text attributes that are applied as part of paragraph and character formats, and since all other aspects of paragraph and character formatting are ignored by the spelling checker, it would seem reasonable to think that they could figure out a way to make it check subscripted and superscripted text as well, but apparently not. The FrameMaker documentation recommends that you change the formatting of subscripted or superscripted text to normal, check the spelling, and then change it back to subscript or superscript again, and I'm afraid I don't have a better suggestion. This is not too difficult if all your subscripts and superscripts were applied via character or paragraph format tags—just edit the tag to remove the sub- or superscript and apply it to all tagged paragraphs or characters, check the spelling, then re-edit and reapply the tag to return the sub- or superscript. If you've applied the sub- or superscripts with format overrides, you have more work to do. Your best bet is probably to use the **Find/Change** option (see Chapter 8) to search for character formats that include sub- or superscripts and replace them with something harmless as a marker (for example, a rarely used font), check the spelling, and reverse the process. It is, in any case, a poor show on Frame's part to leave a documented problem such as this uncorrected and recommend time-consuming work-arounds to the user. (No Frame, it's *not* a feature, it's a problem.)

Making Automatic Corrections

Optionally, you can have FrameMaker automatically correct all subsequent occurrences of a spelling or typing error the same way. When the first instance of the error is discovered, make sure that the proper replacement appears in the Correction box, then check the **Automatic Correction** check box before clicking on the **Correct** button. (This turns on Automatic Correction *for the current spelling error only;* you must repeat the process for each spelling error you want to correct automatically.) FrameMaker replaces all subsequent occurrences of the error with the text in the Correction box, without asking your permission. This option can cause problems if the same misspelling represents more than one word, but you are unlikely to know in advance how you have misspelled words, or you wouldn't have done it in the first place. The process is a bit more automatic for typing errors, correcting all the occurrences of a class of errors the same way. For example, if you replace the double word *the the* with the single word *the* and select **Automatic Correction**, FrameMaker will replace all subsequent double words with the corresponding single word; if you replace a period with a leading space with a period with no space, FrameMaker will replace all designated characters with leading spaces with the same characters without leading spaces. Although this is usually a good idea, there are exceptions, and it's generally worth the extra time to correct typing errors one by one, rather than take the shortcut and perhaps create another error that you might fail to catch in proofreading.

Automatic corrections persist only for the current work session. When you close FrameMaker, all Automatic Correction settings are cleared.

N O T E

If you want to clear the automatic corrections during a session without closing and reopening FrameMaker, you can do so by selecting the **Clear Automatic Corrections** option in the Dictionary Options dialog box (described later in this chapter).

Setting Spelling Checker Options

FrameMaker's spelling checker has several configuration options that determine which typing errors it flags and which items it ignores. To edit or examine these options, click the **Options** button in the Spelling Checker window. The Spelling Checker Options dialog box (Figure 11.2) appears.

The left column of the dialog box, labeled "Find," contains typing errors that the spelling checker will look for:

- **Repeated Words**—finds two instances of the same word in a row.

- **Unusual Hyphenation**—finds hyphenations that are not stored in the dictionaries. If this option is on, FrameMaker will treat hyphenated compounds as single words. If it is off, the program will ignore the hyphens and check the individual words in a compound.

Figure 11.2   The Spelling Checker Options dialog box

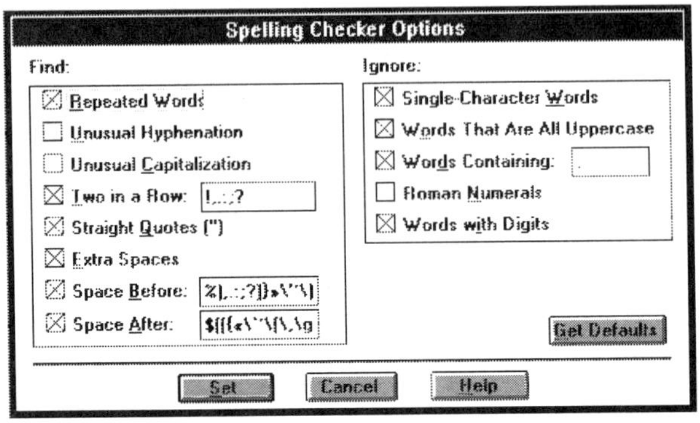

- **Unusual Capitalization**—finds words with non-standard capitalization, such as FrameMaker(!). (See the note following about learning words with uppercase characters.)

- **Two in a Row**—finds two consecutive instances of any of the characters in the text box. (The defaults are the exclamation point, comma, period, colon, semicolon, and question mark.)

- **Straight Quotes**—finds instance of straight quotes (" ") where opening and closing quotes (" ") are required. It can usually distinguish between inch marks and quotation marks from the context. This is a useful feature when importing text created in other word processors, because Frame-Maker does not automatically convert quotes when importing text, as most other desktop publishing applications do.

- **Extra Spaces**—finds instances of two or more consecutive *standard* spaces. It does not find instances of non-breaking spaces, or fixed em, en, thin, or numeric spaces—if you want to find duplicates of these kinds of spaces, add them to the Two in a Row list. Again, this is a good feature to use when importing text created in other word processors. Many writers and typists have the habit of typing two spaces after a period. This is okay in manuscripts, but is incorrect in typeset copy. You can easily remove extra spaces from a document with this feature and the Automatic Correction feature described earlier. (When typing a document in Frame-Maker, use the **Smart Spaces** option in the Document Preferences dialog box to prevent the typing of extra spaces.)

- **Space Before**—finds instances of spaces before characters in the text box. The defaults are the exclamation point, percentage, right parenthesis, comma, period, colon, semicolon, question mark, right bracket, right brace, right double guillemet (»), close quote, right single quote, and right single guillemet (›). You might consider adding the em dash and en dash, which should be set either with thin spaces or no spaces.

- **Space After**—finds instances of spaces after the characters in the text box. The defaults are the dollar sign, left parenthesis, left bracket, left brace, left double guillemet («), open quote, left single quote, left single guillemet (‹), base single quote (‚) and base double quote („). You should probably add the em dash and en dash to this list too.

NOTE When you tell FrameMaker to learn a word that includes uppercase letters, it learns the word with that capitalization. If you have **Unusual Capitalization** turned on and it encounters the same word with a different capitalization, it will flag it as an error. Unless a word will *always* be capitalized, it's best to have FrameMaker learn it as all lowercase. Then it will accept either an initial capital or all caps version of the word.

The right column of the Spelling Checker Options dialog box, under the heading "Ignore," contains a list of items you can have the program skip while checking spelling:

- Single-character words.

- Words that are all uppercase.

- Words Containing—ignores instances of words containing the characters in the text box. The default is a period, which will prevent FrameMaker from flagging DOS file names.

- Roman numerals.

- Words with Digits—this option is indispensable for all kinds of technical writing. Anyone who has had the experience of having a spelling checker flag dozens of hexadecimal numbers or part numbers in a document will understand why. Amazingly, the spelling checkers in some competing programs still don't offer this option.

NOTE You can have the spelling checker ignore entire paragraphs by setting their languages to "none" via the Advanced Properties group in the Paragraph Designer (see Chapter 5). If you do this, FrameMaker will not automatically hyphenate the paragraphs. You can have the spelling checker ignore text lines (see Chapter 12) by setting their language to "none" in the Object Properties dialog box.

Managing Your Dictionaries

You can select a different personal dictionary, import word lists from other sources, or perform a number of other useful operations on your dictionaries and/or document via the Dictionary Functions dialog box (Figure 11.3). This dialog box is accessed by clicking the **Dictionaries** button in the Spelling Checker dialog box.

Figure 11.3 The Dictionary Functions dialog box

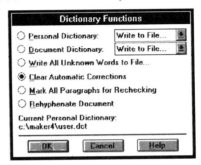

Your Personal Dictionary

The file name of your current personal dictionary is displayed at the bottom of the dialog box. By selecting the **Personal Dictionary** radio button and using the pop-up menu to its right, you can perform several useful operations on your personal dictionary:

- **Set to None**—don't use your personal dictionary in checking spelling (the language, site, and document dictionaries will be used).

- **Write to File**—writes the dictionary to an ASCII text file. Use this option if you want to edit your dictionary or merge it into another (described later).

- **Merge from File**—incorporates words from another text file into your dictionary. Any word list can be added to a FrameMaker dictionary, provided that it is an ASCII text file, each word is followed by a carriage return, and the first item in the file is the header <MakerDictionary 2.0>.

- **Change Dictionary**—select a different personal dictionary. Several people who work on the same machine could have different personal dictionaries, or you could develop different dictionaries for different technical or scientific disciplines.

The Document Dictionary

You can perform some of the same operations on your document dictionary, which exists only for the document you are currently editing.

- **Clear**—empty the document dictionary. You might want to do this if you accidentally told FrameMaker to allow some words in the document that were really errors.

- **Write to File**—writes the dictionary to an ASCII text file. Use this option if you want to merge the dictionary into your personal dictionary, as described previously.

- **Merge from File**—incorporates words from another text file into your dictionary. Any word list can be added to a FrameMaker dictionary, provided that it is an ASCII text file, each word is followed by a carriage return, and the first item in the file is the header `<MakerDictionary 2.0>`. To be fully functional, a file to be merged into a dictionary should include hyphenation points, although FrameMaker will merge a file that doesn't.

Writing Unknown Words to a File

This is one of the most novel and useful options in FrameMaker's spelling checker. If you are working on a document (especially a large one) that you know contains many words that are not in any of the dictionaries (for example, an engineering manual full of technical terms and component names, or a historical article with lots of personal and place names), you can speed up the spell checking process by using this option.

Place the insertion point at the beginning of the document, then select the **Write All Unknown Words to File** radio button in the Dictionary Functions dialog box and select **OK**. The spelling checker will go through the document and write all the words that aren't in the dictionary to an ASCII file with the name and path you specify. You can then load the file into FrameMaker or a text editor and remove or correct any words that are in error. Correct the hyphenation points of the words if necessary and add the header `<MakerDictionary 2.0>` as the first line of the file. Save the file as ASCII or Text Only, with a carriage return at the end of each line. You can now merge the file into your personal dictionary, as described earlier, and have correct spellings and hyphenations of all the new words for use in checking the current and subsequent documents.

Clearing Automatic Corrections

As mentioned previously, you can clear any automatic corrections you have previously set, without closing and reopening FrameMaker, by selecting the **Clear Automatic Corrections** radio button. When you continue checking spelling, you will have to confirm all corrections manually.

Marking a Document for Rechecking

Normally, when FrameMaker rechecks the spelling of a document that has previously been checked, it checks only the paragraphs that have been edited since the last checking. This is generally a good thing, as it speeds up the process of checking spelling. However, there are times when you will want to recheck an entire document; for example, when you have merged new words into one of your dictionaries or you have changed the settings of some of the spelling checker options. It is probably also a good idea to recheck all the paragraphs just before printing a final version to send to a service bureau or submit to a client. To recheck all the paragraphs, select the **Mark All Paragraphs for Rechecking** button in the Dictionary Functions dialog box before running the spelling checker. (It's probably a good a idea to also clear the document dictionary before doing a final check, just in case you inadvertently let a mistake slip in. One can't be too careful.)

Deleting Words from the Dictionary

You can delete any single word from your personal and document dictionary by typing it in the text box at the top of the Spelling Checker window and selecting **Unlearn**. You can also delete words from your personal dictionary by writing it to a text file and editing it, as described previously. (You can use the same technique with the Site Dictionary if you have access to it.)

Managing Hyphenation

The various FrameMaker dictionaries store the hyphenation points for words as well as their spellings. FrameMaker uses these hyphenation points when it automatically hyphenates a paragraph (see Chapter 5 for information on turning automatic hyphenation on or off and setting hyphenation options). You can check the hyphenation points of any word in FrameMaker's dictionaries by typing it in the Word box at the top of the Spelling Checker window and clicking the **Show Hyphenation** button. Hyphens will be added to the word at all its possible hyphenation points. If you want to change the hyphenation points, edit the word, adding or deleting hyphens as necessary. If you never want the word to be hyphenated, type a hyphen before the first letter and delete all other hyphenation points. To store the edited hyphenation points, click the **Learn** button. You can also suppress hyphenation for a single appearance of a word by typing the suppress-hyphenation character (**Esc n s**) before the first letter in regular text.

After you have edited the hyphenation points in one or more words, it is a good idea to rehyphenate the document. Select the **Rehyphenate Document** button in the Dictionary Functions dialog box, then click **OK**. (Best to do this at an early stage; rehyphenating a few words may occasionally have a drastic effect on a carefully tweaked layout.)

Adding Hyphenated Compounds to the Dictionary

Normally, FrameMaker checks the components of hyphenated compound words as separate words, ignoring the hyphen. By turning on the **Unusual Hyphenation** option and storing hyphenated compounds in the dictionary, you can force Frame-Maker to check the hyphenated compounds as units. To add a hyphenated compound to the dictionary, type the word in the Word box in the Spelling Checker dialog box, adding a backslash (\) before the hyphen that connects the words, then click the **Learn** button.

N O T E   Adding a hyphenated compound to the dictionary is not useful as a way to enforce the hyphenated over the non-hyphenated form. The spelling checker still accepts an unhyphenated version of the same term, provided both components are in the dictionaries and spelled correctly. If your object is to ensure that a hyphenated form is used consistently, use the **Find/Change** option (see Chapter 8).

Managing the Site Dictionary

According to Frame's documentation, the System Administrator is responsible for maintaining the Site Dictionary. This is all well and good in networked corporate environments, but what if, like the author, you work in a home office or small business and are not blessed with (or plagued by) such entities as system administrators or MIS managers? If you're the only person who uses your machine, or one of a small number, forget the Site Dictionary and add any special terms you need to your personal dictionary—you'll never know the difference.

If you are a systems administrator and you want to make the Site Dictionary useful, you'll need to do some work. When you first install FrameMaker 4.0, the Site Dictionary contains mostly FrameMaker terminology and some general computer industry terms. Just what you need if you're going to write another book about FrameMaker (good luck!). The Site Dictionary is initially stored in the MAKER4\ DICT subdirectory with the file name SITE.DCT. You can change the location or name of the Site Dictionary file by editing the MAKER.INI file. To edit the Site Dictionary, you must first make it your personal dictionary. To do this, use the **Personal Dictionary** option in the Dictionary Functions dialog box, as described earlier, selecting **Change Dictionary** from the pop-up menu. Once the Site Dictionary has been selected as your personal dictionary, you can write it to a text file for editing or merge other files into it, as described previously.

You could add your site-specific terms to the dictionary by typing a list of words with hyphenation points and merging it, but it will probably be easier to generate site-specific word lists by loading some of your existing documents and/or your corporate style guide into FrameMaker and using the **Write All Unknown Words to File** option in the Dictionary Options dialog box, as described earlier. You may also be able to merge dictionaries created by other applications, depending on the format in which they store dictionaries. (If you are upgrading from FrameMaker 3.0, you can use your existing dictionaries without performing any conversion.) I had no difficulty in merging my supplemental dictionary from WordPerfect 5.1, which contained several years' accumulation of specialized terms, into my FrameMaker personal dictionary. I just loaded the file into FrameMaker, added the header <MakerDictionary 2.0>, saved it as text only with carriage returns between paragraphs, and merged it as described in previously. You should be able to do this with any dictionary that can be loaded into FrameMaker or its originating program and resaved as an ASCII file.

Spelling checkers are useful tools, but they should not be used a substitute for traditional proofreading. Spelling checkers won't find misused homophones (such as are for our or your for you're), nor will they tell you that you're using too many passive constructions or too much techno-jargon. If the quality of your writing is important (and if it isn't, why are you doing it?), it should be carefully proofed at every stage by the author and by at least one other person—preferably a trained proofreader or copy editor. If a trained proofreader is not available, try to get someone who has a thorough knowledge of English grammar, usage, and punctuation and who is not overly familiar with the content of the document. (The author and others who are familiar with the content of a document are apt to see what it *should* say, rather than what it actually says.)

Using the Thesaurus

First, a confession: I am no great fan of thesauruses, whether the printed or electronic variety. If one is a competent writer with a good vocabulary, one will usually be able to find the right word (or at least a suitable one) to express a particular thought without resorting to artificial stimuli. If, on the other hand, one lacks the necessary skills and knowledge, a thesaurus will be of limited help, as one is unlikely to make the correct choice from among the many words offered for any given topic. This being said, FrameMaker's on-line thesaurus is probably no worse than any other: It identifies a word as a part of speech (noun, verb, adjective, etc.), gives a brief definition, and lists synonyms, related words, and antonyms. (Many of its synonyms strike me as ill-chosen, or downright ridiculous, but this is true of every thesaurus I have ever owned.) It can replace a selected word with a word found by the thesaurus or insert a word from the thesaurus into text. FrameMaker's thesaurus uses hypertext links to locate additional information on synonyms, related words, and antonyms.

Looking Up a Word

You can look up a word by selecting it in text or by typing it in the Thesaurus Look Up dialog box. To access the thesaurus, select **Thesaurus** from the Edit menu or use the keyboard shortcut **Esc e t**. If a word is selected, FrameMaker will look up the word. If there is an insertion point in the text but no word is selected, Frame-Maker will ask you to confirm that you want to look up the word nearest the insertion point. If there is no insertion point, you will be prompted for a word to look up. If FrameMaker finds the word you specified in the thesaurus, it displays the Thesaurus window (Figure 11.4). If it can't find the word, it displays a prompt box indicating this fact.

F i g u r e 1 1 . 4 The Thesaurus window

The Thesaurus window displays the word that you looked up, followed by a short definition, a list of synonyms, a "see also" list of related words, and a list of antonyms (opposites). If there is too much information to fit in the window, a page down button like that in the document window will appear in the lower left corner to indicate that more information is available.

To replace a selected word in your document with a synonym, related word, or antonym, or to place such a word at the insertion point, **Ctrl**+click on the word, then click the **Replace** button. If a word was selected when you started the thesaurus, it will be replaced; if not, the word will be added at the insertion point. (If there is no insertion point, FrameMaker will notify you of this fact.)

To look up a synonym, related word, or antonym, click on the boldfaced word in the Thesaurus window. FrameMaker will look up the word and display its definition, synonyms, related words, and antonyms. If you want to go back to a word you looked up previously, open the Word pop-up menu at the top of the window and select the word. FrameMaker remembers the last ten words you looked up. To look up a word that is not in the Thesaurus window, click the **Look Up** button at the bottom of the window. This opens the Thesaurus Look Up dialog box (Figure 11.5), which also appears when you start the thesaurus without first selecting a word in your document. Type the word you want to look up in the Word text box. If you want to use a thesaurus for a different language than that displayed in the Language box, open the box and select it. (FrameMaker offers dictionaries and thesauruses for most Western European languages; contact Frame customer support for information on obtaining additional foreign language support.) Click the **Look Up** button to look up the word. If you want to look up a phrase, rather than a single word, type the phrase in the box with hyphens between the words. You cannot look up a phrase by selecting it in your document; FrameMaker will look up only the first word.

Figure 11.5   The Thesaurus Look Up dialog box

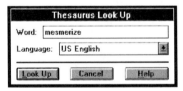

CHAPTER 12

Creating and Editing Graphics

Most desktop publishing applications have a set of tools for drawing lines (rules), boxes, and a few other types of simple graphic objects. FrameMaker has a much more extensive set of drawing tools and editing procedures than its competitors. If you are experienced with object-oriented drawing programs, you will find most of FrameMaker's drawing tools and their operation familiar. Some of its editing techniques, however, are unique in my experience, and would make welcome additions to some high-end drawing programs. Taken as a whole, FrameMaker's drawing capabilities probably won't cause you to throw away your copy of Adobe Illustrator or CorelDRAW, but they are sufficient to allow you to create many figures of low to moderate complexity without the necessity of running another program and importing the resulting graphics file.

Except for the addition of dashed lines and the ability to rotate objects freely, there are no significant differences in the drawing tools in FrameMaker 4.0 compared to those in version 3.0 (FrameMaker 4.0 can use many more colors that 3.0, but that is the subject of Chapter 15). However, there is a difference in the way the tools can be accessed. The Quick Access Bar has two groups of buttons, 28 total, which duplicate most of the commands on the Graphics menu and add some novel variations. The operation of these buttons will be explained in conjunction with the commands they activate, throughout this chapter.

The Tools Palette

FrameMaker's drawing tools are found on the Tools Palette (Figure 12.1). Open the Tools Palette by clicking on the (right triangle) △ button on the left margin of the document window, selecting **Tools** from the Graphics menu, or using the keyboard shortcut **Esc t g**. As shown in the figure, the top two buttons on the palette are used for selecting objects. The next 11 buttons are the drawing tools: You can draw arcs, lines, rectangles, rounded rectangles, polylines, ovals (including circles), polygons, freehand curves, text columns, text lines, and unanchored frames. The remaining buttons are for selecting properties, such as fill pattern, pen pattern, line width, line ends, dash pattern, and color. (The property buttons are on the left row of the palette; the corresponding buttons in the right row are indicators of the current settings of the properties.)

Figure 12.1   The Tools Palette

Setting Up a Grid

Before you begin creating drawings, you may find it useful to set up a grid to help you align and position objects on the page. There are two types of grids in FrameMaker, a visible grid and an invisible "Snap" grid. When Snap is turned on, objects that you draw or move on the page snap to the nearest intersection on the Snap grid.

Both grids are set up in the View Options dialog box (select **Options** on the View menu or press **Esc v o**). You turn on the two grids by selecting their respective check boxes. There are a limited number of choices available for the spacing of the visible grid: 2cm, 1cm, 1/2cm, 1", 1/2", 1/3", and 1/4". You can specify any spacing for the invisible Snap grid, but, if you're going to use the

Snap grid, the practical approach is make it the same as or an equal subdivision of the visible grid. Once the Snap grid is set up, you can turn Snap on and off from the Graphics menu. The origin (0, 0) point for both grids is the upper left corner of the page. When you draw a frame on the page (described later in this chapter) it has its own independent grid(s) with origin(s) at its upper-left corner. When you draw text columns on the page, they normally cover up the grid, but you can make the grid visible by setting the fill pattern of the columns to "None" (see later).

Drawing Objects

The techniques for each of the individual drawing tools are simple and straightforward. To select any tool from the palette, click on it with the mouse. When you move any tool except the Text Line tool over the page, the mouse pointer turns into a +. For the Text Line tool, the pointer turns into an "I-beam" cursor. When you finish drawing an object and release the mouse button, the pointer normally reverts to the Smart Selection tool. (This is different from the way most drawing programs behave and may take some getting used to; I find it an annoyance rather than a useful feature.) If you want a tool to remain selected after you release the mouse button (for example, you want to draw several rectangles), **Shift**+click on the tool. To release the tool, click on the selection tool or any other tool.

Drawing Lines

To draw a straight line, select the Line tool. Move the pointer to the starting point for the line, click and hold the left mouse button and drag the mouse to the end point, and release it. If you want to constrain the line to horizontal, vertical, or a 45° angle, press and hold the **Shift** key while drawing the line. The line will be drawn with the current Pen Style, Line Ends, Dash Pattern, and Color (see "Properties," later in this chapter).

Drawing an Arc

To draw a arc, select the Arc tool. Move the pointer to the starting point for the arc, click and hold the left mouse button, drag the mouse to end point, and release it. To draw a circular arc, hold the **Shift** key while dragging. If you aren't satisfied with the arc, don't release the mouse; drag the pointer back to the starting point and redraw the arc. The arc will be drawn with the current Pen Style, Line Ends, Dash Pattern, and Color (see "Properties," later in this chapter).

Drawing a Rectangle

To draw a rectangle, select the Rectangle tool. Move the pointer where you want to position one corner of the rectangle. Press and hold the left mouse button, drag to the opposite corner, and release it. To draw a square, press and hold the **Shift** key while dragging. The rectangle will be drawn with the current Fill Pattern, Pen Style, Dash Pattern, and Color (see "Properties," later in this chapter).

Drawing a Rounded Rectangle

To draw a rounded rectangle (a rectangle with rounded corners), select the Rounded Rectangle tool. Move the pointer where you want to position one corner of the rectangle. Press and hold the left mouse button, drag to the opposite corner, and release it. To draw a rounded square, press and hold the **Shift** key while dragging. The rounded rectangle will be drawn with the current Fill Pattern, Pen Style, Dash Pattern, and Color (see "Properties," later in this chapter).

You can set the radii of the corners of a rounded rectangle in the Object Properties dialog box.

N O T E

Drawing a Polyline

To draw a polyline (a line with a number of connected segments), select the Polyline tool. Move the pointer to the starting point for the line and click the left mouse button. Move the mouse button to the next point and click again. Continue clicking as many points as you want to connect with the line. Double-click the left mouse button or single-click the right mouse button to end the line. The line will be drawn with the current Pen Style, Line Ends, Dash Pattern, and Color (see "Properties," later in this chapter).

Drawing an Oval

To draw an oval, select the Oval tool. Move the pointer to the location where you wish to position one side of the oval, click and hold the left mouse button, drag to stretch the oval to the desired size and shape, and release. To draw a circle, press and hold the **Shift** key while dragging. The oval will be drawn with the current Fill Pattern, Pen Style, Dash Pattern, and Color (see "Properties," later in this chapter).

Drawing a Polygon

To draw a polygon, select the Polygon tool. Move the pointer to the point where you want to anchor one vertex of the polygon and click the left mouse button. Move the pointer and click on the other vertices in succession. Double-click or right-click on the last vertex. To constrain the segments to horizontal, vertical, or 45° angles, hold the **Shift** key while moving the pointer. The polygon will be drawn with the current Fill Pattern, Pen Style, Dash Pattern, and Color (see "Properties," later in this chapter).

NOTE   You can create a regular polygon (one with equal sides and equal angles) more easily by drawing a circle or rectangle and transforming it with the **Set # Sides** option of the Graphics menu. See "Transforming an Oval or Rectangle into a Regular Polygon," later in this chapter.

Drawing Freehand Curves

Use the Freehand tool to create smooth curves that follow the path of the mouse pointer. Position the pointer at the starting point, press and hold the left mouse button, and drag along the path that you want the curve to follow (except for the starting point, the Freehand tool ignores the Snap grid). When you release the button, FrameMaker creates a smoother version of the rather shaky line you have created. The curve will be drawn with the current Fill Pattern, Pen Style, Line Ends, Dash Pattern, and Color (see "Properties," later in this chapter).

The curve is equipped with control points and reshape handles with which you can further refine the shape of the curve. (See Figure 12.2). Drag a black reshape handle to reposition the point on the curve to which it is attached, changing the length, height, or orientation of the curve between it and the next handle. Each reshape handle is equipped with a pair of white control points which become visible when it is selected. The two control points act as a lever for reshaping the attached segment of the curve. The combination of the reshape handles and control points gives you almost unlimited control over the shape of the curve. How they work together is very difficult to describe in print but easily observed on the screen. If your work requires you to draw smooth curves in documents, take some time to practice with the Freehand tool before you need to use it in a rush job.

Figure 12.2 A freehand curve with reshape handles and control points

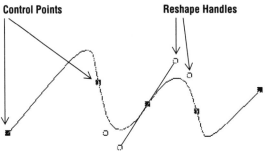

You can add more handles and control points to a freehand curve (dividing it into shorter segments) by **Ctrl**+clicking on the point where you want to place the handle. You can remove a handle (simplifying the curve) by the same method.

N O T E

In many cases, it is easier to create a smooth, regular curve by creating a polyline or polygon and applying the **Smooth** command on the graphics menu. See "Smoothing and Unsmoothing Objects," later in this chapter.

N O T E

Using Text in Graphics

FrameMaker provides two options for using text in graphics: text columns and text lines. Draw a text column when you want to place text that occupies several lines and flows automatically from line to line as part of a graphic, or when you want to include a variable, cross-reference, marker, or anchored frame, or to use conditional text. Text columns placed in graphics are really no different than those used for the main flows on body pages, except that they are drawn directly on the page rather than being generated from templates on master pages and they are not connected to the main text flow(s). Text in text columns can be formatted by applying character formats and paragraph formats (see Chapter 5), or via the options on the Format menu or the Formatting Bar.

A text line is a single line of text that is independent of the text flows in the document. A text line will expand horizontally (or vertically, if rotated) as you type, but it will not wrap to a new line. Use a text line to create a single-line callout in a figure. You can format a text line by applying a character format, or by using the options on the Format menu, but you cannot apply a paragraph format to a text line. A text line cannot contain a cross-reference, anchored frame, variable, marker, or conditional text.

▣ Drawing a Text Column

To draw a text column, use the Text Column tool. Move the pointer to the position where you want to place one corner of the column, press the left mouse button and drag diagonally to position the other corner, then release the button. A column you create this way has a disconnected flow. You can type text in the column like any other and format the text using any of the methods described in Chapter 5. A text column is initially drawn without a border or fill pattern, but you can add them later using the properties buttons.

Ⓐ Drawing a Text Line

To draw a text line, use the Text-Line tool. Click at the position where you want the line to begin (the origin point), then type the text. You can apply a character format either before you start typing or by selecting the text and applying the format after you finish typing. By default, text lines are left aligned at their origin points, but you can change the alignment in the Object Properties dialog box.

▦ *Drawing a Frame*

The last of FrameMaker's drawing tool is the Frame tool. Frames are used to hold, group, and crop other graphic objects, including graphics imported from other programs (see Chapter 13), as well as those drawn with FrameMaker's drawing tools. Drawing a frame is similar to drawing a rectangle: Select the frame tool and move the pointer where you want to position one corner of the frame. Press and hold the left mouse button and drag diagonally to position the opposite corner of the frame, then release the button. The frame will be drawn with the current Fill Pattern, Pen Style, Dash Pattern, and Color (see "Properties," later in this chapter).

Frames drawn with the Frame tool are *unanchored* frames. Paradoxically, unanchored frames stay where you put them until you cut and paste them or drag them to new locations. There is another class of frames, called *anchored* frames, which are attached to particular locations in text and move automatically as the text is edited. Anchored frames form the subject of Chapter 14.

Drawing Properties

Objects drawn with FrameMaker's drawing tools have the following properties: Fill Pattern, Pen Pattern, Line Width, Line Ends, Dash Style, and Color. With the exceptions noted in the previous section, most objects have all these properties.

You can select the properties for an object before you draw it, and you can select an object and edit its properties at any time. Each of the property buttons opens one or more selection menus from which you can set the properties, as detailed in the remainder of this section. As mentioned earlier, the buttons in the left column of the Tools Palette select the properties. The corresponding buttons in the right column serve only to indicate the current settings and nothing will happen if you click on them. Normally when you select a property and use it to draw a object, the properties revert to their defaults when you select another tool. If you want to keep one or more properties active through several operations (for example, you want to draw a number of objects with dashed blue lines) **Shift**+click on the properties you want to use.

Selecting a Fill Pattern

Fill patterns fill any object that wholly or partially encloses a space (including polylines and curves). Polylines and open curves are filled as though their ends were connected by straight lines, as in Figure 12.3. Click the **Fill Pattern** button to select a fill pattern. This displays a palette of patterns (Figure 12.4). Click on the pattern you want to use. If you want the object to be unfilled but to cover up objects placed behind it, select the white pattern. If you want objects placed behind it to show through, select "None" (the default).

Figure 12.3   A filled polygon and polyline

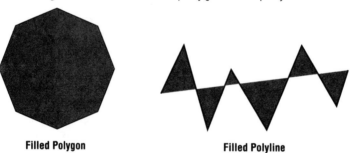

Filled Polygon   Filled Polyline

Selecting a Pen Style

Pen patterns are used by all objects that involve lines or borders, except text columns. Click the **Pen Pattern** button to select a pattern. This displays a palette similar to that for fill patterns. Click on the pattern you wish to select.

Figure 12.4 The Fill Patterns palette

Fill
None

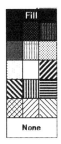

Selecting a Line Width

The Line Width selection process has two levels. When you click on the **Line Width** button, you open a palette from which you can select one of four predefined line widths (Figure 12.5). The line widths in the palette *do not* accurately reflect the lines that will result from selecting among the options—they are purely symbolic of the four different widths. However, the selected line width is displayed to the right of the button. To see the actual widths of all four options or to change them, select the fifth choice, **Set**. This selection opens the dialog box in Figure 12.6, in which you can specify the width in points of the four line width options. Click the **Get Defaults** button to restore the widths to their default values. Click **Set** to save the edited line widths.

Figure 12.5 The Line Widths palette

Line Widths
Set...

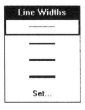

Figure 12.6 The Line Width Options dialog box

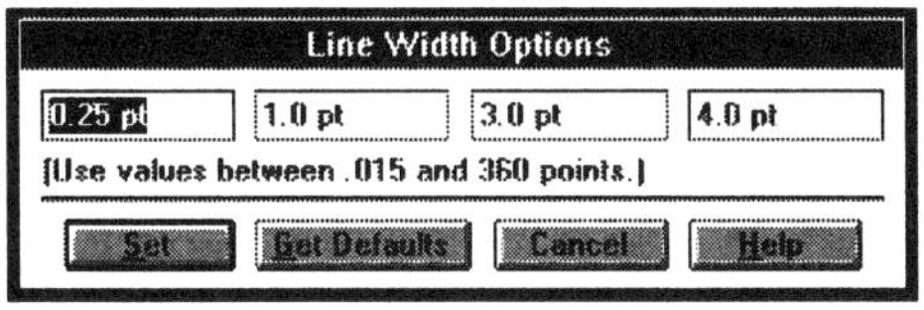

Line Width Options
0.25 pt
1.0 pt
3.0 pt
4.0 pt
(Use values between .015 and 360 points.)
Set
Get Defaults
Cancel
Help

Selecting Line Ends

The Line End property is used by objects with open line ends: straight lines, polylines, arcs, and freehand curves. It has no effect on closed figures such as rect-angles, ovals, and polygons. The line end selection process also has two levels. Clicking the **Line End** button opens a palette from which you can select one of four predefined line-end styles: one plain and three with single or double arrowheads. The fifth option, **Set**, opens the dialog box in Figure 12.7. In this dialog box, you can select one of eight predefined arrowhead styles, define a custom arrowhead style, or select one of three line cap styles. The arrowhead and cap styles you select apply to all four line-end styles in the palette.

Figure 12.7 The Line End Options dialog box

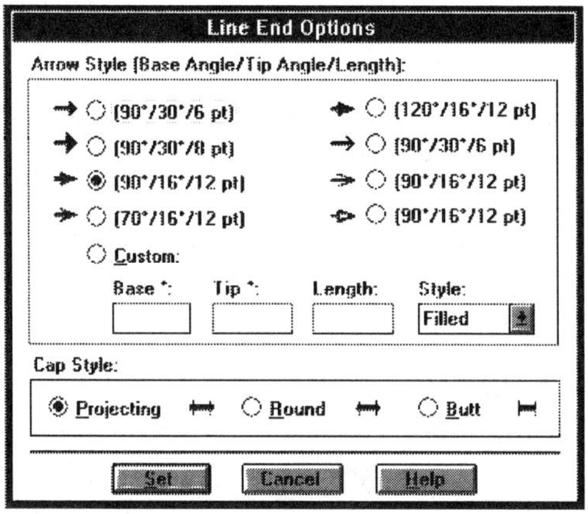

Creating a Custom Arrowhead Style

In the event that none of the eight arrowhead styles are suitable for your purposes, you can create a custom arrowhead style. The shape of a custom arrowhead is defined by three parameters: base angle, tip angle, and length, as shown in Figure 12.8. These parameters are subject to the following limits:

■ Base Angle—between 10° and 175°, and at least 5° greater than the tip angle.

■ Tip Angle—between 5° and 85°.

■ Length—between 0 and 255 points. (The specified length is for an arrow-head used with a one-point line. The actual size of the arrowhead will vary in proportion to the line width with which it is used.)

Figure 12.8   The defining parameters for a custom arrowhead

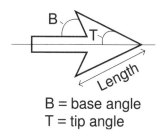

B = base angle
T = tip angle

The arrowhead can also have one of three styles—Filled, Stick, or Hollow—as shown in Figure 12.7.

Selecting a Cap Style

The Cap style determines the shape of line ends that do not terminate in arrowheads and the way lines are joined. FrameMaker provides three cap styles—Projecting, Round, and Butt—as shown in Figure 12.8. Projecting and butt line ends are both square, and there is little difference between them in the case of unconnected lines, except that a line with projecting ends will be slightly longer. End caps become significant when you connect fairly thick lines at a common end point. If you connect lines with butt caps, the ends will not join cleanly (see Figure 12.9). For lines of equal thickness joined at right angles, projecting line caps produce clean corners. Rounded caps will work well with lines joined at a variety of angles. Joining lines with radically different thicknesses is more difficult, regardless of their cap styles. It may be helpful to turn off Snap in order to get the best results in joining unequal lines.

Figure 12.9   Joined lines with different cap styles

Selecting a Dash Pattern

Selecting a dash pattern is another two-level process. Clicking the **Dash Pattern** button opens a palette from which you can select a dashed or a solid line. Selecting **Set** on the palette opens the dialog box in Figure 12.10, from which you can select one of eight predefined dash patterns. For some reason, Frame neglected to include an option for a custom dash pattern; you can create a custom dash pattern by editing your configuration file, but that is an unwieldy process for non-programmers.

Figure 12.10   The Dashed Line Options dialog box

Selecting a Color

Clicking on the **Color** button opens the color palette (Figure 12.11), which contains eight predefined spot colors, plus any additional colors you have defined using the **Color** option on the View menu. See Chapter 15.

Figure 12.11   The Color palette

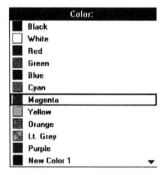

If you select a color and the objects you draw with it are not visible, be sure the color is not set to "Cutout" or "Invisible" in the Define Color Views dialog box (View>**Color**>**Views**). See Chapter 15.

N O T E

Editing Graphics

Selecting Objects

Before you edit graphics in FrameMaker, you must select one or more objects to edit. A selected object has eight handles located at the corners and the centers of the sides of its bounding box (see Figure 12.12). Whenever you finish drawing an object (unless you have "locked" the drawing tool by **Shift**+clicking on it), Frame-Maker automatically selects the object.

Figure 12.12 Selected objects

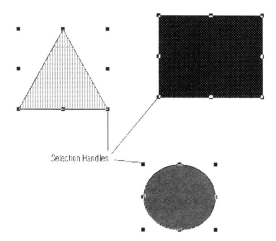

FrameMaker has two selection tools: The Smart Selection tool and the Object Selection tool. The Smart Selection tool knows the difference between text lines and text columns and all other graphic objects. When placed over an empty space on the page, the Smart Selection tool appears as a black arrow. When placed over a graphic object that can be selected, it changes to a hollow arrow. When placed over a text column or text line, it turns into an I-beam cursor for editing text. Except where text columns and text lines are concerned, the Object Selection tool behaves exactly the same way as the Smart Selection tool. The Object Selection tool treats text lines and columns exactly the same as other objects.

To select an object, move the selection tool over the object until it turns into a hollow arrow, then click the left mouse button. To select additional objects, **Shift**+click on them. Another way to select a group of adjacent objects is to place the pointer at one corner of the group, then click and drag to draw a box around the group. When you release the button, all the objects *completely within the box* will be selected. When you use this technique, make sure that the starting point where you click and start to drag is outside any object (i.e., the pointer is a solid rather than a hollow arrow). If you click and drag with the pointer inside an object, you will move the object rather than dragging a box. If you accidentally move an object, press **Ctrl+Z** to undo the move. Once you have selected a group by dragging a box around it, you can add objects to or remove objects from the group by **Shift**+clicking on them. To select a text column or line with the Smart Selection tool (rather than placing an insertion point in it for editing text), press and hold **Ctrl** and click on it. To select all the objects on the current page, press **Ctrl+A** or choose **Select All on Page** from the Edit menu.

Frames form an exception to the rule as regards selection; you cannot have a frame and another object selected at the same time. Selecting a frame automatically deselects any other objects that were selected, and vice versa. When a frame is selected, the objects inside it can be regarded as selected for certain purposes; for example, if you move or rotate a frame (see later) the objects it contains move or rotate with it. To select all the objects *inside a frame*, first select the frame, then press **Ctrl+A** or choose **Select All in Frame** from the Edit menu. The objects in the frame will be selected, but the frame itself will not. You might use this option if you wanted to move, rotate, or flip all the objects in the frame while the frame itself remained stationary.

To deselect one of a group of selected objects while leaving the others selected, **Shift**+click on the object. To deselect a group of adjacent objects, stretch a box around them while holding the **Shift** key. (Observe the precautions mentioned earlier in regard to stretching a box around a group of objects to select them.) When you release the mouse button, all the objects completely within the box will be deselected. To deselect all the objects currently selected, place the pointer outside any object (i.e., anywhere that the pointer appears as a solid arrow) and click.

Cutting, Copying, and Pasting

Objects drawn with FrameMaker's drawing tools can be cut, copied, and pasted at different locations in a document, or in other documents that are open, just like any other FrameMaker objects. Select the object(s), as described earlier, then select **Cut** or **Copy** from the Edit menu, or use their respective keyboard shortcuts, **Ctrl+X** and **Ctrl+C**.

To paste the graphic, select **Paste** or press **Ctrl+V**. Where the graphic will appear on the page depends on what is currently selected:

- ■ If nothing is selected, the graphic will be pasted at the same location it was cut or copied from.

- If another graphic is selected, the new object will be pasted on top of it.

- If a frame is selected, the graphic will be pasted in the frame.

- If there is an insertion point in a text column, the graphic will be pasted in an anchored frame, anchored at the insertion point.

When an object has been cut or copied to the clipboard, it remains there until it is replaced by another cut or copy operation. Hence, you can easily paste multiple copies of the same object at different locations.

N O T E

Moving Objects

There are three ways to move an object: You can drag it with the mouse, you can move it in small increments with the keyboard or the helicopter buttons on the Quick Access Bar, or you can edit its offsets from the upper-left corner of the page in the Object Properties dialog box. To drag an object with the mouse, select it, position the pointer over the object so that it turns into a hollow arrow (not over a handle), press the left mouse button, and drag. As you drag the object, the X, Y coordinates of the upper-left corner of the bounding box will appear in the status area. If the rulers are displayed, guidelines indicating the positions of the edges of the bounding box will appear on the rulers and move as you drag the object. When the object is positioned correctly, release the button. When the Snap grid is on, you can achieve accurate positioning this way. When working with Snap turned off, you may need to use one of the other methods to achieve a precise position.

The four helicopter buttons on the Quick Access Bar (Figure 12.13) move a selected object up, down, left, or right respectively by one point each time you click on the button. You can also move an object by small increments by pressing and holding the **Alt** key and pressing one of the four arrow keys on the cursor key pad. The exact increment by which the object moves depends on the current magnification of the screen. The greater the magnification, the smaller the increment of movement. Movements made with the helicopter buttons and the keyboard are not affected by the Snap setting.

Figure 12.13   The helicopter buttons on the Quick Access Bar

The greatest precision can be achieved by editing the object's offsets in the Object Properties dialog box (see Figure 12.14—the exact contents of the dialog box depend on the type of object selected). Select the object and select **Object Proper-**

ties on the Graphics menu (keyboard shortcut **Esc g o**) or press the **Object Proper-ties** button on the Quick Access Bar. You can control the position of the selected object by typing values in the Offset From Top and Left boxes. These values specify the distance between the upper-left corner of the object's bounding box and the upper-left corner of the page.

Figure 12.14 The Object Properties dialog box

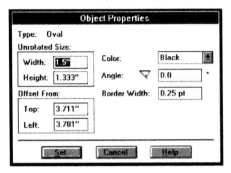

N O T E You can only edit the properties of a single object or a number of objects that have been grouped. If you want to position several objects at one time via the Object properties dialog box, select them and group them with the **Group** command on the Graphics menu (see later). In this situation, the top and left offset values will position the upper-left corner of the collective bounding box for the grouped objects.

Rotating Objects

With the exception of frames, which can only be rotated in 90° increments, all FrameMaker objects can be rotated in almost infinitesimal increments. There are several ways to rotate an object:

- Click and drag one of the object's handles while holding the **Alt** key. If Snap is on and you have entered a Snap Rotate value in the View Options dialog box, the object will rotate only by multiples of the specified value.

- Select the **Rotate** option on the Graphics menu (keyboard shortcut **Esc g t**). In the dialog box that appears, type a rotation value and a direction (clockwise or counterclockwise).

- Open the Object Properties dialog box and edit the object's Angle.

- Use the one of the two rotation buttons on the Quick Access Bar. Each click on the button rotates the selected object by 15°.

Flipping Objects

In addition to rotating them, you can flip most objects on their horizontal and vertical axes via the **Flip Up/Down** and **Flip Left/Right** options on the graphics menu or the corresponding buttons on the Quick Access Bar (keyboard shortcuts **Esc g v** and **Esc g h**, respectively). You cannot flip a frame or a text column.

Scaling Objects

There are several ways to scale or resize an object:

- Use the **Scale** command on the Graphics menu (keyboard shortcut **Esc g z**), or the corresponding button on the Quick Access Bar. This opens the Scale dialog box (Figure 12.15). To scale the object uniformly, select the **Scale** radio button and type a percentage value. 100% represents the current size of the object; a value greater than 100% enlarges the object and a value less than 100% reduces the object. To scale the object non-uniformly, select the **Unrotated Size** radio button and edit the Width and Height values.

Figure 12.15   The Scale dialog box

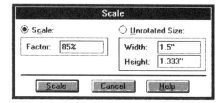

- Click and drag one of the object's handles with the mouse. Place the pointer near a handle, so it turns into a black arrowhead, then press and hold the left mouse button and drag. To resize an object uniformly (that is, to maintain the object's original aspect ratio), hold the **Shift** key and drag one of its corner handles.

- Open the Object Properties dialog box and edit the object's Width and Height.

Grouping and Ungrouping Objects

Often, it is useful to perform an operation on several objects at the same time. You may have created a figure or illustration by drawing several different objects, and you may want to move, resize, or rotate the whole illustration without having to select all the component parts every time you work on it. You can do this by grouping all the objects that make up the illustration.

To group a number of objects, select them using one of the methods described earlier in this chapter, then select **Group** on the graphics menu (keyboard shortcut **Esc g g**) or click the corresponding button on the Quick Access Bar. When the objects are grouped, they will have a single bounding box and set of handles. You can combine grouped objects with other objects of groups to create still larger groups.

To break up a group into its original constituents, select it and choose **Ungroup** from the graphics menu (keyboard shortcut **Esc g u**) or click the corresponding button on the Quick Access Bar. If the group contains other groups, it will be broken into its constituent groups when you ungroup it. Each of these can then be ungrouped into its constituent groups or parts.

Restacking Objects

As you draw, FrameMaker automatically layers new objects on top of older ones. You can change this "stacking" order by selecting one or more objects and using the **Bring to Front** or **Send to Back** options on the Graphics menu (keyboard shortcuts **Esc g f** and **Esc g b**, respectively) or their corresponding buttons on the Quick Access Bar. If two or more overlapping objects are selected, they retain their current order relative to one another, but change their position relative to other layers.

It can be a bit tricky to select the object you want when several objects are stacked one on top of another and their edges are in close proximity. As a first step, it may be useful to select all the objects in an area, just to see where all their bounding boxes and handles are. This is a good way to see the locations of any objects that are completely hidden behind others. Once you know where the object(s) you want to select are located, you may be able to drag a narrow horizontal or vertical box across an area to single out the one you want, or it may be necessary to select two or more closely spaced objects and then **Shift**+click to unselect the ones you don't want. It may also be necessary to temporarily select some objects and send them to the back in order to get at the objects you want to work on.

Aligning and Distributing Objects

These two operations, which rearrange the positions of objects relative to one another are, as far as I know, unique to FrameMaker.

Aligning

The **Align** command repositions selected objects relative to a horizontal or vertical line, or both. Objects can be aligned vertically on their tops, centers, or bottoms, and/or aligned horizontally on their left sides, centers, or right sides. In either case, the last of the objects selected remains stationary and all the others are aligned with reference to it. The **Align** command on the Graphics menu (keyboard shortcut **Esc g a**) opens the Align dialog box (Figure 12.16), in which you can change both the horizontal and vertical alignment of the selected objects. In addition, six buttons on the Quick Access Bar are devoted to alignment, one for each of the possible horizontal and vertical alignments (see Figure 12.17).

Figure 12.16 The Align dialog box

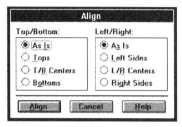

Figure 12.17 The Align buttons on the Quick Access Bar

Distributing

Use the **Distribute** command on the Graphics menu (keyboard shortcut **Esc g d**) to achieve even spacing among several objects. The command opens the Distribute dialog box (Figure 12.18). Selected objects can be spaced either vertically or horizontally, or both. There are three spacing options for either dimension: Equidistant Edges, Equidistant Centers, and Edge Gap. The first two options evenly distribute the objects within the space they currently occupy; that is, the outermost objects in the dimension in question remain stationary and the remaining objects are evenly spaced between them. The Edge Gap option changes the spacing between the edges of the objects to the value you specify. Hence, it can be used to loosen or tighten the spaces among the objects in a group. The **Distribute** command can also be accessed via a button on the Quick Access Bar, which is just another way to open the dialog box.

Reshaping Objects

The **Reshape** command reactivates certain objects so you can edit their shapes. What happens after you select an object and choose **Reshape** from the Graphics menu (keyboard shortcut **Esc g r**) or click the **Reshape** button on the Quick Access Bar depends on the type of object selected.

Figure 12.18   The Distribute dialog box

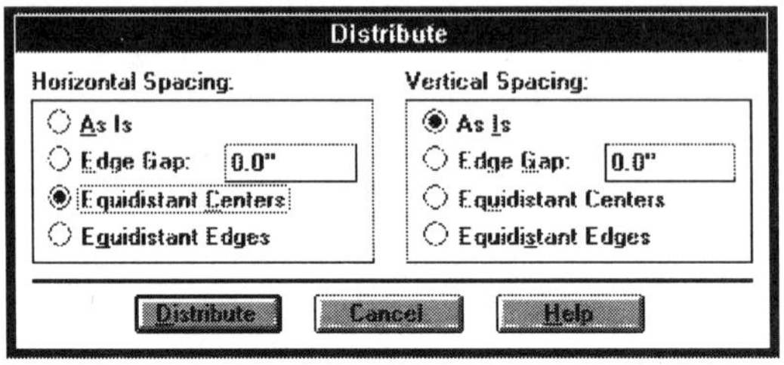

Polylines and Polygons

When you apply the **Reshape** command to a polyline or polygon, its corner points become active and you can drag them to reshape the object. In addition, you can **Ctrl**+click at any point on the object to create a new corner or on any existing corner to remove it. The **Reshape** command has no effect on rectangles or ovals (you can stretch or resize these objects without applying it). You can turn a rectangle or oval into a regular polygon with the **Set # Sides** command (see later). Once this has been done, the resulting polygon can be reshaped like any other.

Curves

You can use the **Reshape** command on curves drawn with the Freehand tool or created by applying the **Smooth** command to a polyline (see later). When you apply the **Reshape** command to one of these curves, you activate its reshape handles and control points, which you can use to manipulate the curve, as described earlier in this chapter.

Smoothing and Unsmoothing Objects

The **Smooth** command transforms a selected object with sharp corners, such as a polygon or polyline, into a smooth open or closed curve. You can select the **Smooth** command from the Graphics menu, use the keyboard shortcut **Esc g s**, or click the **Smooth** button on the Quick Access Bar. In many cases, it is easier to create a smoothly curved but controlled figure this way than by using the Freehand tool. Once an object has been smoothed, it acquires a set of reshape handles and control points and can be reshaped just like a curve created with the Freehand tool. (There is one exception to this: You can smooth the corners of a rectangle to create something similar to a rounded rectangle, but the resulting figure will not acquire reshape handles and control points.)

The **Unsmooth** command has, not surprisingly, the opposite affect as the **Smooth** command; that is, it turns smooth curves into sharp-cornered polygons or polylines.

Select the **Unsmooth** command from the Graphics menu, use the keyboard shortcut **Esc g m**, or click the **Unsmooth** button on the Quick Access Bar. This command can be applied either to objects that have previously been smoothed, or to curves drawn with the Freehand tool. However, you cannot unsmooth a circle or oval into a polygon (use the **Set # Sides** command for this purpose—see next).

Transforming an Oval or Rectangle into a Regular Polygon

You can turn an oval or rectangle into a regular polygon by applying the **Set # Sides** command. (Strictly speaking, only squares and circles produce regular polygons, with equal angles and equal sides; a rectangle or oval will produce a distorted version of a regular polygon.) Select the command from the Graphics menu or use the keyboard shortcut **Esc g n** (there is no button for this command on the Quick Access Bar). The Set Number of Sides dialog box (Figure 12.19) appears. Use this dialog box to specify the number of sides and the start angle for the polygon. The start angle orients one vertex of the figure (what would be the uppermost vertex if the angle were 0˚).

Figure 12.19   The Set Number of Sides dialog box

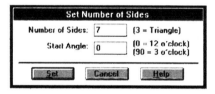

Connecting Objects with Gravity

Gravity is a property that attracts graphic objects to one another. It is turned on by selecting **Gravity** on the Graphics menu (keyboard shortcut **Esc g y**) or clicking the **Gravity** button on the Quick Access Bar. Gravity attracts objects that are being stretched or drawn to other objects that are already present on the screen. It does not have any effect on objects that are being moved. As you drag the handle of an object or move the pointer attached to an active object, the pointer will jump when brought into close proximity to an another object. The attraction is strongest at the corners of objects. Straight sides have weaker gravity, and curves have little, if any, gravity. If Snap is on, gravity can overcome the power of the Snap Grid, causing objects to connect at points that don't correspond to intersections on the grid.

Measuring Objects

You can measure any graphic object by selecting it, then moving the pointer to one of its handles and pressing and holding the left mouse button. The dimensions of the object appear in the status area at the lower left corner of the document window (the dimensions are those of the object's rectangular bounding box).

To check the position of any object, select it and open the Object Properties dialog box. For most types of objects, the position is expressed as the offset of the upper-left corner of the object from the upper-left corner of the page. For text lines, the distance is measured from the upper-left corner of the page to the alignment point on the baseline.

To measure the distance between any two points on a page, move the pointer to the first point, press **Ctrl** and drag to the second point while holding the *right* mouse button. The horizontal and vertical distances between the two points appear in the status area.

CHAPTER 13

Importing Graphics Created in Other Programs

Although you can do a lot with the drawing tools built into FrameMaker, sooner or later you will probably need to import a graphic image created by another program, either because you need to do something that is beyond the capabilities of FrameMaker's drawing tools, or because you need to use images that originate elsewhere, such as screen captures, scanned photos, CAD drawings from the engineering department, a corporate logo produced by an outside ad agency, or the like.

About Graphics File Formats

FrameMaker, and computers in general, deal with two basic types of graphic files: vector (or outline) files and bitmap (or raster) files. A third type of graphics file, called a metafile, can contain both bitmapped and vector information. Vector files are produced by object oriented drawing and illustration programs, CAD programs, and business and presentation graphics programs. They contain mathematical descriptions of the images to be produced. Vector files generally have *device independent resolution;* that is, they can be printed on any compatible output device at any size and will take full advantage of the output device's resolution.

Bitmapped images commonly originate in paint programs, or as screen captures or scanned photographs. A bitmapped image contains a numerical representation of the rows of dots or pixels that made up the image on the device on which it was created. The resolution of bitmapped images is *device dependent.* Enlarging a bitmapped image beyond its original size will make its resolution appear coarser, and scaling it to a size such that its original dot patterns don't match those of the output device can result in data loss, making the image even coarser.

Encapsulated PostScript Files

The most versatile and popular metafiles at present are Encapsulated PostScript (EPS) Files. EPS files contain PostScript code that will create the desired image on a Post-Script printer or image setter. They also typically contain a bitmapped *preview image* that is displayed on the screen when the EPS file is imported into another application, such as FrameMaker. To print EPS files satisfactorily, you must have a PostScript printer. When printing to a non-PostScript output device, most applications will print only the bitmapped *preview image*, which is typically much cruder than the PostScript image.

FrameMaker imports and prints EPS files created on a variety of platforms, but may not be able to display the preview image of an EPS file created on a different platform. For example, some Windows applications create EPS files with Windows Metafile preview images. These preview images display correctly in FrameMaker for Windows but not in FrameMaker on the Macintosh. Conversely, some Mac applications create EPS files with PICT previews; these display correctly in FrameMaker on the Mac, but not in Windows. EPS files with TIFF previews will display correctly on either platform. When FrameMaker cannot display the preview image of an EPS file, it will display a gray box where you place the graphic.

Desktop Color Separations

Desktop Color Separation (DCS) files are created by image manipulation programs such as Adobe Photoshop and Letraset Color Studio. FrameMaker 4.0 can import DCS graphics. A DCS image consists of five files: a master file that contains the preview image and four files for the four separated colors (cyan, yellow, magenta, and black). How the five files are named depends on the application that created them. To import a DCS image into a FrameMaker document, import only the master file. For the image to print correctly, you must keep the four separation files in the same directory as the master file and not rename them. (For more information on color separations, consult Chapter 15.)

Graphics Filters

As with importing text files from other applications, what kinds of graphic image files you will be able to import into FrameMaker depends on which filters you have installed. When you first installed FrameMaker on your system, you were given the option of selecting which filters to install. If you find that you need filters that you did not initially install, you can run the Setup program again and check only the **Filters** option.

A definitive list of graphics filters was not available at the times of this writing, but FrameMaker 4.0 will have filters for at least the graphics formats listed in Table 13.1.

Table 13.1 FrameMaker graphics file filters

File Format	Extension	Type
Computer Graphics Metafile	CGM	Metafile
AutoCAD Drawing Exchange Format	DXF	Vector
Encapsulated PostScript	EPS	Metafile
Compuserve Graphics Interchange Format	GIF	Bitmap
Hewlett-Packard Graphics Language	PGL	Vector
PC Paintbrush	PCX	Bitmap
Macintosh PICT 1 and PICT 2	PCT	Metafile
Sun Raster	RAS or SUN	Bitmap
Tagged Image File Format	TIF	Bitmap
Windows Bitmap	BMP	Bitmap
WordPerfect Graphics	WPG	Metafile
X-Windows Bitmap	XWD	Bitmap

As with text filters, the creation of FrameMaker graphics filters is an ongoing process. If the filter you need was not included in FrameMaker 4.0, you may be able to obtain it from Frame as part of an optional filter pack, or from a third-party vendor. If you have graphics files that use an obscure format, you may be able to obtain a third party conversion utility that will convert them to a more common format for which FrameMaker has a filter.

Importing a Graphic

The first step in importing a graphic is to decide where you're going to put it. Imported graphics can be placed in anchored frames, in unanchored frames, in rectangles drawn with FrameMaker's drawing tools, or directly on the page.

If you want the graphic to move with a particular text line or paragraph as text is edited and revised, use an anchored frame. You can either create an anchored frame with the **Anchored Frame** option on the special menu, as described in Chapter 14, or you can click an insertion point in a paragraph before importing the graphic and an anchored frame will be created automatically. An anchored frame created this way can be edited like any other.

If you want the graphic to stay at a fixed location on a page, place it directly on the page. To import a graphic directly onto the page, click in the page margins, outside of any text column or frame, before importing the graphic. Once the graphic is imported, you can position it on the page by dragging it with the mouse or by editing its offsets from the upper-left corner of the page in the Object Properties dialog box. If you want to use a graphic at the same location on many pages in a document (for example, a company logo in a report), you can import it onto a master page.

Graphics in unanchored frames are used mainly on *Reference Pages* (see Chapter 4). Unanchored frames can also be used to crop graphics on body pages. To place a graphic in an unanchored Frame, draw the frame with the Frame tool (see Chapter 12) and be sure it's selected before importing the graphic. A rectangle can be used to scale a graphic to a predetermined size. To place a graphic in a rectangle, draw the rectangle with the Rectangle tool and be sure the rectangle is selected before importing the graphic.

When you are ready to import the graphic, open the File menu and select **Import**, then select **Files** from the submenu or use the keyboard shortcut **Esc f i f**. This opens the Import dialog box (Figure 13.1). Use the drive, directory, and files selection boxes to locate the file to import. (To make it easier to locate files of a particular format, type a wildcard specification, such as *.EPS, *.TIF, or *.BMP, in the File text box and press **Enter**. Now only files of the appropriate type will appear in the file list box.) When you have found the file you want to import, select the appropriate radio button to import the file by copying or by reference (see the discussion of these two methods later in this chapter) and click the **Import** button.

If you are importing a vector file, this completes the importation process. If you are importing a bitmap file, an additional dialog box (Figure 13.2) will appear. Use this dialog box to select the resolution and size at which the graphic will be imported. The size at which a bitmapped graphic will appear depends on the resolution in dots per inch you select (remember, a bitmapped image consists of a fixed number of dots. Hence, the higher the number of dots per inch you specify, the smaller and more finely grained the image.) For the best results, pick a resolution that is an even submultiple of your printer's resolution; for example, choose 75, 100, 150, or 300-dpi if you're printing to a 300-dpi laser printer. If you want to scale the image to a selected rectangle, select **Fit in Selected Rectangle**. This scales the image so that the larger of its width or height exactly matches that of the rectangle.

Figure 13.1   The Import dialog box

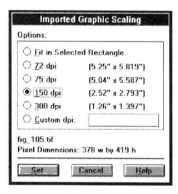

Working with bitmapped images, especially ones you didn't create for use at a particular size, generally involves a tradeoff between placing the image at a size that suits your page layout and one that gives the best resolution that the image file is capable of. If you have a choice, it is almost always preferable to use a vector, rather than a bitmapped image.

Figure 13.2   The Scale Imported Graphic dialog box

If FrameMaker does not recognize the format of the file you are trying to import, it displays the Unknown File Type dialog box, with the choice it considers most likely highlighted. Confirm the file format if it is correct, or select another.

N O T E

Replacing a Graphic

The process of replacing a graphic is almost exactly the same as that described previously for importing a graphic. The only difference is that before beginning the process, you must select an existing imported graphic by clicking on it with the mouse. Proceed as described previously. Observe that what was previously labeled the **Import** button is now labeled **Replace**. When you complete the operation, the old graphic will be replaced with the new one.

N O T E

If you import a graphic by reference, there is no need to replace an old version of a graphic with a new one. Provided the revised graphic has the same file name and path as the original, FrameMaker will automatically import the most recent version whenever it redraws the page that contains it.

Importing by Reference vs. Importing by Copying

There are two ways to import a graphic image file into FrameMaker: by copying or by reference. Importing a graphic by copying permanently incorporates a copy of the graphic file into the FrameMaker document. Importing by reference copies only the path to the graphics file into the document. When FrameMaker loads a document file with graphics imported by reference, it searches the disk for the necessary files and loads them. Each method has its advantages and disadvantages.

The main advantage of importing files by copying is that it makes the document file fully self-contained. You can move the file to another directory, another drive, or another system without having to worry about maintaining the links to graphics files; all the necessary files are part of the document. One of the main disadvantages of copying is that it makes for large document files. Bitmapped files such as TIFFs tend to be especially large; nothing bloats a document file like importing a lot of large TIFF files by copying. If you need to move files between systems via floppy disks ("sneaker net"), you may find that the document files are too large to fit on a floppy. Of course, you may be able to overcome this limitation by using a file-compression utility such as PKZIP. (Every PC user should have a copy of PKZIP; it's available on most bulletin boards as shareware.) Another approach to the oversized file problem is to break up large documents into multi-file "books" (see Chapter 18). Importing graphics by copying also wastes disk space. Suppose, for example, that you have a 300K TIFF file that you need to use in three different documents. If you copy the TIFF file into each of the documents, you've used up 900K of disk space, in addition to the original 300K. If you import the image into each of the documents by reference, you've only used the few dozen bytes required to store its path.

The main advantages of importing graphics by reference are smaller document file size and ease of updating the graphics files. Because FrameMaker loads the graphic images anew every time the program redraws the pages containing them, the document always contains the latest versions of the images (assuming that, when you revise your graphics, you always store them in the same directories with the same file names). It also allows an unlimited number of documents to import the same graphic by reference. The price for these advantages is that you must keep track of the graphic files. You cannot rename them or move them to other directories or disks or FrameMaker will lose track of them. When you move a document from one system to another, you must be sure to include all the necessary files, and they must be stored at analogous locations at their new location or you will have to reconstruct all the links. Unfortunately, FrameMaker has nothing comparable to Ventura's Manage Publication feature for copying all the files required for a publication from one location to another. However, you can generate a list of all the graphics in a document (see "Generating a List of References," in Chapter 16).

Relative vs. Absolute Paths

When FrameMaker imports a graphic by reference, it stores a path that it uses to locate the graphic file. The paths FrameMaker uses are of two kinds: relative paths and absolute paths. A relative path indicates the position of the file relative to the directory in which the FrameMaker program files are stored. An absolute path specifies the location of the files beginning with the drive designator of a particular disk. By default, FrameMaker will store a relative path for any file that is located on the same disk as the FrameMaker program files. By necessity, it always stores an absolute path for files stored on other physical or logical drives. You can see the path for any graphic imported by reference by selecting the graphic and opening the Object Properties dialog box.

If a graphic is imported with a relative path, both the document and the graphic can be moved to different drives and directories, provided they retain the same relative locations, and FrameMaker will still find the graphic. However, if one of the files is moved and the other is not, the path will no longer be valid and the connection will have to be reestablished, as described later in this chapter. If a graphic is imported with an absolute path, the document can be moved to another directory or drive and FrameMaker will still be able to find the graphic, but if the graphic is moved, the path will no longer be valid and the connection will have to be reestablished.

All this really matters only if you do a lot of moving of documents back and forth between systems. If your documents start and end their lives on the same disk, you really needn't think much about relative and absolute paths. If you frequently move documents between systems, and you can persuade all the parties involved to create analogous directory structures (what are the odds of this happening outside of a corporate, MIS-managed environment?), the use of relative paths can simplify the process of moving the documents and keeping the connections to imported graphics intact.

Importing Graphics via OLE

In addition to importing graphics by copying or by reference, you can also import graphics into FrameMaker documents from other Windows applications via Windows Object Linking and Embedding (OLE). To do this, the program in which the image originates must be an OLE server. (Windows uses the term *server* to describe programs that create files that can be exported via OLE; programs such as FrameMaker, that can import files via OLE, are called OLE *clients*. FrameMaker 4.0 is strictly a client; it cannot act as an OLE server.)

To import an image via OLE, use the following procedure:

1. Select the location in the FrameMaker document where you want to place the image (the same considerations described earlier in the chapter for placing imported graphics apply here).

2. Open the server application and load or create the image.

3. Copy the image to the Windows clipboard using the **Copy** option in the server application.

4. Switch back to FrameMaker.

5. Open the Edit Menu and select **Paste Special** or use the keyboard shortcut **Ctrl + Shift + V**. In the list box that appears, select OLE. The graphic will be placed just as if you had imported it via the Files>**Import** method.

Editing an OLE Image

To edit an image imported via OLE, double-click on the image. This loads a copy of the application that created the image (the server). Edit the image using whatever tools the server application provides. When you have finished editing, close the server. You will be asked whether you want to update embedded object. Select **Yes** to replace the image with the edited version.

N O T E

The preceding is a simplified description of how OLE operates. For more details, consult Chapter 13 of the *Microsoft Windows User's Guide*.

Scaling and Manipulating Imported Images

Once a graphic is imported into a document, you can manipulate it in a number of ways using tools on the Tools Palette or commands on the Graphics menu.

Scaling

There are several ways to scale a graphic:

- Use the **Scale** option on the Graphics menu. In the Scale dialog box, you can either specify a percentage for rescaling the graphic uniformly in both dimensions, or you can select the **Unrotated Size** radio button and type separate values for width and height.

- Use the Object Properties dialog box to set width and height values, as well as various other factors such as rotation and offset.

- Stretch the graphic to the desired size with the mouse. Select the graphic and move the pointer to one of its handles. The pointer changes to a black arrowhead. Drag the handle to stretch the graphic.

- To stretch a graphic uniformly in both dimensions, press and hold the **Shift** key while stretching. When you move the mouse pointer near one of the graphic's selection handles, it turns into an arrow head at the lower right (Figure 13.3). Drag the handle to stretch the graphic.

Figure 13.3   Stretching a graphic

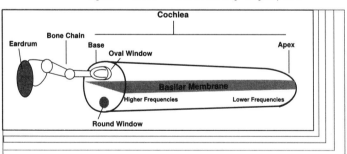

N O T E

If Snap is turned on and you resize a graphic by dragging with the mouse, you will only be able to resize the graphic so that its borders correspond to the snap grid. The snap grid has no effect when you resize a graphic via the Scaling or Object properties dialog box.

WARNING

FrameMaker has no option for restoring a graphic to its original aspect ratio after it has been distorted by stretching. You must re-import the graphic to restore its aspect ratio. If you are working on a document that originated on another system and has graphics that were imported by copying, you won't be able to do this. In such a case, you should be extra careful; use the **Scaling** option on the Graphics menu to rescale graphics uniformly and you won't run into this problem.

Rescaling Bitmaps

In addition to the techniques described previously, you can rescale a bitmapped image that was imported by copying by changing its dots-per-inch specification. To do this, select the graphic, then open the File Menu and select **Import>Files** (keyboard shortcut **Esc f i f**). The Imported Graphic Scaling dialog box (Figure 13.2) will appear. Select a dpi setting as described previously. If a bitmapped image was imported by reference, you must replace the image to change its dpi specification.

Rotation

You can rotate an imported graphic by specifying its angle of rotation in the Object Properties dialog box, or by dragging one of its handles while holding the **Alt** key. If you have Snap turned on and have specified a Snap Rotate value, the graphic will rotate only by multiples of the specified value.

You can also flip a graphic on its horizontal or vertical axis with the **Flip Left/Right** and **Flip Up/Down** commands on the Graphics menu.

Adding a Border

You can easily add a border to an imported graphic:

1. Select the graphic.

2. Open the Tools Palette if it is not already visible on the screen.

3. Click on the Pen Pattern tool and select a pattern. A border in the selected pattern will appear around the graphic.

4. You can optionally change the width, dash pattern, or color of the border by changing its line width, dash pattern, or color properties.

For additional information about these and the other drawing options, consult Chapter 12.

Cropping a Graphic

Cropping a graphic hides a portion of the image from view without actually changing the image (the complete image is still there on the page and can be revealed if you wish, but only part of it is visible). To crop a graphic, it must be placed in an anchored or unanchored frame. If you did not import the image into a frame, draw an unanchored frame with the Frame tool or create an anchored frame with the **Anchored Frame** command, then drag the image into the frame. When the pointer crosses the frame border, you will see the graphic "pop" into the frame. Resize the frame and/or move the graphic within the frame until only the desired portion of the graphic is showing.

When a graphic is cropped in a frame, it can be difficult to select and drag the frame to move it. Intuitively, you might expect, based on the way other Frame-Maker objects behave, that you should select the frame and then place the mouse pointer in the middle of the frame before clicking and dragging to move the frame. This will not work; you will only succeed in dragging the graphic out of the frame. To move the frame, move the pointer close to the outside edge of the frame, until it turns into a hollow arrow, then click to select it. With the pointer still outside the frame and still close enough to appear as a hollow arrow, press and hold the mouse button and drag. This will move the frame and its contents together.

To make it easier to select the cropping frame instead of its contents, it's a good idea to leave a little slack at one edge of the image (that is, don't bring the edge of the frame quite flush with the edge of the image). Then you can see clearly, when selecting, whether you have selected the frame or its contents. Otherwise, the only way you can tell for sure is to look in the Object Properties dialog box.

Cutting, Copying, and Pasting

Like any other class of FrameMaker objects, imported graphics can be moved or duplicated using the **Cut**, **Copy**, and **Paste** commands on the Edit menu. Just select the graphic(s) you want to copy, then select the **Cut** or **Copy** command from the Edit menu (or use the keyboard shortcuts **Ctrl+X** or **Ctrl+C**). Go to the page where you want to paste the graphic and select the location where you will paste it. You can paste the graphic in an anchored or unanchored frame, in a rectangle, or directly on the page. Use the methods described earlier in this chapter to select the location to paste the graphic. Select **Paste** on the Edit menu or press **Ctrl+V** to paste it.

When you copy or cut a graphic to the clipboard, it remains there until you replace it by performing another cut or copy. Thus, you can easily paste multiple copies of a graphic at different locations in a document.

Finding Missing Graphics Files

If graphics files that are imported by reference are moved, renamed, or deleted, FrameMaker will not be able to find them when it loads a document that uses them (this can be an especially big problem when you move a document with lots of imported-by-reference graphics to a different system with a different directory structure.) When FrameMaker is unable to find one or more imported graphics files on opening a document, it displays the Missing Graphics File dialog box (Figure 13.4). If the document has been moved or renamed and you know the new name and path, you can type them in the New Filename box and select the **Update Document to Use New Path** radio button. You can also use the drive, directory, and file selection boxes to search for the file if you don't know the correct name and path. If the graphics file is no longer valid, select the **Skip This Graphics File** radio button. If there are likely to be many missing files and you don't want to deal with searching for them at the moment, select the **Ignore All Missing Graphics Files** radio button. Select the **Update** button to exit the dialog box and resume loading the document.

When you skip graphics files that FrameMaker cannot find, it will display shaded boxes where the graphics were formerly placed. When you move to the pages where the graphics are located, FrameMaker may display a prompt box indicating that it is unable to display some imported graphics.

Figure 13.4   The Missing Graphic File dialog box

CHAPTER 14

Anchoring Graphics
Working with Anchored Frames

What Is an Anchored Frame?

In Chapter 12 we explained, among other things, how to draw frames to hold other objects with the Frame tool. Frames created this way are *unanchored* frames. Unanchored frames stay where you draw them on the page unless you cut and paste them or drag them to new locations. Sometimes, this is what you want, but at other times, you may want a graphic to always appear on the same page or in the same column as the text that refers to it. In this case, you need to create an *anchored* frame. An anchored frame is attached to a marker at a particular location in text (the anchor). As you edit and revise your text, the anchored frame will move when necessary to maintain the position you specify relative to its anchor. You can position the frame directly in the text line with the anchor, below the line, at the top or bottom of the column, or in the margin. A variety of options are available to control the exact position of the frame, as will be explained later in this chapter.

Creating an Anchored Frame

You don't draw anchored frames with the Frame tool. Anchored frames are created with the **Anchored Frame** option on the Special menu. Before you create an anchored frame, you must click an insertion point in the text at the location where you want to anchor the frame. After you place the insertion point, select the **Anchored Frame** command (keyboard shortcut **Esc s a**). This opens the Anchored Frame dialog box (Figure 14.1). This dialog box is used both to create new frames and edit existing ones. Use the controls in this dialog box to specify the position and size of the frame. The eight radio buttons for selecting the position of the frame are divided into three groups, as indicated by the borders within the dialog box. Use one of the buttons in the top group to place the frame in the text column that contains the anchor. Use the lone button in the middle group to place the graphic directly at the anchor point in the text line. Use one of the buttons in the lower group to place the frame in the margin. (The functions of each of the groups will be explained in detail in the following section.) Use the **Width** and **Height** text boxes to specify the size of the frame (you can easily change the size of the frame later, if necessary). Select the **New Frame** button to create the frame. The frame will appear at the specified location and the frame anchor (like an upside down, sans serif "T") will appear in the text at the insertion point.

Figure 14.1   The Anchored Frame dialog box

Anchored Frame		
Anchoring Position:		
○ Below Current Line	Alignment:	☐ Cropped
◉ At Top of Column	Center ▾	☒ Floating
○ At Bottom of Column		
○ At Insertion Point - Baseline Offset:	0.0 pt	
○ Left Side of Column	Baseline Offset:	
○ Right Side of Column	0.0"	
○ Side Closest to Page Edge	Near-Side Offset:	
○ Side Farthest from Page Edge	0.0"	
Size:		
Width: 1.0"	Height: 1.0"	
New Frame	Cancel	Help

NOTE An anchored frame is created automatically when you insert a table (see Chapter 20) or import a graphic file with an insertion point in a text column (see Chapter 13). Anchored frames created by these methods can be edited using the methods described later in this chapter.

Placing a Frame in a Text Column

The options for placing a frame in the text column are straightforward. Use one of the three radio buttons in the top group to select the position for the frame: **Below Current Line**, **At Top of Column**, or **At Bottom of Column**. Use the pull-down Alignment menu to align the frame at left, right, or center in the column.

Check the **Cropped** box if you want to limit the width of the frame to the width of the column with the insertion point. Uncheck this box if you want a frame to overlap several columns in a multi-column format. The **Floating** box controls the way the frame will move as text flows from column to column. If the box is not checked, the frame must always stay in the same column as the anchor. This means that in a multi-column format, the frame and the graphic may jump together to a new column in order to stay together (as in Figure 14.2a), leaving a large white space at the bottom of the preceding column. To prevent this, check the **Floating** box. When the box is checked, the frame floats to the next column, leaving the anchor behind and allowing text from the next column to flow back to fill the space vacated by the frame (as in Figure 14.2b).

Figure 14.2a and b   The effect of the Floating option on an anchored frame

Floating OFF

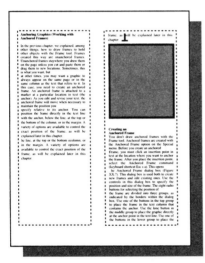

Floating ON

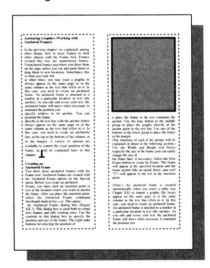

N O T E

If you want to keep frames in the same columns as their anchors, but don't want to have empty space at the bottom of columns, the **Feathering** option in the Flow Properties dialog box may prove useful (see Chapter 7).

Placing a Frame at the Insertion Point

If you want to place a small anchored frame directly in a text line at the insertion point (as in Figure 14.3), select **At Insertion Point**. A frame placed this way will flow from line to line like a word when text is revised. Optionally, you can adjust the vertical position of the frame relative to baselines of the text by typing a value in the **Baseline Offset** box. When you place a graphic at the insertion point, the text in the lines above and below does not move to make room for it. Hence, the graphic may cover up text in adjacent lines. To cause the text lines to spread to make room for an in-line graphic, use the Character Designer or the Formatting Bar to turn off Fixed Line Spacing for the paragraph in which the graphic is placed. Unfortunately, there is no way to make text automatically wrap around an in-line graphic.

Figure 14.3 An in-line graphic placed at the insertion point

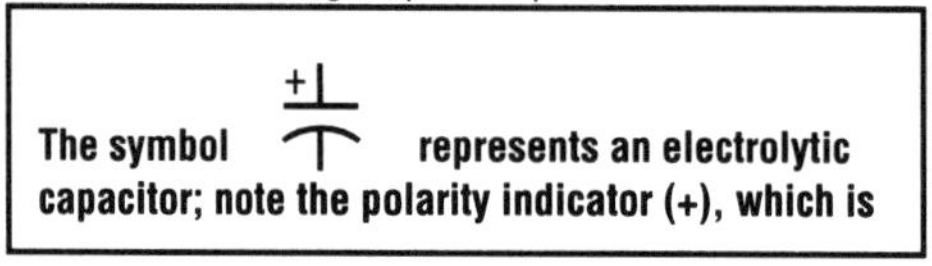

The symbol ⊤ represents an electrolytic capacitor; note the polarity indicator (+), which is

Placing a Frame in the Margin

To place an anchored frame in the margin, select one of the four options in the bottom group to choose the margin in which the frame will be placed: **Left Side of Column**, **Right Side of Column**, **Side Closest to Page Edge**, or **Side Farthest From Page Edge**. These settings are relative to the column in which the anchor is located (not to the entire block of columns on the page). Note that the Left Side and Right Side settings are fixed, so that the position of the frame relative to the column won't change as the anchor moves from column to column and page to page. However, a frame with a Closest or Farthest setting may flip from the left to the right margin or vice versa when the anchor is repositioned.

The exact position of a frame in the margin can be controlled by typing values in the **Baseline Offset** and **Near-Side Offset** boxes. The Baseline Offset is a vertical shift relative to the baseline of the text line in which the anchor is placed. The Near-Side Offset is a horizontal shift relative to the nearest edge of the text column in which the anchor is placed (see Figure 14.4). By default, the frame is placed with its lower edge aligned with the baseline of the text line with the anchor and the edge nearest the text column flush with the column border. Both of the offsets can have either positive or negative values. Regardless of the Baseline Offset value, an anchored frame cannot be placed above the top or below the bottom of the column containing the anchor. If the Baseline Offset value would push the frame above or below the column, it will be positioned flush with the top or bottom of the column. However, FrameMaker will not hesitate to shift a frame horizontally so that it is beyond the left or right margins of the page if you enter an excessive Near-Side Offset.

If you want to position a frame so that it is partly in the margin and partly overlaps the text column (for example, to place a graphic that is too wide to fit entirely in the margin), you can do this by specifying a negative Near-Side Offset; however, the text will not move to make room for the portion of the frame that overlaps the text column. You must make room for the frame by changing the indent of the adjacent paragraphs or by splitting and adjusting the column.

Figure 14.4   A frame placed in the margin, showing baseline and near-side offsets

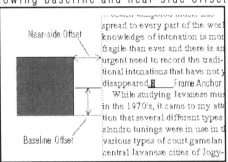

Using frames in the margin can be awkward in a multi-column format. Because the frame position is relative to the border of the column with the anchor rather than to the page margins, a text edit that moves the anchor to a different column may cause the frame to move from the margin to the middle of another text column (see Figure 14.5). I know of no workaround for this, except to either refrain from using frames in margins in multi-column formats or to spend a lot of time manually relocating anchors to keep the frames where you want them (which rather vitiates the purpose of using anchored frames).

Using Frames in the Margins in Combination with Side Heads

If you use anchored frames in the margins in combination with Side Heads (see "Pagination Properties," in Chapter 5)—a common layout strategy these days—keep in mind that the Near-Side Offset value will position the frame relative to the true margin of the text column, rather than the edge of the normal text area. Hence, if you want to place a frame outside the text area but wholly or partly within the Side Head area, you must use a negative Near-Side Offset to shift the frame into the Side Head area.

Using Anchored Frames in Multi-Column Formats

FrameMaker's anchored frames are reasonably useful in formats with a single text column per page, but in multi-column formats, their liabilities often outweigh their assets. The problems seem to stem from the fact that all of the placement controls position the frame relative to the column, rather than the page.

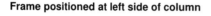

Figure 14.5 The effect of a change in anchor position on a frame placed in the margin

Frame positioned at left side of column

Text revised; anchor moves to right column; frame overlaps left column

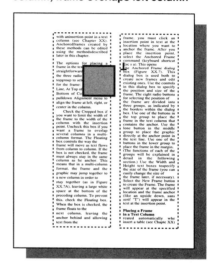

Frames that are less than or equal to one column in width work satisfactorily, but consider what happens if you want to place a frame that is more than one column wide (see Figure 14.6). The frame in the figure is positioned at the bottom of the column and centered in the column. The anchor is in the central column. The text in the center column breaks to make room for the frame, but the text in the outer columns does not. To make the text in these columns break for the frame, we must intervene manually. We could shorten the outer columns, add forced line breaks, or change the formats of the paragraphs that run over the frame to force them to start at the top of the column. Any of these methods, however, could lead to unsatisfactory results if it causes the anchor to move to the next column, as shown in the figure. Now the frame is shifted into the margin and partially off the page, and you must change its alignment to Left in order to get it back. If your text undergoes a lot of editing such that the location of the anchor changes positions, you will have to keep fiddling with the frame position to keep it in the desired location. There is really no wholly satisfactory workaround for this. You can probably save yourself some trouble by not placing anchored frames in this kind of situation until the text is fairly stable, assuming you have control over such matters. You can, of course, place your graphic in an unanchored frame and adjust your columns around it, or use an anchored frame in a separate, disconnected text column, which amounts to the same thing. If you do this, you lose the benefit of the anchored frame, in that the frame does not move with the text, but at least the frame will remain wholly on the page and won't get overrun by text.

Figure 14.6 The behavior of an anchored frame in a multi-column format

1. Frame anchored in center column

2. Frame anchored in right column

Look Out for Split Columns!

Another situation in which anchored frames can cause trouble is in conjunction with split columns. Split columns are created to solve a variety of layout problems, such as creating runarounds for graphics, pull quotes, or drop caps, or placing full-page headings in multi-column formats. (For information on splitting columns, consult Chapter 7.) Split columns are useful, but they are potentially troublesome when combined with anchored frames.

Suppose you have an anchored frame with a graphic placed at the bottom of a column on a normal, multi-column page. Suppose also that on an adjacent page there is a column that has been split into lines to run around a graphic. If, in the course of editing your document, the text with the anchor moves to the next page and ends up in the vertically split column, the frame will no longer appear at the bottom of the page. It will still be, technically, at the bottom of the column; that is, at the bottom of the split-column segment in which the anchor is located, but this will not produce the results you desire—the frame may appear anywhere vertically in the visual column, depending on the segment where the anchor lands.

There is no entirely satisfactory workaround for this situation either. You can move the anchor to a new position on the page that produces the desired result (and you may have to do this more than once if your text changes), you can put the graphic in an unanchored frame at the desired position, or you can draw a disconnected text column at the desired position and anchor the frame there. Again, you lose the benefit of using an anchored frame, i.e., having your graphic move as text reflows.

Filling an Anchored Frame

You fill an anchored frame by drawing in it with the drawing tools (see Chapter 12), by cutting objects and pasting them, or by importing graphics files (see Chapter 13). You can place text in a frame with the Text Line tool, or by drawing a text column with the Column tool and typing into it (see Chapter 12).

Editing Anchored Frames

You can change the size and position of an anchored frame in a number of ways. You can select the frame and open the Anchored Frame dialog box. In the dialog box, you can change any of the settings you entered when you created the frame. You can change the size of the frame by editing the Height and Width values, you can change its positioning by selecting a different radio button, or you can alter other settings, such as offset and alignment, that are associated with a particular position setting.

In some cases, a frame can be moved by dragging with the mouse. An in-line frame can be dragged vertically (the same as changing its Baseline Offset), but it cannot be dragged horizontally. A frame positioned in the margin can be dragged either horizontally or vertically (the same as changing its Baseline and Near-Side Offsets). A frame that is positioned in the column cannot be relocated by dragging. An Alert box will appear to inform you of this if you try it. You cannot change the position of an anchored frame in the Object Properties dialog box; you can only view its current settings. However, you can use the Object Properties to edit the size of a frame.

Rotation

Unlike most graphic objects, frames can be rotated only in 90° increments. You can rotate an anchored frame by selecting the **Rotate** command on the Graphics menu or by opening the Object Properties dialog box and changing the **Angle** setting. When you rotate a frame, all of its contents rotate with it. However, you can still select one or more of the objects within the frame and rotate them independently. Graphics within a frame can be rotated by fractions of a degree.

Adding a Border

You can easily add a border to an anchored frame:

1. Select the frame.

2. Open the Tools Palette if it is not already visible on the screen.

3. Click on the Pen Pattern tool and select a pattern. A border in the selected pattern will appear around the frame.

4. You can optionally change the width, dash pattern, or color of the border by selecting the line width, dash pattern, or color properties. For additional information about these and the other drawing options, consult Chapter 12.

Moving a Frame's Anchor

To anchor a frame at a new location, select the frame, then select **Cut** from the Edit menu. Place the insertion point where you want to re-anchor the frame, then select **Paste**. The anchor will appear at the insertion point and the frame will reappear at a position relative to the new anchor point. You can also copy the frame and paste the anchor point at one or more different locations to place multiple copies of the frame. (Although you can perform these operations by cutting or copying the anchor itself rather than the frame, it is awkward to do so; it is difficult to select the anchor without also selecting some of the surrounding text.) Cutting or copying and pasting a block of text that contains a frame anchor produces analogous results: The frame appears relative to the position where you paste the text block with the anchor.

As an alternative to placing graphics in anchored frames, it is often preferable to place graphics in table cells. Using a table as a frame for a graphic can work well in situations where you want to place graphics with titles or captions in a consistent format. For information on this technique, consult Chapter 21.

N O T E

CHAPTER 15

Working with Color

The competition between desktop publishing applications in the area of color pre-press support has been fierce in recent years. FrameMaker 3.0 was definitely behind the pack in this regard, offering support for only eight predefined spot colors. FrameMaker 4.0 represents a major advance over the previous version. It supports both process color and spot color, and allows you to define colors using one of several color models, including RGB, CYMK, HLS, and also allows you to specify spot colors from the Pantone Matching System (PMS). (If you're unfamiliar with color printing, don't worry; all these terms will be defined in the course of the chapter.) Despite these improvements, FrameMaker is certainly not the leader in color support, but its features in this area are adequate for the kind of content-driven technical or academic publications for which it is most commonly used.

What Do You Need to Know about Color Printing?

If you're new to the craft of designing and producing color publications, the answer to the above question is "plenty"—far more than one chapter of this book can possibly tell you. The best single piece of advice I can give is to select your printing method and your commercial printer *before* you start designing your publication. Likewise for the prepress service bureau that performs your color scanning, tweaks your color separations, produces your final image-setter output, and the like. Shop around for a printer and a service bureau that are willing to take the time to help you become familiar with the color printing process and advise you on how to design your publication to produce the best results at the lowest cost. The surest way to waste time and money is to design and produce a color publication without considering the printing process and then look for a printer to reproduce it.

Two Kinds of Color

In commercial printing, there are two types of color, *process color* and *spot color*. The term process color refers to color created by means of the *four-color process*. The four-color process uses four printing plates and four colored inks (cyan, magenta, yellow, and black—CMYK for short) to reproduce full-color, continuous tone artwork (for example, color photographs or illustrations). The term *spot color* refers to one or more additional colors added to a black and white publication, usually for contrast, accent, or decoration. A typical example would be the use of a second color in a book for rules, display type, and shading in tables. Spot color requires an additional printing plate for each additional color. The precise colors are those of the inks used on the additional plates, with variations being produced by using different percentage screens and/or by mixing two or more spot colors.

A Little Color Theory

The retina, the light sensitive region at the back of the eye, is equipped with two kinds of receptor cells, rods and cones. Rods are sensitive to differences in intensity and insensitive to differences in color. They are active only at low light levels, where we see mainly black, white, and shades of gray. The cone cells are responsible for color vision. There are three types of cones, which respond most strongly to light with three particular wavelengths. These three wavelengths correspond to red, green, and blue-violet. Any color sensation can be produced in the human eye by an appropriate mixture of these three *primary colors*. Any two of these primary colors combine to produce a complementary secondary color: red + blue = magenta; blue + green = cyan; and red + green = yellow. The combination of all three primaries produces white, and the total absence of all three produces black. This model is referred to as *additive* color mixing, and applies to situations in which colored light is transmitted directly to the eye or reflected from a white surface. This is exactly the way color is produced on televisions and video monitors, where triads of red, blue, and green phosphor dots are turned on at varying intensities to produce a full range of colors.

A different but related color model applies when pigments such as paint or ink are used to break up white light and transmit particular wavelengths to the eye. Pigments are chosen for their abilities to absorb certain wavelengths and reflect others. Although a painter may choose from an almost infinite variety of pigments, the printing industry has chosen to use four in reproducing full-color images: cyan (a greenish blue), magenta, yellow, and black. We'll temporarily ignore the black and consider the behavior of cyan, magenta, and yellow first.

As you may have observed, cyan, magenta, and yellow are the three secondary colors obtained by mixing the three possible pairs of the additive primary colors, red, green, and blue. Cyan, magenta, and yellow are each capable of reflecting the two light primaries that compose it and absorbing the third primary that does not:

- Cyan reflects green and blue and absorbs red.
- Magenta reflects red and blue and absorbs green.
- Yellow reflects red and green and absorbs blue.

Just as all the possible colors can theoretically be created by mixing the proper portions of red, green, and blue light, so also can they be created by mixing the proper proportions of cyan, yellow, and magenta pigments, in a process that is known as *subtractive* color mixing. Here, the roles of the primaries and secondaries are reversed: yellow + cyan = green; cyan + magenta = blue; and magenta + yellow = red. The equal combination of all three subtractive primaries produces black and the total absence of all three produces white (assuming they are applied to a white surface).

If, as we just said, an equal combination of all three subtractive primaries produces black, where does the black ink come in? As usual, there is a little discrepancy between theory and practice. If the cyan, magenta, and yellow inks were perfect absorbers and reflectors of their respective colors, they would, indeed, produce solid blacks and pure neutral grays, and no black ink would be required. In practice, they fall a bit short of perfection, producing blacks that are rather muddy and grays that have a slight brownish cast. Then there is the matter of text on the same page as a full color graphic. You could produce the black text by overlapping all three primaries. However, if there were any slight misregistration of the color plates, the text would have a colored "halo," which would be highly annoying to the reader. It is much easier to use black ink both for text and to produce true blacks and neutral grays in artwork.

Choosing a Color Model

FrameMaker supports three color models: CMYK (cyan, yellow, magenta, black), RGB (red, green, blue), HLS (hue, lightness, saturation), plus PANTONE spot colors. Each of these models is useful for a particular purpose or in a particular situation. CMYK is the system used in four-color process printing. Use this model if your document contains full-color, continuous-tone art work and will be produced by commercial four-color printing. RGB is the model used in color monitors and television. Use this model if you are creating a document for on-line viewing. The details of how these two models work were explained in the previous section.

The HLS model is not associated with a particular output technology; it attempts to mimic the way artists have traditionally viewed and mixed colors. This model treats colors as three components:

- **Hue**—the wavelength or position on the spectrum or color wheel of the color, expressed in degrees, from 0 to 360.

- **Lightness**—the amount of white or black added to the color to produce a tint or shade. This is expressed as a value from 0 to 100; 0 = black, 100 = white, and 50 = the pure color.

- **Saturation**—the purity of the hue, in terms of freedom from admixture of its complement. This is expressed as value from 0 to 100, with 0 being neutral gray and 100 being the pure, saturated color.

The PANTONE Matching System (PMS) is not really a color model in the sense that RGB, CMYK, and HLS are; rather, it is a method for precisely specifying spot colors. PANTONE, Inc., publishes color reference guides used by designers, and ink formulas that commercial printers use to match these colors. PANTONE colors are picked from a palette or specified by number. The use of PANTONE spot colors is independent of your choice of the CYMK, RGB, or HLS color model.

Creating or Choosing a New Color

FrameMaker comes with eight predefined colors: black, white, red, green, blue, cyan, magenta, and yellow. If you want to use any other colors, you must create or choose them, using one of the following procedures:

Mixing a New Color

1. From the View menu, select **Color**; select **Definitions** from the submenu. This opens the Color Definitions dialog box (Figure 15.1).

2. Choose a color model by selecting the appropriate radio button.

3. Mix the color by manipulating the sliders and/or typing values for the color components. (The appearance of the dialog box and the labels of the sliders will vary depending on which color model you select, but the principles remain the same—the figure shows the dialog box for the CMYK model.)

4. Type a name for the color in the Name text box.

5. Select the **Set** button to store the new color.

6. You can create as many colors as you wish by repeating steps 3–5 before selecting the **Done** button to exit the dialog box.

Figure 15.1 The Color Definitions dialog box

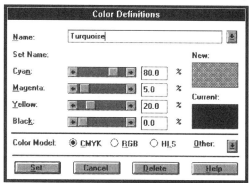

Editing a Color

You can also use the above procedure to edit existing colors. Select the color to edit in the Name box, then perform steps 3–5 in the preceding section. You cannot edit any of FrameMaker's eight predefined colors.

Deleting a Color

You can delete a color in the Color Definitions dialog box by selecting its name in the Name box and clicking the **Delete** button. You cannot, however, delete any of FrameMaker's default colors.

You cannot undo the deletion of a color. The only way to get a deleted color back is to revert to the saved version of the document (if you haven't saved it since the deletion) or to import the colors from another document that has the same color set (if one exists).

WARNING

Picking a Color

As an alternative to mixing a color in the Color Definition dialog box, you can use the Common Color Picker (Figure 15.2).

1. Open the Color Definitions dialog box, as described previously.

2. Open the "Other" menu at the lower right corner of the dialog box and select **Common Color Picker**.

3. The Common Color Picker is similar in operation to the HLS model. Drag the selection sight across the larger color box to select hue (left to right) and saturation (top to bottom). Drag the pointer up or down next to the tall, thin color box at the right of the dialog box to select the lightness. The HLS and RGB values for the color will appear in the text boxes in the dialog box.

4. Select **Done** to return to the Color Definition dialog box.

5. Name and store the color as described previously.

Figure 15.2 The Common Color Picker

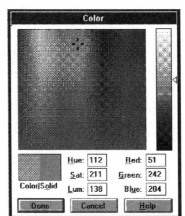

Selecting a PANTONE Color

You don't mix PANTONE colors; you select them from a palette or specify them by the numbers from a PANTONE color reference book:

1. Open the Color Definition dialog box, as described previously.

2. Open the "Other" menu at the lower right corner of the dialog box and select **PANTONE**. This opens the PANTONE Colors dialog box (Figure 15.3).

3. In the PANTONE Colors dialog box, you can either type the number of a specific color in the Find PANTONE text box, or scroll through the possible

colors by manipulating the slider at the bottom of the dialog box. In the latter case, click on the color you want to use.

4. When you have chosen a color, select **Done** to return to the Color Definition dialog box.

5. In the Color Definition dialog box, select **Set** to store the color. You do not need to type a name for the color, as the PANTONE color number is automatically placed in the Name box. You should not change the name without making a note of it, so you can give the proper information to your printer.

F i g u r e 1 5 . 3 The Pantone Colors dialog box

```
                    PANTONE Colors

 Find PANTONE  35                              CV

 PANTONE 344 CV            PANTONE 351 CV

 PANTONE 345 CV            PANTONE 352 CV

 PANTONE 346 CV            PANTONE 353 CV

 PANTONE 347 CV            PANTONE 354 CV

 PANTONE 348 CV            PANTONE 355 CV

 PANTONE 349 CV            PANTONE 356 CV

 PANTONE 350 CV            PANTONE 357 CV

                        © PANTONE, Inc. 1986, 1988

    Done          Cancel          Help
```

N O T E You can edit the definition of a PANTONE color in the Color Definition dialog box, but it is clearly not a good idea to do so. The whole object of using PANTONE colors is to allow your printer to mix an ink that precisely matches the color you specify. If you change the definition of a PMS color, you will lose this ability.

Importing Color Definitions

In addition to creating color definitions as described in the preceding section, you can import color definitions from other FrameMaker documents. When you import a set of definitions, they are added to the existing color definitions. If any of the definitions in the source document have the same names as those in the destination document, the definitions from the source replace those in the destination. Use the following procedure to import color definitions:

1. Open the document into which you want to import the definitions (the destination) and the document from which you wish to import the definitions (the source).

2. Make the destination the active document by clicking in its window or selecting it from the Window menu.

3. Select **Import** from the File menu; select **Formats** from the submenu (keyboard shortcut **Esc f i o**). This opens the Import Formats dialog box.

4. Select the name of the source document in the **Import from Document** list box.

5. Check the **Color Definitions** check box. Unless you want to import other characteristics at the same time, uncheck the other check boxes.

6. Select the **Import** button to import the definitions.

Applying Colors

You can apply a color, either one of the eight defaults or one you create, to any object that FrameMaker can display and print. The process for applying a color depends on the type of object. The procedures are summarized in Table 15.1:

Table 15.1   Procedures for applying colors to FrameMaker objects

Object	Procedure
A paragraph	Create and apply a paragraph format (see Chapter 5).
A selected word or phrase in a paragraph	Create and apply a character format (see Chapter 5).
A text line	Use a character format, the pop-up color menu on the Tools Palette, or the color menu in the Object Properties dialog box (see Chapter 12).
An object drawn with the drawing tools	Use the pop-up color menu on the Tools Palette, or the color menu in the Object Properties dialog box (see Chapter 12).

An imported black and white or grayscale image	Use the pop-up color menu on the Tools Palette, or the color menu in the Object Properties dialog box (see Chapter 12).
Text in a table	Same as for a paragraph or a word or phrase in a paragraph.
Table cells	Use the pop-up color menu in the Custom Ruling and Shading dialog box (see Chapter 20).
Change bars	Use the pop-up color menu in the Change Bar Properties dialog box (see Chapter 5).
Equations or elements in an equation	Use a character format.

Setting Up Color Views

Color views are a rather unusual feature of FrameMaker. Color views determine which of FrameMaker's colors (default or user-defined) will be visible on the screen. You can create up to six different color views. If you are using spot colors, you can create the equivalent of color separations on the screen. (You can't simulate four-color process separations on the screen with views.) This can be helpful in checking that colors have been correctly assigned to different objects. For example, if you use black for body text and a spot color for rules and headings, you could create one view with only black visible, and another with only the spot color visible. By paging through the document in each view, you could verify that the correct colors had been applied.

Creating a View

Use the following procedure to create up to six color views:

1. Select **Color** from the View menu; select **Views** from the submenu (keyboard shortcut **Esc v c v**). This opens the Define Color Views dialog box (Figure 15.4).

2. Select a radio button to choose the view to define (1–6).

3. There are three list boxes in the dialog box: Normal, Cutout, and Invisible. Normal means display the color on the screen; Cutout means display the color as white where it overlaps other colors; Invisible means don't display the color. To move a color from one list to another, highlight the color and use the arrow buttons to move it.

4. If you want to restore the default settings for the view, select the **Get Defaults** button.

5. When you have all the colors in the lists where you want them, select the **Set** button to store the view.

Figure 15.4 The View Definitions dialog box

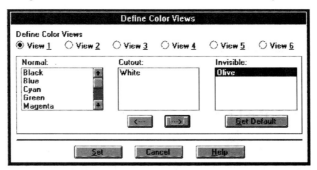

Changing the View

Once you have defined one or more color views, use the following procedure to select a different view:

1. Open the View Definitions dialog box, as described above.

2. Select the radio button for the view you want to use.

3. Select **Set** to close the dialog box and activate the view.

Printing Color

There are two ways to print color: as a composite or "comp" (all the colors printed on a single page) or as separations (a separate page for each process color and/or spot color). Print a composite to see a preview of your document. If you have a color printer installed under Windows with an appropriate driver, your composite will print in color, *approximating* the appearance of the final printed document. If you have a black and white printer, the colors in your document will print as gray screens.

Print separations when you have finished producing your document and want to create the final output from which your printer will prepare plates. (You may also want to print test separations on a laser printer to verify that your colors are being separated properly.) Unless you have a high-resolution laser printer (600+ dpi) or a PostScript image setter, you will probably want to print your separations to a file, so you can send your output to a service bureau for high-resolution output. Consult your service bureau before printing separations to see if they have any special requirements.

Printing a Composite

Printing a composite image of a document is simple. Just select **Print** from the File menu and uncheck the **Print Separations** check box in the Print Document dialog box. If you're printing in black and white, colors are printed as gray screens by default. If you want colors printed as solid black, check the **Print Spot Colors as Black/White** check box. Select the **Print** button to print the comp.

Printing Separations

FrameMaker prints two types of color separations: process color and spot color. You can use either or both together, depending on what is appropriate for your publication. Printing process separations breaks each color into its CMYK components and prints four separate pages for each page of your document. Printing spot color separations produces a separate page for each spot color you have defined.

If your document contains imported, full-color images and also uses a spot color for rules and headings, you will probably want to separate both process and spot colors. Note, however, that this will require five printing plates (C, M, Y, and K, + 1 spot color) and increase the cost of your print job. You might save some money by simulating your spot color with process color, thereby eliminating one printing plate, but at the risk of some reduction in the accuracy of the color match. Consult your printer. If your document contains only black text, plus one spot color for headings, rules, table shadings, and tinted grayscale images, you would separate your document as spot color only, resulting in only two printing plates per page.

To print separations:

1. Select **Print** from the File menu (shortcut **Ctrl+P**).

2. Check the **Print Separations** check box.

3. Select **Set Up Separations**; this opens the Set Print Separations dialog box (Figure 15.5).

4. Use this dialog box to select which colors will be separated as process color (broken down into their CMYK components) and which will be separated as spot colors (printed to their own separate pages). The dialog box has three lists: Print As Process, Print As Spot, and Don't Print. Select the colors you want to move and use the two arrow buttons to move them to the appropriate lists.

5. (Optional) Select the **Halftone Screens** button to set the frequencies and angles of the screens used for the four process colors and spot colors. This opens the dialog box in Figure 15.6. See the next section for an explanation of these settings. Select **Set** to return to the Set Print Separations dialog box.

6. Select **Set** again to return to the main **Print Document** dialog box.

7. (Optional) You may want to check the **Skip Blank Pages** check box so your service bureau doesn't charge you to output blank plates. You may also want to turn on Registration Marks. Consult your service bureau and/or your printer for information on these matters.

8. If you want to output to a file to transmit to your service bureau, check the **Print Only to File** box and type a path and file name.

9. Click **Print** to print the separations.

Figure 15.5   The Set Print Separations dialog box

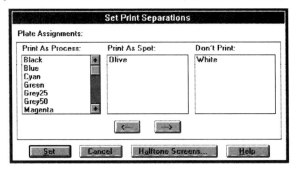

Figure 15.6   The Halftone Screens dialog box

Halftone Options

When you print a full-color image by means of the four-color process, you don't have the option of using different shades of ink on different parts of the printing plate. The only way the four-color process can produce different shades is to use patterns of dots that apply more or less ink to different parts of the page. The dot patterns that form the images for each of the colors are known as halftones. Halftone dots are placed on a consistent grid on each plate. The individual dots vary in size, running together at one extreme to form solid areas of color, and vanishing entirely at the opposite extreme to show the white paper. Halftones have two important characteristics that you can control in Frame-Maker: frequency and angle.

The frequency of a halftone screen (expressed in lines per inch) is the spacing of adjacent rows of halftone dots. FrameMaker automatically selects a halftone frequency based on the resolution of the selected printer. Halftone frequency is not the same as the dpi resolution of the printer—several printer dots are required to form each halftone dot. Selecting the correct halftone frequency depends, in part, on the type of press and paper that will be used to produce your publication. Consult your printer for advice on selecting the optimal halftone frequency.

Halftone screens are set at different angles so that the different colored dots do not stack up on one another, but rather spread out in a "rosette" pattern, which has been found to give the best color mixing. You can see an example of this pattern by examining a good quality full-color image in a book or magazine under a magnifying glass. If halftone angles are set incorrectly, a disturbing moiré pattern (a repeating geometric pattern that has nothing to do with the image) may result. Traditionally, halftone screens have been set at black = 45°, magenta = 75°, yellow = 90°, and cyan = 105°, but FrameMaker does not use these settings as defaults. Again, consult your printer and/or prepress service bureau for advice on halftone angles. The angle setting for spot colors is not really important, since spot colors are not usually intended to be mixed with other colors.

Other Printing Options

Depending on how your document is being output, it may be necessary to print your document as a negative image (the usual practice if you're printing directly to the film that will be used in producing the printing plates) or as a mirror image. You can select either of these options by checking their check boxes in the Advanced Options dialog box (select **Print Setup** from the File menu; select **Options** in the Print Setup dialog box; select **Advanced** in the Options dialog box). Consult your service bureau to determine if either of these options is necessary.

Separating Imported Graphics

FrameMaker 4.0 separates only three types of imported graphics files: color EPS, Desktop Color Separations (DCS), and CMYK TIFF. All other imported images are printed as comps, duplicated on each separation (not very useful). Since all full-color, continuous-tone images are imported (you can't scan a photograph or paint a continuous-tone image in FrameMaker), you need to take this into account in choosing the programs you use to create the images you will import into your documents and in specifying their output formats. If you already have images in another format, such as PCX or RGB TIFF, you may be able to convert them to color EPS or CMYK TIFF by means of a third-party conversion program, such as HiJaak Pro.

Knockouts and Overprinting

Normally, when FrameMaker creates separations for a page in which different colored objects overlap, it creates *knockouts;* for example, if you are printing an image that includes a pure magenta object in front of a pure cyan object, there will be a hole or knockout in the cyan plate that corresponds to the magenta object. If the plates are not registered properly, you may get a white edge around one side of the magenta object. This situation is less of a problem if the overlapping objects share a common color component. For example, if an orange object (magenta + yellow) overlapped a violet object (magenta + cyan), any misregistration will result in a magenta shadow, rather than a white one. This is less likely to distract the viewer, but it is still undesirable.

Where darker objects overlap lighter ones, you may be able to avoid this problem by overprinting the object. Select the darker object, then select **Overprint** from the Graphics menu. In the dialog box that appears, select the **Overprint** radio button, then select **Set**. When the separation is printed, the background object will not have a knockout that corresponds to the foreground object; hence the foreground object will overprint on the background object and there will be no possibility of a shadow from misregistration.

N O T E   Although it is possible to overprint a light object on a darker one, it is not a good idea to do so. The darker background will probably show through the lighter object, resulting in a color other than that which you desire. Traditionally, printers use a method called *trapping* to avoid the problems described above. Before resorting to overprinting, consult your prepress service bureau and/or your printer to see what options are available to trap your color images to ensure clean registration.

Who Can You Trust?

Using a desktop computer for designing and producing full-color publications presents considerable difficulties. These difficulties stem from the fact that neither color monitors nor desktop color printers can be depended upon to give you an accurate representation of what your document will look like when printed via offset lithography, whether in four-color process or with PANTONE specified spot colors.

As far as display accuracy is concerned, the first consideration is your video display adapter (the circuit board that interfaces between your computer and monitor). Different display adapters support varying numbers of colors at varying display resolutions, with the number of colors often decreasing with increased resolution. Screen resolutions appropriate for desktop publishing at present are 800×600, 1024×768, and 1280×1024. Color depth (as it is called in industry jargon) may be expressed in the number of simultaneous colors displayed, or in bits per pixel (n bits can represent 2^n colors). Table 15.2 shows popular color depths in the PC display adapter market at the time of this writing. The current standard for producing and viewing high-quality continuous tone images is 24-bit color.

Table 15.2 Color depths available from PC display adapters

Bits per pixel	Number of simultaneous colors
8	256
15	32,768 (32K)
16	65,636 (64K)
24	16,777,215 (16M)

Another factor is the Windows driver provided with your display adapter (the software that interfaces between Windows and the adapter). To get the maximum color depth, your adapter must come with a driver that supports the maximum color depth at the resolution at which you choose to work. Display driver programming is one of the black arts; it takes a lot of time and effort and the number of programmers who know how to do it well is limited. Thus, it is quite possible to purchase a display adapter capable of providing the resolution and color depth you need, only to find that it comes equipped with a driver that falls short of this ideal. A call to the manufacturer informs you that new drivers are in the works and will ship "any time now." If you are unlucky, "any time now" may turn into months. It pays to inquire into the state of an adapter's Windows drivers before you buy.

Obviously, the more colors your display adapter can display, the better chance you will have in representing color accurately, whether it is the color in a piece of continuous-tone artwork such as scanned photograph, or a PANTONE spot color. If your display adapter and driver don't display enough colors, FrameMaker (and other applications) resort to *dithering*—creating a pattern of dots of different colors to simulate the desired color. Dither patterns don't give you very accurate representations of final output colors.

Even if your display adapter and driver give you 24-bit color at the highest resolution your monitor is capable of, there are other potential pitfalls. All monitors use analog technology, and hence are capable of displaying infinite variations in color, so the color depth of your monitor is not an issue. However, color *accuracy* is another matter. Your monitor produces colors by striking triads of red, blue, and green phosphor dots on the screen with electron beams of varying intensities. The intensities with which the three beams strike the dots in a given triad determine the color of one pixel. Obviously, there's some room for error here: The intensities of the beams may not be calibrated correctly, or the beams may not be aimed accurately. The settings of the brightness and contrast controls on your monitor also have an effect, as does the lighting in your work space. It is possible to calibrate a monitor for color accuracy if you have the appropriate hardware and software, but even this does not provide absolute reliability. Color monitors and four-color process printing are each capable of reproducing only a portion of the color spectrum that the human eye can see; unfortunately, the portions of the spectrum that these two technologies can reproduce overlap but do not match exactly. That is, there are colors that can be displayed on an RGB monitor but not printed via four-color process, and vice versa.

What is the solution to this dilemma? First, consult with your printer and prepress service bureau both before and during the process of creating a color publication. Second, use color proofs, such as Dupont Cromalins or 3M Matchprints, to verify that your colors are correct. Finally, if at all possible, approve a press check (a sample of your document printed with the actual press, plates, and inks that will be used for the final version) before allowing the press run to go ahead.

CHAPTER 16

Creating Tables of Contents and Other Lists

FrameMaker can create tables of contents, lists of figures or tables, lists of paragraphs, glossaries, lists of imported graphics and/or cross-references, and just about any other kind of list you might care to define. Collectively, FrameMaker refers to these as *generated* lists (because the program generates them, based on information you provide) and uses similar procedures to create all of them. (FrameMaker also generates indexes, but this process is more elaborate and will be treated separately in Chapter 17.)

Two Types of Lists

There are two basic types of generated lists in FrameMaker: paragraph lists and marker lists. A paragraph list uses paragraph tags that already exist in the document to find the items to be included in the list. For example, a table of contents usually uses section titles, chapter titles, and one or two levels of headings as entries. These items are readily identified by their paragraph format tags; a list of figures or tables could be based on paragraphs that are tagged as figure captions or table titles. Paragraph lists normally use the complete text of the tagged paragraphs as list entries. Marker lists can list anything you choose, but they are normally used when it would be impractical to use the complete content of a paragraph, such as for entries for a glossary. Before you generate a list based on markers, you must place the markers in text and select or type the text that will be associated with them (see later). Whichever type of list you generate, FrameMaker initially generates it as a separate document in a window of its own. Some kinds of lists can be pasted into other files, but lists such as tables of contents are best incorporated into larger documents via the book building procedures described in Chapter 18.

Preparing for a Paragraph List

The basic step in preparing to generate a paragraph list is one that you should have been performing since you first started work on your document, namely, using your paragraph tags consistently. For example, if you want to include chapter titles, A-heads, and B-heads in a table of contents, all chapter titles, A-heads, and B-heads must have been tagged with the appropriate paragraph tag and none of these three paragraph tags should have been applied to anything else but the appropriate title or head. You should never, for example, use a B-head with format overrides to serve as a C-head or some other type of display type, nor should you do something like using different tags for A–heads depending on whether they have one or two text lines. If your tagging has been inconsistent, you will find out when you generate a table of contents or other type of generated list: items that don't belong in the list may show up there and/or items that belong in the list may be missing. Indeed, generating paragraph lists is a good way to determine whether you (or others) have been consistent in the use of paragraph tags.

The other thing that may interfere with the generation of proper paragraph lists is breaking a line in a title or heading into two lines with a carriage return (¶). This also is a practice that you should eschew regardless of whether you plan to incorporate the heading or title in a table of contents or other list. If a heading is broken into two lines with a carriage return, it becomes two tagged paragraphs, and hence will appear as two separate entries in a table of contents or other list. The proper way to break a heading or title that does not naturally break in an aesthetically appealing way is to use either a forced line break (**Shift+Enter**) or alter the left and/or right indents of the heading with a format override to make it break at the desired location.

Preparing for a Marker List

Before you can generate a marker list, you must place the necessary markers at the appropriate locations in your document. FrameMaker recognizes 26 different types of markers. Some of these, including Conditional Text, Header/Footer, Hypertext, and Cross-Reference markers, are dedicated to particular purposes, as described elsewhere in this book. It is alright to generate lists of these markers (for example, you might want to generate a list to see where all the cross-reference targets in your document are located), but you should not *insert* markers of any of these types for the purpose of generating a list independent of their primary uses. You can freely use Comment, Subject, Equation, Author, or Glossary markers or any of the type 11–25 markers for lists of any kind.

Whichever type of marker you choose, the process of placing markers is the same:

1. Place the insertion point at the location in the text where you want to place the marker. If you want to use a text string in the document as the marker text, highlight the string.

2. Select **Markers** from the Special menu, or use the keyboard shortcut **Esc s m**. This opens the Marker dialog box (see Figure 16.1).

3. Select the marker type from the pop-up Marker Type menu.

4. If you did not begin by highlighting a text string in the document, type the text you want to appear in the list in the Marker Text box.

5. Click the **New Marker** button to insert the marker. If text symbols are turned on, the Marker symbol (like a large sans serif T) will appear in text at the insertion point. The Marker window will remain on the screen. You can page or scroll to other locations in the document and place additional markers.

Figure 16.1 The Marker dialog box

For readability, it's best to place markers at the ends or beginnings of paragraphs, but if you want to list page numbers on which particular words or phrases occur, this can cause problems; the paragraph with the marker may break across two pages, placing the marker on one page and the text on the other. At minimum, avoid placing markers in the middle of words.

SHORTCUT

If you want to use a single word in the document as the marker text (for example, as a glossary entry), place the insertion point immediately before the first letter of the word, and don't type any marker text. When the list is generated, the word following the marker will be used as the list entry. (*Don't* put the marker *in* the word, or you'll get only the letters following the marker.)

N O T E

You can generate two different kinds of marker lists: a List of Markers and an Alphabetical Marker List. A List of Markers lists the markers in the order in which they appear in the document; an Alphabetical Marker List presents them in alphabetical order of the marker text.

Generating a Table of Contents or Other List

Although we will work with a table of contents in this example, the process of generating and formatting any type of generated list is essentially the same:

1. Select **Generate/Book** from the File menu (keyboard shortcut **Esc f g**). This opens the Generate/Book dialog box (see Figure 16.2). This dialog box is also used to generate indexes and multi-file books, as described in chapters 17 and 18, respectively.

2. Select the **List** radio button and select the type of list from the pop-up menu. In this example, we will select Table of Contents, but the other options include List of Figures, List of Tables, List of Paragraphs, List of Markers, Alphabetical Marker List, Alphabetical Paragraph List, and List of References.

3. Click the **Generate** button to go to the next stage. This opens the Set Up Table of Contents dialog box (Figure 16.3) or whatever Set Up dialog box is appropriate for the type of list you have chosen to generate.

4. In the Filename Suffix text box, type the extension for the file that will be generated. FrameMaker adds the extension to the file name of the source document to create the name of the generated list file. By default, it will use an extension that matches the initials of the type of file to be generated, such as TOC for a table of contents. You should probably accept the extension FrameMaker suggests, as this will make it easier to keep track of and update the list files.

5. Select the paragraph formats to be included in the list by moving them into the Include Paragraphs Tagged list box. Select the tags in the Don't Include list box and use the arrow button to move them.

6. Check or uncheck the **Create Hypertext Links** check box. Although you might think this box should be used only when creating hypertext documents for on-line reading, it is actually useful for any kind of document, because it allows you to jump from list entries to their sources with a mouse click, which can be extremely helpful in tracing errors in generated lists.

7. Click the **Generate** button to generate the list. The list will appear in its own document window.

Figure 16.2 The Generate/Book dialog box

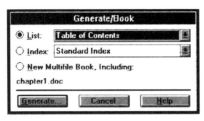

Figure 16.3 The Set Up Table of Contents dialog box

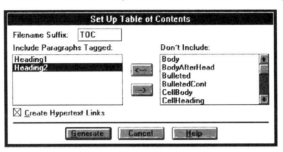

Generating a List of References

FrameMaker can create one important type of generated list that is really neither a marker list or a paragraph list. This item, which hides in the pop-up menu in the Generate/Book dialog box under the rather uninformative name *List of References*, can include one or more of the following items:

- **Condition Tags**—what condition tags are used in the document and which pages they occur on.

- **External Cross-References**—the source file name, the cross-reference marker text, and the page number of the reference for each external cross-reference in the document.

- **Fonts**—which fonts occur on each page of the document.

- **Imported Graphics**—the path name for each graphic imported by reference, the dpi resolutions for imported bitmaps, and the page numbers where the graphics are located.

- **Unresolved Cross-Refs**—the locations of all unresolved cross-references.

A list of references can be a very useful tool, if you are moving a document to another system or another platform. It can tell you which files need to be moved with the document in order for it to print correctly (all graphics imported by references and all other documents that are the sources of external cross-references). By telling you what fonts are included, it can help you determine whether any font substitutions are required when migrating to another platform. If the document is to be sent to a service bureau for image setter output, the List of References can be used to determine whether any font substitutions are needed or whether any special fonts need to be installed on the image setter.

Formatting a List

Once a list has been generated, you can format it to give it the appearance you want. Formatting a generated list is a bit different than formatting a normal FrameMaker document. When FrameMaker generates a list, it applies different generated paragraph format tags to each of the different classes of items in the list (that is, to the different paragraph tags in a paragraph list or the different marker types in a marker list.) The generated tags can be readily recognized because they end in the same three letters as the file extension for the list, for example, TOC for a table of contents, LOF for a list of figures, LOM for a list of markers, or the like. Initially, all the generated tags will have the same type specs, so there will be no visible distinctions, for example, between different levels in a table of contents. You can edit these generated format tags like any other paragraph format tags in order to change the appearance of the list (see Chapter 5), but you should not change their names or you will not be able to update your list successfully after editing your document.

In addition to format tags, the items in a generated list have *definitions*, similar to the definitions of variables, cross-references, or autonumbering formats. These definitions, which are composed of building blocks and additional text, determine what items will appear in the list entry (for example, page numbers, paragraph text, paragraph autonumbers, or tabs) and how they will be ordered. The definitions reside in a special text flow on a reference page that is part of the list document (not the document from which the list was extracted).

To examine the definitions for a generated list of any kind, make the list the current document and switch the view to Reference Pages (**Esc v R**). The reference page containing the special flow will not be the first for the generated list, so you will have to page or scroll down to it. The name of the reference page will be the same as the file extension for the list; this also serves as the flow tag for the flow that contains the definitions.

A typical generated table of contents entry has the definition `<$paratext>` `<$pagenum>`. If you've read the chapters on variables and cross-references, you will recognize these two building blocks, which indicate the text of the specified paragraph and its page number. You could modify this definition in a number of ways: You could switch the order of the two building blocks if you wanted the number to appear before the heading; you could add a tab to position the page number (see later for details); you could add the <$paranum> building block to include the number of an autonumbered paragraph; or you could add a character format tag to change the appearance of the text. *For any changes you make in the list definition to take effect, you must update the list.*

Using Tabs and Leaders in a List

Adding tabs and tab leaders in a generated list is a three-step process. First, place the tab at the desired location in the definition on the reference page (for example, between <$paratext> and <$pagenum>). You might expect that you would do this by typing the symbolic code \t as you do in other kinds of definitions, but no, you place a tab in list item definition by pressing the **Tab** key. The second step is to edit the paragraph format for the list item to place the tab stop and select an optional leader character. (See "Default Properties" in Chapter 5 for details on setting tab stops and selecting leader characters.) The final step is to update the list (see later); the changes you have made will not appear on the body pages until the list is updated.

Using Character Formats in a List Definition

You can include a character format tag in a list item definition if, for example, you want to use different typefaces for the entries and page numbers. First, use the Character Designer to create the format if it doesn't already exist (see "Character Formats" in Chapter 5). Then, type the format tag name in angle brackets (< >) at the location in the definition where you want the typeface to change. For example, to set the page numbers in boldface, you might add the Emphasis character format to the definition shown previously:

<$paratext> <Emphasis><$pagenum>

If you wanted, instead, to have the entry in boldface and the page number in the default paragraph font, you would use a definition such as the following:

<Emphasis><$paratext><Default Para Font> <$pagenum>

Adding a Title to a List

Add a title to a table of contents or other generated list by typing the title on the body page that contains the list (not the reference page). Format the title like any other by applying an appropriate paragraph tag. To ensure that your title is not replaced when you update your list, *don't* give it a paragraph tag with a name like that of a generated list tag. For example, don't give a table of contents title a tag such as Title TOC—all paragraphs with tags that end in the extension for the list file are automatically replaced when you generate a new list (TOC Title would be okay).

Depending on the margin and indent settings of the page and the lengths of the entries, a list entry may wrap so that the page number appears on a line by itself. If you don't want this to happen, you can keep the page numbers together with the last words of their respective entries by inserting a non-breaking space (**Ctrl+Space**), en space (**Esc space n**), or em space (**Esc space m**) between the `<$para-text>` and `<$pagenum>` building blocks in the list item definition.

Using a Template to Format a List

As an alternative to generating a list and then applying formats, you can use a template to control the layout and format of a generated list. A template for a generated list must be derived from another generated list that has the properties you want to use. It should include the paragraph and character formats, the reference page with the special flow containing the definitions, and the page layout(s) for the list. Once you have created such a file, copy it into the directory in which the source document is stored and give it the name of the source document and the extension denoting the type of list for which it is to be used (for example, `CHAP-TER1.TOC`). When the list is generated, it will automatically use the formats from the template. As with any other FrameMaker document, you can also modify a generated list by importing character or paragraph formats or page layouts via the File>**Import**>**Formats** option.

Updating a Generated List

If you edit or revise your document after generating a table of contents or other list, some items in the list may no longer be valid (for example, some of the items that serve as table of contents entries may have moved to other pages, or you may have edited or deleted some of the items). You can easily update your table of contents or other list; all the formatting you have applied to the list will be retained. The process of updating a list is exactly the same as that you used to generate the list. To update a list successfully, the list file must be kept in the same directory as the source document (the document from which the list was extracted) and have the same file name and extension that FrameMaker initially gave it. If the file has been moved or renamed, FrameMaker will just generate a new copy of the list; if this occurs, none of the layout or formatting changes you made in the original list will be used.

Fixing Problems in Generated Lists

When you first generate a list, you may discover a variety of problems: Items that you want in the list may be absent, and items that you don't want may be included. In addition, in the case of a paragraph list, you may find page numbers in the list without corresponding entries or double entries for a single item. Each of these problems is the result of a particular failure to prepare the document properly before generating the list.

If an item you expect to appear in a list is absent, one of two things must be the case: Either the item doesn't have the correct paragraph tag or marker type, or you have failed to include the paragraph tag or marker type when setting up the list. If only a few items are missing in a lengthy list, it is probably due to the former cause; use the **Find/Change** option to find the missing items and make sure they are tagged or marked correctly. If many items are missing, it is most likely due to an error in setting up the list. Repeat the process of generating the list and be sure to include and exclude the right types of paragraph tags or markers.

As with missing items, so also with extraneous ones. A few stray items in a list are probably the result of misapplied tags or misplaced markers; a large number are more likely due to the inclusion of an incorrect tag or marker type in the list set-up. If you checked the **Create Hypertext Links** box in the Set Up dialog box before generating your list (always a good idea), you can trace the extraneous items to their locations in the source document by **Ctrl+Alt**+clicking on their list entries. If the list is a paragraph list, check the item's paragraph tag in the status area and change it if necessary; if the list is a marker list, select a block of text that includes the marker, open the Marker dialog box to view the marker type and marker text, and change these if necessary.

Empty entries in a list, such as page numbers without headings in a table of contents, result from the improper use of the Enter key to add space after a paragraph. While this may be the proper way to add blank lines on a typewriter or in your word processor, it is not the way to do things in FrameMaker or most other desktop publishing programs. The space below a heading (or any other type of paragraph) should be set with the **Space Below** option in the Basic group of the Paragraph Designer (see Chapter 5). If you need to add extra space below one or more paragraphs, use the designer to create a format override. If you find empty entries in a generated list, use the Hypertext Links to trace them to their locations in the source document. If you find extra carriage returns, delete them and use the method described above to replace them with the appropriate amount of extra space.

A paragraph that produces two list entries on separate lines, such as that in Figure 16.4, is the result of using a carriage return (¶) to break a title or heading into two lines. The solution to this problem is to delete the carriage return and use another technique to control the line break. Either use a format override to change the indents for the line or use a forced line break (**Shift+Enter**). (The former technique is preferable, as it allows the entry to wrap freely in the list; if you use a forced line break, you may have to edit the list entry to make the line break appropriately in the list.)

Figure 16.4   A double list entry

Introduction **1**

How This Manual is . . . .**2**———— **A Double Entry**
Organized. . . . .**2**—⌐
The README.TXT File **4**
Software Installation **5**
Testing. **7**

CHAPTER 17

Creating Indexes

What Is an Index?

The question raised by the heading above may seem like a foolish one; we have all used indexes countless times, so surely we know what they are. However, when confronted for the first time with the need to *create* an index, we may find that we know far less about these familiar creatures than we thought. Hence, a short definition seems in order.

An index is an alphabetical list of every *pertinent* statement in a work (pertinence, of course, being determined by the context). An index comprises a series of *entries*, each of which consists of a heading with one or more references. Index headings are usually nouns or noun phrases: names of people, places, objects or concepts. The references are typically to page numbers, but in some types of publications they may be to section and paragraph numbers. Index headings are sorted alphabetically, with all references for a given heading being grouped together under the heading. The entry for a given heading may be broken into subentries, and even sub-subentries. An index also usually includes cross-references to other, related entries. These various subjects will be described in greater detail in the course of this chapter.

How FrameMaker Creates an Index

The process of creating an index in FrameMaker is similar to that of creating a marker list, as described in the previous chapter. You insert markers in text to identify index entries—the marker text determines how the entries will be sorted; FrameMaker searches for the markers and extracts and sorts the marker text, then compiles the index as a separate document; the program gives the entries generated paragraph format tags that you can edit to change the appearance of the entries; the formats of the entries are also controlled by definitions that reside in a special text flow on a reference page in the index file.

Before You Start Indexing

Creating an index is a task for which software can be of only limited help. FrameMaker (or any other application) can compile and sort the entries that you mark, and format them as you specify, but it cannot perform the most difficult and important tasks in creating an index: deciding which items should be selected as entries and how they should be organized—which should be principal entries and which should be subentries, and which should be cross-referenced and in what manner. These tasks still fall squarely on the shoulders of the indexer.

To index a book or other large publication successfully requires both a knowledge of the subject matter and skill in the craft of indexing. Traditionally, indexes have been created either by experienced authors or by professional indexers. Now, because of the inclusion of indexing features in word processing and desktop publishing applications, people without experience or training in this craft are often expected to create indexes. *The Chicago Manual of Style* (University of Chicago Press, Thirteenth Edition, 1982, pg. 518) prescribes that an indexer should be "...intelligent, widely read, and well acquainted with publishing practices—also level-headed, patient, scrupulous in handling detail, and analytically minded." (A tough bill to fill—if you can't find such a person, you may have to do it yourself!) The aforementioned volume includes a detailed description of the indexing process as traditionally performed, and is highly recommended to novice indexers. I have tried to incorporate some of its most pertinent advice into the appropriate sections of this chapter.

If you're both the author and the indexer, you could place index markers in your text as you write, but that is probably not the best approach. Designing an index requires an overview of the text that is difficult to attain while it is still being written. A better idea would be to wait until you have individual chapters or other major units at least to the first draft stage before you begin adding index markers. Then you can read and mark up chapters and make well-informed decisions about primary entries and subentries, cross-references, and other important matters.

It is essential that, in designing an index, you be consistent in the spelling, punctuation, and formatting of the headings for your entries. For example, if you use a singular form of a term in one location and the plural in another, or capitalize an entry in one location and use a lowercase version in another, the result will be multiple, inconsistent entries. Similarly, if you use a heading like "indexes, subheadings in" in one location, you must be careful not to mark the same concept as "subheadings, in indexes" in another. These and hundreds of other analogous decisions go into making an orderly, well-designed index. To keep track of all of them, some kind of record keeping is required. The traditional method is to use index cards (is that how they came to be so called?), but since you're indexing on a computer, some kind of simple, flat-file data base seems the obvious way to go.

Marking a Document for Indexing

The first step in creating an index is to place markers in the text to identify the locations of the index entries. FrameMaker has a marker type specifically for indexes, and if you are going to generate only a single index for the publication, this is the marker type you should use. If you need to generate more than one index, as is the case with some kinds of scholarly or technical books (for example, historical works often have separate indexes of personal or place names), you can use Author, Subject, Equation, Glossary, or Comment markers for additional indexes, assuming that you haven't already used these markers for other purposes. *Don't* use Cross-Ref, Hypertext, Conditional Text, or Header/Footer markers— FrameMaker uses these markers for other purposes.

The actual practice of placing the markers is the same as for any other type of marker list:

1. Place the insertion point at the location in the text where you want to place the marker. If you want to use a text string in the document as the marker text, highlight the string.

2. Select **Markers** from the special menu, or use the keyboard shortcut **Esc s m**. This opens the Marker dialog box (see Figure 17.1).

3. Select **Index** or another appropriate marker type from the pop-up Marker Type menu.

4. If you did not begin by highlighting a text string in the document, type the text you want to appear in the list in the Marker Text box. (The marker text for an index entry determines how the entry will be sorted and alphabetized, whether it will be a primary entry or subentry, and the like. These matters will be explained in the following section.)

5. Click the **New Marker** button to insert the marker. If text symbols are turned on, the Marker symbol (like a large sans serif T) will appear in text at the insertion point. The Marker dialog box will remain on the screen. You can page or scroll to other locations in the document and place additional markers by repeating steps 3–5.

Figure 17.1 The Marker dialog box

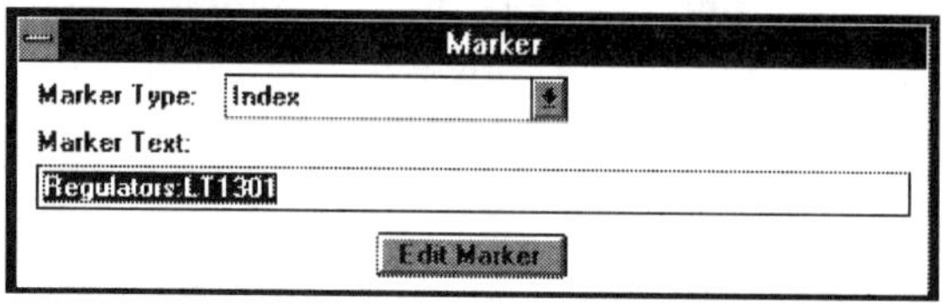

Marker
Marker Type: Index ▼
Marker Text:
Regulators:LT1301
Edit Marker

Primary Entries and Subentries

An index entry that has many page references is typically broken up into several subentries. Provided that the headings for the primary entry and subentries have been properly chosen, this format makes it easier for the reader to find information on specific aspects of a topic. As a rule of thumb, if a topic has more than five or six references, they should be divided into subentries.

To create a subentry in FrameMaker, type the primary entry and subentry with a colon (:) between them as the marker text for the subentry. For example, the marker text des Pres, Josquin:secular songs would be indexed as a subentry under *des Pres:*

> des Pres, Josquin
>   life of   44
>   masses   45–49
>   motets   52, 55–59
>   secular songs   75, 77

You can create a sub-subentry by adding a second colon followed by additional text, such as des Pres, Josquin:secular songs:texts. More than two levels of subentries, while possible, should be avoided.

Referring to a Range of Pages

When FrameMaker generates an index, it collects all the page numbers where you have placed markers for a particular heading under a single entry for that heading and lists the numbers sequentially, separated by commas:

> Active filters   33, 34, 35

If you prefer, you can have the program show a range of pages for an entry:

> Active filters   33–35

You mark a range of pages for a single index entry by placing two markers in the text with the building blocks <$startrange> and <$endrange>. On the first page of the range, place a marker with the <$startrange> building block at the beginning of the marker text, such as `<$startrange>Active filters`. On the last page of the range, place the second marker with the `<$endrange>` building block, such as `<$endrange>Active Filters`. When FrameMaker generates the index, it will create an entry with a reference to the range of pages, as shown previously.

Traditionally, an index entry refers to a range of pages only when those pages contain a continuous discussion of the topic. Separate references to a topic on consecutive pages receive separate references in the index.

There is another way to make FrameMaker display index entries for the same topic on consecutive pages as a range, without using the `<$startrange>` and `<$endrange>` building blocks. This method involves editing the index entry definition in the special text flow, as described later in this chapter. Note, however, that this method cause *all* such entries to be displayed as ranges, vitiating the distinction between continuing discussion and isolated references.

Creating Cross-References

Cross-references are used to refer the reader to related topics in the index. (Cross-references in indexes should not be confused with the cross-references created with FrameMaker's Cross-Reference feature—see Chapter 10—and placed on document pages to refer readers to other locations in the document.) Two types of cross-references are typically used in indexes, *see* cross-references and *see also* cross-references. See cross-references are used in several situations: when a topic is indexed under one of several possible headings; when a topic is indexed as a subentry (sometimes the form *see under* is used in this situation); when a topic is listed under one of several possible spellings or alphabetizations; or when a person or place is listed under one of several possible names or titles. See also cross-references should be used only to refer the reader to related information under a different heading, *not* to refer the reader to the same information differently indexed.

FrameMaker can create either type of cross-reference. To create a see cross-reference, place the building block `<$nopage>` at the beginning of the marker text:

```
<$nopage>Troubadour songs. See Plaint, Rondeau, Virelai
```

This causes the entry to be printed without a page number. Of course, it is up to you to see that the items referred to are indexed under the proper headings.

To create a see also reference, use the `<$nopage>` building block in conjunction with a subentry:

```
<$nopage>Troubadours:See also Trouveres, Minnesingers [Trou-
     badours:aaa]
```

The last item in the example above causes the see also cross-reference to be listed first among the subentries under the heading "Troubadours" (see "Changing the Sort Order," later in this chapter). Traditionally, see also references are listed either first or last among the subentries under a given heading (there are good arguments in favor of either method, which I won't enumerate here); pick one or the other and use it consistently. If you want the cross-reference to be listed last, change the aaa building block in the preceding example to zzz. If you don't include a sort order building block, the cross-reference will be alphabetized among the subentries under "see," which is not acceptable.

Creating Several Entries with One Marker

You can combine several index entries that appear on the same page in the same marker by typing the entries in the marker text separated by semicolons (;). You can type up to 255 characters in a given marker, so you could include several different entries of any of the types described previously in a single marker. This, however, is less useful than you might think. In correcting or modifying your index (and any substantial index is going to need some correction), you must edit marker text in the text box in the Marker window, which holds only about 55 characters. Therefore, it is probably best that you combine no more than two or three simple entries in a single marker. If you include a `<$nopage>` marker in an entry to create a see cross-reference, and want to follow it with a normal primary entry or subentry in the same marker text, insert a `<$singlepage>` marker at the beginning of the normal entry.

Changing the Sort Order of an Entry

Normally, FrameMaker sorts index entries word by word, placing special symbols first, numbers second, and alphabetic characters last. The details of how FrameMaker alphabetizes index entries and how you can change the sorting order for a whole index will be explained in detail later in this chapter.

You can change the sorting order of any individual index entry by adding the word to sort by in square brackets ([]) at the end of the marker text. We have already seen an example of this technique used to determine the position of a cross-reference in a series of subentries. Another possible use would be to make a number, such as a year, appear among alphabetical entries as though it had been spelled out

(*The Chicago Manual* recommends that all numbers in indexes be sorted as though spelled out):

```
1066 [ten sixty-six]
```

You could also use this option for a book title beginning with an article, where you want the title to appear in its complete form, but to be sorted by the second and following words of the title:

```
The Conquest of Mexico [Conquest of Mexico]
```

You can change sort order for subentries, but with the following limitation: The sort string you use for a subentry must duplicate the primary entry before the text by which you want the subentry sorted, for example:

N O T E

```
Decisive years in history: 1066 [decisive years
in history:ten sixty-six]
```

If you just put [ten sixty-six] as the sort text, the whole entry will appear under "T" for ten, rather than "D" for decisive.

Using Different Typefaces in Index Entries

The default typefaces for index entries are controlled by the generated paragraph format tags that are created the first time the index is generated (see later). You can change the typeface (or any other characteristic) for all index entries of a particular level (e.g., primary entries, subentries, sub-subentries) by editing the paragraph format for that level.

If you want to change the typeface *within* an index entry, for example, to set the references *see* and *see also* in italics (a common practice), you must insert a character format tag in angle brackets (< >) at the appropriate location in the marker text, as in the following example:

```
Madness: <Emphasis>See also<Default Para Font> Dementia,
    Lunacy
```

This assumes that the <Emphasis> paragraph format has been defined as italic, with all other characteristics being set appropriately. The <Default Para Font> character format tag is included to change the typeface back to the default, as specified in the paragraph format, after *See also*. (See Chapter 5 for information on creating character formats.) Another situation where you might want to change the typeface within an entry is to use a different style of page number to specify a particular type of entry, such as the location of a figure or photograph, or the definition of a term:

Oldstyle typefaces   12, 14–16, *19*

In the preceding example, the bold italic reference for page 19 might indicate the presence of an illustration. To create such an entry, place a character format tag as the last item in the marker text:

                    Oldstyle typefaces <Refnum>

This assumes that you have designed a character format called <Refnum> with the appropriate characteristics. Note that, in this case, it is not necessary to use the <Default Para Font> tag to return the entry to the default font—the <Refnum> tag applies only through the end of the particular index entry.

N O T E   An alternate way of applying different character tags to parts of index entries to distinguish different types of entries, and one that is probably more efficient if you have many such entries, is to use different marker types for different types of entries, and to include character formats in the definitions for the different types of entries. See "Editing Index Entry Definitions" later in this chapter for details.

Generating an Index

If the process of marking a document for indexing seems long and complex, that of actually generating the index is short and straightforward:

1. Select **Generate/Book** from the File menu or use the keyboard shortcut **Esc f g**. This opens the Generate/Book dialog box (Figure 17.2).

2. Select the **Index** radio button.

3. From the pop-up menu, select the type of index to generate. The options are **Standard Index**, **Author Index**, **Subject Index**, **Index of Markers**, and **Index of References**. Normally, if you were generating only one index for the publication, you would select **Standard Index**.

4. Click the **Generate** button to proceed to the next step. This opens the Set Up Standard Index dialog box (Figure 17.3), or whichever set up dialog box is appropriate for the type of index you have chosen.

5. The Set Up Standard Index dialog box is set up by default to search for the Index marker type and to generate an index with the file extension IX. This is what you want in most cases. If you want to search for additional types of markers, add them to the Include Markers of Type list by double-clicking on them in the Don't Include list. Note that the **Create Hypertext Links** check

box is also checked by default; you should definitely leave this setting on, as it allows you to jump from an index entry to its marker with a mouse click, an indispensable aid in tracking down and correcting problem entries.

6. Click **Generate** to create the index. It will appear in a new document window and be selected as the current document. The Index has not been saved at this point, so you should save it before making any modifications.

Figure 17.2 The Generate/Book dialog box

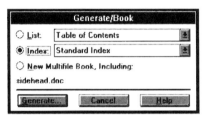

Figure 17.3 The Set Up Standard Index dialog box

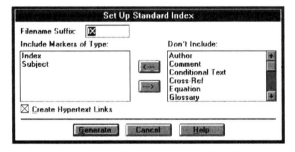

N O T E

An Index of References is similar to a List of References, described in the previous chapter. It can include information on the fonts, external and/or unresolved cross-references, condition tags, and imported graphics in a document. It differs from a List of References in that it is organized alphabetically, with all the page references for each type of item grouped together in a single entry.

An Index of Markers differs from a List of Markers in the same way. Whereas a List of Markers has one entry for each marker, organized in order of appearance, an Index of Markers is organized alphabetically by marker text, with all the page references for each item grouped together in a single entry.

Formatting an Index

As mentioned previously, the appearance of index entries is determined by both their generated paragraph format tags and their definitions in the special text flow located on a reference page in the index file.

Generated Paragraph Formats

When an index is generated, each *level* in the index has a generated paragraph format tag—there will be different tags for primary entries, subentries, and sub-subentries. In a standard index, these tags are called `Level1IX`, `Level2IX`, and `Level3IX`, respectively. Another class of items in the index that has its own tag is the Group Titles—the capital letters that divide the index into sections corresponding to the letters of the alphabet—tagged `GroupTitlesIX`. Observe that all these tags end in IX, the extension of the generated index file (if we had generated some other type of index, the file extension and the termination of the tags would not be IX, but both would still be the same).

Initially, the paragraph formats for all the generated tags are the same, except that different first and left indents are used to identify the different levels. You can edit the generated paragraph formats just like any others to change the appearance of your index entries (see Chapter 5 for details). What you should not do, however, is change the names of any of the generated formats or apply any other, non-generated formats to any of the index entries. If you do, any formatting changes you make will be lost when you update the index (and you are sure to have to update the index a few times in order to get it right, even if the document doesn't undergo major revisions).

Type Specs for an Index—there are some fairly firm traditions as to how an index is formatted. The typeface is usually the same as that used for body text, but the type size is typically two points smaller, since the index is not designed for sustained reading. (Of course, you shouldn't set *anything* smaller than 8 points, assuming you want anyone over 40 to be able to read it at all.) Indexes are normally set in two or more columns; if the page format is large, as many as four can be used. Indexes are commonly set left-aligned (ragged right). The indents FrameMaker applies by default to different indent levels are rather excessive for a multicolumn index set in 8- or 9-point type. An indent of one em per level makes a good starting point.

Indexing Styles

There are essentially two indexing styles in common use: run-in indexes and indented indexes. Most other types are variations on one or the other, or a combination of elements from both. The two types are illustrated in Figure 17.4. In a run-in index, all the subentries under a given entry are formatted as a single text block, which wraps from line to line as required by the column width. In an indented index, each subentry starts a new, indented line under the primary entry. The indexes generated by FrameMaker are formatted as indented indexes. This is more or less inescapable, since each index entry is a separate paragraph, and Frame-Maker has no provision to place paragraphs side by side on the same line, except for the special case of Run-In Heads, which isn't really applicable in this situation. You can transform a generated, indented index into a run-in index with a great deal of manual labor (i.e., by removing all the carriage returns between subentries). If you decide to do this, wait until you are *absolutely certain* that you have the final version of the publication and the index. If you have to update the index after making the modifications, all your labor will be lost and you will have to start from scratch with an indented index.

Figure 17.4 A run-in index and an indented index

Run-in Format	Indented Format

Capacitors: Absorption losses in, 95; Ceramic, 46–47; Effective series resistance (ESR), 102; Electrolytic, 49, 52; Testing 203	Capacitors
	    Absorption losses in 95
	    Ceramic 46–47
	    Effective series resistance (ESR) 102
	    Electrolytic 49, 52
	    Testing 203

Editing the Special Text Flow

Much of the appearance of a generated index is determined by definitions included in a special text flow found on a reference page in the generated document. To view these definitions, switch the view in the index document (not the source document from which the index was extracted) to Reference Pages (**Esc v R**). The special flow will not normally be on the first reference page; you will have to scroll or page down to find it. The reference page and the special flow will both have the same name as the extension of the generated file, such as IX for a standard index.

When you find the correct reference page, you will see something similar to Figure 17.5, only without the explanatory text (the exact number of elements and the order in which they appear may vary, depending on how you design your index). You can identify each of the elements in the flow by clicking an insertion point in that paragraph and reading its paragraph tag in the status area.

Figure 17.5   The special flow containing index definitions

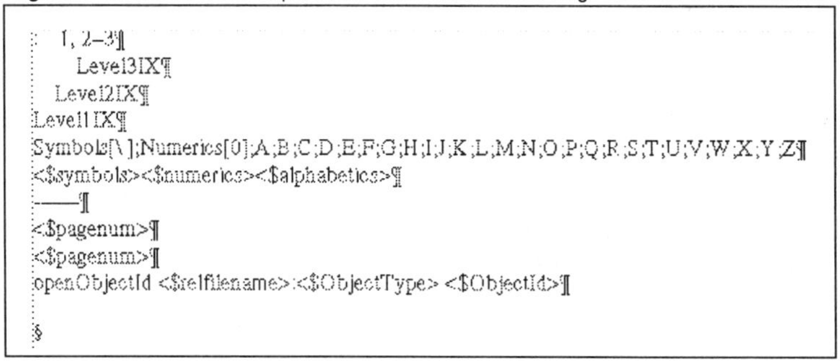

```
  1, 2–3¶
     Level3IX¶
  Level2IX¶
Level1IX¶
Symbols[\];Numerics[0];A;B;C;D;E;F;G;H;I;J;K;L;M;N;O;P;Q;R;S;T;U;V;W;X;Y;Z¶
<$symbols><$numerics><$alphabetics>¶
——¶
<$pagenum>¶
<$pagenum>¶
openObjectId <$relfilename>:<$ObjectType> <$ObjectId>¶

§
```

Every index flow will have at least the following elements:

- **Separators paragraph**—determines how page numbers and ranges are formatted.

- **Index entry paragraphs**—one for each level in your index (for example, primary entry, subentry, sub-subentry), formatted with their respective paragraph formats.

- **Group titles paragraph**—determines the headings under which index entries are grouped (normally uppercase alphabetic characters).

- **Sort order paragraph**—determines the relative positions of numeric, alphabetic, and symbolic characters in the index.

- **Ignore characters paragraph**—determines which characters will be ignored in sorting the index.

- **Index entry definition(s)**—(one for each marker type included in the index) determine what elements (other than the marker text) will appear in the index entries.

- (Optional) **Hypertext link paragraph**—determines what happens when you click on an index entry to jump to its marker in the source document (present only if the Generate Hypertext Links box was checked when you generated the index). Consult Chapter 23 for information on editing this paragraph.

You can change the format of the index in a variety of ways by editing one or more paragraphs in the special flow. *Any changes you make by editing the flow won't take effect until you update the index.*

Changing the Numbering Format

By default, the page numbering format for a standard index has a single space between the heading and the first page number, a comma and a space between subsequent page numbers, an en dash between the numbers delimiting a page range, and nothing following the last page number. You can change any aspect of this format *for all index entries* by editing the Separators paragraph. For example, it is common practice to use a comma or a colon after the heading in an index. To do this, add the comma or colon as the first character in the Separators paragraph. You might also want to use a fixed space (an en, em, or numeric space) between the heading and the first page number, rather than a standard space. To do this, select the space before the first page number and type the keyboard shortcut for whichever type of space you want to use (that is, type **Esc space m** for an em dash, rather than the symbolic code **\sm**). The comma and space between page numbers, the en dash denoting a range, and the absence of a trailing character after the last reference are all standard practice in an indented index, though, of course, you can edit any of these if you so choose. (A run-in index normally uses semicolons between subentries, but you had best add these manually if you're going to the trouble of constructing a run-in format.)

The FrameMaker documentation indicates that you can also replace the space between the entry and the first page number with a tab in order to right-align the page numbers, and even shows an example using dot leaders. (To use this method, you would also have to include the appropriate tab stop in the paragraph formats of each of the index levels.) Although there is no question that you *could* do this, you probably shouldn't, if you want to produce something that looks like a standard index. A random survey of my library revealed no indexes with right-aligned page numbers, let alone dot leaders, and this is certainly not among the formats recommended in *The Chicago Manual of Style*. The use of right-aligned page numbers and dot leaders seems to be strictly a feature of tables of contents, *not* of indexes.

Changing Grouping and Group Titles

When FrameMaker generates an index, it groups entries by default into 28 groups: symbols (all entries beginning with non-alphanumerics), numerics (all entries beginning with a digit), and the 26 letters of the English alphabet. The Group Titles paragraph shown in Figure 17.5 yields this result. (Note, however, that FrameMaker doesn't display or print a group title for a group that has no entries.)

You can change either the way entries are grouped or the group titles be editing the paragraph.

For example, if you have a relatively short publication, with few index entries for certain letters, you could edit the paragraph so that Q–R and X–Y–Z (or any other ranges of characters you choose) formed single groups. To do this, you would modify those portions of the paragraph thus:

```
… P; Q-R [Q]; S; … W; X-Y-Z [X]
```

(The ellipses in the preceding example represent omitted characters, and are not to be typed as part of the paragraph.) Although it is not clear why you would want to do so, except perhaps to torment your readers, you can create an index without group titles by placing each character in the Group Titles paragraph in separate square brackets. This eliminates the titles, but preserves spaces between the groups. To eliminate even the spaces, thus causing readers to curse your name even more loudly, delete the whole paragraph *except for its paragraph mark* (¶).

To change the appearance of the group titles (for example, their typeface, size, or alignment), edit their paragraph format in the Paragraph Designer (see Chapter 5). Their paragraph format tag is GroupTitlesIX.

Selecting Characters to Ignore when Sorting

Normally, FrameMaker ignores hyphens, non-breaking hyphens, en dashes and em dashes when sorting index entries. These characters are found in the Ignore characters paragraph. (You'd better zoom in at high magnification if you want to distinguish among them—there are no spaces between them, so they appear, at a glance, as a single horizontal line.) You can add to or delete from this list if you want FrameMaker to ignore other characters.

Sorting Letter by Letter vs. Word by Word

There are two systems of alphabetization in current use for indexing: letter by letter and word by word. The two systems produce exactly the same result with single-word headings; they differ only in their treatment of headings with two or more words. The word-by-word method alphabetizes headings up to the end of the first word. The second word is considered only when the first words of two or more entries are identical. This is the default alphabetization method in FrameMaker. The letter-by-letter method ignores any spaces between words and alphabetizes single-word and multi-word entries the same way, considering each letter in succession. You can use this method in FrameMaker by adding a space to the Ignore characters paragraph. Each system has its advocates and detractors, and each may, in some cases, produce results that strike the reader as absurd. *The Chicago Manual of Style* prefers letter-by-letter alphabetization, but finds the word-by-word method acceptable.

Modifying the Sort Order

You can easily change the relative positions in the sort order of symbols, numerics, and alphabetics by changing the positions of their respective building blocks in the sort order paragraph. However, if you want to change the order *within* one of these three blocks, you have your work cut out for you; you must type a complete list of the characters in the group in the order in which you want them sorted. The default order is shown in Figure 17.6. (Why Frame doesn't provide a list you can edit, I don't know, since such a list must obviously exist inside the program—not a very friendly feature.)

About the only situation I can think of in which you would want to edit the sort order of the alphabetic characters is to index in a foreign language. (Although FrameMaker can check spelling and set hyphenation based on foreign language dictionaries, it alphabetizes indexes only in English.) For example, if you are indexing a publication in Spanish, you need to treat CH and LL as separate letters from C and L. To cause FrameMaker to treat two letters as a single letter for sorting purposes, place them in angle brackets (< >) and insert them in the appropriate location in the sort order, as in Figure 17.7.

If you are certain that the publication you are indexing uses only one language and is free of foreign words (or doesn't use them as index entries), you can save yourself much time by omitting letters with unnecessary diacritical marks and accents from the sort order list.

N O T E

Figure 17.6   The default sort order for alphabetic characters

> AÁÀÂÃÅaáàâãåª Bb CÇcç Dd
> EÉÈÊËeéèêë Ff*f* Gg Hh IÍÌÎÏiíìîï Jj Kk
> Ll Mm NÑnñ OÓÒÔÖÕØoóòôöõøº
> Pp Qq Rr Ss Tt UÚÙÛÜuúùûü Vv
> Ww Xx YŸyÿ

Figure 17.7   The sort order modified for Spanish

> AÁÀÂÃÅaáàâãåª Bb CÇcç
> <CH><Ch><ch> Dd EÉÈÊËeéèêë Ff*f*
> Gg Hh IÍÌÎÏiíìîï Jj Kk Ll <LL><Ll><ll>
> Mm NÑnñ OÓÒÔÖÕØoóòôöõøº Pp
> Qq Rr Ss Tt UÚÙÛÜuúùûü Vv Ww
> Xx YŸyÿ

Editing the Definitions

The form of an index entry is controlled both by the marker text and by the index entry definition. The special flow contains one definition for each marker type included in the index. You can distinguish among the definitions by clicking in them and reading their tags in the status area; they will have names such as IndexIX, AuthorIX, SubjectIX, and the like. By default, each definition consists simply of the `<$pagenum>` building block, with the result that the entries refer to the page numbers where their markers are placed (with the exception of entries that use the `<$startrange>` and `<$endrange>` building blocks, as explained previously). This, of course, is what you want in most situations. However, you can edit the definitions if you require something different.

For example, if you are using different marker types for different types of entries (say, Author markers for entries referring to photographs and Subject markers for entries referring to maps) and you want to distinguish among them by printing the page numbers in different typefaces, you can do this easily by adding character format tags before the `<$pagenum>` building blocks. For example, you might do something like the following:

<Photoref><$pagenum>
<Mapref><$pagenum>

where `<Photoref>` and `<Mapref>` are character formats that you have previously defined as, say, boldface and italic. This is a much less time-consuming method than adding the character format tags to the marker text on an entry-by-entry basis, and makes it easier to ensure consistency.

In publications that are organized in numbered sections and subsections, such as some types of reference works and technical documents, you may want to index by section and subsection numbers, rather than by page numbers. Assuming you have numbered your sections by using paragraph autonumbering formats (see "Numbering Properties" in Chapter 5), you can easily do this by replacing the `<$pagenum>` building block with the `<$paranum>` building block (for the complete numbering format) or the `<$paranumonly>` building block (for the counters only).

If you want all the references on consecutive pages for each entry to be expressed as ranges, without having to use `<$startrange>` and `<$endrange>` building blocks, include the `<$autorange>` building block before the `<$pagenum>` building block in the definition.

Index References to Footnotes—you can place an index marker in a footnote in FrameMaker just as you can at any other location in text. However, when the index is generated, the entry will show the page number, but no indication that the reference is to a note rather than to the body of the document. Convention requires that an index reference to a note include a lowercase *n* following the page number to indicate that reference is to a note; if there is more than one note on the page, the *n* should be followed by the note number. You can make FrameMaker generate the *n* after the page number by using a different marker type that is not used elsewhere (for example, Author or Subject) for all the markers in footnotes. Edit the index entry definition for that marker type and add a thin space and the lowercase *n* after the `<$pagenum>` building block. When you update the index, the *n* will appear in the appropriate locations after the page numbers. This will not get you the note numbers, however—you will have to add them manually where required. This should not be too onerous a task if you use the hypertext links to jump from the index entries to their markers to find the note numbers. Don't add the note numbers until you are sure you have otherwise created the final version of your index—they will be lost if the index is updated.

Adding a Title

To add a title to an index, type the title at the top of the index and apply an appropriate paragraph format. To ensure that the title is retained when the index is updated, be sure *not* to give the title a paragraph format tag that ends in the extension of the generated file, such as `TitleIX`. All items with tags ending in the generated file extension will be replaced when the index is updated. A tag such as `IXTitle` is okay.

NOTE

If you are using special text formatting to distinguish different types of entries in your index, be sure to include an explanation of your system below the index title.

The Page Format

By default, a generated index uses the normal page layout of the document from which it was extracted. However, since indexes are usually set in a multicolumn format, you will probably want to create a special page layout for your index that is different from your normal left and right master pages. The best approach is probably to modify the left and right master pages in the index document (*not* the source document) so that the proper format will be used whenever the index is updated. (See Chapter 4 for information on modifying master pages and on page layout generally.) Of course, if you already have an index in another file that has the proper page format, you can import the format via the **Import Files** command (**Esc f i o**).

Maintaining an Index Format

Once you have generated your index for the first time and made any necessary modifications to the format by editing the paragraph formats, the special flow, and/or the page layout, FrameMaker will use the modified format whenever you update the index, provided that you save the index file in the same directory as the source document and with the name and extension that the program initially gave it. By the same token, you can change all the aspects of an index's format by copying an index file that was previously generated from another publication into the directory that contains the source document and giving it the source document's file name with the IX extension. When you update the index, FrameMaker uses the paragraph formats, page layouts, and definitions from *whatever* file is located in the same directory as the source document and has the appropriate file name.

Updating an Index

Update your index whenever you make significant revisions to your document and want to be sure your page references are correct, or whenever you make modifications to the index format by editing the special flow and want them to take effect.

The process of updating an index is no different from that of initially generating it: Open the Generate/Book dialog box, make sure that it is set up for Index and that the right type of index is selected, and click **Generate**. In the Set Up dialog box, check to make sure that the right types of markers are selected, and click **Generate** again. If you have followed the instructions in the previous section, the index will be generated with all the formatting changes you created in the previous version.

Correcting Errors in an Index

An index for a significant publication is bound to contain some errors the first time it is generated, just as a major program is bound to have bugs the first time it is compiled. There are just too many entries (anywhere from five to 20 per page for a scholarly book) for there to be any likelihood that all of them were entered correctly the first time. So allow adequate time to make the necessary revisions and corrections; it may take several generations to get all the details right, but your readers will thank you.

All the many and varied problems that occur in a generated index boil down to a single cause: failure to type the marker text correctly. And the cure, obviously, is to edit the marker text. Fortunately, this task is much easier in FrameMaker than in most other desktop publishing publications, thanks to hypertext links. If you had the **Generate Hypertext Links** box checked when you generated your index (and didn't I tell you that you should do this?), you can jump from the index entry to its marker by **Ctrl+Alt**+clicking on the entry (if there is more than one reference for the entry, click on the page number to go to a particular marker). Open the Marker dialog box and you will see and be able to edit the marker text. You can leave the Marker dialog box open while switching back and forth between the index and the source document (or, if your screen is big enough and its resolution high enough, place the index and the source document side by side). To save keystrokes while revising an index, lock the index document by pressing **Esc F l k** (the second character is a lowercase L, not the numeral 1). When the document is locked, you can dispense with the **Ctrl+Alt** and just click on the entries to jump to their markers.

When checking your index, look for the following common errors:

Inconsistent Headings

The most common type of error results from simple inconsistency in typing the marker text. You may have used a plural form for a heading in one location and a singular in another; you may have mixed capitalized and lowercase versions of a heading; you may have inadvertently typed an extra space between two words in an entry (unfortunately, the **Smart Spaces** option does not apply to typing in dialog boxes); or you may have just misspelled the heading on one or more occasions. Any of these errors will result in multiple, slightly different entries for the same heading, where you want all the references gathered together under a single heading:

> Op amps   23
>
> op amps   14–16
>
> op amps   19, 24
>
> Op-amps   25
>
> op amp   24

The solution, obviously, is to decide which form is the correct one and to edit all the others to match it. When you update the index, all the references will be grouped under a single heading:

> Op amps   14–16, 19, 23, 24, 25

A more insidious version of this kind of error is the use of a straight version of the heading in one location and an inverted one in a different location:

> Piano sonatas   25–29
>
> Sonatas, piano   23, 27, 28

If these were both subentries under the same primary entry, they would be easy enough to spot and correct. If they were both primary entries, however, they might be separated by several pages, and only an editor with a sharp eye and a retentive memory would be likely to catch them. The best solution, then, is to catch these problems before they occur; make a note of each new heading when you use it for the first time, and consult your notes as to the correct version of the heading when it recurs. You will spend more time in marking your index this way, but considerably less in correcting mistakes.

Missing Range Markers

If you have placed a `<$startrange>` marker and failed to place the corresponding `<$endrange>` marker, or vice versa, or if you have placed both markers but used variant versions of the heading, you will get entries with double question marks (??) in place of page numbers:

Filters	??–24	(missing `<$startrange>` marker)
Op amps	19–??	(variant headings for `<$startrange>` and `$endrange>`
op amps	??–22	
Regulators	12–??	(missing `<$endrange>` marker)

If a marker is missing, click on the page number of the marker that is present, then page or scroll forward or back to find the proper location and place the appropriate marker. If you have typed variant headings, decide which is the correct form, then jump to the incorrect one and edit the marker text.

N O T E   You will get two entries with missing markers if you happen to place the `<$endrange>` marker before the `<$startrange>` marker. This is easy to do if you cut and paste a block containing one of the markers. This is another good reason not to try to place index markers while a document is being written.

Missing Subentries

Missing or misplaced subentries are the result of failing to type the colon between the primary entry text and the subentry text. If no character or a space is typed between the primary entry and subentry, the two will simply run together into a single primary entry. This should be easy enough to spot, especially if there is another instance of the primary entry in close proximity, as will likely be the case. However, if a semicolon is accidentally typed in place of a colon (an easy error to make),

FrameMaker will format the entry as two different primary entries and sort them accordingly. This can be much harder to spot, as the two entries may appear on different pages. Again, it will take an editor with a sharp eye and a retentive memory (and adequate time to do a proper job) to recognize a misplaced subentry masquerading as a primary entry.

Mis-Sorted Cross-References

As mentioned earlier, *see also* cross-references should be consistently sorted as either the first or the last subentry under a given primary entry. If you see a see also cross-reference sorted in the middle of a group of subentries, such as the following, you have probably failed to include sorting information or have failed to place it as the last item in the entry:

> Semiconductors
> > Bipolar transistors   23
> > FETs   25–27
> > Rectifier diodes   44
> > *See also* Integrated circuits
> > Zener diodes   48, 49

In this case, the cross-reference is sorted under *S* for "See." In order for it to be sorted correctly, you must add the correct sorting information to the end of the marker text: either `[Semiconductors:aaa]` or `[Semiconductors:zzz]`, depending on whether you have decided to sort cross-references first or last.

Superfluous Page Numbers

A *see* cross-reference should not have a page number. If you find examples of see cross-references that do include page numbers, you have presumably omitted the `<$nopage>` building block, or have failed to place it at the beginning of the entry. Jump to the entry and add the building block at the proper location.

Bad Breaks

Bad line breaks and bad column or page breaks can both be problems in an index. Bad line breaks can be prevented easily enough. Breaks after en dashes separating the two page references for a range can be avoided by removing the en dash from the Allow Line Breaks After list in the Document Properties dialog box (see Chapter 2); do this in the index document, *not* the source document. (The en dash is represented in the list as \=.) Breaks between the last word in a heading and the first page reference can be avoided by editing the Separators paragraph in the special flow and replacing the space before the first number with a nonbreaking space, em space, or en space.

By default, FrameMaker defines the paragraph format for the group titles as "keep with next," so, provided you don't edit this property, you will not be troubled with widowed group titles. However, since each index entry is a separate paragraph, you cannot apply widow/orphan protection to them—you can widow/orphan protect each type of entry, so that a two-line entry is not split across a column or page break, but you can't use this method to prevent the last single-line entry for a letter from appearing at the top of a column. You must manually tag such entries "keep with last" or tag the preceding entry "start at top of column" to keep the two together. Another kind of page/column break problem that FrameMaker doesn't deal with automatically is groups of subentries split across a page or column break. The solution to this problem, which must be performed manually, is to start the new column with a repeat of the primary entry with the word *continued* in parentheses. Like any other manual modification of an index, this should not be done until the final version, as it will be lost if the index is updated.

Other Problems

If you have managed to find and correct all the mechanical problems just described, you have accomplished the least important part of editing your index. The far more important task, which is beyond the scope of this book to describe in detail, is checking to be sure that all your entries and subentries are meaningful and helpful to the reader, that all your cross-references lead to useful information, that all the essential information has been included, and that superfluous or redundant items have been omitted. For this, one needs all the qualities of the professional indexer enumerated earlier in this chapter. At least one aspect of the traditional process of editing and index has been eliminated by FrameMaker—performing a rigorous check of the page references against the actual pages. I think you can be relatively confident that FrameMaker will extract the page numbers correctly when generating an index. However, it cannot hurt to do a little spot checking, just to assure yourself of this.

CHAPTER 18

Building Complex Documents ("Books")

Book building is FrameMaker's term for creating and maintaining documents that consist of two or more files. A book need not be a particularly long document; any document in which you need to use different page numbering schemes in different sections, such as lowercase Roman numerals in front matter and Arabic figures in the body, or in which chapter numbers are prefixed to page numbers, and for which you need to generate a table of contents and/or index, should be managed as a book. In addition to managing page numbering and generating lists and indexes across multiple files, FrameMaker's book building features update external cross-references, control paragraph autonumbering, and enable you to change formats and layouts in several files with a single operation. Even if you don't need to do any of these things, it is easier to work on a long document if it is broken into several smaller files. Smaller files are quicker to open and save and to navigate in, and easier to transport to other systems. Building a book allows you to write and edit small files, then manipulate and print them as a single entity, with continuous page numbering, paragraph numbering, and so on.

All the major league Windows desktop publishing applications except QuarkXPress have some kind of book building feature. FrameMaker's book building features, used in combination with its cross-referencing and index and list generation features (described in previous chapters), constitute the most powerful set of large-publication management tools currently available on the Windows platform.

Creating a New Book

The first step in book building is to create a book file. A book file is not a document, it's just a list of the files that comprise the book, showing the order in which they occur:

1. Open one of the documents that will be included in the book.

2. Select **Generate/Book** from the File menu, or use the keyboard shortcut **Esc f g**. This opens the Generate/Book dialog box (Figure 18.1).

3. Select the **New Multifile Book** radio button and click **Generate**. This opens a Book window, like that in Figure 18.2. Initially, there is only one file in the book, the one that was open when you started, and the book has the same name as the file, with the extension .BK. Observe also that the menu bar at the top of the screen has changed, showing only File, View, Window, and Help.

4. Add other existing files to the book. Select **Add File** from the File menu or use the keyboard shortcut **Esc f f**. This opens the Add File to Book dialog box (Figure 18.3).

5. Use the radio buttons to select the type of file to load: **Generated List, Generated Index**, or **Document File**. In this section, we'll assume that you want to add another document file. The procedures for adding generated files will be explained later.

6. Select the file name to add from the scroll box on the left side of the dialog box. You can add a single file, or you can add all the files in the scroll box by checking **Add All Listed Files to Book**. Unfortunately, there is no way to select a group of files to add. If you want to load a file from another drive or directory, type the path and an optional file spec in the File text box and press **Enter**. To restrict the type of files displayed in the scroll box, type a file spec with a wildcard, such as *.DOC, in the File text box and press **Enter**.

7. Select the location to place the file in the book. Select a file name in the scroll box on the right side of the dialog box (initially, there will only be one, the file that was open when you started the book). Use the pop-up menu to determine whether the new file will be placed before or after the selected file (you can easily change to position of the file later, if necessary).

8. Click the **Add** button to add the new file to the book.

9. Repeat steps 4–8 to add other files to the book.

Figure 18.1 The Generate/Book dialog box

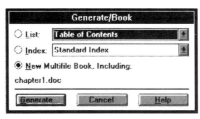

Figure 18.2 A Book window

Figure 18.3 The Add File to Book dialog box

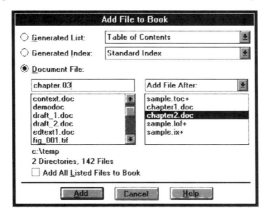

Naming and Saving a Book File

The book created in the previous section has not yet been saved, so before proceeding, you should save it. Initially, FrameMaker gives the book the same name as the document file that was open when you created it, with the .BK extension appended. If this is not satisfactory, use the **Save As** command (keyboard shortcut **Esc f a**) to save the file under a different name. Otherwise, use the **Save** command (**Ctrl+S**) to save it with its current name. When the active window contains a book file, the **Close**, **Save**, **Save As**, **Revert to Saved**, **Import**, and **Print** commands all apply to the book file and behave accordingly.

When you save the book file, you save only the list of the elements that comprise the book. The document files themselves are not affected. If you hold the **Shift** key when you open the File menu, the **Open**, **Close**, and **Save** commands appear as **Open All Files in Book**, **Close All Files in Book**, and **Save All Files in Book**. Use these commands to act on all the files in the book, and the book file itself, simultaneously.

The **Open All Files in Book** command opens the book files as icons and places them in a row along the bottom of the FrameMaker program window. If you have another document file maximized, you might fail to notice them there.

N O T E

You can open any file in a book, if it is not currently open, or make it the active window if it is, by highlighting the file name in the Book window and pressing **Enter** or by double-clicking on it.

SHORTCUT

Adding Generated Files

The procedure for adding generated files to a book begins in the same way as adding a document file:

1. With the book file active, select **Add File** from the File menu (**Esc f f**).

2. In the Add File to Book dialog box, select the radio button for **Generated List** or **Generated Index**. Use the pop-up menu next to the radio button to specify the precise type of list or index. (Although you can add a preexisting index or table of contents as a document file, **don't!** FrameMaker won't update a generated file that was added to the book as a document file.)

3. What happens next depends on whether you want to add an existing index or table of contents to the book file, so that FrameMaker will use it as a template when generating files from the book, or you want FrameMaker to generate the table of contents and index for the new book from scratch.

    a. If you're adding an existing generated file, select the file name from the scroll list just like you would a document file (FrameMaker doesn't check the type of file you selected, so make sure you have selected a generated file of the proper type). Click the **Add** button to add it to the list. This ends the process.

b. If you want FrameMaker to generate a new list or index from scratch, make sure that the File text box is empty, then click **Add**. FrameMaker responds by opening the appropriate Set Up dialog box for the type of list or index you specified (Figure 18.4 shows the Table of Contents Set Up dialog box).

4. If you selected option B, above, select the appropriate settings and select **Set** to add the file.

Figure 18.4 The Table of Contents Set Up dialog box

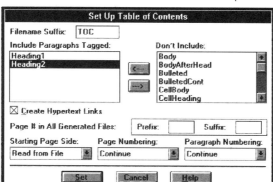

For the most part, the set-up procedures for generating an index or a list from a book are the same as those described in chapters 16 and 17 for generating these files from a normal document, so they won't be repeated here. However, there are some controls in the lower portion of the Set Up dialog box that are unique to the book building process. These controls, which affect pagination, page numbering, and paragraph numbering, are the same as those that can be applied to document files. See "Setting Up Numbering and Pagination," later in this chapter, for an explanation of these controls.

When you add new generated files to a book's file list, the file names appear in the list but the actual files aren't created until you generate or update the book (see later).

You can skip setting up the numbering and pagination for generated lists when you first add them to the book and set them up later when you set up the other files, as described later in this chapter.

N O T E

Moving or Copying a Book

FrameMaker has no simple, straightforward way of moving or copying all the files in a book to a different drive or directory. If you want to copy all the files to a floppy to move them to another system, copy them to another directory so you can create a variant version while preserving the original, or move them all to a different directory for organizational reasons, you will have to do most of the work manually. Saving the book file itself to a different drive or directory with the **Save As** command copies *only* the book file itself, not any of the component files. You must copy the component files to the new directory using the Windows File Manager or the **DOS COPY** command. (You don't necessarily *have* to copy generated files; if it doesn't find them in the new directory, FrameMaker will generate new ones the next time you update the book. However, if you want to use the formats of your existing generated files, you must copy them. And you *must* copy all the document files.) After you have copied the files and resaved the book file in the new directory, one more step is necessary. FrameMaker still thinks the document files in the book are those in the original directory (note that they now appear in the book list with path specs). You must delete the document files from the book list and add them again so that the program knows that you want to use the files in the new directory. And don't forget to save the book file after you have finished all these operations.

Renaming a Book File That Includes Generated Files

If you change the name of an existing book file by resaving it with the **Save As** command, FrameMaker changes the names of all the generated files *in the Book window* to match the new book file name. However, if the generated files already exist, their names are not changed on the disk. If you generate or update the book after changing its name, FrameMaker will generate new lists and indexes. In so doing, it will not use any format changes you have made in the generated files prior to the name change. If you want to continue to use the formats of existing generated files, you must copy or rename them to match the new book file name before you update the book. (Use the Windows File Manager or the **DOS COPY** or **REN** command.)

Rearranging or Deleting the Files in a Book

To change the order of the files in a book or to delete files from the list, select the book window, then select **Rearrange Files** from the File menu (keyboard shortcut **Esc f e**). This opens the Rearrange Files dialog box (Figure 18.5). In the dialog box, highlight the file you want to move, and use the **Move Up** or **Move Down** button to move it to the desired location. To delete a file, highlight it and click the **Delete** button. When you have made all the necessary changes, click the **Done** button.

Figure 18.5   The Rearrange Files dialog box

Rearrange Files

Files:

sample.toc+

chapter1.doc
chapter2.doc
sample.lof+
sample.ix+

| Move Up | Move Down | Delete |

| Done | Cancel | Help |

NOTE   If you have given the chapters in your book chapter numbers, or if you have assigned chapter-number prefixes to the page numbers as they appear in generated lists, you may need to edit these items manually if you change the order of the files in your book.

Setting Up Numbering and Pagination

One of the most useful features of book building is the ability to control page numbering and paragraph numbering. You can have page numbering run continuously through a book, restart for each file, or some combination, such as having lowercase Roman numerals for the front matter and Arabic figures restarting from one and running consecutively through the remaining chapters. Paragraph autonumbers, if used, can be similarly and independently controlled. You can also control the starting pages of your chapters, forcing them to begin on left or right pages, or allowing them to start on the next available page. FrameMaker will add blank pages where necessary to achieve the correct pagination.

Some aspects of pagination and numbering are set up in the individual documents or generated list files, by means of their document properties (**Esc o d**). The Document Properties dialog box (Figure 18.6) has settings for the **First Page #**, **Numbering Style**, and whether to **Restart Paragraph Numbering**. The **First Page #** and **Restart Paragraph Numbering** settings can be overridden by settings in the book file, but the **Numbering Style** settings (numeric, upper- or lowercase Roman, or upper- or lowercase alphabetic) from the individual files will be used in the book. Hence, if you want to use lowercase Roman numerals in the front matter (title page, table of contents, preface, etc.), as is customary, and Arabic figures (numeric style) in the body chapters, you must make these respective settings in the various files.

Figure 18.6   Page numbering options in the Document Properties dialog box

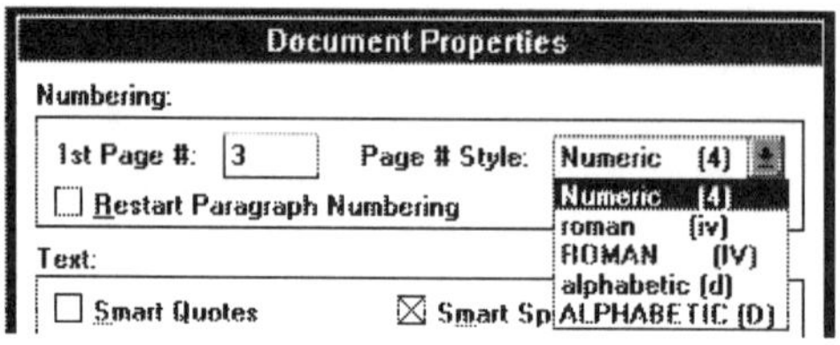

Another aspect of page numbering that is controlled in the individual files is the prefixing of page numbers with chapter numbers, such as 3–1, meaning page 1 of chapter 3. This is done by means of system variables on master pages. (See "Placing Chapter Numbers in Headers or Footers," later in this chapter.)

Those aspects of numbering and pagination that are controlled at the book level are how the page numbers appear in generated lists, such as indexes and tables of contents, what pages new chapters start on, and whether page and paragraph numbering restart in each file or continue from the preceding file. These properties must be set individually for each file in the book—use the following procedure:

1. Highlight the file name in the Book window.

2. Select **Set Up File** from the File menu. This opens the Set Up File dialog box (Figure 18.7). (The set up dialog box in the figure is for a document file. If the file you selected was a generated file, you would see a different set up dialog box, such as that in Figure 18.4, with options for selecting the items to be included in the list, as well as for numbering and pagination.)

Figure 18.7   The Set Up File dialog box

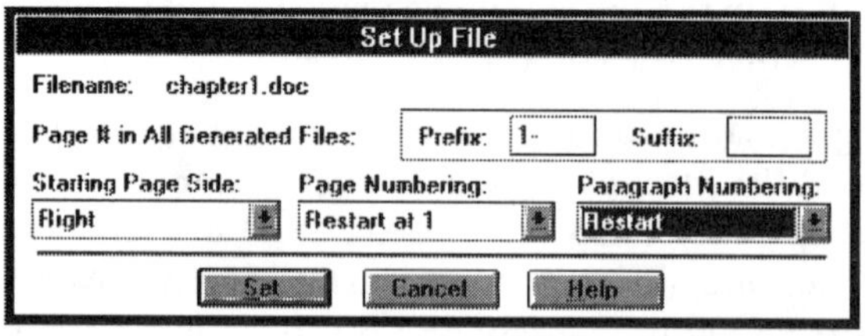

3. (Optional) Type a prefix or suffix to be added to the page numbers when they appear in generated lists in the **Page # in All Generated Files** boxes. For example, if you prefix the page numbers in your document with chapter numbers by means of Running Header/Footer variables, FrameMaker will not extract the prefixes when generating an index or table of contents, just the page numbers. To have the prefixes for the files appear in generated lists, you must type them here for each file. If you use a hyphen to separate

the prefix from the page number, type a non-breaking hyphen (/+) in the text box so the list entries can't break after the hyphen.

4. Select the starting page for the file from the pop-up menu. There are four options:

   ■ **Read from File**—make the first page whatever kind of page it is in the file. In a double-sided document, this is determined by the **First Page** setting in the Normal Page Layout; in a single-sided document, all pages are right pages.

   ■ **Next Available Side**—put the first page of the file on the page immediately following the last page of the preceding file.

   ■ **Left**—make the first page a left page.

   ■ **Right**—make the first page a right page.

   Any of these settings except **Next Available Side** may cause FrameMaker to insert blank pages in order to paginate the document as indicated.

5. Select a page numbering option from the Page Numbering pop-up menu:

   ■ **Continue**—continue the numbering from the preceding chapter.

   ■ **Restart at 1.**

   ■ **Read from File**—use the setting in the Document Properties dialog box in the file.

6. If your book uses autonumbered paragraphs, select a paragraph numbering option from the Paragraph Numbering pop-up menu:

   ■ **Continue**—continue the paragraph numbering from the preceding file.

   ■ **Restart**—restart all paragraph numbering as determined by the numbering–format definitions (see Chapter 5).

7. Select **Set** to save your settings.

8. Repeat steps 1–7 for each file in the document.

N O T E

In order for the options you selected in the Set Up dialog box to take effect, you must generate or update the book (see the following section).

Including Chapter Numbers in Headers or Footers

To refer to chapter number in headers or footers, use one of the Running Header/ Footer system variables on master pages. The variable definition should include the paragraph tag for the chapter number, for example:

```
<$paratext[Chapter#]>
```

If you are using an autonumbering format to create your chapter numbers, use the `<$paranum>` or `<$paranumonly>` building block instead of `<$paratext>`, for example:

```
<$paranum[ChapterTitle]>
```

For more information see "Using the Running Header/Footer Variables," in Chapter 9.

If you don't use autonumbered paragraphs within the chapters of a book, or you are willing to have your paragraph numbers run continuously, you can use the autonumbering feature to maintain chapter numbers, so that if you change the order of the chapters within a book, the numbers will be adjusted automatically when you update the book. Just create a paragraph format tag for your chapter numbers that includes autonumbering and use a simple counter such as `<n+>` or `<R+>` (see "Numbering Properties" in Chapter 5). If you use other autonumbering formats in the same documents, be sure to give the chapter number format a series label.

Including Chapter Numbers in Cross-References

If you use a page numbering format that prefixes chapter numbers to page numbers, such as 3–5, meaning page 5 of Chapter 3, you will, presumably, want to include chapter numbers in cross references. You can do this by creating a cross-reference format similar to the Running Header/Footer definition described in the preceding section, such as the following example:

```
See page <$paratext[Chapter#]>\=<$pagenum>
```

or

```
See page <$paranum[ChapterTitle]>-<pagenum>
```

For more information, see "Understanding Cross-Reference Formats" in Chapter 10.

Updating Formats Globally

Just as you can import paragraph and character formats, page layouts, table formats, color definitions, and a host of other formatting features from one document into another, you can also import these formats into *all* the documents in a book with a single operation. For example, you could edit the paragraph formats in one of the documents in a book, then apply these formats uniformly to all the files by importing them into the book. This is both a powerful feature for achieving uniformity in a publication, and a dangerous one which, if mishandled, can undo much careful "tweaking" and manual adjustment in a document. Be sure you thoroughly understand its consequences before you use it. And for extra safety, save all the files in the book (make the Book window active, hold **Shift** while opening the File menu, and select **Save All Files in Book**) before using it so that you can **Revert to Saved** if something goes wrong.

To import formats into a book:

1. Make the Book window active.

2. Select **Import** from the File menu (**Formats** will be the only option on the submenu), or use the keyboard shortcut **Esc f i o**. This opens a special version of the Import Formats dialog box (Figure 18.8).

3. From the Import From Document pop-up menu, select the source (the document from which to import the formats). You can only import formats from a document that is currently open.

4. By default, all the types of formats are checked. Uncheck those you don't want to import.

5. Determine whether to remove format overrides. You have two options: **Manual Page Breaks** and **Other Format/Layout Overrides**. This is the most dangerous aspect of the import process. Any large, complex document will likely contain many format and layout overrides for various purposes. Before choosing to override them, make sure you know where they are and what purposes they are serving. (This is especially important in a document that many people have worked on.) If you do opt to remove overrides, be sure to heed the advice given earlier about saving all files, in case the results aren't what you expect.

6. Select the files that you want to apply the selected formats to by placing them in the appropriate list. Initially, all the files appear in the Update list,

but you might, for example, want to update only the body chapters of a book with paragraph and/or character formats created in one of the chapters and leave the generated files as they are. Move any files that you don't want to apply the formats to into the Don't Update list. Double-click on a file name to move it, or highlight it and click on the arrow button. To move all the files from one list to the other, **Ctrl+Shift**+click on an arrow button.

7. Click **Import** to import the formats.

Figure 18.8   The Import Formats dialog box

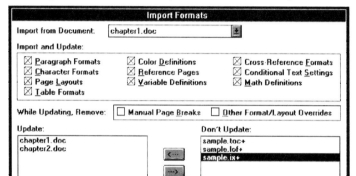

There is no undo for this operation except by reverting to saved files.

WARNING

Generating or Updating a Book

Once you have added all the necessary files to a book and set up the page numbering and pagination for the individual files, a further step is necessary before the book can be printed: It must be generated (if it is a new book) or updated (if it is a preexisting book that has been revised). Generating or updating a book updates all page numbers and paragraph numbers in the constituent files, creates or updates all generated lists (table of contents, index, list of figures, and so on) and updates all external cross-references (those in which the reference is in one file and the source is in another). It also adds blank pages, if necessary, to force the component documents to start on the pages that you specify.

You can update a book at any time, but you should definitely update in any of the following situations:

- You have added files to or deleted files from the book.

- You have changed the order of the files in the book.

- You have edited one or more of the document files in the book so that generated file entries or cross-references are no longer valid.

- You have edited the special flows for one or more of the generated files and want to see the results.

- You have changed the pagination or numbering with the **Set Up File** option.

The actually process of generating or updating a book is simple:

1. (Optional) Open all the files in the book. You can do this quickly by opening the File menu while holding the **Shift** key and selecting **Open All Files in Book**. Having all the book files open allows FrameMaker to update the files more quickly. However, you must be sure to save all the files after the update, as they will have been updated in memory only, and not on the disk.

2. With the Book window active, select **Generate/Update** from the Files menu (keyboard shortcut **Esc f g**). This opens the Generate/Update Book dialog box (Figure 18.9).

3. The dialog box shows only the generated files for the book (not the document files). By default, FrameMaker will update all the generated files, but you can opt to have it not update one or more of the files by moving them to the **Don't Generate** list. (FrameMaker always updates page numbering, paragraph numbering, and cross-references in the document files.) Double-click on the file you want to move. If you want to move all the files, press and hold **Ctrl+Shift** and click one of the arrow buttons.

4. Click the **Update** button to begin the update process.

5. While the book is being updated, messages indicating the progress of the process are displayed at the bottom of the Book window. (Depending on the speed of your system and the size of your files, you may or may not be able to read these messages as they pass by.) If FrameMaker encounters any problems during the update, it will display error messages in this location.

6. (Optional) If your document was updated in memory, rather than on the disk, save all the components by holding the **Shift** key while opening the File menu and selecting **Save All Files in Book**.

Figure 18.9   The Generate/Update Book dialog box

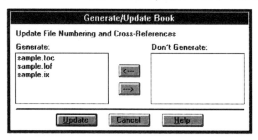

Error Messages

FrameMaker may display the following messages while generating or updating a book:

- **Unresolved Cross-Refs**—the indicated file has unresolved external or internal cross-references. Consult Chapter 10 for information on repairing unresolved cross-references.

- **Inconsistent Show/Hide Settings**—you have different show/hide settings for conditional text in different files. For information on correcting this problem (assuming it *is* a problem and not what you intend), consult Chapter 22.

- **Couldn't Open File**—FrameMaker couldn't open the indicated file. (This error halts the generation or updating at the indicated file.) The file may have been moved, renamed, or deleted; or the file may have been created by an earlier version of FrameMaker; or it may include unavailable fonts. If the file exists at the specified location, open and examine it. If it was created with an earlier version of FrameMaker, resave it. If it includes unavailable fonts, opening and resaving it will effect font substitutions.

- **Book Not Self-Consistent**—some aspect of the book, such as the contents of generated files, the page count, or cross-references, changed while the book was being generated. FrameMaker tried to generate the book again, but the book continued to change.

If FrameMaker Fails to Update a File

If FrameMaker doesn't generate the files you expected, you may have added generated files to the book as document files. Check the Book window to see if the generated file names are followed by plus signs (+). If they are not, this indicates that the files were added as document files rather than as generated files. Delete the files from the book, as described earlier, and add the files again as generated files.

Printing a Book

1. To print some or all of the files in a book, make the Book window the active window, then select **Print** from the File menu (keyboard shortcut **Ctrl+p** or **Esc f p**). This opens the Print Files in Book dialog box (Figure 18.10).

2. By default, all the files in the book are set up to print. If you don't want to print some of the files, move them to the Don't Print list. Double-click on the name of a file to move it from one list to the other. To move all the files, press and hold **Ctrl+Shift** and click one of the arrow buttons. If you want to print only one or two files from a large book, it will be quicker to move all the files to the Don't Print box this way, then move the ones you want to print back to the print box.

3. When the proper files are selected, click on **Print**. This opens the Print Book dialog box.

4. The Print Book dialog box is similar to the normal Print dialog box. You can select any of the print options, as described in Chapter 2, or set up color separations, as described in Chapter 15. The only options that are not available are thumbnails and printing a selected range of pages.

5. Click on **Print** to print the book.

Figure 18.10 The Print Book dialog box

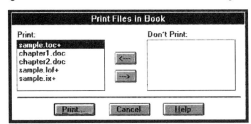

CHAPTER 19

Working with Footnotes

Footnotes are a standard feature of scientific, scholarly, and technical writing. Just about every PC/Windows word processing or desktop publishing program has some kind of automatic footnoting feature, though their flexibility and ease of use varies greatly. FrameMaker's footnoting facilities are among the best I have seen to date.

Types of Footnotes

FrameMaker supports two types of footnotes: standard footnotes and table footnotes. Standard footnotes refer to locations in normal text paragraphs and appear at the bottom of the text columns where their references are located. They are separated from the rest of the column by a *separator*, a line or other graphic device that you specify. If there are too many footnotes in a column, FrameMaker will move some of them to the bottom of the next column or page. You can adjust the amount of space available for footnotes at the bottom of the column in the Footnote Properties dialog box, described later in this chapter. Table footnotes refer to table cells and appear directly below the tables to which they refer. FrameMaker automatically updates and maintains the numbering of both types of notes as you add or delete them or cut, copy, or paste the text that contains them.

FrameMaker also indirectly supports *endnotes*, notes that appear at the end of a chapter or document rather than at the bottoms of the text columns with the paragraphs to which they refer. Endnotes are not really a formal feature of FrameMaker, but you can create them using autonumbered paragraphs and cross-references, as described later in this chapter.

Placing Footnotes

Placing a footnote of either type is simple:

1. Click an insertion point in the text where you want the footnote reference (the note number) to appear—in a text paragraph for a standard footnote or in a table cell for a table footnote.

2. Open the Special menu and select **Footnote** (keyboard shortcut **Esc s f**). The insertion point will move to the appropriate location (either at the bottom of the text column for a standard footnote or below the table for a table footnote) and the note number will appear.

3. Type the text of the footnote, just as you would type any other text.

4. After you have typed the footnote, click an insertion point in a regular text column or select **Footnote** from the Special menu again.

Placing Two Footnotes at the Same Location

If you want to place two footnotes at the same location in text, you must place a space, comma, or other character between them (a comma seems the best choice). Otherwise, the procedure for placing the second note is exactly the same as for the first, as described previously.

Referring to the Same Note at Two Different Locations

One you have placed a footnote, you can refer to it at other locations in your document by using cross-references (see Chapter 10 for a detailed discussion of cross-references). A footnote is a type of autonumbered paragraph, so you can make it the source of a paragraph cross-reference that displays its number, just as you can any paragraph. This is the technique for referring to an extant footnote at another location in a document:

1. Place the insertion point where you want the reference to appear.

2. Open the Special menu and select **Cross-Reference**.

3. In the Source Type list box, select **Footnote**.

4. In the Reference Source list box, select the footnote to which you wish to refer.

5. Select an appropriate format. If you haven't used this technique before, you may need to create a new format. If so, select the **Format** button. For a standard footnote style, create a format such as `<superscript><$paranu-`

`monly>`. This format uses a superscript character style and the `<$paranumonly>` building block, which displays only the counter from an autonumbered paragraph.

6. Insert the cross-reference.

You can use this technique to create as many references as you like to a single note; however, unlike the original footnote, FrameMaker will not automatically update the reference numbers as you edit and revise your document. You must use the procedure described in Chapter 10 for updating cross-reference numbers whenever you revise your document so as to change the note numbers.

Editing Footnote Text

Once a footnote has been created, you can edit the note text just like any other text in a FrameMaker document. Just click in the footnote text and use the text editing techniques described in Chapter 2. The appearance of the footnote text is controlled by the Footnote paragraph format, which is automatically applied to all footnotes by default. Every FrameMaker document has a Footnote paragraph format, even those created from a blank paper or custom template. You can change the appearance of footnotes by editing the format, by applying a different paragraph format manually, or by selecting a different format for all footnotes in the document by editing the Footnote Properties, as described later in this chapter.

You can also edit the text containing the footnote references in the normal manner. If you cut and paste a block of text that contains a footnote reference, the note will move to the bottom of the column where you paste the text and the note number will change if necessary to reflect the new location of the note.

Deleting a Footnote

You can delete the *text* of a footnote by selecting it and pressing the **Delete** key, but the note will remain. To delete a note entirely, you must delete the reference (the note number) from the text or table cell. When you delete the reference, the note text also disappears.

The Separator

A standard footnote is separated from its text column by a separator, which normally consists of a frame and a horizontal rule. Table footnotes also have separators, but by default the table footnote separator is an empty frame. The separators are supplied as part of the FrameMaker template and are found on a reference page. To examine the separators and other reference graphics, select **Reference**

Pages on the View menu. Use the techniques for editing graphics described in Chapter 12 to modify the separators.

Editing Footnote Properties

Many aspects of the appearance of footnotes are controlled by the settings in the Footnote Properties dialog box (Figure 19.1). Access this dialog box by selecting **Footnote Properties** on the Format menu (keyboard shortcut **Esc o f**). There are separate Footnote Properties for standard footnotes and table footnotes. FrameMaker will open the correct dialog box depending on whether the insertion point is in a standard paragraph or a table cell. The two dialog boxes are quite similar. We will describe the standard footnote properties first, then the differences in the table footnote properties.

Figure 19.1   The Footnote Properties dialog box

Footnote Properties	
Maximum Height Per Column:	Paragraph Format:
4.0"	Footnote
Numbering Style:	
⦿ Numeric [4]	○ Start Over on Each Page
○ Custom: *\d\D	⦿ Sequentially From: 1
Number Format:	
In Main Text:	In Footnote:
Position: Superscript	Position: Baseline
Prefix:	Prefix:
Suffix:	Suffix: .\t
Set Cancel Help	

Maximum Height per Column

This setting determines how much vertical space FrameMaker allows for footnotes. If you have many footnotes per page or long footnotes, and you want to keep the notes on the pages where their references occur, increase this setting. Whatever setting you use, FrameMaker will not use more space than it needs for the actual notes plus the separator.

A text column that contains more footnote than body text is disturbing to the eye and is likely to intimidate the reader. If footnotes are taking up an excessive portion of your text columns, you may want to reduce their size. Consider reducing the type size and line spacing used in the footnote text format. Typically, footnotes are set in the same typeface as the body paragraphs, at a size one or two points smaller than body text. If it is available, consider using a more condensed version of your body typeface. If these techniques are not sufficient, consider integrating more of the text from the notes into the body paragraphs (assuming you have such editorial authority) or using endnotes instead of footnotes.

Paragraph Format

The paragraph format tag automatically applied to all footnotes—this is set to Footnote by default, but you can type the name of another paragraph format. It makes better sense to edit the footnote paragraph format than to replace it with a different format.

Numbering Style

You can select one of five predefined numbering styles from a pull-down list box, or design a custom format. The predefined formats are Numeric (Arabic figures, the default), lower- and uppercase Roman numerals, and lower- and uppercase alphabetic characters. To design a custom format, select the Custom radio button and type the characters in the text box. (Use the symbolic codes for special characters.) The default custom format uses the asterisk (*), dagger († [\d]), and double dagger (‡ [\D]). Traditionally, the section symbol (§) would come next in this series. If you use a custom format and the number of notes exceeds the number of symbols that you specify, the series of symbols will be repeated with the symbols doubled. With the custom series described above, the sequence would be: *, †, ‡, **, ††, ‡‡, ...

You can also opt to have the numbering sequence restart on each page or use a sequence that starts with a specified value and runs sequentially throughout the document.

Number Format

Use these settings to specify the format for the note numbers in the main text (the references) and the footnotes. For each type of number, you can specify the vertical position of the number (baseline, superscript, or subscript), and a prefix and/or suffix for the number. Typically, the number in the note is followed by a period and a fixed space or tab. A right parenthesis is another possibility. In some styles, the reference may be enclosed in brackets or parentheses.

Table Footnote Properties

The Table Footnote Properties differ from those described previously only in that they lack a Maximum Height per Column setting (table footnotes appear directly beneath the tables to which they refer) and a restart/sequential option (table foot-note numbers automatically restart with each new table). By default, table foot-notes use a Table Footnote paragraph format and a lowercase alphabetic numbering format.

Creating Endnotes

An endnote is a note that is placed at the end of a document or chapter, rather than at the bottom of the column that contains the reference. Traditionally, end-notes were preferred by book designers because they were much easier to set than footnotes. In FrameMaker this is not the case; as you will see, true footnotes require much less effort to create and maintain than do endnotes. Still, there may be other reasons for choosing endnotes. For example, in a publication with many figures, tables, and other graphics that must be placed on the same page spreads as their explanatory text, using endnotes can help an already complex layout problem from getting totally out of hand. Some types of publications require *both* footnotes and endnotes. One common practice is to use footnotes for substantive notes and endnotes for bibliographic references. When this is done, the footnotes normally use a symbolic numbering format, such as was described previously, and the refer-ences use a numeric style. Another situation where both types of notes may be required is a translation, where it is necessary to distinguish between the original author's notes and translator's notes.

FrameMaker doesn't really support endnotes (it doesn't automatically update them or have a predefined paragraph format for them), but you can create and maintain endnotes by using two other FrameMaker features: cross-references and paragraph autonumbering. Use the following technique to create an endnote:

1. Create an autonumbered paragraph format for whatever numbering and type style you want to use for your endnotes. Name the format "Endnote." (See Autonumbering Properties, in Chapter 5, for information on creating a paragraph autonumbering format.)

2. Go to the end of your document and type your note, then apply the format you created in the previous step.

3. Go to the location where you want to place the reference (the note number) and place the insertion point.

4. Open the Special menu and select **Cross-Reference (Esc s c)**.

5. In the Source Type list box, select **Endnote**.

6. In the Reference Source list box, select the endnote to which you wish to refer.

7. Select an appropriate format. If you haven't used this technique before, you may need to create a new format. If so, select the **Format** button. For a standard endnote style, create a format such as `<superscript><$paranumonly>`. This format uses a superscript character style and the `<$paranumonly>` building block, which displays only the counter from an autonumbered paragraph.

8. Insert the cross-reference.

Assuming you designed the autonumber format correctly, FrameMaker will automatically update the numbers of the notes where you have placed them at the end of the document. However, it will not automatically update the reference numbers as you edit and revise your document. You must use the procedure described in Chapter 10 for updating cross-reference numbers whenever you revise your document so as to change the note numbers. If you cut and paste blocks of text that contain the endnote numbers, updating the cross-references may not be sufficient. If you move the text that contains note #1 after the text that contains note #2, then update the cross-references, the numbers will stay the same, because reference #1 still points to note #1 and reference #2 still points to note #2, regardless of the order of the references in the text. In order to put things right, you must cut note #1 and paste it after note #2. FrameMaker will update the autonumbers of the notes; now updating the cross-references will produce the correct results. Sounds like a lot of bother, doesn't it? Maybe FrameMaker 5.0 will support *real* endnotes.

CHAPTER 20

Working With Tables

Almost any kind of scholarly or technical publication will need at least occasionally to format information in rows and columns. Row/column formats are also useful for schedules, catalogs, parts lists, forms, and a host of other applications. In the early days of desktop publishing, creating tables was a major torture. The only way to format text in rows and columns was to use tabs, and this usually required several increments of trial and error to get the tab stops positioned correctly. Positioning paragraphs that involved multiple lines required breaking the lines with forced returns and tabbing each line into the position. Fortunately, the preceding description is ancient history. Every Windows desktop publishing application has a table building feature, and most word processors do also.

FrameMaker's table features are among the most extensive in any Windows application, as witness the length of this chapter, one of the longest in the book. Although FrameMaker's table building features are flexible and powerful, they are by no means easy to understand and use. There are lots of controls, distributed through a number of different dialog boxes and windows, and the way they interact is not exactly intuitive. I have attempted to organize the information in this chapter so as to make them a little easier to master.

Terminology

A table comprises a number of cells. Table cells can contain text, special items such as variables, cross-references, and footnotes, graphics, and even other tables. The cells are organized in rows and columns. Three kinds of rows can occur in a Frame-Maker table: heading rows, body rows, and footing rows. Heading rows are typically used to indicate the contents of the columns. Footing rows are less common, but can be used to duplicate headings on tables with many rows. When a table splits across a page break, heading and footing rows are duplicated on the second and subsequent pages. The remaining rows that contain data are termed body rows. Tables can also have autonumbered titles; these, too, are duplicated when a table is split across a page break. You can add rules and/or shadings to a table to make it easier to read or to improve its appearance.

How Table Properties Are Controlled

One of the most confusing aspects of working with tables is keeping track of how the various properties of a table are controlled and modified. FrameMaker has scattered these controls over a number of different dialog boxes and windows and developed a rather confusing nomenclature to describe them:

Default Properties—these properties are stored as part of a table format, but can't be edited in the Table Designer. (Why not? I don't know, you'll have to ask Frame.) The default properties of a table include the total number of rows and columns, the number of heading and footing rows, the paragraph format of the first paragraph in the title (if present), and the paragraph format of the first paragraph of the heading, footing, and body cells in each column.

You can override the default number of heading, footing, and body rows and the total columns when you place a new table, and you can freely add and delete rows and columns as you work on a table. However, you can only alter these properties of a stored format, and those mentioned previously having to do with paragraph formats, by creating a table with the desired properties and using it to update the stored format (see "Applying and Storing New or Modified Formats," later in this chapter).

Table Designer Properties—these properties are created and edited in the Table Designer, and can be applied to individual tables or to all tables with a particular format tag, or stored in the catalog as part of a named format. Thus, these properties are analogous to those created with the Paragraph Designer. The properties in the Table Designer are divided into three groups: Basic Properties, which include indents, alignment, spacing, position, and cell margins; Ruling Properties; and Shading Properties.

Custom Settings—these properties involve alterations to the formatting of individual rows, columns, or cells that override the properties described previously. These settings are created mainly by means of commands on the table menu, but the Table Properties group in the Paragraph Designer also plays a role here. Custom settings are not stored as part of a table format, even when a format in the catalog is updated from a table that includes them, and they are not affected when a format from the catalog is applied to an existing table. Custom settings include cell rotation and "straddling," custom ruling and shading, custom cell heights, custom cell margins and vertical alignment, and custom page breaks.

Paragraph and Character Formats—the appearance of text in table cells, like that of all other text in a FrameMaker document, is controlled with character and paragraph formats. When you insert a new table, certain paragraph formats are included in cells of different types as part of the default properties, described earlier. You can use these formats as you find them, edit them in the Paragraph Designer, or replace them with other formats. The Table Properties group in the Paragraph Designer can be used to modify the vertical alignment of text in table cells or the table cell margins. Character formats can be applied to selected characters in table cells.

Inserting a New Table

To insert a new, empty table, use the following procedure:

1. Place an insertion point in a text column; this is where the table's anchor will be placed.

2. Select **Insert Table** from the Table menu, or use the keyboard shortcut **Esc t i**. This opens the Insert Table dialog box (Figure 20.1).

3. Select one of the table formats from the Table Format list. The number and variety of formats offered depends on the template upon which the document is based. A document based on a blank paper template has two table formats, A and B.

4. If you wish, you can edit the number of columns, body rows, heading rows, and footing rows in the dialog box.

5. Click **Insert** to insert the table.

Figure 20.1 The Insert Table dialog box

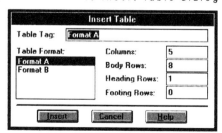

The position of the table relative to the location of its anchor will be determined by setting in the Basic Properties group of the Table Designer (see "Positioning a Table," later in this chapter).

NOTE

You cannot place a table in a footnote. You can however, place a footnote in a table cell (see later).

Tables and Anchored Frames, a Marriage Made in...?

Strange though it may seem, FrameMaker can place a table only in a text column. When you place a new table, FrameMaker creates an anchored frame with its anchor at the insertion point in text. Any attempt to place a table in an unanchored frame or directly on the page is doomed—the **Insert Table** command is simply not available unless there is an insertion point in a text column. Nor can you drag a table out of its anchored frame once it has been placed—you can't select a table independent of its frame. You can cut or copy a table, but to paste it, you must place an insertion point in a text column.

Because tables are always in anchored frames, they are affected by all the problems exhibited by anchored frames in multi-column formats (see Chapter 14 for details). If you want a table to stay in a fixed location on a page, rather than being dragged along with its anchor as text is revised, or if you want to place a table that is wider than a column in a multi-column format and not have it overwrite or be overwritten by text, you will need to draw a disconnected text column (see Chapter 4) and insert the column therein.

Filling In a Table

Each cell in a table is like a disconnected text column. You can type text in a cell, or cut or copy it from another location and paste it in a cell. The horizontal (column) borders of a cell are fixed (unless you edit them), but a cell will expand vertically to make room for new lines of text as you type. Text wraps automatically from line to line as you type, just as in any other text column.

To type or edit text, you can place the insertion point in any table cell with the mouse, or you can use the key combinations in Table 20.1.

Table 20.1   Key combinations for navigating in a table

Key	Action
Tab or **Esc t m r**	Move to the next cell
Shift+Tab or **Esc t m l**	Move to the previous cell
Ctrl+Alt+Tab or **Esc t m d**	Move down one cell
Ctrl+Alt+Shift+Tab or **Esc t m u**	Move up one cell
Esc t m e	Move to rightmost cell in row
Esc t m a	Move to leftmost cell in row
Esc t m t	Move to top cell in column
Esc t m b	Move to bottom cell in column
Esc t I	Move to the table's anchor

(To insert a tab in a table cell, press **Esc Tab**.)

The position of text within a cell is determined by the default margins of the cell, set in the Table Designer. In addition, you can set custom margins and vertical alignment in the Table Cell properties group in the Paragraph Designer. The appearance of text in tables, like any other FrameMaker text, is controlled by paragraph and character formats.

In addition to text, you can place graphics (either imported or drawn in Frame-Maker) in a table cell. You can even place another table in a table cell (see later).

Converting Text to a Table

In addition to placing a table and filling it in by typing or pasting text, you can create a table by converting existing text, either text that is already in a FrameMaker document, or an ASCII text file that you import into FrameMaker. When you convert text to a table, you decide whether paragraphs will be converted to rows or cells. Use the former option when you have text lines that are divided by tabs, spaces, or other separators into separate items. Use the latter option when you have a number of different paragraphs that you want to convert to table cells, as, for example, in a bulleted list or an outline. If you treat the paragraphs as cells, you specify the number of columns to use in creating the table and FrameMaker creates the appropriate number of rows based on the material to be converted. If you treat the paragraphs as rows, FrameMaker chooses the numbers of rows and columns based on the number of paragraphs and separators per paragraph.

Converting Text in FrameMaker

1. Select the material to be converted.

2. Select **Convert to Table** from the Table menu, or use the keyboard shortcut **Esc t v**. This opens the Convert to Table dialog box (Figure 20.2).

3. Select the appropriate radio button to determine whether each paragraph in the selection will be treated as a cell or a row. If you choose to treat paragraphs as rows, select the separator character that FrameMaker will use to break the row into cells. You can specify, tabs, a minimum number of spaces, or any other character that you type in the text box, such as a comma, colon, or dash. If you choose to treat the paragraphs as cells, specify the number of columns.

4. Select the table format to apply to the new table.

5. Choose the number of heading rows. If the headings are not part of the selected material, check **Leave Heading Rows Empty** and type the headings after the table is created.

6. Click **Convert** to create the table. FrameMaker inserts the table in the paragraph directly above the text that was converted. (You can easily cut the table from this location and paste it elsewhere in the document if you wish—see later.)

Figure 20.2   The Convert to Table dialog box

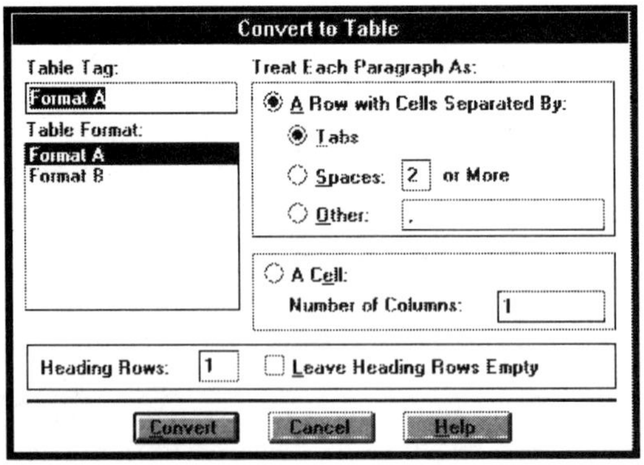

After the text is converted, you may have to do a bit of manual repair work to put it in good order. For example, if the text that you converted contained any extraneous tabs or carriage returns, the table may contain extra, empty rows or cells that you will have to delete.

Converting Imported ASCII Text

1. Click an insertion point where you want to anchor the new table.

2. Select **Import** from the File menu and select **File** from the submenu, or use the keyboard shortcut **Esc f i f**.

3. If FrameMaker is not sure of the file type, it will display the Unknown File Type dialog box. If it does so, confirm that the file is a text file.

4. FrameMaker displays the Reading Text File dialog box. Select the **Convert to File** radio button and then click **Read**. The Convert to Table dialog box appears.

5. Follow steps 3–6 in the previous section to convert the text into a table.

N O T E FrameMaker can also import tables intact from other applications that have table features. Thus, it may not be necessary to turn tables created in your word processor into tabbed text before importing them into FrameMaker and then convert them back into tables, as it is with most other desktop publishing applications.

Converting a Table to Text

In addition to converting normal paragraphs into table cells, FrameMaker can convert the contents of a table into normal text. When you convert a table to text, you have the option of converting the cells column by column or row by row.

1. Click an insertion point in the table you want to convert.

2. Select **Convert to Paragraphs** from the table menu, or use the keyboard shortcut **Esc t v**.

3. Select the appropriate radio button to convert the table by rows or columns.

4. Click **Convert**.

Placing a Graphic in a Table Cell

Placing graphics in table cells can be a powerful technique for organizing and manipulating figures with complex callouts, or for managing a series of similar figures that you want format consistently. Graphics in table cells are placed in anchored frames (see Chapter 14). The following instructions describe the process of placing a single graphic in a cell, but you can also place graphics and text together or more than one graphic.

1. Click an insertion point in a paragraph in the table cell where you want to place the graphic.

2. The position of the graphic in the cell can be controlled, in part, by the alignment of the paragraph where you place the insertion point. (This is important only if the graphic is smaller than the cell in which you're placing it.) You can position the paragraph horizontally by specifying its alignment (Left, Right, or Center), in the Basic Properties Group in the Paragraph Designer (see Chapter 5). You can position the paragraph vertically (Top, Middle, or Bottom) with the **Cell Vertical Alignment** option in the Table Cell Properties group in the Paragraph Designer.

3. If you are going to place the anchored frame for the graphic **At Insertion Point** (see next step), turn off Fixed Line Spacing for the paragraph in the Basic Properties group of the Paragraph Designer.

4. Place an anchored frame in the paragraph by selecting **Anchored Frame** on the Special menu or using the keyboard shortcut **Esc s a**. Frame recommends you anchor the frame **At Insertion Point**, but you can potentially use any of the anchored frame positioning options described in Chapter 14 to achieve different effects.

5. Draw or import the graphic in the cell (see Chapters 12 and 13, respectively).

6. Make any adjustments required to the size and position of the graphic and/ or the anchored frame to achieve the desired visual effect. You can position the graphic by dragging, editing its top/left offsets in the Object Properties dialog box, or using the **Align** command on the Graphics menu. Use the settings in the Anchored Frame dialog box to adjust the position and size of the frame.

Placing a Table in a Table Cell

Occasionally, you may want to place a table inside a table cell. This technique is useful if you need to produce irregular rows or columns, or to subdivide a cell without subdividing the whole row or column. Placing a table within a table involves creating an anchored frame in the cell, drawing a text column in the frame, and then inserting the table in the text column, thereby creating another anchored frame (that's a table in a frame in a column in a frame in a cell in a table in a frame in a column!). It sounds more complicated than it is to do, and, in any event, you're unlikely to need to do it very often.

1. Click in the cell where you want to insert the table.

2. Select **Anchored Frame** from the Special menu, or use the shortcut **Esc s a**. In the Anchored Frame dialog box, specify the position of the frame as **Below Current Line**, set the horizontal alignment (Left, Center, or Right) as you wish, and specify the size of the frame. It's a good idea to make the frame a bit oversized, as you have to draw the column in the frame and place the table in the column. You can fine-tune the sizes and positions of all these items later.

3. Draw a text column in the frame with the Text Column tool from the Tools Palette (see Chapter 12).

4. Click an insertion point in the text column and insert the table, as described earlier in this chapter.

5. Make any necessary adjustments in the frame, column, and table to achieve the desired visual effect.

Placing a Footnote in a Table Cell

You can insert a footnote in a table cell just as you do in body text:

1. Click an insertion point in the cell where you want the footnote reference (the note number) to appear.

2. Open the Special menu and select **Footnote** or use the keyboard shortcut **Esc s f**. The insertion point will move to the appropriate location, below the last row of the table, and the note number will appear in the cell.

3. Type the text of the footnote, just as you would type any other text.

4. When you are done typing the footnote, click an insertion point in a regular text column or select **Footnote** from the Special menu again.

Table footnotes always appear below the last row of the table to which they refer. Their appearance is controlled by the Table Footnote Properties (consult Chapter 19 for details).

Editing a Table

Selecting Table Cells

In working with a table, one must distinguish between selecting a table cell and selecting its contents. You select text within a table cell just as you select any other

FrameMaker text, using any of the methods described in Chapter 2. As long as you don't drag the mouse over a cell border, only the contents of the cell are selected (see Figure 20.3a). To select a cell or group of cells, click in one cell and drag across the cells you want to select. A cell or row of cells that is selected shows a selection handle on its right border (see Figure 20.3b). To select a single cell, drag across its right boundary, then back into the cell before releasing the mouse button. To select an entire column, select the topmost cell, then drag down into the cell below before releasing the button. To select a whole table, drag across its top row, then drag down into the next row before releasing the button, or select the table's anchor symbol. Alternatively, you can use the keyboard shortcuts in Table 20.2 to select various combinations of table cells.

Figure 20.3a and b   Selecting the contents of a cell/Selecting a cell

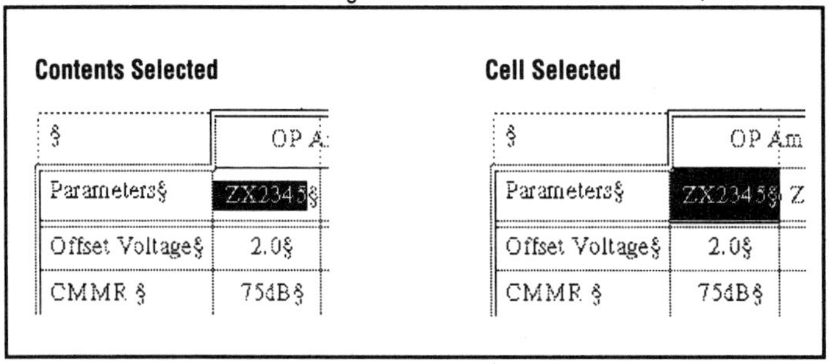

Table 20.2   Keyboard shortcuts for selecting table cells

Keys	Action
Ctrl+click	Select the cell
Esc t h r	Select the row
Esc t h c	Select the column
Esc t h b	Select the body cells in the column
Esc t h t	Select the whole table

Copying a Table

To copy a table, select all the cells, as described previously, and select the **Copy** command from the Edit menu (**Ctrl+C**). Place the insertion point in a text column where you want to anchor the table, and select **Paste** from the Edit menu (**Ctrl+V**). (You can also copy selected rows or columns from a table and paste them in another table—see later.)

Copying, Cutting, and Pasting Cells, Rows, and Columns

In addition to cutting or copying entire tables, you can cut or copy individual cells, rows, or columns and paste them at different locations in the same table, in other tables, or in text as new, independent tables.

If you want to copy or cut only the contents of a single cell, select the contents as described previously (no selection handle should appear) and select **Cut** or **Copy**. You can paste the text either in another table cell or in normal text.

If you cut or copy a whole cell, several adjacent cells, or one or more rows or columns, you cut or copy both the contents and any custom formatting that was applied to the cells (see later). If you cut one or more cells, but less than a whole row or column, FrameMaker cuts the contents of the cells to the clipboard without asking you for confirmation and leaves the empty cells. If you paste one or more cells but less than a whole row or column, either at a different location in the same table or in a different table, FrameMaker overwrites the cells at the destination, again without asking you for confirmation. (You can reverse this operation with the **Undo** command.)

When you select one or more whole rows or columns in a table and attempt to cut it, FrameMaker displays a dialog box like that in Figure 20.4, so you can indicate whether you want to remove the contents of the cells, leaving the blank cells in place, or to remove the cells and their contents. Select **Leave Cells Empty** to remove the contents and leave the empty cells. Select **Remove Cells from Table** to remove both the cells and their contents.

Figure 20.4 The Cut Table Cells dialog box

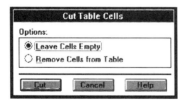

Having cut one or more rows or columns, you can paste them at a different location in the same table, in a different table, or at the insertion point in text, as a new table. When you attempt to paste the rows or columns at a different position in the same table, or in another table, one of the dialog boxes in Figure 20.5 or 20.6 appears, depending on whether you are trying to paste rows or columns. Choose the location to paste the new cells: in the case of rows, above, below, or in place of the current row; in the case of columns, to the left of, to the right of, or in place of the current column.

Figure 20.5   The Paste Rows dialog box

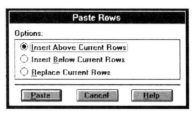

Figure 20.6   The Paste Columns dialog box

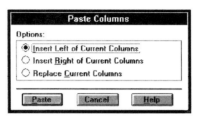

N O T E

To paste a row in a different table, the destination table must have the same number of columns as the original table; to paste a column, the destination must have the same number of rows as the original table. If there is a mismatch between the source and destination, the cells from the source will overwrite those in the destination, rather than being inserted between the rows or columns.

Moving or Deleting a Table

To move a table, select all of its cells, as described earlier, and select **Cut** from the Edit menu (**Ctrl+X**). FrameMaker responds with the dialog box in Figure 20.7, asking whether you want to **Leave Cells Empty** (that is, cut the contents and leave the empty cells) or **Remove Cells from Table** (that is, cut the whole table, with its contents). Select the latter radio button and click **Cut**. Place the insertion point at the new location where you want to anchor the table, then select Paste (**Ctrl+V**).

Figure 20.7   The Clear Table Cells dialog box

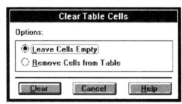

To delete a table, select all the cells and select **Clear** on the Edit menu or press **Del**. A dialog box similar to that in Figure 20.7 appears. Select **Remove Cells from Table** and click **Clear** to delete the table.

Deleting Cells, Rows, or Columns

To delete the contents of a single cell, select the contents and press **Del** or select **Clear** on the Edit menu. The contents of the cell are deleted like any other text. You can also use the **Del** and **Backspace** keys within a table cell just as in any other text column.

To delete the contents of one or more cells but less than a full row or column, along with any custom formatting, select the cells so that their selection handles are visible, as described earlier, and press **Del** or select **Clear** from the Edit menu. FrameMaker deletes the contents and custom formatting of the cells without asking for confirmation. You can recover the cells with the **Undo** command (**Ctrl+Z**).

When you delete one or more full rows or columns, you have a choice of deleting the contents and formatting of the cells and leaving the empty cells behind, or of removing the cells from the table. Select one or more full rows or columns, as described earlier, press **Del** or select **Clear** from the Edit menu. FrameMaker displays a dialog box like that in Figure 20.7, so you can indicate whether you want to delete the contents of the cells, leaving the blank cells in place, or to delete the cells and their contents from the table. Select **Leave Cells Empty** to delete the contents and leave the empty cells. Select **Remove Cells from Table** to delete both the cells and their contents.

Adding Rows or Columns

Although you specify the number of rows and columns when you insert a new table, you can easily add more rows or columns later if you need to add more data or change the format. Use the following procedure:

1. Place the insertion point in a cell in a row or column next to which you want to add the new row(s) or column(s).

2. Select **Add Rows or Columns** from the **Table** menu, or use the keyboard shortcut **Esc t a**. The dialog box in Figure 20.8 will appear.

3. Use the radio buttons to specify whether to add rows or columns, and enter the number of them to add in the adjacent text box.

4. Use the pop-up menus to select the location at which to add the new row(s) or columns(s): for rows, above or below the selection (the row with the

insertion point) or to the heading or footing; for columns, to the left or right of the selection.

5. Click the **Add** button to add the new row(s) or column(s).

Figure 20.8 The Add Rows or Columns dialog box

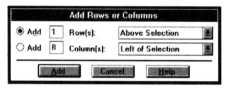

SHORTCUT

Use the keyboard shortcuts in Table 20.3 to add or delete rows or columns in a table.

Table 20.3 Keyboard shortcuts for adding or deleting rows or columns

Keys	Action
Esc t R a	Add one row above the selection
Esc t R b or **Ctrl+Enter**	Add one row below the selection
Esc t c l	Add one column to the left of the selection
Esc t c r	Add one column to the right of the selection
Esc t c e	Delete the contents of the selected cells
Esc t c x	Delete the selected rows or columns from the table

Resizing Rows and Columns

Changing Columns Width

When you create a new table in FrameMaker, the columns are initially all the same width. When you type or paste text in the table cells, the text wraps at the cell margins and the rows grow vertically to accommodate the text. Depending on the type of information you have to display, you may need to increase or decrease the width of selected columns to better fit their contents. FrameMaker provides several ways to do this:

By Dragging with the Mouse

You can stretch or shrink the width(s) of one or more table columns by selecting them and dragging with the mouse. Select a cell in the column you want to stretch or shrink. Move the pointer near the handle, until it turns into a black arrowhead, then press the mouse button and drag the handle to stretch or shrink the column. As you drag, the changing width of the column is displayed in the status area. The other columns move as necessary to accommodate the resized column, but their widths do not change—the width of the whole table increases or decreases. If you want to increase the width of one column while decreasing that of its neighbor, press and hold the **Alt** key and drag as described previously. The border between the two columns moves, one shrinking and the other growing. If you select two or more columns before dragging (either with or without the **Alt** key), the selected columns grow or shrink together, maintaining their original proportion to one another.

N O T E

If Snap is active when you drag to resize a column, you can position the column borders only on grid lines.

Resizing with a Dialog Box

The Resize Selected Columns dialog box (Figure 20.9) gives you several options for precisely controlling the widths of columns. Select the columns you want to resize and select **Resize Columns** from the Table menu or use the keyboard shortcut **Esc t z** to open the dialog box. Select one of the radio buttons to choose how the columns will be resized, type the required value, as indicated, and click **Resize**:

Figure 20.9 The Resize Selected Columns dialog box

Resize Selected Columns	
⦿ **T**o Width:	0.5"
○ **B**y Scaling:	80.0 %
○ To **W**idth of Column Number:	5
○ To **E**qual Widths Totalling:	0.5"
○ By **S**caling to Widths Totalling:	6.25"
○ To Width of Selected **C**ells' Contents	
(Maximum Width:	5.0")

[Resize]   [Cancel]   [Help]

■ **To Width**—make all the selected columns the width indicated in the text box.

- **By Scaling**—rescale all the selected columns by the percentage in the text box. (100% = no change; a percentage greater than 100% means increase the width(s) of the column(s); a percentage less than 100% means decrease the width(s) of the column(s)).

- **To Width of Column Number**—resize the selected columns to match the width of the column whose number appears in the text box.

- **To Equal Widths Totaling**—resize the selected columns to equal subdivisions of the value in the text box. (To make all columns equal, select a full row, then use this option.)

- **By Scaling to Widths Totaling**—resize the selected columns to the width in the text box while maintaining their relative widths.

- **To Width of Selected Cells' Contents**—resizes the column so that the text in the selected cell will fit without wrapping (or, if a frame for a graphic or another table is in the cell, resizes the column to accommodate the frame). This is the only one of the options for which the specific cell you select, rather than just the column, is significant. You can specify a maximum width beyond which the column will not expand.

By Copying and Pasting

You can copy the width of a table column and paste it to one or more other columns:

1. Place the insertion point in the column from which you wish to copy the width.

2. Select **Copy Special** from the Edit menu and select **Table Column Width** from the submenu, or use the keyboard shortcut **Esc e y w**.

3. Select one or more columns into which to paste the width setting.

4. Select **Paste** from the Edit menu, or use the keyboard shortcut **Ctrl+V**.

Increasing the Height of a Row

Normally the height of a row increases or decreases automatically to accommodate the text that is typed in it. The only constraints on the height of a row are minimum and maximum values, which, by default, are a rather ample 0.0" minimum and 14.0" maximum. (Of course, the overall height of a table is constrained by the page on which it is placed and its starting location. If a table is too tall, it will break to a second page—see later.)

Sometimes, you may want to increase the height of a row beyond what is required to accommodate the contents of the tallest cell. You can do this by increasing the row's minimum height value:

1. Click an insertion point in the row whose height you want to change.

2. Select **Row Format** from the Table menu or use the keyboard shortcut **Esc t r**. This opens the Row Format dialog box (Figure 20.10).

3. Type a new minimum height value and click **Set**.

The other controls in the Row Format dialog box will be explained later in this chapter.

Figure 20.10 The Row Format dialog box

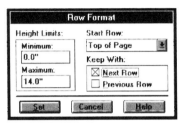

If you want to make all the row heights equal, measure the tallest row by pressing and holding **Alt+Shift** while dragging a selection box around the row (read the height in the status area). Then select the whole table and set the minimum to the height of the tallest row, as **N O T E** described previously.

Rotating a Table

You can rotate a table in one of two ways. You can create a rotated master page and apply it to the body page on which the table is located (see Chapter 4). Use this method when the table is the only item on the page, as, for example, when you want to place a wide, landscape-oriented table in a portrait-oriented publication, or when you want to rotate every item on the page. Or, you can draw a disconnected text column on a page, place the table in the column, then rotate the column. Use this method if you want other items on the page to retain their normal orientation and only the table to be rotated. (The FrameMaker documentation says that you should draw a column in an anchored frame, but this is an unnecessary step unless you want the table to move as text reflows.)

To rotate a table in a text column:

1. Adjust the other columns on the page, if necessary, to make room for the new text column.

2. Draw the new column with the text column tool (see Chapter 12).

3. Click an insertion point in the column and create or paste the column.

4. Select the column (not the table), then select the **Rotate** command for the Graphics menu (**Esc g t**).

5. In the Rotate Selected Objects dialog box, enter the number of degrees and direction of rotation, then select **Rotate**.

When you use this method, you are not limited to rotation in 90° increments; you can rotate the column and table freely (although I can't see why you would want to do so).

N O T E

Rotating Table Cells

In addition to rotating whole tables, you can rotate selected cells. Although you can rotate any cell, the most common practice is to rotate heading cells by 90° in order to accommodate wide headings to narrow columns, as in Figure 20.11. To rotate one or more table cells:

1. Select the cells, as described earlier in this chapter.

2. Select **Rotate** from the Graphics menu, or use the keyboard shortcut **Esc g t**.

3. Select one of four rotation angles from the Rotate Table Cells dialog box. (A table cell can be rotated only in 90° increments.)

4. Click **Rotate** to apply the selected rotation.

Figure 20.11   A table with rotated headings

Input (Volts)	ISET(ma)	Differential Gain	Differential Phase	Signal-to-Noise
0.03	1.88	0.3%	0.8°	50db
0.08	2.25	0.5%	1.0°	55db
0.12	2.50	0.8%	1.5°	62db

If you rotate cells by 90° or 270°, text typed in the cell(s) will be set on a vertical baseline. The height of the cell will expand to accommodate the text and the text will not wrap. If you want to force the text to wrap at a certain point, set the maximum row height in the Row Format dialog box, as described earlier.

"Straddling" Cells

Straddling is FrameMaker's term for combining two or more adjacent cells in a row or column. This is often useful for tables that have multiple levels of headings, as in Figure 20.12. You can straddle any rectangular block of cells, but you can't straddle an irregular shape, such as an L. If you straddle cells that contain text, the text from the different cells appears as separate paragraphs in the combined cell.

Figure 20.12 A table with straddled cells

Straddled Cells

	OP Amps		Video Difference Amps	
Parameters	ZX2345	ZX2347	XY1128	XY1130
Offset Voltage	2.0	1.0	2.0	2.5
CMMR	75dB	78dB	80dB	85dB
Supply Current	24mA	28mA	30mA	32mA
Slew Rate	±450	±475	±450	±500

To straddle two or more cells:

1. Select two or more adjacent cells in a row or column.

2. Select **Straddle** from the Table menu or use the keyboard shortcut **Esc t l** (the last character is a lowercase L).

To unstraddle a cell:

Select the cell and select **Unstraddle** from the Table menu (**Esc t l**). The items in the straddled cell will all be placed in the upper left cell. If you want to return them to their original locations in the unstraddled cell, you must cut and paste them.

The Table Designer

Many aspects of a table's formatting can be controlled with the Table Designer (Figure 20.13). The Table Designer is similar in operation to the Paragraph and Character Designers, described in Chapter 5. The designer has three groups of properties: Basic (shown in Figure 20.13), Ruling, and Shading. As with the Paragraph and Character Designers, the properties set in the Table Designer can be applied to the current selection, used to update all the tables with a particular format tag, applied to tables with a variety of different format tags, or stored in the catalog as a new format or as a modification of an existing format.

To open the Table Designer, select it from the Table menu, or use the keyboard shortcut **Esc t d** or **Ctrl+d**. Use the designer when you want to set any of the following properties, whether for a single table or a number of tables with the same table format tag (the process for setting each of these properties will be explained in subsequent sections):

Figure 20.13   The Basic Properties group in the Table Designer

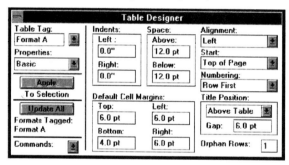

- The position of the title
- The position of the table relative to the column or page
- The default cell margins
- The default ruling and shading for the table
- The way autonumbering formats are applied to the contents of table cells

N O T E   Some of these properties, such as cell margins or ruling and shading, are set for the whole table from the designer, but can also be modified on a cell-by-cell basis with other controls located outside the designer. Frame refers to the controls that operate on individual cells as custom settings. The custom settings for the various properties will be explained in subsequent sections, along with the settings made from the designer.

Applying and Storing New or Modified Formats

The process of applying and storing new or modified table formats is exactly the same as that of applying and storing paragraph and character formats with the Paragraph and Character Designers. Therefore, a detailed description of the process will not be included here. Consult "Applying and Storing New or Modified Formats" in Chapter 5 if you are not already familiar with these operations.

Table Titles

The presence or absence of a table title, and its position relative to the table, if present, are Basic Properties set in the designer. These properties can be stored in the Table Catalog as part of a named format. The format of the title, including its numbering style, is an aspect of its paragraph format, set via the paragraph designer. By default, table titles have the form "Table n:", where n is the table number. You can add descriptive text to this basic title.

To add or remove the title or change its position, use the Title Position pop-up menu in the designer to select **No Title**, **Above Table**, or **Below Table**. The space between the title and the table is controlled by the **Gap** setting.

To change the numbering format, for example, to use Roman numerals or alphabetic characters rather than Arabic figures, or to append chapter or section numbers to the table numbers, edit the numbering properties of the table title paragraph format in the Numbering Properties group of the Paragraph Designer (see "Numbering Properties" in Chapter 5).

A table title can also include system variables to indicate continuation and specify the sheet number in multi-page tables (see "Working with Multi-page Tables," later in this chapter).

Controlling a Table's Position

A table's position relative to the page and columns where it is anchored is controlled by the **Indents**, **Space**, **Alignment**, and **Start** settings in the designer. These properties can all be stored in the Table Catalog as part of a table format. When a new format is applied to an existing table, these properties affect the table's position.

Indents

Table indents, in conjunction with the **Alignment** setting, determine a table's horizontal position in the column. If a table is left aligned, its left edge is set at the left indent position, or, if the indent is 0.0", at the left edge of the column. If a table is right aligned, its right edge is set at the right indent position, or, if the indent is 0.0", at the right edge of the column. If a table is center aligned, it is centered between the left and right indents, or, if both indents are 0.0", it is centered in the column. The indents are taken relative to the true edge of the column, regardless of whether a side-head format is in use (see "Side Heads," in Chapter 5).

Alignment

A table can be aligned at the left, in the center, or at the right in the column. As mentioned previously, if left or right indents have been specified, alignment is relative to the indents rather than to the column borders.

Space Above and Below

The vertical position of a table is determined by its **Space** and **Start** settings and by the position of its anchor. The **Space Above** and **Below** settings determine the space between the table and paragraphs above and below. These settings interact with those of the preceding and following paragraphs: The space inserted above a table is the greater of the preceding paragraph's **Space Below** setting and the table's **Space Above** setting; the space inserted below a table is the greater of the table's **Space Below** setting and the following paragraph's **Space Above** setting. The **Space Above** setting has no effect when the table is at the top of the column. The **Space Below** setting has no effect when the table is at the bottom of the column.

Start Position

By default, a table is normally placed immediately below the line where its anchor is located. You can control the position of a table in a column or on a page with the **Start** option. The Start pop-up menu in the designer shows several options: **Anywhere**, **Top of Column**, **Top of Page**, **Top of Left Page**, **Top of Right Page**, and **Float**. **Anywhere** is the default setting; unless prevented by other constraints, such as **Start** settings for particular rows (see later) or **Orphan** settings, this setting usually results in the table starting directly below the anchor row. Most of the other settings are more or less self-explanatory. Note, however, that the **Top of...Page** and **Top of Column** settings always mean the top of the page or column *following* the anchor position; there is no way to force a table to the top of the page or column with the anchor. The **Float** setting allows FrameMaker to move the table to the next column or page that can hold it. If the table moves to the next column or page, text from the next column flows back to fill the space between the table and the anchor.

The **Start** option leaves much to be desired. When you set a table to start at the top of a column or page, the table moves to the desired location, but all the text after the anchor moves after it! In the case of a **Top of Left Page** or **Top of Right Page** setting, this can, in some situations, result in a blank page being inserted between the anchor and the table. It is hard to imagine any circumstance in which this would be desirable. What is obviously needed is to make **Float** a check box to be used in combination with the other **Start** settings, as is the case with other anchored frames (see Chapter 14). In the absence of such a feature, in many cases the only practical way to deal with tables that you want positioned at the top or bottom of the page is to draw a disconnected text column at the desired location and anchor the table there. Trying to manage the position of a table that is more that one column wide in a multi-column format is a nightmare, especially where split columns are involved (see Chapter 14). Again, the only practical solution in many cases is to create a disconnected text column and anchor the table there.

Getting Rid of the "Phantom Space"—even when a table is at the top of an empty column and has a **Space Above** setting of 0.0", there will still be some blank space above the table. The problem is that FrameMaker regards the location with the anchor point as a paragraph, even when there is no paragraph mark there. Being a paragraph (usually a Body paragraph), it has its own **Space Below** and **Default Font Size** settings, which both contribute to the "phantom space." You can select the insertion point paragraph and use the Paragraph Designer to set its **Space Below** to zero, but you can't set a type size of zero points; whatever you enter for the Default Font Size, FrameMaker won't allow a size less than 2 points. So far as I have been able to discover, there is no way to reduce the Phantom Space below this minimum, which is, fortunately, acceptable in most situations.

Working With Multi-Page Tables

Controlling Page Breaks

If it can't fit a table entirely on one page, FrameMaker will split the table across the page break. Heading and footing rows will be duplicated on the next and subsequent pages, and the continued and sheet number variables, if used, will appear in the table titles. You can affect the way a table breaks between rows with the **Orphan Rows** setting in the designer and the **Start Row** and **Keep With** settings in the Row Format dialog box.

Orphan Rows

The **Orphan Rows** setting determines the minimum number of body rows (exclusive of heading and footing rows) that must be kept together on the page. The **Orphan Rows** setting can be stored as part of a table format. If a new format is applied to an existing table, this setting will be affected. You can enter an **Orphan**

Rows setting of 1 to 255. If you want to prevent a table from breaking, set a value equal to or greater than the number of rows in the table.

Keep With

Sometimes, it may be necessary to keep certain groups of rows together on a page in order for their meaning to be intelligible. If this is the case, you can ensure that the rows will stay together by using the **Keep With** option in the Row Format dialog box:

1. Select one or more rows that you want to keep on the same page with the next or previous row.

2. Select **Row Format** from the Table menu, or use the keyboard shortcut **Esc t r.**

3. Check **Next Row** and/or **Previous Row** in the Keep With box. (For example, you could keep three rows together by selecting the center row and checking both **Next Row** and **Previous Row.**

4. Click **Set** to apply the settings.

Keep With is a custom setting. It cannot be stored as part of a table format. When a new format is applied to an existing table, **Keep With** settings are not affected.

Start Row

Another way to control the way a table breaks between pages is with a **Start Row** setting in the Row Format dialog box. As with the **Start** setting for the whole table in the designer, a **Start Row** setting can be used to force a row to a particular location on the page. The available options are **Anywhere**, **Top of Column**, **Top of Page**, **Top of Left Page**, and **Top of Right Page**. The default setting is **Anywhere**. To apply a **Start Row** setting:

1. Select the row to which you want to apply the setting.

2. Select **Row Format** from the Table menu, or use the keyboard shortcut **Esc t r.**

3. Select a setting from the Start Row pop-up menu.

4. Click **Set** to apply the settings.

Start Row is a custom setting. It cannot be stored as part of a table format. When a new format is applied to an existing table, **Start Row** settings are not affected.

Using the "Table Sheet" and "Table Continuation" Variables

If you wish, you can insert the Table Sheet and/or Table Continuation system variables in the title or heading row of a table. (You will probably want to use one or the other, but not both.) If the table is continued across a page break, the message(s) specified by the variable definition(s) will be displayed as part of the table title or heading on the second and subsequent pages of the table. By default the Table Sheet Variable is defined as `Sheet <$tblsheetnum> of <$tblsheetcount>`, which will display something like "Sheet 2 of 3." The Continued variable has a default definition of `(Continued)`. You can change the definitions of either of these variables if you wish (see Chapter 9).

To insert either of the variables:

1. Place the insertion point in the title or heading of the table where you want the variable to appear (if the table is already split across a page break, do this on the first page).

2. Select **Variable** from the Special menu, or use the keyboard shortcut **Esc s v**.

3. Select the variable you want to insert from the scroll box in the Variable dialog box.

4. Click the **Insert** button to insert the variable.

Consult Chapter 9 for more information on working with variables.

Ruling and Shading

You can apply ruling (horizontal and vertical lines) and shading to your tables to make them more attractive and legible (or, if you don't use good judgment, with the opposite result). By default, FrameMaker applies horizontal and vertical rules to tables, but no shading. Shading is needed mainly in tables with very long rows or columns, to keep the reader's eye "on the track." It's also useful in situations where there are gaps in the rows and/or columns. Small tables with only three or four rows or columns don't really need rules or shading to be legible, but you may want to include them to maintain consistency.

FrameMaker uses two types of ruling and shading. Regular ruling and shading are set in the table designer and affect whole rows or columns. Regular ruling can be applied to tables as part of a stored format and is affected when a new format is applied to an existing table. Custom ruling and shading are applied to selected cells, rows, or columns via the **Custom Ruling & Shading** command on the Table menu. Custom rulings and shadings cannot be stored as part of a format, and are not altered when a table's format is updated.

Regular Ruling

You set up regular ruling for a table in the Ruling Properties group of the Table Designer (Figure 20.14). The Ruling Properties group allows you to select from six predefined ruling styles: **None**, **Double**, **Medium**, **Thick**, **Thin**, and **Very Thin**, plus any others you may have created. These predefined styles can be viewed and edited in the Custom Ruling and Shading dialog box (see later). The different types of Regular Rulings, described in subsequent paragraphs, are shown in Figure 20.15.

Figure 20.14   The Ruling Properties group in the Table Designer

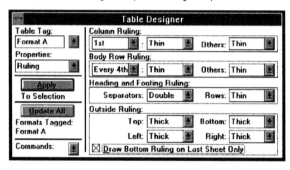

Figure 20.15   The various types of regular rulings

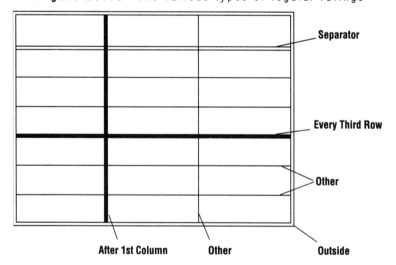

Column Ruling

In the Column Ruling section, you can select a special ruling to be placed after one particular column, for example, to separate a heading column from the body. Select the position for this rule from the pop-up menu that initially displays "1st" (the rule will appear to the right of the specified column). Select the weight for this rule from the next pop-up menu to the right (if you don't want to use this rule, select "None"). Select a weight for the rule to go between every pair of columns from the pop-up menu labeled "Others."

Body Row Ruling

In the Body Row Ruling section, you can select a ruling style to divide rows into regular groups, and another to use between every pair of body rows. To divide the rows into groups, select a frequency from the pop-up menu that initially displays "Every 4th." Select a weight for this rule from the next pop-up menu to the right (if you don't want to divide rows into groups, select a weight of "None"). Select a weight for the rule to go between every pair of body rows from the pop-up labeled "Others."

Heading and Footing Ruling

In the Heading and Footing Ruling section, you can select a separator to divide heading and/or footing rows from body rows, and a ruling to separate heading and footing rows if there is more than one of either. Select the weight for the separator from the pop-up menu labeled "Separators"; select the weight for the ruling to go between heading and/or footing rows from the pop-up menu labeled "Rows."

Outside Ruling

In the Outside Ruling section, you can select border rules for the table. There are separate pop-up menus for Top, Left, Bottom, and Right, though, in most cases, you will probably want to use the same line weight on all sides. If you don't want the bottom rule to appear at the bottom of the first page when a table is split across a page break, check the **Draw Bottom Ruling on Last Sheet Only** box.

Regular Shading

Use the Shading Properties group in the Table Designer (Figure 20.16) to apply shading to selected rows or columns in a table. For each of the options in the Shading Properties group, you select a percentage screen for the fill and a color from pop-up menus.

Figure 20.16   The Shading Properties group in the Table Designer

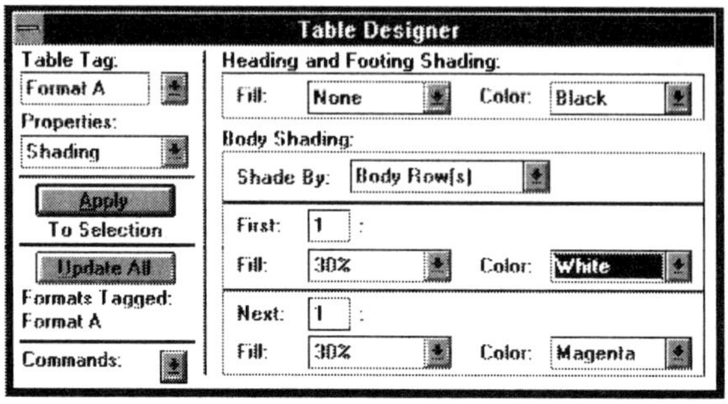

The first option in the group is **Heading and Footing Shading**. If your table includes heading and/or footing rows, you can specify a separate fill for these rows. You cannot specify separate shadings for headings and footings. If you wish to do this, you must use custom shadings. The remaining options in the group are concerned with body shading. The setting in the **Shade By** box determines whether shading in the body of the table will be applied to rows or columns. You cannot shade *both* rows *and* columns via the designer, but you can do this with custom shading (but who wants a plaid table?). The **First** and **Next** settings create a repeating pattern of shading in the rows or columns of the table. For example, if **Shade By** is set to Rows, the **First** settings are 1, 30, and magenta, and the **Next** settings are 2, None, and any color. This means the first body row will have a 30% magenta screen, the next two rows will have no shading, the fourth row will have the 30% magenta screen, the fifth and sixth rows will be unshaded, and so on to the bottom of the table (see Figure 20.17).

Figure 20.17   An example of regular shading

Parameters	OP Amps		Video Difference Amps	
	ZX2345	ZX2347	XY1128	XY1130
Offset Voltage	2.0	1.0	2.0	2.5
CMMR	75dB	78dB	80dB	85dB
Supply Current	24mA	28mA	30mA	32mA
Slew Rate	±450	±475	±450	±500
Gain Bandwidth	50MHz	55MHz	70MHz	72MHz
Output Current	50mA	55mA	60mA	66mA

Using Custom Ruling or Shading

In addition to the regular rulings and shadings created in the designer, you can apply custom rulings and shadings to any cells, rows, or columns that you want to draw attention to. Figure 20.18 is an example of a table with custom ruling and shading. Custom rulings and shadings cannot be stored as part of a format, nor are they affected when a new format is applied to an existing table. Custom rulings and shadings can only be removed in the way they are applied, with the Custom Rulings & Shadings dialog box, as described herein. To apply a custom ruling or shading:

1. Select the cells to which you wish to apply the custom ruling and/or shading.

2. Select **Custom Ruling & Shading** from the Table menu or use the keyboard shortcut **Esc t x**. This opens the Custom Ruling and Shading window (Figure 20.19).

3. In the Custom Ruling and Shading window, you can specify a custom ruling, a custom shading, or both. Specify which you want by checking the **Custom Cell Ruling** and/or **Custom Cell Shading** boxes.

4. If you selected a custom ruling, select a ruling style from the Apply Ruling Style list, and use the check boxes to specify where you want to apply the ruling: to the outside edge of the selection, to the borders of the cells inside the selection, or both.

5. If you selected a custom shading, select a screen percentage and a color from the pop-up menus at the bottom of the window.

6. Click the **Apply** button to apply the custom settings. The Custom Ruling and Shading window remains on the screen. You can select other cells and apply additional rulings and/or shadings, or close the window by double-clicking on its control box.

Figure 20.18   A table with custom ruling and shading

	OP Amps		Video Difference Amps	
Parameters	ZX2345	ZX2347	XY1128	XY1130
Offset Voltage	2.0	1.0	2.0	2.5
CMMR	75dB	78dB	80dB	85dB
Supply Current	24mA	28mA	30mA	32mA
Slew Rate	±450	±475	±450	±500

Figure 20.19 The Custom Ruling and Shading window

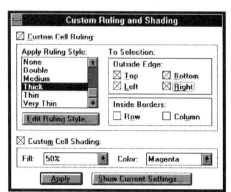

Removing a Custom Ruling or Shading

To remove a custom ruling or shading, select the cells with the ruling or shading and open the Custom Ruling and Shading window. To remove a custom ruling, check Custom Cell Ruling and select **From Table** in the Apply Ruling Style list. To remove a custom shading, check Custom Cell Shading and select **From Table** on the Fill and Color pop-up menus. Click **Apply** to remove the ruling and/or shading.

Creating or Editing a Ruling Style

You can also use the Custom Ruling and Shading dialog box to create a new ruling style or edit an existing ruling style:

1. Open the Custom Ruling and Shading window, as described earlier.

2. If you want to edit an existing ruling style, select the style in the Apply Ruling Style list. If you're going to create a new style, select anything except From Table.

3. Click the **Edit Ruling Style** button. This opens the Edit Ruling Style dialog box (Figure 20.20).

4. If you want to create a new style, type a new name in the Name box.

5. Select a color and a pen pattern (screen percentage) from the pop-up menus, and type a line width in the Width box.

6. Use the radio buttons to specify a single or double line. If you specify a double line, type a value for the gap between the lines.

7. Click the **Set** button to add the new or edited style to the list.

Figure 20.20 The Edit Ruling Style dialog box

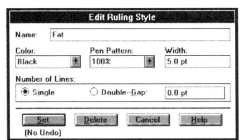

Deleting a Ruling Style

1. Open the Custom Ruling and Shading window, as described earlier.

2. Select the style to delete in the Apply Ruling Style list.

3. Click the **Edit Ruling Style** button. This opens the Edit Ruling Style dialog box.

4. Click the **Delete** button. If the style you are attempting to delete is used in the document, FrameMaker will warn you and prompt you to confirm the deletion.

Positioning Text in Table Cells

The position of text in table cells is controlled by the **Default Cell Margins** settings in the Basic Properties group of the Table Designer. The **Default Cell Margins** affect all the cells in a table, and can be stored as part of a table format. When a new format is applied to an existing table, the cell margins are affected. In addition, **Custom Cell Margins** can be applied to selected cells via the Table Cells group in the Paragraph Designer. The vertical alignment of text in table cells can be specified via the **Cell Vertical Alignment** option, also in the Table Cells group. And, of course, the horizontal alignment of text in table cells is affected by the **Alignment** setting in the Basic Properties group of the Paragraph Designer.

Default Cell Margins

Cell margins are the distances between the boundaries of the table cells and the edges of the table text columns. The margins are set in the Basic Properties group in the Table Designer, and apply to all cells in the table. You can set separate Top, Bottom, Left, and Right margins for the cells.

Custom Cell Margins

In addition to the default cell margins set in the Table Designer, you can set custom cell margins in the Table Cell Properties group of the Paragraph Designer (Figure 20.21). You can set separate Top, Bottom, Left, and Right margins for selected paragraphs. There are two types of custom margins, which you select from pop-up menus in the Cell Margins section. If you select **From Table Format Plus**, the value you enter is added to the default cell margin. Hence, if you change the default cell margins later, the margins will change, with the values you entered being added to the new defaults. If you select **Custom**, the value you enter is absolute; if you change the default margins later, the custom margins won't change.

Applying a custom top or bottom margin to a single paragraph may cause all the cells in the row to increase in height, but only the text in the selected cells will change its vertical alignment. Increasing the left or right margins of a cell will not affect the column width; it will just make the text column in the cell narrower and thus cause text to wrap sooner.

Figure 20.21   The Table Cell Properties group in the Paragraph Designer

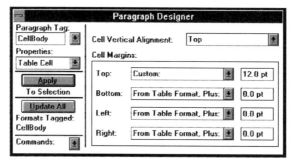

Custom Vertical Alignment

In addition to using custom cell margins, you can control the vertical position of text in table cells by applying a custom **Cell Vertical Alignment** in the Table Cell Properties group in the Paragraph Designer. The three options for this setting, Top Middle, and Bottom, are selected from a pop-up menu at the top of the Table Cell Properties group. These settings position the paragraphs to which they are applied relative to the top and bottom cell margins, whether default or custom.

Storing Custom Margins and Vertical Alignments in a Table Format

Custom cell margins and vertical alignments are part of the cells' paragraph formats, rather than of the table format. However, when you store the format of an existing table in the Table Catalog, FrameMaker stores the paragraph formats of the first (topmost) paragraph in each column's heading, footing, and body rows. If these paragraphs have custom margins and/or alignments as part of their paragraph formats, these are also stored. To clarify, only the format of the first paragraph in each column in each different type of row is stored. Hence, if you have a table with several body rows, only the formats from the cells in the first (topmost) row are stored. When you create a new table using the stored format, the paragraph formats from the top row of the previous table are applied to *all* body rows in the new table.

Numbering Order

If you use autonumbering formats in paragraphs in table cells, you have two choices for how numbers are applied to the cells: **Row First** or **Column First**. These options are selected from the Numbering pop-up menu in the Basic Properties group of the Table Designer. **Row First** means number the successive cells from left to right across a row before moving down to the leftmost cell in the next row. **Column First** means number the successive cells from top to bottom down a column before moving to the top cell in the next row to the right.

C HAPTER 21

Working With Equations

As recently as ten years ago, typesetting mathematics was an extremely rarefied discipline, a specialty within a specialty. Although computerized typesetting systems were then well on the way to replacing older, metal type technologies, these systems ran on expensive minicomputers and required highly trained operators. Mathematical typesetting was costly, difficult, and to be avoided wherever possible. Today, the situation has changed radically. With a little practice, and some examination of traditional models, anyone who can type can set complex mathematics on an inexpensive desktop computer, using FrameMaker's equation features.

Creating an Equation

The first step in creating an equation is placing an *equation object*. An equation object is a special kind of anchored frame in which you can place and manipulate math elements. Equation objects can be placed within body paragraphs (in-line equations), as separate paragraphs (display equations), or in frames with other objects. The three types are shown in Figure 21.1. Before placing an equation object or performing any of the other operations described in this chapter, you must open the Equations Palette (Figure 21.2) by clicking the Σ button at the right margin of the document window or selecting **Equations** from the Special menu.

Figure 21.1 Three types of equations

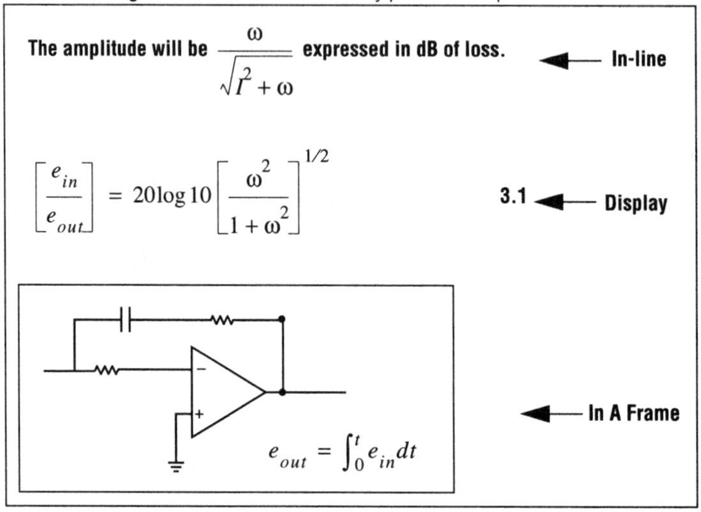

The amplitude will be $\dfrac{\omega}{\sqrt{\Gamma^2 + \omega}}$ expressed in dB of loss. ◀── **In-line**

$$\left[\frac{e_{in}}{e_{out}}\right] = 20\log 10 \left[\frac{\omega^2}{1 + \omega^2}\right]^{1/2}$$

3.1 ◀── **Display**

◀── **In A Frame**

$$e_{out} = \int_0^t e_{in}\,dt$$

Figure 21.2 The Equations Palette

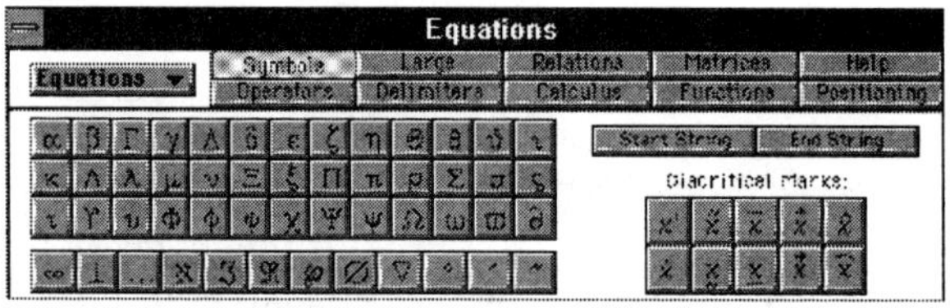

Placing an In-Line Equation

1. Click an insertion point in the text where you want to anchor the equation.

2. Open the Equations menu on the Equations Palette and select one of the three **New Equation** commands: **Small**, **Medium**, or **Large**. The sizes refer to the font sizes used for various elements in the equation; you can change the default sizes, as described later in this chapter.

3. The equation object appears as an empty frame below the line with the insertion point, with a highlighted question mark prompt in the center. The question mark will be replaced by the first math element you insert.

4. Insert the math elements in the equation. The procedures for placing the math elements will be described later in this chapter.

5. Open the Equations menu on the palette, and select **Shrink-Wrap**. This shrinks the frame around the equation to the minimum size necessary and places the equation in the text line at the anchor point.

6. If necessary, add spaces on either side of the equation to separate it from the surrounding text. FrameMaker treats an in-line equation as a character and doesn't automatically add extra space around it.

N O T E If the equation is too tall for the text line, either because it involves multiple lines, or because you have chosen a type size larger than your body type, it will overlap the lines above and/or below. To prevent this, you can select the body paragraph and turn off Fixed Line Spacing in the Paragraph Designer. This causes the line spacing to increase, making room for the equation. However, it is generally considered better typographic practice to set multi-line equations in display format.

Placing a Display Equation

1. Create an empty paragraph by pressing the **Enter** key at the end of the paragraph below which you wish to place the equation. Leave the insertion point in the new paragraph.

2. Apply an appropriate paragraph format to the empty paragraph. The **Horizontal Alignment**, **Left Indent**, and **Space Above** and **Below** settings for the paragraph affect the position of the equation, and you can use the autonumbering properties to number display equations. (See Chapter 5 for information on creating and applying paragraph formats.)

3. Open the Equations menu on the Equations Palette and select one of the three **New Equation** commands: **Small**, **Medium**, or **Large**.

4. The equation object appears as an empty frame below the insertion point, with a highlighted question mark prompt in the center. The question mark will be replaced by the first math element you insert.

5. Insert the math elements in the equation.

6. Open the Equations menu on the palette, and select **Shrink-Wrap**. This shrinks the frame around the equation to the minimum size necessary and places the equation in the empty paragraph.

N O T E

The **Space Above** and **Space Below** settings for the paragraph add space relative to the height of the paragraph's default font, not to the height of the equation. Hence, you will need to create much larger than normal **Space Above** and **Space Below** settings for the empty paragraph than you would for a normal text paragraph.

TIPS &
TECHNIQUES

Equation Numbering—equation numbers for display equations are normally right-aligned in the column. It is not necessary to number all displayed equations, only those that will be referred to by number in the text. However, it is good practice to display all numbered equations (that is, rather than set them in line).

Placing an Equation in a Frame

To place an equation as part of a figure, such as a graph of a function or a schematic diagram, place it in a frame (anchored or unanchored) with the graphic:

1. Select the frame or an object within the frame. The equation will initially be placed centered in the frame, but you can move it if you wish.

2. Open the Equations menu on the Equations Palette and select one of the three **New Equation** commands: **Small**, **Medium**, or **Large**.

3. The equation object appears as a highlighted question mark prompt in the center of the frame. The question mark will be replaced by the first math element you insert.

4. Insert the math elements in the equation.

5. Select the equation (**Ctrl**+click on it) and drag it to the correct position in the frame. If Snap is on, you will only be able to position the equation on snap grid ticks. You can also position the equation in the Object Properties dialog box. The top and left offsets refer in this case to the upper left corner of the frame, rather than of the page.

Inserting Math Elements

The main task in creating an equation is inserting the math elements: alphanumeric characters, operators, symbols, and text strings. You type alphanumeric characters and strings on your keyboard. Symbols, operators, and other special characters are inserted from the Equations Palette. You can also add symbols and other special characters by typing codes on your keyboard, and you will probably want to learn the codes for your most frequently used symbols to save time, but the great advantage of FrameMaker's equation feature is that you don't *have* to learn any abstruse codes in order to create even the most complex equations.

Adding Elements from the Keyboard

There are two ways to add math elements from the keyboard: with shortcuts, i.e., **Control**, **Alt**, or **Shift** key sequences, and backslash sequences, consisting of a strings of characters with a leading backslash (\). Most of the symbols on the Equations Palette have both shortcuts and backslash sequences. For example, you can insert a lowercase alpha (α) by pressing **Ctrl+Alt+a** or by typing `\alpha`. For a complete list of shortcuts, see the Shortcuts portion of the FrameMaker help system. You can also insert those elements that are on the keyboard, including Arabic figures, parentheses, brackets, braces, arithmetic operators, and alphabetic characters, by typing their normal keys.

The Equations Palette

The Equations Palette (Figure 21.2) has eight groups or pages of different special characters, grouped according to function, plus a ninth group for micro-positioning equation elements (new in FrameMaker 4.0). Use the buttons at the top of the palette to select the different pages:

- **Symbols**—Greek characters, atomic symbols, diacritical marks, and strings.

- **Operators**—addition, subtraction, multiplication, division, roots, exponents, subscripts, superscripts, and logic symbols.

- **Large**—sum, product, integral, intersection, and union signs.

- **Delimiters**—parentheses, brackets, braces, and substitution signs.

- **Relations**—equal, greater than, less than, and other comparison symbols; subset of, superset of, and proportional to signs.

- **Calculus**—integral, derivative, partial derivative, and limit signs.

- **Matrices**—matrices and matrix commands.

- **Functions**—trigonometric, hyperbolic, and logarithmic functions; commands for evaluating expressions and for creating and applying rules.

- **Positioning**—commands to micro-position equation elements, adjust spacing, align elements, and add or remove line breaks.

The Scope of an Operation

When you insert math elements in an equation, FrameMaker decides where to place them and how to adjust the positions of other elements based on the *scope* of the operation. FrameMaker determines the scope based on where the insertion point is placed or what elements are selected. For example, if you type the expression "$3ab$" followed by a slash ("/") and a *c* to create a fraction, you get the result $3a\frac{b}{c}$. If, on the other hand, you select the "$3ab$" and then type the slash and the *c*, you'll get the result $\frac{3ab}{c}$. In the first case, the scope of the division represented by the slash is only the *b*, whereas in the second case, it is the whole expression $3ab$. For another example, if you type the expression "$2x + 3y$," that is exactly what you get. If, on the other hand, you type "$2x + 3$," then select that expression before typing the *y*, you get $(2x + 3)y$. In the first case, the scope of the *y* is just the 3; in the second case, it is the expression $(2x + 3)$.

Inserting Symbols

The symbols page has Greek characters, other symbols, and diacritical marks. It does not include those Greek characters that are exactly the same as their Roman equivalents, such as the uppercase A, B, and E. It also has the commands for starting and ending a text string. To insert a symbol in an equation object, place the insertion point or select a range, depending on the scope to which you want the symbol to apply, and click the symbol on the palette.

 If you want FrameMaker to be able to evaluate your equations, don't use Greek characters from the symbols page for summation, product, or partial differential symbols. Insert these elements from the Calculus page.

N O T E

Inserting a String

A string is a group of characters in an equation that FrameMaker treats as a group. In Figure 21.3, "Ohms," "Volts," and "milliamperes" are strings. To type a string:

1. Click the **Start String** button on the symbol page, or type an apostrophe (') or quotation mark ("). A pair of quotation marks appear at the insertion point.

Figure 21.3 An equation containing strings

$$Ohms \ = \ \frac{Volts \times 10^3}{milliamperes}$$

2. Type the string. The quotation marks disappear when you start typing.

3. To end the string, click the **End String** button, or press **Enter**.

NOTE Strings have no mathematical meaning to FrameMaker, hence it cannot evaluate them as parts of equations. You should insert functions that are represented by strings of alphabetic characters, such as trig and log functions, from the functions page on the palette, rather than typing them as strings.

Inserting an Operator

Use the Operators page (Figure 21.4) to insert arithmetic operators (+, −, ×, ÷), exponents, signs, subscripts, superscripts, and logic symbols. To insert an operator in an equation object, place the insertion point or select a range, depending on the scope to which you want the operator to apply, and click the operator on the palette. Some operators produce two question mark prompts for the required elements; use the **Tab** key to move between the prompts.

Figure 21.4 The Operators page

FrameMaker has three division operators: a horizontal bar (—), a slash (/), and a division symbol (÷). When you select the horizontal bar or the slash, FrameMaker creates a fraction. You can change the division signs in an existing expression without retyping it by selecting the relevant portion of the expression and clicking the **Toggle Format** button above the division operator. FrameMaker will add parentheses when changing from a horizontal-bar fraction to a slash or division symbol if it is necessary to maintain the intelligibility of the expression.

It is often possible to fit a tall expression into an in-line equation without increasing the line spacing by substituting slashes or division symbols for horizontal bar fractions.

The Operators page has buttons for both superscripts and exponents in the leftmost group. The superscript button is in column 1, row 2; the exponent button is in column 4, row 3. The two buttons look alike, as do their results, but FrameMaker only evaluates exponents; it does not evaluate superscripts.

Inserting a Horizontal or Vertical List

Normally, an equation object contains a single expression or equation, but it is possible to create a horizontal or vertical list of equations, as in Figure 21.5. The buttons for creating lists are on the Operators page (Figure 21.4), where they appear as the first two buttons in the top row of the leftmost group. To create a list, select the expression that is to be the first item in the list and click the horizontal or vertical list button. The ? prompt appears to the right of or below the selection, as appropriate. Type or insert the new element and it will replace the prompt. To add new elements to an existing list, select the element to the left of or above the location where you want to add the new item and click one of the list buttons. FrameMaker aligns the expressions in a list automatically. For information on changing the alignment of expressions in a list, see "Aligning Items in a List or Multi-line Equation," and "Aligning Items in a Horizontal List," later in this chapter.

Figure 21.5   Horizontal and vertical lists of equations

$$Ra = \frac{3 \times 2}{11} = 0.545\Omega$$

$$Rb = \frac{3 \times 6}{11} = 1.64\Omega \quad \textbf{Vertical List}$$

$$Rc = \frac{2 \times 6}{11} = 1.09\Omega$$

$$\frac{K\omega_0}{S + \omega_0} \qquad \frac{K\omega_0^2}{S^2 + \frac{\omega_0}{Q}S + \omega_0^2} \qquad \textbf{Horizontal List}$$

Inserting a Large Element

Use the Large Element page on the palette (Figure 21.6) to insert sum, product, integral, contour integral, intersection, and union signs. (Integral and contour integral signs are also found on the Calculus page.) Each of these elements is available in several versions with one to three operands, as is evident from the figure. To insert a large element in an equation object, place the insertion point or select a range, depending on the scope to which you want the element to apply, and click the element on the palette. If you have selected an element with two or more operands, use the **Tab** key to move from one to another of the ? prompts.

Figure 21.6 The Large Element page

![The Large Element page palette]

To add operands to an existing sign, click on the **Add Operand** button. To change the vertical positions of the operands, click the **Toggle Format** button.

If you need to fit a large sign in an in-line equation, use the format that places all operators in front of, rather than above and below the sign.

Inserting Delimiters

The Delimiters page on the palette (Figure 21.7) includes delimiters such as parentheses, brackets, braces, and angle brackets, substitution signs, and other paired elements. To insert a pair of delimiters in an equation object, place the insertion point to insert an empty pair, or select an expression to place the delimiters around the expression, and click the expression on the palette. You can also insert a single parenthesis, bracket, or brace. FrameMaker automatically adjusts the height of the delimiters to accommodate the expression they enclose.

To change the format of delimiters among parentheses, braces, and brackets, select an expression and its delimiters and click the **Toggle Format** button. To remove a pair of delimiters, select the expression and the delimiters and click **Remove Parentheses**.

Figure 21.7 The Delimiters page

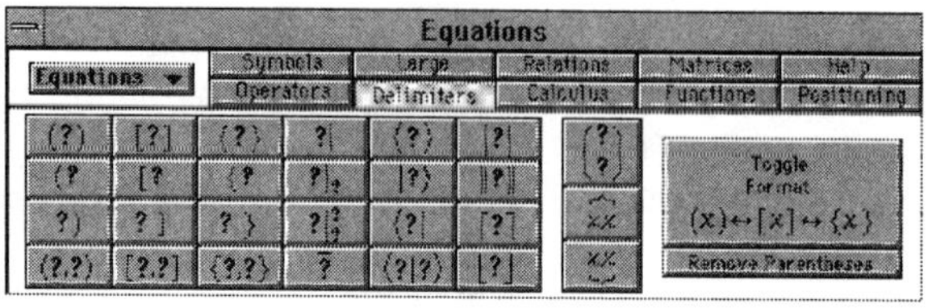

Figure 21.7 — the Equations palette showing the Delimiters page

NOTE

If the delimiters are added one at a time, rather than as a pair, the **Toggle Format** command doesn't work properly (it toggles only one of the pair) and the **Remove Parentheses** command has no effect.

TIPS & TECHNIQUES

The preferred order for delimiters is {[( )]}. This is the opposite of the order in which these characters are used in ordinary text. Angle brackets (<>), bars (I), and double bars (II) have special meanings in mathematics, and should not normally be used as delimiters.

Inserting Relations

Use the Relations page on the palette (Figure 21.8) to insert signs of numerical or set-theory relations. To insert a relation sign in an equation object, place the insertion point or select a range, depending on the elements to which you want the sign to apply, and click the sign on the palette. Except for the binary equal sign (? = ?), all relation signs apply to the elements to the left and right of the insertion point or to the selection. A sign inserted between multiplied elements applies to the elements on either side of the insertion point.

Figure 21.8 The Relations page

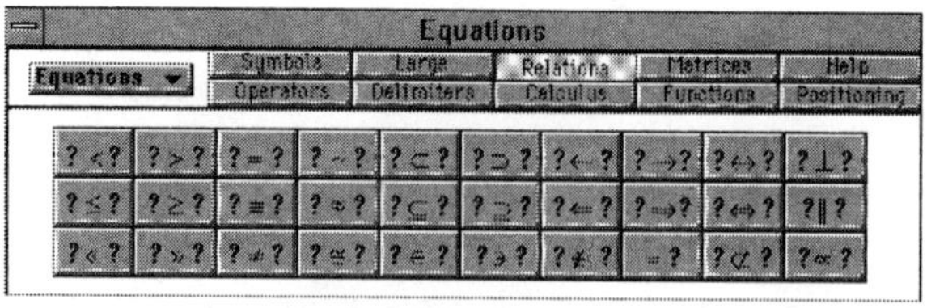

Figure 21.8 — the Equations palette showing the Relations page

When the insertion point is in an expression, a binary equal sign appears to the right of the expression. If the insertion point is in a subscript, the equal sign appears in the subscript. To insert an equal sign in an expression, press **Esc m =**.

Inserting Calculus Signs

Use the Calculus page in the palette to insert calculus signs, including integral, contour integral, derivative, gradient, and limit signs. To insert a calculus sign in an equation object, place the insertion point or select a range, depending on the scope to which you want the sign to apply, and click the sign on the palette. If you have selected a sign with two or more operands, use the **Tab** key to move from one to another of the ? prompts.

To add operands to an existing sign, click on the **Add Operand** button. To change the vertical positions of the operands, click the **Toggle Format** button.

Figure 21.9 The Calculus page

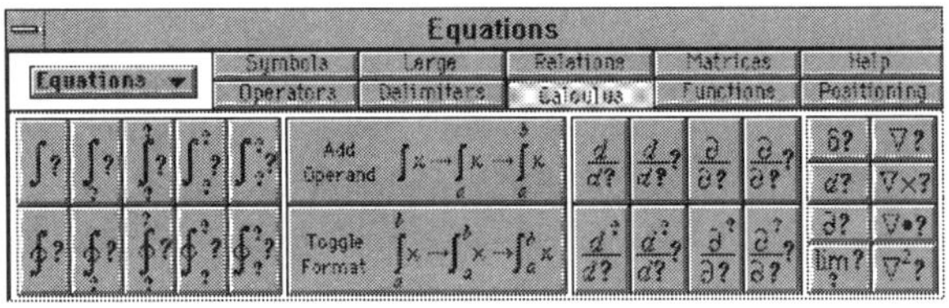

Inserting and Changing Matrices

The Matrix page on the palette (Figure 21.10) has commands for inserting and changing matrices. You can insert matrices ranging in size from 1×1 to 3×3 and add rows or columns to an existing matrix. To insert a matrix in an equation object, place the insertion point or select an expression, and click the desired matrix size on the palette. If an expression is selected, it becomes the first cell in the matrix. Use the **Tab** key to move among the ? prompts in the matrix.

Figure 21.10 The Matrix page

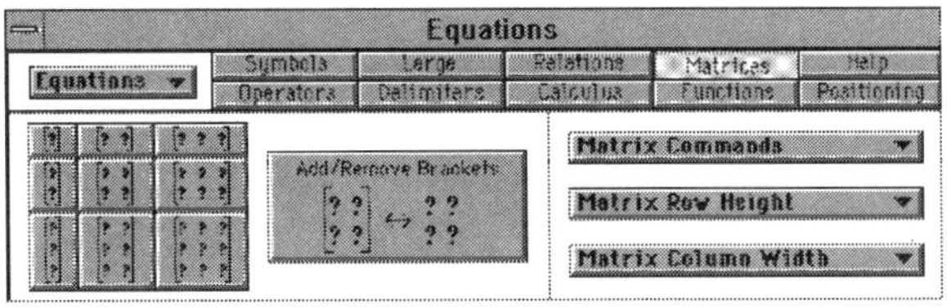

Adding and Deleting Rows or Columns

To add rows or columns to a matrix, place the insertion point in the matrix and open the Matrix Commands menu, then select **Add Row** or **Add Column**. Regardless of where the insertion point is located, new rows are added at the bottom and new columns are added at the right side of the matrix. To delete a row or column, select it and press the **Del** key.

For information on editing matrix row height and column width, see "Aligning Rows and Columns in a Matrix"; for information on performing matrix algebra and matrix transpositions, see "Matrix Commands" (both later in this chapter).

Inserting Functions

Use the Functions page on the palette (Figure 21.11) to insert trigonometric, hyperbolic, logarithmic, and other functions in equation objects. (The Function page also includes commands for addition, multiplication, division, evaluation, rules, and other rewrites, which will be described later.) To insert a function in an equation object, place the insertion point or select a range and click the function on the palette. If you have selected an expression, it becomes an argument of the function, except in the cases of the limit and general functions.

Figure 21.11   The Functions page

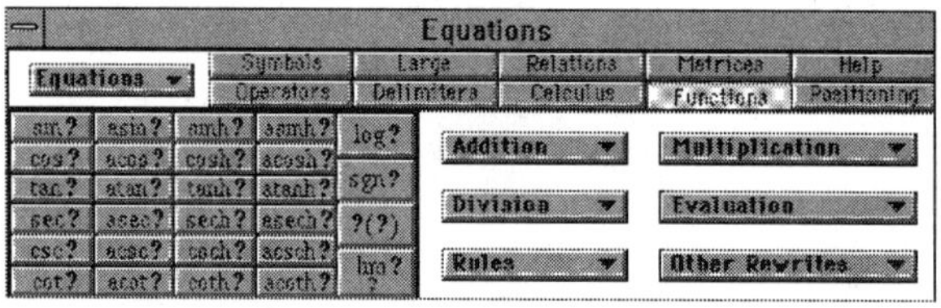

Creating and Inserting Custom Math Elements

If you need a special symbol or sign that is not provided on the equation palette, you can create it. However, FrameMaker cannot mathematically evaluate custom elements that you create. You can also change the definitions of some elements provided by FrameMaker, but you can't change the behavior of built-in elements, just their appearance.

Use the following procedure to create a custom math element or modify an existing element:

1. Display or create a FrameMath reference page. If this is the first custom math element you have attempted to create, your document will probably not include a FrameMath reference page. To create one, switch the view to Reference Pages (**Esc v R**), and select **Add Reference Page** from the Special menu (**Esc s p a**). In the Add Reference Page dialog box, give the new page the name FrameMath1.

2. Using the Frame tool on the Tools Palette, draw an unanchored frame on the reference page. The frame need only be large enough to accommodate the character(s) for the custom element.

3. In the dialog box that appears, type the name of the custom element as the name of the frame. If you're modifying the definition of an existing element, you must use the exact name that FrameMaker uses for that element. To see the list of names, select **Insert Math Element** from the Equations menu on the Equations Palette. Uncheck the **Show Custom Only** check box to show the complete list of names in the scroll box. (You must display a body page and place an insertion point in an equation to display the list.)

4. In the frame you have created, use the Text Line tool on the Tools Palette to create a text line. Type the character(s) comprising the custom element on the text line. The operands for the element are determined by the element's type in step 6. If you're defining a pair of delimiters, leave a space between them to indicate the location of an operand. You can use any characters for the element, and you can format them with the **Font**, **Size**, or **Style** options on the Format menu or via the Character Designer. You can also shift the positions of the characters horizontally or vertically using the **Alt**+arrow keys.

5. Select the frame.

6. Select **Add Definition to Catalog** from the Equations menu on the palette. If you're adding a new custom element, select a type from the pop-up menu (you can't change the type of an existing element). An element's type determines the number and position of its operands (see Table 21.1 for an explanation of types).

7. Click **Add**.

Inserting a Custom Element

1. Place the insertion point in an equation, or select existing elements. (How the custom element interacts with a selection depends on its type.)

2. Open the Equations menu on the palette and select **Insert Math Element** (**Esc m i**).

3. In the Insert Math Element dialog box, select the name of the custom element in the scroll box. To make it easier to find your custom definition, check the **Show Custom Only** check box.

4. Click **Insert**.

Table 21.1 User-definable math element types and their operands

Type	Example	Number of operands
Atom	α	None
Infix	$\alpha \times \beta$	Two, to left and right of element
Prefix	$\pm\alpha$	One, to left of element
Postfix	$\alpha!$	One, to right of element
Delimiter	(α)	One
Large	$\int_0^t e$	One to three, above, to right of, and below element
Vertical list	α β γ	Variable
Function	$\cos\theta$	One, to right of element
Limit	$\lim_{x\to\infty}\dfrac{1}{x^2}$	One or two, below and to the right of element

Editing Equations

You edit an equation much as you edit ordinary text; You can cut, copy, delete, and paste elements, and also use the delete and backspace keys to remove elements. As you cut, delete, and paste elements, FrameMaker adjusts the syntax of the equation as required. Some special editing commands found on the various pages of the palette, such as those for changing the division operator, removing parentheses, adding rows and columns to a matrix, adding operands to various calculus signs, and toggling the formats of various elements, were described in the previous section.

Editing an equation differs from editing normal text in the way that insertion-point movement and element selection work. FrameMaker treats the elements in an equation as meaningful expressions and sub-expressions. Hence, it will not necessarily allow you to arbitrarily select and cut or delete any sequence of characters, or paste it in any location you wish. You select elements in an equation by dragging through them, as with normal text, but the results may not always be what you expect. As you drag, the selection expands by incorporating additional sub-expressions; thus it sometimes expands in the opposite direction to that in which you are dragging, or it may expand vertically when you drag horizontally, or vice versa. Another way to expand a selection is to select a single character or expression, then press the **Spacebar**. Each successive press incorporates additional expressions until the entire equation is selected.

You can also move a selection around in an equation with the arrow keys. Select a single character or expression, then press an arrow key to move it.

Unwrapping an Equation

If the equation you want to edit has been "shrink-wrapped," as is normally the case with in-line or display equations, you will probably want to unwrap the equation before editing it, so you will have adequate working space.

1. Select the frame containing the equation (**Ctrl**+click on it).

2. Open the Equations menu on the palette and select **Unwrap Equation** (**Esc m e**).

Deleting an Element

To delete an element, select it and press **Del**. The element disappears and is replaced by a ? prompt. If you're not going to replace the element with something similar, press **Del** again to delete the prompt. Any elements that are no longer needed, such as a sign connecting the deleted element to other elements in the equation, will also be deleted when you delete the prompt.

Deleting an Equation

To delete a whole equation, select all the elements and press **Del**. This deletes the equation, but leaves the empty frame. If you want to delete everything, select the frame and press **Del**.

Replacing an Element

Another way in which editing an equation differs from editing text is in the way you replace an element. If you select an element and then type or click on the replacement, the new element is added to the old (the selected element is assumed to be the scope of operation to which you want to apply the new element). You must delete the old element first, then insert the replacement.

Cutting, Copying, and Pasting Elements

You can cut or copy an element from one location and paste it at a different location in the same equation, or in another equation:

1. Select the item to cut or copy, as described previously.

2. Select **Cut** (**Ctrl+X**) or **Copy** (**Ctrl+C**) from the Edit menu. If you select **Cut**, the element that is cut may be replaced by a ? prompt.

3. Move the insertion point to the location where you want to place the element. If you want to replace an existing element, select it.

4. Select **Paste** from the Edit menu (**Ctrl+V**).

N O T E

Because of the rules regarding scope, it may not be practical to paste certain elements at certain locations in an equation, and you may have to add them from the palette instead.

Formatting Equations

Although the way it formats equations by default is usually satisfactory, FrameMaker offers a variety of options for modifying equation formats. You can adjust spacing and position within equations, microposition individual elements, select different fonts for different types of elements, control line breaks, and control how lines in a multi-line equation or multiple equations on a page are aligned.

Micropositioning Elements

FrameMaker positions the elements in an equation according to their mathematical meaning and adds spacing based on their definitions, but you may want to "fine-tune" the positions of certain elements, either for aesthetic reasons or to achieve greater clarity. You can position individual elements or expressions with the controls on the Positioning page (Figure 21.12—new in FrameMaker 4.0)

Figure 21.12 The Positioning page

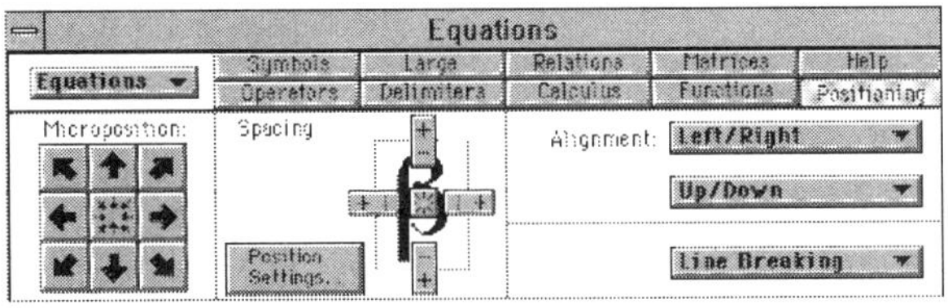

To reposition an element or expression, select it, as described previously, then click one of the micropositioning arrows (the matrix of outward-pointing arrows at the left side of the Positioning page—see Figure 21.12) to move it in the desired direction. Only the selected elements move. For example, if you select the middle element in a group and press the left arrow, the selected element will move toward the element to its left and away from that on its right. Each click on an arrow moves the selected element(s) one pixel in the desired direction on the screen, so larger magnifications result in smaller movements, and vice versa. Select your magnification accordingly, i.e., use higher magnification for greater precision. To return an element to its default position, click the button on the center of the matrix. You can also examine the position of an element or expression, relative to its default position, and/or adjust its position numerically via the Math Element Position Settings dialog box (Figure 21.13). To open the dialog box, click on the **Position Settings** button on the Positioning Page. To change an expression's position in the dialog box, type new values in the **Left/Right** and/or **Up/Down Microposition Offset** boxes, then click **Set**.

Adjusting Spacing

The four buttons surrounding the oversized "beta" (β) on the Positioning page can be used to increase or decrease the white space around an element or expression. Select the element, then click the plus sign on one of the buttons to add space in the desired direction, or click the minus sign to subtract space in the desired direction. As with the micropositioning matrix, the amount of space added depends on the magnification. Each click adds or subtracts one pixel in the indicated direction, so use a low magnification for coarse adjustments and a high magnification for fine ones. To restore the original spacing of the selected elements, click the center button. You can also examine the spacing of an element or expression, relative to its default spacing, and/or adjust its spacing numerically via the Math Element Position Settings dialog box. To open the dialog box, click on the **Position Settings** button on the Positioning page. To change an expression's spacing in the dialog box, type new values in the **Top**, **Bottom**, **Left** and/or **Right Spacing** boxes, then click **Set**.

Figure 21.13 The Math Element Position Settings dialog box

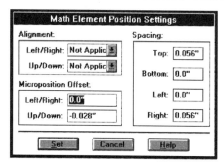

Editing the Spacing in a Math Element Definition

In addition to changing the spacing around selected elements and expressions, you can edit the spacings in the definitions of certain math elements. You can edit the spacings of elements of the following types: infix, prefix, postfix, large, scripts, and the division bar (see Table 21.1 for an explanation of the element types):

1. Adjust the spacing around the selected element in one equation.

2. Open the Equations menu on the palette and select **Update Definition** (**Esc m U**).

3. In the Update Definition dialog box, make sure that the name of the correct element is displayed, then click **Update**. The spacing in the definition is updated with the spacing from the selected item on the screen.

To restore the spacing for a selected element to its default, follow the preceding instructions, but click the **Get Default** button in the dialog box.

You can also edit the horizontal and vertical spacing ("spread") for all the characters in equations of a given size (Small, Medium, or Large); see "Setting Standard Character Sizes," later in this chapter.

N O T E

Aligning Equations

Alignment involves several independent factors, including the setting of automatic or manual line breaks in multi-line equations, the horizontal alignment of display equations within their anchored frames, the horizontal alignment of items in multi-line equations or vertical lists, or of multiple equations in a text column, the vertical alignment of items in horizontal lists, and the alignment of cells in matrices.

Controlling Line Breaks

There are two types of line breaks in equations: automatic and manual. An automatic line break setting takes the form of a width value after which an equation will wrap to a new line. Automatic line break is on by default, and is based on the width of the frame in which the equation is placed. To set automatic line break for an equation, place the insertion point in the equation or select it, then select **Object Properties** from the Graphics menu (**Esc g o**). If necessary, check the **Automatic Line Break After** check box and type a value in the text box at the right. Click **Set** to exit the dialog box and activate the new setting. If required, FrameMaker will try to break the equation between expressions, as is proper.

To place a manual line break, place the insertion point at the desired location, open the Line Breaking menu on the Positioning page of the palette, and select **Set Manual** (**Esc m b s**). To remove a manual line break, select elements on both sides of the break, open the Line Breaking menu, and select **Clear Manual** (**Esc m b c**).

If an equation is shrink wrapped, unwrap it before adding line breaks to prevent material from being pushed below the bottom of the frame. After you have set the line breaks, rewrap the equation.

N O T E

Changing the Horizontal Alignment of a Display Equation

The alignment of the frame containing a display equation in the text column is controlled by the properties of the paragraph in which the frame is anchored. To change the alignment of a display equation, select the paragraph mark for the empty paragraph where the frame is anchored. Use the alignment button on the Formatting Bar or the Alignment pop-up menu in the Basic Properties group of the Paragraph Designer to set the alignment to **Left**, **Center**, or **Right** (**Justified** alignment has no meaning in this context; it produces the same result as **Left** alignment). As mentioned earlier in this chapter, the **First Line Indent** setting of the paragraph also affects the horizontal alignment of a display equation.

To simplify the placement of display equations, create a paragraph format with the appropriate alignment and indent settings and apply it whenever you create an empty paragraph in which to anchor a display equation.

Aligning Items in a List or a Multi-Line Equation

You can horizontally align the lines of a multi-line equation or the items of a vertical list along their left or right edges or their centers, along the left or right edge of the equal sign, or to a manual alignment point that you select. (You can also align multiple equations in a text column, but that involves a different technique, as described later.) To align the lines of a multi-line equation or vertical list:

1. Place the insertion point anywhere in the equation or list.

2. Open the Alignment Left/Right menu on the Positioning page of the palette.

3. Select one of the options from the menu.

Use a manual alignment point to make items in a vertical list or lines in a multi-line equation left-align at a selected point in one of the lines. If you put the alignment point in the top line of the list or equation, all the other lines will left-align to that point. You can put manual alignment points at different locations in different lines, and those points will align along a vertical line. Only one manual alignment point can be placed in a given line or list item. To manually align a list or multi-line equation:

1. Click an insertion point where you want to place the alignment point.

2. Open the Alignment Left/Right menu on the Positioning page and select **Set Manual (Esc m a s)**. A manual alignment symbol (I) will appear at the insertion point and the lines will align as appropriate.

To remove a manual alignment point:

1. Select the portion of the line(s) where the alignment symbol(s) to be removed are located.

2. Open the Alignment Left/Right menu on the Positioning page and select **Clear Manual (Esc m a d)**. Adding a new alignment point in a line also replaces any existing alignment point in that line.

Aligning and Spacing Multiple Equation Objects in a Frame

You can use the **Align** and **Distribute** commands on the Graphics menu to arrange a group of equations in a single frame. Use the **Align** command to horizontally or vertically align a group of selected equations:

1. Select the equation objects that you want to align (**Ctrl**+click on the first object, then **Ctrl+Shift**+click on the remaining objects). Select the object to which you want to align the others *last*.

2. Select **Align** on the Graphics menu or use the keyboard shortcut **Esc g a**.

3. In the Align dialog box, select a **Left/Right** or **Top/Bottom** alignment. In most cases, you will probably want to set a **Left/Right** alignment (Left, Center, or Right) and leave the **Top/Bottom** alignment As Is; however, if you have a number of vertical lists side by side, it may be useful to set a **Top/Bottom** alignment.

4. Click **Align** to set the alignment.

Use the **Distribute** command to achieve even spacing between equations in a frame. Consult Chapter 12 for information on using the **Distribute** command. You can also use the **Rotate** command on the Graphics menu to rotate an equation in 90° increments.

Aligning Equations in Different Frames

You can use the **Offset From Left** setting in the Object Properties dialog box to align a number of equation objects in different frames. (This technique also works with equations that are in the same frame, although the technique described previously is quicker, but it is the *only* technique for aligning objects that are in different frames.) You can align equation objects Left, Center, Right, or at Manual Alignment points in this way.

1. (Optional) If you are going to use manual alignment points, place the alignment points at the desired locations in each of the objects you want to align, as described previously.

2. Select the first of the equation objects that you want to align (**Ctrl**+click on the object).

3. Select **Object Properties** from the Graphics menu, or use the keyboard shortcut **Esc g o**.

4. In the Object Properties dialog box, set the desired alignment (**Left**, **Center**, **Right**, or **Manual**) and enter an **Alignment Point Offset From Left** value. You can also set an **Offset From Top** value if you wish.

5. Click **Set**.

6. Repeat steps 2–5 for each of the objects you want to align, using the same alignment and offset.

The **Offset from Left** setting is relative to the left edge of the frame, so the left edges of all the frames holding the equations must be aligned for the preceding technique to work properly. To be sure, select the

N O T E

frames one at a time and check their **Offset from Left** settings in the Object Properties dialog box.

Aligning Items in a Horizontal List

Items in horizontal lists can be vertically aligned along their tops, bottoms, or baselines:

1. Select all or part of one of the list items you want to align.

2. Open the Alignment Up/Down menu on the Positioning page of the palette.

3. Select one of the three options: **Top (Esc m a t)**, **Baseline (Esc m a b)**, or **Bottom (Esc m a B)**.

When one of the items in a list that is being **Baseline** aligned is a horizontal-bar fraction, other items will be center-aligned vertically on the bar.

N O T E

Aligning Rows and Columns in a Matrix

You can align the elements (cells) in a matrix horizontally and/or vertically using the Alignment Left/Right and Up/Down menus on the Positioning Page of the palette:

1. Place the insertion point anywhere in the matrix that you want to align.

2. To align the columns, select an option from the Alignment Left/Right menu. The command will align all the columns in the matrix, regardless of the location of the insertion point.

3. To align the rows, select an option from the Alignment Up/Down menu. The command will align all the rows in the matrix, regardless of the location of the insertion point.

Changing Row Height or Column Width in a Matrix

There are two options for row height and column width in a matrix: All Equal and Proportional. These settings apply to all rows and columns in a matrix. All Equal means make all rows tall enough to accommodate the tallest element in any row and make all columns wide enough to accommodate the widest element in any row. Proportional means make each row tall enough to accommodate its tallest element and make each column wide enough to accommodate its widest element. To apply these settings, select the matrix, and open the Matrix Row Height or Matrix Column Width pop-up menu on the Matrices page of the palette. Select **All Equal** or **Proportional** from the menu.

Selecting and Changing Equation Fonts

FrameMaker 4.0 offers increased flexibility over version 3.0 in selecting fonts for use in equations. You can apply character formats to individual elements in an equation and choose from a variety of fonts for your Greek and symbolic characters, in addition to selecting defaults for the fonts used for different types of elements.

Setting Standard Character Sizes

FrameMaker uses predefined sets of character sizes for the three standard equation sizes (Small, Medium, and Large). You can modify these predefined character sizes. When you do so, you change the character sizes in all current and future equations in the document. To edit the standard character sizes:

1. Open the Equations menu on the palette and select **Equation Sizes** (**Esc e p**). This opens the Equation Sizes dialog box (Figure 21.14).

2. In the dialog box, edit the default sizes of any elements you wish. You can also edit the Horizontal Spread (the horizontal spacing between characters—what typesetters call letter spacing) and the Vertical Spread (one aspect of the vertical spacing around elements).

3. Click **Set** to activate the new settings.

To restore the default size and spread settings, open the Equation Sizes dialog box, click **Get Defaults**, then click **Set**.

Figure 21.14 The Equation Sizes dialog box

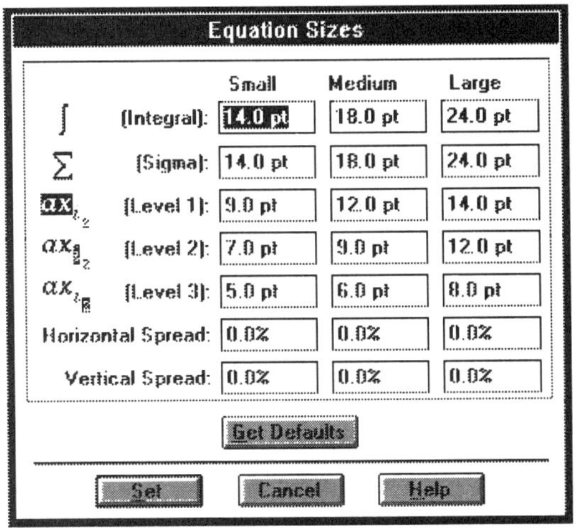

Setting Standard Fonts

FrameMaker can use different fonts for math symbols, functions, numbers, strings, and equation variables. By default, it uses the Symbol font for symbols, Times Roman for functions, numbers, and strings, and Times Italic for variables. To change any of these font selections, open the Equations menu on the palette and select **Equation Fonts**. This opens the Equation Fonts dialog box (Figure 21.15). Select a new font for any of the items described previously from their respective pop-up menus. The Math Symbols pop-up menu shows only appropriate math fonts, such as Lucida Math, Mathematical Pi, Universal Greek and Math Pi, or the like. If no such fonts are installed on your system, it will show only Symbol. The remaining pop-up menus show character formats rather than specific fonts. Any character format that was in the template upon which your document is based or that you created with the Character Designer will appear on these menus. Select the fonts for the various elements, then click **Set**.

Figure 21.15 The Equation Fonts dialog box

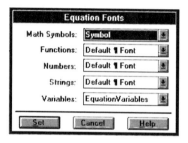

Select one font family for use in all the math elements except the symbols. You might want to select a contrasting family from that used for your body type, for example, a sans serif face for use with a serif body type. However, if you're using in-line equations, be sure to take into account how the two fonts look together in a line. Unless you have a good reason for doing otherwise, use italic for variables and Roman/regular for functions, as is conventional. Roman should probably be used for strings also, although I know of no firm rule on this point.

Applying Character Formats to Selected Elements

In addition to selecting character formats for classes of items, as described in the preceding section, you can also apply character formats directly to selected elements, albeit with certain restrictions. You can't apply underline, overline, strikethrough, change bars, superscript/subscript, or pair kerning to an expression with a character format. Most of these attributes can be applied to expressions via the Equations Palette. (Subscripts and superscripts are on the Operators page; underline and overline are among the diacritical marks on the Symbols page; use micropositioning in place of pair kerning.) Neither can you change the font or other properties of Greek and symbol characters or some operators with a character format. The font for all symbol characters must be set in the Equation Fonts dialog box, as described previously. Within these restrictions, you can apply any character format property in elements in equations. For example, you might want to use a character format to set certain items in a script or blackletter font where appropriate.

Evaluating Equations

Unlike other desktop publishing and word processing applications, which treat equations as static pieces of typographic art, FrameMaker has a variety of commands for evaluating and manipulating equations mathematically. Except for those involving matrices, these commands are located on a group of six pop-up menus on the Functions page of the Equation Palette. All these commands require that you first select an expression or group of expressions. To work properly, the selected expression(s) must contain elements appropriate to the command.

Addition Commands

Add Fractions (Esc m m a)—adds the selected fractions and expresses the result as a single fraction; like terms are combined.

Order Sum (Esc m a o)—arranges polynomials in order of decreasing powers of a selected variable. Select the variable in the equation before selecting this command.

Order Sum Reverse (Esc m a O)—arranges polynomials in order of increasing powers of a selected variable. Select the variable in the equation before selecting this command.

Multiplication Commands

Factor (Esc m u f)—factors a selected term out of a product. Select the desired term before executing this command.

Factor Some (Esc m u F)—factors the selected term from only those items that contain it. Select the desired term before executing this command.

Multiply Out (Esc m u m)—simplifies the selected expression, distributes multiplication over division, and expands a selected term raised to a positive integral power.

Multiply Out Once (Esc m u M)—multiplies the first pair of factors on the left side of a selected expression.

Distribute (Esc m u d)—performs a variety of operations, depending on the selection, including distributing division over addition, distributing multiplication over addition, and transforming products and quotients involving radicals or exponents to single expressions raised to a power.

Distribute Over Equality (Esc m u D)—performs the same operation on both sides of an equation.

Division Commands

Long Division (Esc m d l)—performs long division on fractions with a polynomial numerator and denominator.

Remove Division (Esc m d d)—converts division to multiplication in the selected expression by changing positive exponents to negative and vice versa.

Remove Division 1 Level (Esc m d D)—converts division to multiplication as in the previous command, but applies only to the first level of operators.

Remove Negative Powers (Esc m d n)—converts negative exponents to positive by replacing multiplication with division and vice versa.

Remove Negative Powers 1 Level (Esc m d N)—converts negative exponents to positive, as in the previous command, but applies only to the first level. If the selected expression has no negative powers at the first level, the command has no effect.

Evaluation Commands

Number Crunch (Esc m v n)—changes the integers in the selection to floating point numbers and evaluates the expression. If evaluation results in undefined value, Number Crunch displays "NaN" ("Not a Number"); if evaluation would result in a value too large to calculate, it displays infinity.

Show All Digits (Esc m v.)—displays up to 15 decimal places for a floating point number.

Evaluate (Esc m v e)—evaluates the selected expression. This command performs a variety of operations, depending on the selection:

- Displays an expression raised to a power less than 20 as a product
- Computes the factorial of an integer

- Computes the determinant of a matrix

- Extracts a term from a sum or product

- Computes a substitution like the Evaluate Substitution command (see next)

- Rewrites an "evaluate between" operator as a difference

- Rewrites a logarithm of a product as a sum of logarithms, or rewrites a logarithm of a power as a product

- Rewrites a logarithm to a base in terms of natural logarithms

- Rewrites a "choice" function in terms of factorials

Evaluate Substitution (Esc m v s)—performs the specified substitution and then simplifies the expression. If an "evaluate between" expression is selected, it is rewritten as a difference.

Evaluate Integrals (Esc m v i)—rewrites a selected integral with a polynomial integrand. This turns a definite integrand into an indefinite integrand. Repeat the command several times to fully integrate a polynomial.

Evaluate Derivatives (Esc m v d)—evaluates a selected derivative, applying the chain rule to complex expressions when necessary. It evaluates a partial derivative only when all dependencies are explicitly written. This command treats elements in a total derivative as if they depend on the variable of differentiation. Use the Evaluate command to evaluate an nth derivative before applying this command.

Evaluate Derivatives 1 Level (Esc m v D)—evaluates only the first level of the selected derivative.

Rules Commands

Enter Rule (Esc m r e)—stores a rule for substituting one expression for another. Select the expression you want to store as a rule before you select the command. You can store only one rule at a time.

Apply Rule (Esc m r a)—substitutes one term or set of terms for another based on a rule stored with the previous command.

Designate Dummy (Esc m r d)—designates a selected term as a dummy variable. A dummy variable in a rule allows you to substitute the expression on the right side of the rule for any variable, not just the variable named in the rule. Select the term you want to be a dummy variable before you select the command.

Other Rewrite Commands

Simplify (Esc m o s)—simplifies the selected expression. This command may take a variety of actions, depending on the selection:

■ Performs integer arithmetic

■ Groups terms in a sum or product

■ Cancels common factors in a fraction

■ Interprets the complex number i

■ Distributes exponentiation across multiplication and division

Simplify Some (Esc m o S)—simplifies the selected expression, like the previous command, but does not multiply fractions.

Isolate Term (Esc m o i)—isolates a selected expression on one side of the equal sign. This command does not combine terms or solve for the selected term.

Expand First Term (Esc m o e)—expands the first term of a selected summation or product.

Expand All Terms (Esc m o E)—expand all terms of a selected summation or product.

Matrix Commands

The matrix commands are located on the Matrix Commands menu on the Matrices page of the Equations palette (they include the commands for adding and formatting rows and columns described earlier).

Matrix Transpose (Esc x t)—interchange the rows and columns of the selected matrix (the whole matrix must be selected).

Matrix Algebra (Esc x a)—performs matrix multiplication and addition, and evaluates dot and cross products in a selected matrix. After you have performed matrix algebra, you can remove like terms with the **Simplify** command on the Other Rewrites menu, described earlier.

CHAPTER 22

Creating Multiple Versions with Conditional Text

What Is Conditional Text?

Conditional text is a unique FrameMaker feature that allows you to create multiple versions of a document in a single file. Different elements in the document, including text, graphics, tables, table rows, cross-references, footnotes, and variables, can be assigned *condition tags*. All the elements with a given condition tag can be hidden or revealed with a simple command. Hidden conditional text has no effect on the format of a document. You can assign different attributes and/or colors to the different condition tags (*condition indicators*) to make it easy to distinguish among them when you are writing and editing, and you can turn off the indicators when you are ready to print your document(s). You can even merge two existing versions of a document to create a single, conditional version. Figure 22.1 shows three versions of a conditional paragraph: one with both versions showing and condition indicators turned on, the other two with one tag hidden and the other showing, and with the indicators turned off.

Use conditional text whenever you need to create two or more versions of a document that have much text in common but also differ significantly in some respects; for example, manuals for versions of a program that run on different platforms, or wholesale and retail catalogs for the same group of products. You can also use conditional text to add non-printing comments to a document, either to remind yourself of things that need to be added or revised, or to alert your editors or reviewers to important issues.

Figure 22.1 Three versions of a conditional document

Both Conditions

~~Boot your system~~Start Windows as you
normally do and proceed as follows:

1. Place diskette one in the appropriate
   diskette drive (A or B).

2. <u>Open the File menu in the Windows</u>
   <u>Program Manager or File Manager and</u>
   <u>select Run, then</u> ~~At the DOS prompt,~~
   type **[drive]:setup**, where [drive] is

Condition 1

Start Windows as you normally do and
proceed as follows:

1. Place diskette one in the appropriate
   diskette drive (A or B).

2. Open the File menu in the Windows
   Program Manager or File Manager and
   select Run, then type **[drive]:setup**,
   where [drive] is

Condition 2

Boot your system as you normally do and
proceed as follows:

1. Place diskette one in the appropriate
   diskette drive (A or B).

2. At the DOS prompt, type **[drive]:setup**,
   where [drive] is

Creating a New Condition Tag

The first step in working with conditional text is to create the necessary condition
tags for your document. (All FrameMaker documents start life with the single con-

dition tag "Comment," so if you only want to use conditional text for comments, you can skip this step.)

1. Select **Conditional Text** from the Special menu, or use the keyboard short-cut **Esc s C**. In the Conditional Text dialog box, click **Edit Condition Tag**. This opens the Edit Condition Tag dialog box (Figure 22.2).

2. Type the name for the new condition tag in the Tag text box.

3. Select the condition indicators for the new tag from the Style and Color pop-up menus. You can use any of the following text styles—overline, strikethrough, underline, or double underline—and/or any of the colors available in the document.

4. Select **Set** to store the new condition tag and to return to the Conditional Text window. The new tag will appear in "Not In" list in the window.

5. You can now close the Conditional Text window or use it to apply your new tag, as described next.

Figure 22.2   The Edit Condition Tag dialog box

Applying a Condition Tag

To make an item conditional, apply a condition tag. Select the item you wish to tag, then use the following procedure (consult Table 22.1 for information on what items can be tagged and how to select them):

1. Select **Conditional Text** from the Special menu, or use the keyboard short-cut **Esc s C**. This opens the Conditional Text window (Figure 22.3).

2. Select the Current Selection is **Conditional** radio button.

3. Move the tag(s) you want to apply to the "In" list. (An item can have more than one condition tag.) Tags in the "Not In" list are removed from selected items if they are currently so tagged. Tags in the "As Is" list are not changed. To move a tag from one list to another, highlight it and click on one of the

arrow buttons, or double-click on it. To move all the tags from one list to another, **Shift**+click on one of the arrow buttons.

4. Select the **Apply** button to apply the tag to the selection.

5. The Conditional Text window remains on the screen. You can use it to tag additional items or close it by double-clicking on its control box.

Figure 22.3 The Conditional Text window

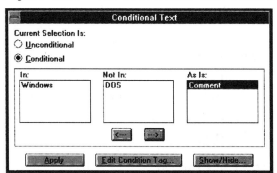

SHORTCUT After selecting the item that you want to tag, press **Ctrl+4**. A "?" will appear at the left side of the status area. Begin typing the condition tag name. You will probably not need to type the full name, just enough letters to identify the unique tag name. The full name will appear in the status area. As an alternative, you can use the up and down arrow keys to step through the list of possible tags. Press **Enter** to apply the tag.

N O T E You can apply a condition tag at the insertion point without selecting text. Any new text you type at the insertion point will receive the condition tag, until you move the insertion point outside the conditional text.

Table 22.1 Items to select to apply a condition tag

To tag	Select
Text in a text column, table cell, or footnote	The text
An anchored frame	The frame's border or anchor symbol
An entire table	The table's anchor symbol

To tag	Select
A cross-reference	The cross-reference text
An entire footnote	The footnote number in the text
A marker	The marker symbol
A variable	The variable text
A table row	The whole row

To be made conditional, a graphic or a table must be in an *anchored* frame, associated with a text column. An unanchored frame, drawn with the frame tool on the Tools Palette, won't do. For information on anchored frames, consult Chapter 14.

N O T E

You cannot make a text line (an object created with the Text Line tool on the Tools Palette) conditional. To be made conditional, text must be in a text column. Keep this in mind when adding callouts to figures in a conditional document.

N O T E

Showing or Hiding Conditional Items

To view a particular version of your document, show the items with the condition tag that belongs to the version and hide those with the tags that belong to other versions. Use the following procedure:

1. Select **Conditional Text** from the Special menu, or use the keyboard shortcut **Esc s C**.

2. In the Conditional Text dialog box, select the **Show/Hide** button. This opens the Show/Hide Conditional Text dialog box (Figure 22.4).

3. In the Show/Hide dialog box, select the **Show** radio button. (If you want to show *all* the tags—for example, to compare versions or to spell-check the document—select **Show All** and skip to step 5.)

4. Move the tag(s) that you want to show to the Show list, and move all the others to the Hide list. To move a tag, highlight it and click an arrow button, or double-click on it. To move all the tags from one list to another, **Shift**+click on an arrow button.

5. (Optional) You may want to uncheck the **Show Condition Indicators** box to make the conditional text indistinguishable from normal text. You should definitely do this before printing a version of your document.

6. Click **Set** to Show/Hide the selected conditional text. This returns you to the Conditional Text window.

7. You can do further work with condition tags or close the window by double-clicking on its control box.

Figure 22.4   The Show/Hide Conditional Text dialog box

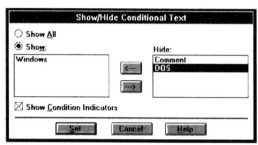

When some condition tags are hidden, you can see the location(s) of conditional text from the presence of marker symbols. (You must have **Text Symbols** selected on the View menu to see the markers.)

Deleting a Condition Tag

Deleting a condition tag from a document removes it from the tag list and either deletes all items that have the tag or makes them unconditional.

1. If it is not already on the screen, open the Conditional Text window (**Esc s C**).

2. Select the tag you want to delete from the tag list and click the **Edit Condition Tag** button.

3. In the Edit Condition Tag dialog box, click **Delete**.

4. A dialog box will appear asking whether you want to delete items with the tag or make them unconditional. Select the appropriate radio button in the box and click **OK**, or click **Cancel** to terminate the operation without deleting the tag.

Removing or Changing a Condition Tag

If you want to change the condition of a selection or make a selection unconditional, you can do so either in the Conditional Text window or from the keyboard.
(This is not the same operation as removing a condition tag from a document.)

In the window:

1. Select the item with the tag you want to change. (See Table 22.1, earlier in
   this chapter, for information on how to select different types of items.)

2. If it is not already one the screen, open the Conditional Text window (**Esc s
   C**).

3. In the window, move the tag(s) that you want to remove from the selection
   from the "In" list to the "Not In" list. If you want to apply a new tag to the
   selection, move the tag name to the "In" list from one of the other lists. To
   move a tag, highlight it and click one of the arrow buttons or double-click
   on it.

4. If you want to remove *all* the tags from a selection, or if a selection has only
   one tag and you want to remove it, select the **Unconditional** radio button.

5. Click the **Apply** button to apply the changed tag(s).

From the keyboard:

1. Select the item with the tag you want to change. (See Table 22.1, earlier in
   this chapter, for information on how to select different types of items.)

2a. To remove *all* tags from the selection, press **Ctrl+6**. You will not be prompted
    to confirm this choice, the tags are removed immediately and the selection
    is made unconditional.

2b. To remove one tag, press **Ctrl+5**. An upside-down question mark will appear
    at the left side of the status area.

3. Begin typing the name of the tag you want to remove. You probably won't
   have to type the whole name, just enough characters to identify it as a
   unique name. The full name will appear in the status area. As an alternative,
   you can use the up and down arrow keys on the cursor keypad to step
   through the available tags.

4. Press **Enter** to remove the tag. A prompt box will appear, asking whether you
   want to delete the selection or make it unconditional. Select the appropriate

radio button in the box and click **OK,** or click **Cancel** to terminate the operation without changing the selection's condition.

5. If you want to give the selection a different tag, press **Ctrl+4**. A "?" will appear at the left side of the status area. Begin typing the condition tag name. You will probably not need to type the full name, just enough letters to identify the unique tag name. The full name will appear in the status area. Press **Enter** to apply the tag.

Importing Condition Tags

You can import a single condition tag from another document by copying and pasting it, or you can import all of another document's tags with the **Import>Formats** option on the File menu. To copy a single condition tag:

1. Place the insertion point in a block of text that has the tag you want to copy.

2. From the Edit menu, select **Copy Special**; select **Conditional Text Settings** from the submenu. (Or use the keyboard shortcut **Esc e y d**.)

3. Switch to the destination document. Click an insertion point or select an item to which to apply the condition tag.

4. Select **Paste** from the Edit menu or press **Ctrl+V**.

5. The condition tag is applied to the selection or made active at the insertion point. It is also added to the list in the Conditional Text dialog box.

To import all the condition tags from a document:

1. Open the destination document (the one into which you want to import the condition tags) and the source document (the one with the tags you want to import).

2. Make the destination the active document.

3. Select the **Import>Formats** option from the File menu or use the keyboard shortcut **Esc f i o**.

4. A dialog box like that in Figure 22.5 will appear. By default, all the import options are checked. Uncheck all the options except those you want to import, such as Conditional Text Settings.

5. Open the list box that says "Current," meaning the document that's currently active, and select the document from which to import the formats (you can only select a document that's currently open).

6. Click the **Import** button to import the condition tags from the source document into the destination document.

Figure 22.5   The Import Formats dialog box

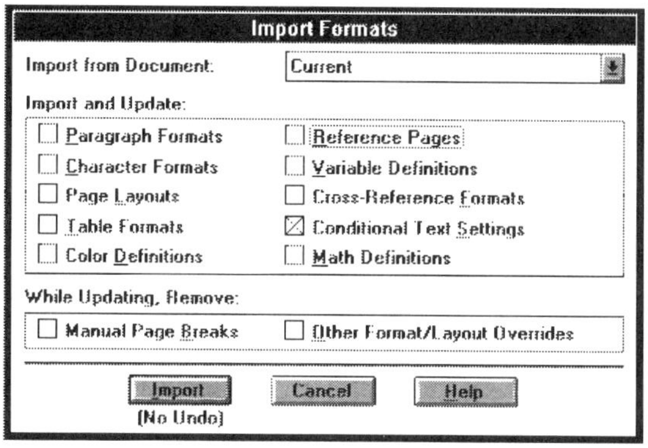

Creating a List of Condition Tags

You can create a list of all the condition tags used in a document, showing the pages on which they are used, by generating a List of References or an Index of References that includes condition tags. A List of References shows all the occurrences of the condition tags, in the order in which they occur in the document. An Index of References lists each of the tags once, in alphabetical order, and lists all the pages on which each tag is used. An Index of References is thus the more practical format for most purposes.

To generate a list or index of references, select **Generate/Book** from the File menu (**Esc f g**). Select either the **List** or **Index** radio button and select the appropriate type of list or index from the pop-up menu. Click the **Generate** button, and, in the Set Up dialog box that appears, place Condition Tags in the list of references to include. Click **Generate** again to create the list. Consult Chapters 16 and 17 for detailed information on generating lists and indexes.

Creating Non-Printing Comments

It is frequently useful to add non-printing or, optionally, printing comments to a document in progress. Such comments can function as "electronic Post-Its"; they can remind you of things you need to add or revise, or they can call the attention of your editor, reviewers, or coworkers to important issues or unresolved questions. Conditional text makes it easy to create such comments. The one condition tag that exists in all FrameMaker documents is "Comment." The predefined indicator for this tag is red underlined text. Although this tag is the obvious choice to use for your comments, it is not mandatory that you so use it—you can create a new tag or select a new indicator if you prefer.

If you don't want your comments to affect your page layouts, as will be the case if you intersperse them in your regular text columns, you can put the comments in anchored frames in the margins. Create and position an anchored frame with the **Anchored Frame** command on the Special menu (**Esc s a**—see Chapter 14.) You must then use the Frame tool to draw a text column inside the frame to hold the comment (see Chapter 12). Type the comment in the frame. You can then either select the text and tag it with the condition tag, or you can select and tag the frame. If you tag the frame, the text inside it won't display the condition indicator associated with the tag. Show or hide your comments as you would any other conditional item.

Editing a Conditional Document

You can work in a conditional document with different versions showing and their condition indicators displayed, or you can hide all the conditional items belonging to other versions while working on one particular version. Which approach is best will depend on your working style and what you're trying to accomplish. If you opt to work with some condition tags hidden, you should turn on **Text Symbols** on the View menu (**Esc v t**), so you can see the markers indicating the locations of hidden text.

Many FrameMaker editing commands work on visible text only or affect hidden and visible text differently. You should consider the effects described in the following sections in deciding whether to show or hide conditional text before using a particular editing command.

Finding and Changing Conditional Items

FrameMaker's **Find/Change** option finds only visible conditional text or other conditional items; it cannot find or change hidden text or other items by searching directly for them as text, variables, anchored frames, or the like, although it can find markers indicating the locations of hidden conditional items. You can find *visible* conditional text with a particular condition tag by searching for it. Open the Find/Change window (**Ctrl+F**), select Conditional Text from the Find pop-up menu, and specify the condition tag to search for in the dialog box that appears.

You can change the condition tags of items you find by using the change **By Pasting** option. Place the insertion point in text that has the condition tag you want to use and copy the tag by using the **Copy Special>Conditional Text Setting** option on the Edit menu (keyboard shortcut **Esc e y d**). Select **By Pasting** from the Change pop-up menu in the Find/Change Window, then search for the item as described in the preceding paragraph. Click the **Change** or **Change All** button, as appropriate.

You can find hidden conditional items by searching for the markers that indicate their locations. Open the Find/Change window and search for Marker of Type: Conditional Text. The program responds by highlighting the location of the marker. You can only search for hidden conditional items this way, not those that are visible. And it's no use trying to find specific items by searching for marker text. The marker text for a conditional text marker is not its hidden text, but a numeric code that is used internally by FrameMaker (you could search for this if you knew what it was, but you would have to have already found the item and looked at its marker text to know what to look for). For more information on the Find/Change options, consult Chapter 8.

Updating Cross-References

FrameMaker cannot update cross-references whose sources are in hidden conditional text. Hence, you should take care, when placing cross-references in a conditional document, that both the reference and the source of the cross-reference have the same condition tag. If you have a paragraph cross-reference (for example, a reference to a heading or chapter title) and part of the paragraph, including the first word, is conditional, the cross-reference marker to the paragraph will also be conditional. If that portion of the paragraph is hidden, you will not be able to update any cross-references to the title, and an unresolved cross-reference will result. You can correct this by making the paragraph visible, selecting the cross-reference marker, and making it unconditional. (It's hard to select a marker without selecting any surrounding text. The best way to do it is to search for it in the Find/Change window; move the insertion point just before the location of the marker and, in this case, search for Marker of Type: Cross-Ref.) For more information on working with cross-references, consult Chapter 10.

Deleting Conditional Text

When conditional text is visible, you can delete it or cut it like any other text. Hidden conditional text, however, behaves differently. You cannot delete hidden conditional text by removing its marker with the backspace or delete key. The insertion point simply moves through the hidden text marker while the text surrounding it is deleted. To delete hidden text, you must select the marker, then press **Delete** or use the **Cut** command on the Edit menu (**Ctrl+X**). A dialog box will appear asking you to confirm that you want to delete the hidden text. It is very difficult to select the marker without also selecting some surrounding text, even at high magnifications. It's much more practical to show the hidden text and then delete or cut it.

Changing Character and Paragraph Formats

You can't change the paragraph or character formats of hidden conditional text by tagging it in the normal manner. For example, if you have a paragraph that contains some hidden conditional text, and you apply a paragraph format that changes, say, the type family or weight, the change will affect only the visible text. When you reveal the hidden text, it will have the same properties as it had before it was hidden. The same considerations pertain when applying a character format to a block of text that contains some hidden text. Even reapplying the format tag after showing the hidden text doesn't always produce the desired effect, and you must change the tag for the paragraph and change it back again in order for the desired format to take effect. It is far simpler to show all hidden text before applying character or paragraph formats and hide it again afterward.

There are two situations in which changes to paragraph or character formats *do* affect hidden conditional text: when updating *all* paragraphs or characters with a particular tag via the **Update All** button in the paragraph or character designer, and when importing paragraph or character formats via the **Import>Formats** option on the File menu.

Index and Other List Markers

If you are going to generate an index or other marker list from your conditional document, be sure to place separate index markers in the different conditional items, where appropriate. When FrameMaker compiles an index or other marker list, it uses only the markers in text that is currently visible.

Working with Conditional Graphics

As mentioned previously, in order to be conditional, graphics, whether they are drawn with FrameMaker's drawing tools or imported from other programs, must be placed in anchored frames. All the considerations described in Chapters 12, 13, and 14 regarding manipulating graphics and frames apply in this situation.

If you wish, you can place two different conditional graphics in the same location in a document. Create an anchored frame for the first graphic, as described in Chapter 14. Import or draw the graphic in the frame, as appropriate. Select the frame and apply a condition tag, then hide the condition tag (the graphic will disappear). Repeat the process for the second graphic. As long as only one graphic is shown at a time, it can be manipulated freely, with no interference from the other, hidden graphic. To simplify matters further, place the anchors for the two frames at different locations in the text, so that you can easily select and move one without interfering with the other.

Merging Two Documents to Create a Conditional Version

When you compare two documents with the **Compare Documents** feature (see Chapter 24) and opt to have a composite document created, you are not simply producing a report in which you can view the differing and common features of the two documents; you are creating a "live" conditional document that can take the place of both preexisting versions and be managed as described in this chapters.

Printing a Conditional Document

Before printing a version of your conditional document, show the condition tag for the version you want to print and hide all the tags for other versions. Turn off condition indicators, so your text will be printed without extraneous attributes. If the text for the two versions differs sufficiently to affect the layout, you should probably save the version under a different name with the **Save As** command before making any necessary manual adjustments, such as forced page or line breaks. (Save the original for future revisions.)

Once you have performed these steps, printing a conditional document is no different from printing any other FrameMaker document.

CHAPTER 23

Creating View-Only
Documents with Hypertext

What is Hypertext?

Hypertext is another unique FrameMaker feature. (Or almost unique. As this book was being completed, Adobe released its Acrobat family of products for creating documents for electronic distribution. These products produce *view-only* documents from other applications, and offer many features that are similar to those of FrameMaker's hypertext documents.) In addition to creating conventional documents for paper distribution, FrameMaker can create locked, view-only documents for distribution on disk or over a network. Such documents need not be merely static images to be read from the screen, page by page. You can embed hypertext commands in a document to enable the reader to jump to related topics by clicking on *active* areas, including headings, text strings with special character formats, buttons or other graphic devices, or entries in lists such as indexes or tables of contents. View-only documents can even include pop-up menus of topics to jump to. In addition to jumping to other locations in the same document file, hypertext commands can open other documents in separate windows and even open other Windows applications. FrameMaker maintains a list of past moves, allowing you to retrace your steps. FrameMaker's on-line help system and on-line manuals are typical FrameMaker hypertext documents.

Unfortunately, FrameMaker does not create "stand-alone" hypertext documents. In order to read a FrameMaker view-only document, the reader must have either a copy of FrameMaker, or a less expensive, companion product, FrameViewer. (In previous releases, the name "FrameViewer" was reserved for the original, UNIX version of this product, and the Windows and Mac versions were called "FrameReader." A new version, compatible with FrameMaker 4.0, to be called FrameViewer and have uniform features on all platforms, is scheduled for release in the first quarter of 1994.) Frame seems to envision this product primarily for use in a networked corporate environment, where everyone on the network has a site-licensed copy of FrameViewer, and all short-lived documents are distributed and updated over the network. This seems like a plausible vision for such environments, but it limits the usefulness of FrameMaker view-only documents in other situations. Certainly, you would not, at today's FrameViewer prices, want to publish your user's group newsletter as a view-only document and provide a copy of FrameViewer to each subscriber.

Basic Concepts

The basic concepts involved in creating a hypertext document are surprisingly simple. Certain objects in a FrameMaker document are designated as active. An active object or area is one on which the user clicks to execute a hypertext command. An active object can be a text string that is set apart by a special character format, a whole paragraph, or a graphic such as a button or icon. A marker of the type "Hypertext" is inserted in the active object or area. The marker text for the Hypertext marker is a particular hypertext command. Some hypertext commands, such as those that jump to other locations or open other files, must have target markers at their destinations; others, such as those that page forward or back, or retrace your steps through the document, do not. A few, such as those that create pop-up menus or "matrices" of commands (see later), refer to special flows on reference pages. The most potentially difficult task in creating a hypertext document—building hypertext links to an index, table of contents, or other list—is performed automatically by FrameMaker when the list is generated.

The complete set of hypertext commands is small, and the function of each is simple and straightforward. Hence, although they look like the commands of a programming language (as, indeed, they are, of a rather limited sort), one certainly need not be a programmer to use them effectively.

Designating Active Areas

As mentioned previously, an active area is a location on which a reader clicks to execute a hypertext command. An active area can be a text string, a paragraph, a graphic, or a portion of a graphic. Each of these items requires a different preparation before a hypertext command is inserted to make it active.

Preparing a Text String

To prepare a text string (that is, a word or phrase within a paragraph) give it a distinct character format. Any character format can be used to distinguish an active string *except* pair kerning, spread, change bars, and case. In most cases you will want to use a distinctive format, such as a different typeface or a different color, to designate active areas, so your readers will readily recognize them. You should not, for obvious reasons, use a character format for active areas that is also used for other purposes; for example, if you use italics for the conventional purposes of designating titles or foreign words, or expressing emphasis, it would not be a good idea to also use italics for active areas. If, for some reason, you don't want your active areas to stand out from other text, you can use a character format in which all the properties are set to "As Is." (See Chapter 5 for more information on character formats.)

Preparing a Paragraph

If you want a whole paragraph to serve as an active area, it must be free of character format changes. If the paragraph is a heading, title, or figure caption, this probably won't be difficult to achieve in most cases. However, if the paragraph must have character format changes and you want it to function as a single active area, you will need to place several hypertext markers with the same command in the different sections created by the format changes.

Preparing a Graphic

You can use graphic devices, such as buttons or icons, to make it easier to navigate through a document. The graphics you use can be created with FrameMaker's drawing tools or created in another program and imported. To prepare a graphic, draw a text column around it with the Text Column tool on the Tools Palette (see Chapter 12). The columns should cover the entire graphic. Set the pen pattern and fill for the column to "none," making the column invisible and transparent. Use the **Bring to Front** command on the Graphics menu to ensure that the text column is in front of the graphic. (This is a change from FrameMaker 3.0, where you could activate a hypertext command even if it was covered up by a graphic.)

Preparing Active Areas on Master Pages

If you want to have the same active area on several different pages, create it on a master page. For example, you could have a pop-up menu in the margin, with commands to go to an index or table of contents or to jump to other chapters, or you could have next page, previous page, backtrack, and quit buttons on each page, as in the FrameMaker help system. There is little difference between preparing an area on a body page or a master page. Just remember that when you draw a text column on a master page, you will be asked whether it is to be a template column or a background column. A column that is to hold the hypertext commands for a graphic must be a background column.

An active area created on a master page can be overridden on selected body pages by drawing another graphic and/or text column in front of the background column. For example, on the last page of a document, you might want to cover up a "next page" button with a blank box, or you might want to leave the button visible, but override it with a command to open a new file for the next chapter. Where one hypertext command is placed in front of another, only the topmost command is active.

Inserting Hypertext Markers

After you have prepared your active areas, the next step is to insert the Hypertext markers and type the hypertext commands. Once the commands have been inserted, the hypertext areas are active.

1. Click an insertion point in the prepared area (text string, paragraph, or text column).

2. Select the **Marker** command from the Special menu, or use the keyboard shortcut **Esc s m**.

3. In the Marker dialog box, type the command and any required parameters. (The commands will be described in the next section.) The hypertext commands must be typed in lowercase. The parameters may be typed in upper- or lowercase, but they are case sensitive, so you must be consistent. For example, in typing a parameter indicating the destination of a jump, you must use exactly the same form in the command and in the marker at the destination.

4. Click **New Marker** to place the marker. If Text Symbols are turned on, the Marker Symbol (like a large, sans serif T) will appear at the insertion point.

Putting Multiple Commands in a Paragraph

If you want to put more than one command in a paragraph, you can do so. Just place the markers in such a manner that they divide the paragraph into logical sections, as illustrated in Figure 23.1.

Figure 23.1 Multiple hypertext markers in a paragraph

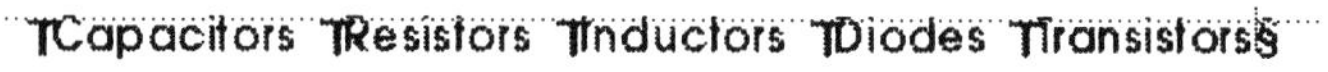

¶Capacitors ¶Resistors ¶Inductors ¶Diodes ¶Transistors§

Editing Hypertext Commands

Editing a hypertext command is similar to inserting one:

1. If you have locked the document, you must unlock it (press **Esc F l k**) before editing a hypertext command (or any other item).

2. Open the Marker window (**Esc s m**).

3. Select the marker for the command you want to edit. If you have difficulty finding or selecting the marker, use the **Find/Change** option to search for Marker of Type: Hypertext, or for the specific marker text. Leave the Marker window open while searching so you can see the commands in the Marker Text box. And remember, if you placed markers on master pages, you must edit them there.

4. Revise the text as required.

5. Click the **Edit Marker** button to replace the command with the edited version.

Deleting Hypertext Commands

To delete a hypertext command, select the marker and delete it. If you have difficulty in locating or selecting the marker that you want to delete, try the suggestions in step 3 of the previous section.

The Hypertext Commands

The following is an alphabetical listing of all of FrameMaker's hypertext commands, with their parameters. Optional parameters are shown in square brackets ([]). The more abstruse commands will be explained in greater detail later in this chapter.

`alert message`—Display an alert box. The `message` parameter represents the message that the alert box will display; it can be up to 249 characters in length.

`gotolink [filename:]linkname`—Jump to and display the topic located at `[filename:]linkname`. The destination of the jump can be in the same file as or a different file than the `gotolink` command. If the destination is in the same file, the `filename:` parameter is not required. The destination for the jump must be marked by a corresponding `newlink` `linkname` command, and the `linkname` parameters must match perfectly.

`gotolink [filename:]firstpage`—Jump to and display the first page of the current file or a different file. To jump to the first page of the current file, no `filename:` parameter is required.

`gotolink [filename:]lastpage`—Jump to and display the last page of the current file or a different file. To jump to the last page of the current file, no `filename:` parameter is required.

`gotopage [filename:]pagenumber`—Jump to and display the material at the specified page number in the current file or another file. If the page is in the current file, no `filename:` parameter is required.

`matrix rows columns flowname`—Select one of the hypertext commands in a matrix (see "Creating a Matrix" later in this chapter for details).

`message system application pathname, windowstate` or `message winexec application pathname, windowstate`—Start another Windows application (see "Starting Another Application" later in this chapter for details). There is no difference between the effects of these two commands.

`newlink linkname`—Marks the destination of a `gotolink` or `openlink` command.

`nextpage`—Jump to the next page of the current document.

`openlink [filename:]linkname`—Jump to and display a new location in the current file or another file. The destination is displayed in a new window, while the original window remains open. If the destination is in the current document, the `filename:` parameter is not required.

`opennew filename`—Open the specified file as a new, unnamed document in a new window, while leaving the current window open.

`openpage [filename:]pagenumber`—Jump to and display the specified page in the current file or another file. The destination is displayed in a new window, while the original window remains open. If the destination is in the current document, the `filename:` parameter is not required.

`popup flowname`—Open a pop-up menu of items containing hypertext commands (see "Creating a Pop-up Menu," later in this chapter, for details).

`previouslink [filename:linkname]`—Display the last location the reader viewed. The `filename:linkname` parameters indicate what page to display if the hypertext stack (see later) is empty. If these parameters are absent, the current page will remain on display.

`previouspage`—Jump to the previous page of the current file.

`quit`—Close the current file.

`quitall`—Close all currently open view-only documents.

N O T E You can use cross-references as hypertext commands. If a reader clicks on a cross-reference in a view-only document, FrameMaker treats the cross-reference the same as a `gotolink` command. If a cross-reference and a hypertext marker are located in the same text area, the cross-reference takes precedence over the hypertext command.

Path Names

Those FrameMaker Hypertext commands that open other files can accept path names as part of the `[filename:]` parameter. FrameMaker prefers to use UNIX-style path names, in which directory levels are separated with forward slashes (/), such as `book/chapters/chapter.01`. If you use UNIX-style path names, they will be recognized by FrameMaker versions on all hardware platforms. If you use DOS-style path names with backslashes (\), such as `book\chapters\chapter.01`, they will be recognized by FrameMaker for Windows, but not by Frame-Maker versions on UNIX or Mac platforms. DOS-style 8-character.3-character file names are acceptable on all platforms.

FrameMaker hypertext commands also distinguish between relative and absolute path names. A relative path name starts in the same directory as the current file (the one from which the hypertext command is being executed). Directories below that directory are named without any leading slash. For example, if the current file is in the `book` directory, and the file you want to open is in `book\chapters`, the relative path would be `chapters/filename`. For a path that must go up a level in the directory structure before going down another branch, use two periods (..) to represent the parent of the current directory. For example, if the current file is in `book\chapters` and the file you want to open is in `book\lists`, use the path name `../lists`.

Absolute path names start at the top of the directory tree. If you're using UNIX-style path names, an absolute path name begins with a slash and doesn't include a drive letter, for example, `/maker/book/chapters/filename`. Hence, when you use these path names on a Windows system, the destination file must be on the same logical drive as the current file. When you use DOS-style path names, you use the normal DOS form of an absolute path name, such as `c:\maker\chapters\filename`.

The most practical approach to path names is probably to put all the files for a given hypertext document in the same directory whenever possible, so you don't have to worry about paths.

The Hypertext Stack

The FrameMaker hypertext system, like most such systems, uses a data structure called a stack to keep track of where you've been in a document so you can retrace your steps. A stack is a "first-in, last out" structure. When a command jumps to a new location, it leaves its previous location on the stack. Successive jumps pile more recent locations on top of older ones. When you execute the `previouslink` command, it jumps to the location on top of the stack, removing it from the stack as it does so. Successive `previouslink` commands remove successive locations from the stack in the reverse of the order in which they were put there, playing back your steps through the document in reverse order. The stack can store up to 69 jumps. If the stack "overflows" (that is, the reader makes more than 69 jumps without using a `previouslink` command), additional jumps are not added to the stack, and the next `previouslink` jumps to the location on the top of the stack.

The following commands affect the stack:

`gotolink`—stores the current location on the stack before jumping.

`gotopage`—stores the current location on the stack before jumping.

`openlink`—starts a new stack for the new window and leaves the stack for the old window unchanged.

`openpage`—starts a new stack for the new window and leaves the stack for the old window unchanged.

`previouslink`—jumps to the top location on the stack and discards the location.

The remaining hypertext commands have no effect on the stack.

Creating a Matrix

A matrix is FrameMaker's term for a graphic with a rectangular array of cells, such that clicking on any given cell executes a different hypertext command. Use the following steps to create a matrix:

1. Draw or import the graphic for the matrix. The graphic you choose should be a rectangle clearly divided into different cells in regular rows and columns, such as that in Figure 23.2.

2. Draw one text column that covers the whole graphic. If you're working on a master page, make the column a background column.

3. Click an insertion point in the text column, open the Marker window, and type the `matrix` command as the marker text. The complete syntax of the command is: `matrix rows columns flowname`, where `rows` and `col-`

umns are the numbers of rows and columns in the matrix, and `flowname` is the name of a special text flow on a reference page that you'll create in step 5. Click **New Marker** to insert the command in the column.

Figure 23.2 A graphic for a matrix

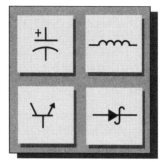

4. Switch the view to Reference Pages. If you're going to use many `matrix` or `popup` commands in your document, you'll probably want to create a new reference page for this purpose.

5. Draw a text column on the reference page and assign it a flow tag that matches the `flowname` parameter you typed in step 3. (See Chapter 12 for information on drawing a text column; see Chapter 7 for information on assigning a flow tag.)

6. In the column, type the hypertext commands that correspond to the cells in the matrix. Each command must be a separate paragraph. Enter the commands that correspond to the cells of the top row from left to right, followed by those in subsequent rows. See Figure 23.3 for an example corresponding to the graphic Figure 23.2.

Figure 23.3 The text flow for the matrix in Figure 23.2

Creating a Pop-Up Menu

Use the `popup` command to create a pop-up menu from which the user can execute other hypertext commands. You create a graphic for the menu and embed the popup command in it. When the user clicks on the graphic and holds the mouse button, the menu opens. For example, you could have a pop-up menu to jump to a variety of related topics. The process of creating a pop-up is quite similar to that for creating a matrix:

1. Draw or import the graphic indicating the location of the menu. You can use any symbol you like, but the standard indicator for a pop-up menu in Windows applications is a downward pointing arrow at the right end of the title.

2. Draw a text column over the graphic. If you are working on a master page, make the column a background column.

3. Click an insertion point in the new column. Open the Marker window and type the command. The full command syntax is popup flowname, where flowname is the name of a special flow on a reference page that you will create in step 5. Click **New Marker** to insert the command.

4. Switch the view to Reference Pages. If you're going to use many matrix or popup commands in your document, you'll probably want to create a new reference page for this purpose.

5. Draw a text column on the reference page and assign it a flow tag that matches the flowname parameter you typed in step 3. (See Chapter 12 for information on drawing a text column; see Chapter 7 for information on assigning a flow tag.)

6. In the text column, type the title of the menu as the first item. Type each menu entry as a separate paragraph, following the title.

7. Insert a hypertext marker in each menu entry with the command you want the menu entry to execute. Don't insert a command in the title.

Figure 23.4 A hypertext pop-up menu

Nested pop-up menus, which were supported as an undocumented feature in FrameMaker 3.0, are not possible in version 4.0. If you port documents with nested pop-ups from version 3.0 to version 4.0, the inner menus will not work and will need to be revised.

N O T E

Executing Other Windows Programs

You can start other programs from within a view-only document with the `message system` or `message winexec` commands. (These two commands have exactly the same effect.) These commands work on windows systems only and are not portable to other platforms. Indeed, it's hard to imagine that they would be very portable even among windows systems, as they presume that you know which programs are installed on the system where the document is being read. Still, they could be useful for in-house documents where you know that the document will be read only on systems with a certain configuration.

The complete syntax for these commands is `message system application pathname,winstate` or `message system application pathname,winstate` where `winstate` is one of the following:

`SW_HIDE`	`SW_MINIMIZE`
`SW_RESTORE`	`SW_SHOW`
`SW_SHOWMAXIMIZED`	`SW_SHOWMINIMIZED`
`SW_SHOWMINNOACTIVE`	`SW_SHOWNA`
`SW_SHOWNOACTIVE`	`SW_SHOWNORMAL`

These options produce far fewer different results than the variety of their names would seem to indicate. With the exception of `SW_HIDE`, they all open the specified application in a window of one size or other, somewhere on the screen. A few minutes of trial and error should suffice to show which is most useful for your purposes.

Adding Hypertext Links to Generated Documents

FrameMaker can generate a variety of lists, including Tables of Contents, Indexes, Figure Lists, and many others. These lists are generated via the **Generate/Book** option on the File menu, and are described in detail in Chapters 16 and 17. When you generate a list, you can easily add hypertext links from the list entries to their sources (the markers or paragraph tags to which they refer). All you need to do is check the **Generate Hypertext Links** box in the Set Up dialog box before generating the list. This is recommended even if you're not creating a view-only document, as it makes it easy to trace and correct errors in tables of contents and indexes. If you are creating a view-only document, it means that you can create an index and/or table of contents in which the reader can click on an entry and jump to its source. At least in the case of tables of contents, which are normally based on paragraph tags, you can do this without having to place hypertext markers and type commands. In the case of an index, you have to place the markers to identify the entries anyway, but you get double duty from them by using them to generate hypertext links.

Changing the Way the Sources of List Entries are Displayed

When you generate a list with hypertext links, you can change the way that Frame-Maker jumps to and displays the sources of list entries. By default, when you click on a list entry, FrameMaker displays the source document in a new window, with the source of the reference highlighted. You can change this by editing the Hypertext Links paragraph in the special flow on the reference page that defines the list entries (see Chapter 17).

1. In the generated document (not the source), switch the view to **Reference Pages** (**Esc v R**). Page down to find the reference page with the special flow. The special flow and the reference page will have names that correspond to the extension of the generated document, such as TOC for a table of contents or IX for an index.

2. In the special flow, find the Hypertext Links paragraph. It will look something like this:

    ```
    openObjectId <$relfilename>:<$ObjectType> <$ObjectId>
    ```

3. Substitute one of the other options, as described in the following section.

4. Save the generated file, then generate it again from the source document. Changes made to the format of a list by editing the reference flow don't take effect until the next time the list is generated.

5. Test the new links by jumping from the list to the source, to make sure the edited command does what you intend.

Display Options

The following are the options you can use to control how the sources of generated lists are displayed. The examples use the `<$relfilename>` building block, indicating that they will use a relative path to search for the file to open. If you want FrameMaker to search for an absolute path, substitute the `<$fullfilename>` building block.

`openObjectId <$relfilename>:<$ObjectType> <$ObjectId>`—Displays the source document in a new window, with the source of the reference highlighted.

`gotoObjectId <$relfilename>:<$ObjectType> <$ObjectId>`—Displays the source document in the current window, with the source of the reference highlighted.

`gotopage <$relfilename>: <$pagenumonly>`—Displays the source document in the current window, with nothing highlighted.

`openpage <$relfilename>: <$pagenumonly>`—Displays the source document in a new window, with nothing highlighted.

`alert <$relfilename>`—Displays an alert box showing the file name of the source document.

Incorporating Generated Lists into On-Line Documents

Generating a list with hypertext links provides an easy way to get from the list entries to their sources in other documents, but it doesn't provide a comparable way to get back from the source document(s) to the list. Neither does it provide a way to navigate *within* the generated list. Both of these additions are necessary to make a generated list a fully functional part of an on-line document. To get back from the source document to the list, you should use a `gotolink` or `openlink` command. You could, for example, create index and/or table of contents buttons in the margin on a master page, as described earlier in this chapter, containing the appropriate commands. Or you could create a pop-up menu with index and table of contents commands, along with other navigation options. Within the list, you might create next page, previous page, and backtrack buttons, as are used in the FrameMaker help system. For an extensive index, you might create a matrix to jump to the group headings (letters of the alphabet), as is also done in the Frame-Maker help system.

Designing a View-Only Document

It is important to recognize that the experience of reading a document on screen is different than that of reading a document on paper, and to take this into consideration in designing a view-only document. Here are a few points to consider:

- The aspect ratio of a monitor is different than a typical printed page (it is closer to being a landscape page than a portrait page). Design your master pages accordingly, so that a full page fits in a maximized program window. (Yes, the scroll bars are active in a view-only document, and the readers could scroll down to view the lower portion of the page, but why force them to do so? It's much more convenient to use the page up/down buttons.)

- Fonts are much cruder on screen, and so are graphics (as low as 72 dpi on screen, compared to a minimum of 300 dpi on a laser printer). Choose your type specs so they'll be readable on screen, which, in most cases, will result in your making them larger than you would on the printed page. And, if your document is going to be widely distributed, limit your document to common fonts. (Everyone presumably has some form of Times and Helvetica, and most ATM users probably have the equivalent of the "basic 35" PostScript fonts that were shipped with the original Apple LaserWriter.)

■ Use color. Just about every Windows user has a color display. You can use color to highlight different elements in a view-only document at no extra expense, whereas it would be very costly to do the same thing in a printed document.

Testing and Debugging a Hypertext Document

Before locking and distributing a document, you should test the hypertext commands to be sure they behave as expected. You can test hypertext commands in an unlocked document by **Ctrl+Alt**+clicking on them. You may find this more convenient than repeatedly locking and unlocking a document while testing and editing.

The most common problems are likely to result from `gotolink` or `openlink` commands with mismatched file names or `newlink` commands. You may also have inadvertently typed hypertext commands using another marker type. These, obviously, won't work.

One way to check all the hypertext commands in a document is to generate a list of markers consisting of hypertext markers. The list will show each hypertext marker, indicating the page on which it occurs. Use the list to cross-check the `gotolink` and `openlink` commands against their corresponding `newlink` commands. (If you need to generate a list that covers several files, assemble them as a book—see Chapter 18.) Another way to check commands is to execute them with the Marker window open—you'll see the marker text at the destination of each jump.

Locking and Unlocking Documents

To lock the document in the active window, press **Esc F l k** (the second character is a lowercase L). When the document is locked, the menu bar at the top of the FrameMaker program window changes to File, Edit, Navigation, Window, and Help (the same thing happens when you open an existing view-only document). The commands on the menus themselves also change; for example, the commands on the Edit menu are limited to **Copy**, **Copy Special**, **Select All on Page**, **Find**, and **Find**

Next. The Navigation menu offers commands for moving through the document that are comparable to those provided by the hypertext commands.

Once a document has been locked, it can be distributed to readers. Readers equipped with FrameViewer will be able to read the document but not edit it. Readers with FrameMaker will be able to read the document as view-only, but can also unlock the file and edit it if they choose. The command to lock a file is the same as that for locking it: **Esc F l k**.

CHAPTER 24

Reports and Revisions

In addition to its host of features for creating, editing, and formatting documents, FrameMaker has several novel features that can help you keep track of revisions in a document, differences in document versions, and details of document structure. You can even combine two versions of a document into a single conditional document.

Using Change Bars

You can use change bars to identify revisions in a document, either for your own information, or to alert your readers, reviewers, or editors to important changes. You can have FrameMaker apply change bars automatically to *all* revisions, or you can apply them manually to revisions you consider important. Change bars appear as vertical lines in the margins of a document. You can select their color, thickness, and exact location.

Applying Change Bars Automatically

To have FrameMaker apply change bars automatically to all changes in text, select **Change Bars** from the Format menu, or use the keyboard shortcut **Esc o b**. In the Change Bar Properties dialog box, check **Automatic Change Bars**. Set the options for **Distance from Column**, **Thickness**, **Color**, and **Position** as you wish (these settings apply both to automatic change bars and to those you apply manually). Click **Set** to activate the change bars. Thereafter, any change, be it as minor as an added or deleted comma, will result in a change bar in the margin.

Applying Change Bars Manually

If you don't want to note all changes, but only those you consider significant, apply change bars manually. You can do this either from the Character Designer or the Paragraph Designer. If you want to apply the change bars only to a range of text within a paragraph, use the Character Designer:

1. Select the revised text.

2. Open the Character Designer (**Ctrl+D**).

3. Check the **Change Bar** check box.

4. Click the **Apply** button.

As an alternative, you can create and store a character format that turns on change bars while leaving all other properties unchanged:

1. Open the Character Designer (**Ctrl+D**).

2. Select **Set Window to As Is** from the Commands menu.

3. Check the **Change Bars** check box.

4. Select **New Format** from the Commands menu.

5. In the New Format dialog box, type a name for the new format, such as "revision." Check the **Store in Catalog** check box, and, if you also want to apply change bars to the current selection, check the **Apply to Selection** check box as well.

6. Click **Create**.

If you want to apply change bars to one or more complete paragraphs, use the Paragraph Designer:

1. Click in the paragraph to which you want to apply the change bar, or select two or more consecutive paragraphs.

2. Open the Paragraph Designer (**Ctrl+M**).

3. Select the Default Font Properties group.

4. Check the **Change Bar** check box.

5. Click the **Apply** button.

For more information on using the Paragraph and Character Designers, consult Chapter 5.

Clearing Change Bars

You can clear change bars in the same ways you add them: either automatically or manually. To clear all the change bars in a document, open the Change Bar Properties dialog box (**Esc o b**), check **Clear All Change Bars**, and click **Set**. All the change bars in the document will be cleared, whether they were applied manually or automatically.

To clear change bars selectively, use the Character Designer or the Paragraph Designer, depending on whether you are removing the change bars from a range of text or from one or more whole paragraphs. Select the text from which you want to remove the change bars, open the appropriate designer, uncheck the **Change Bars** check box while leaving all other properties unchanged, and select **Apply**.

Turning off the change bars on a selection that had them applied by means of a character format does not remove the format. To remove the old format, you must replace it with another, such as the Default ¶ Font.

N O T E

Using Revision Pages

Another way to keep track of revisions in a FrameMaker document is to freeze pagination and allow FrameMaker to create revision pages (also called *point pages*, for reasons explained later). When the pagination of a document is frozen and you add new material (text or graphics) to a page, material that is forced off a page doesn't flow to the next page; instead, it flows to a special revision page, inserted between regular pages. This revision page receives the page number of the overflowing page, followed by a decimal point and a second character, for example 2.a (hence, the term point pages).

Limitations

There are some fairly severe limitations on the situations in which you can use revision pages. The document must have a single body text flow, and no layout overrides on body pages. Freezing pagination may cause problems in documents with multi-page tables or anchored frames that float.

Freezing Pagination

1. Type the key sequence **Esc p z** to open the Freeze Pagination dialog box (there is no menu equivalent for this command).

2. Select a **Point Page # Style** from the pop-up menu. This option determines the style of number after the decimal point on revision pages. The usual FrameMaker numbering options are available: numeric (Arabic figures), upper- and lowercase Roman, and upper- and lowercase alphabetic.

3. Click **Freeze**. A dialog box will appear, warning that the operation cannot be undone, which is not, strictly speaking, true. Click **OK** to freeze the pagination.

Unfreezing Pagination

The process of unfreezing pagination is similar to that of freezing it:

1. Type the key sequence **Esc p z** to open the Unfreeze Pagination dialog box (there is no menu equivalent for this command).

2. Click **Unfreeze**. A dialog box will appear, warning that the operation cannot be undone, which is not, strictly speaking, true. Click **OK** to unfreeze the pagination.

N O T E

You can also use the Unfreeze dialog box to change the point page numbering style. Open the dialog box, select a new page numbering style from the menu, and click **Set Page # Style** rather than **Unfreeze**.

When you unfreeze pagination, the point pages are renumbered so that page numbering is consecutive throughout the document. The forced page breaks between revision pages and subsequent normal pages are eliminated so that text flows continuously from page to page. This may result in one or more empty pages at the end of the document. You can delete the extra pages manually, or you can select **Delete Empty Pages** before printing and saving in the Document Properties dialog box. If you use the latter option, any empty pages will be deleted whenever you save the document.

Generating Reports

Report generation is more of a potential feature in FrameMaker 4.0 than an actual one. Frame has provided an interface for report generators and one sample report generator that counts words, and recommends that you create the generators you need by writing programs with the Frame Developer's Kit. The Frame Developer's Kit for Windows had not been completed when FrameMaker 4.0 was released in

October 1993, so I can't tell you what this involves. It appears that Frame's thinking about this issue is governed by conditions in the UNIX environment, where C programming is a common and essential skill—it seems unlikely that most Windows users have a couple of idle C programmers hanging about to write report generators. In any case, the potential will be there for those that have the necessary skills and resources. Perhaps some more useful generators from third parties will show up on the market or on bulletin boards in the not-too-distant future.

To use a report generator:

1. Select **Utilities** from the File menu and select **Document Reports** from the submenu, or use the keyboard shortcut **Esc f t r.**

2. Select a report generator from the list in the dialog box that appears. (By default, there is only one report generator, WordCount, which counts the words in a document.)

3. Click the **Report** button.

Lists and Indexes of References

A related device, and one that is operative in its current form, is the list or index of references. This is a list or index of internal FrameMaker features; it can include Condition Tags, External Cross-References, Fonts, Imported Graphics, and/or Unresolved Cross-References. The list or index shows all the occurrences of the selected item(s) in the document, with the page numbers on which they occur. Consult chapters 16 and 17 for more information on generating these and other lists and indexes.

Comparing Documents

FrameMaker can compare two open versions of a document and generate a summary of the differences and a composite, conditional document that combines the features of both. The composite can, if you choose, replace both versions. The comparison process checks all items affecting content, but ignores differences of a purely visual nature, such as differences in paragraph and character formats or page layout. In the summary document, text that is present in the newer document but not in the older is described as "Inserted," and text that is present in the older document but not in the newer is described as "Deleted." In the composite document, which contains all the text from both versions, Inserted and Deleted condition tags are used to identify text that is exclusive to one or the other version. For a detailed description of what elements are compared, see "What is Compared," later in this chapter.

The terms "newer," and "older," as used in the document comparison process, are wholly arbitrary. FrameMaker treats as newer whichever document you have open when you select the **Compare Documents** option, even if it has the earlier "last modification" date.

N O T E

The process of performing a comparison is fairly simple (it's understanding the results that can be challenging.)

1. Open both of the documents that you want to compare. Make the newer version the active document. If the documents contain conditional text, all conditional items must be visible (see Chapter 22).

2. Select **Utilities** from the File menu and select **Compare Documents** from the submenu, or use the keyboard shortcut **Esc f t c**. This opens the Compare Documents dialog box (Figure 24.1).

Figure 24.1   The Compare Documents dialog box

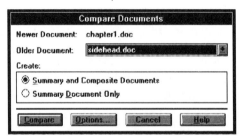

3. From the Older Document pop-up menu, select the name of the other document you want to compare.

4. Use the radio buttons to select whether you want to generate both the summary and the composite document, or only the summary.

5. (Optional) Click **Options** to set up the comparison options. This opens the Comparison Options dialog box. The comparison options will be explained in the following section.

6. Click **Set** to return to the main Compare Documents dialog box.

7. Click **Compare** to begin the comparison. When the comparison is complete, FrameMaker opens the summary and the composite, if created, in separate

document windows. (If the two versions were identical, neither the summary nor the composite will be generated.)

Reading the Composite and Summary Documents

The comparison process opens the comparison and summary documents in their own document windows. The composite document is named `filename.cmp`, where `filename` is the name of the newer document. The summary document is simply called `summary`.

The composite document is a typical FrameMaker conditional document. Text that is common to both of the compared documents has no condition tag and appears with the same character format it has in the newer version; items that are in the newer but not the older version have, by default, the condition tag "Inserted" and the condition indicators green and underline; items that are in the older but not the newer version have, by default, the tag "Deleted" and the condition indicators red and strikethrough. You can change either the condition tags or the indicators (see "Setting Comparison Options" and "Changing Condition Indicators," later in this chapter.

If the two compared documents are versions for different purposes, rather than older and newer versions of the same document, you may be able to substitute the one composite document for both versions. Consult Chapter 22 for more information on working with conditional documents.

The summary document lists the names of the newer and older documents with their last modification dates, and the total numbers of insertions, deletions, and changes of text, markers, cross-references, imported graphics, tables, and equations. This is followed by a complete page-by-page list of what was inserted, deleted, or replaced. If you opted to create hypertext links in the summary, it is created as a view-only document, and you can jump to the location of an insertion or deletion in the newer or older document by clicking on its page number in the list. (For more information on view-only documents and hypertext links, consult Chapter 23.)

Setting Comparison Options

Clicking the **Options** button in the Compare Documents dialog box opens the Comparison Options dialog box (Figure 24.2). The settings in this dialog box determine which condition tags will be used to identify inserted and deleted items in the composite document. The default condition tags "Inserted" and "Deleted" will be appropriate in most cases, but you can substitute other tags if you wish. In the case of insertions, you can also opt to use no condition tag (select **Nothing**). Do this if you want to treat the text in the newer version as the norm. In the case of deletions, you can also opt to have a text string that you type displayed in place of the deleted text. In addition, you can mark changes in the composite with change bars and/or create hypertext links in the summary document (recommended). If you just want to add change bars to the newer version of the document, check the Mark Changes with Change Bars box, set "Mark Insertions With" to **Nothing** and set "Mark Deletions With" to **Replacement Text**. Don't type any text in the replacement text box. The composite document will be the same as the newer version, with change bars indicating the changes.

Figure 24.2   The Comparison Options dialog box

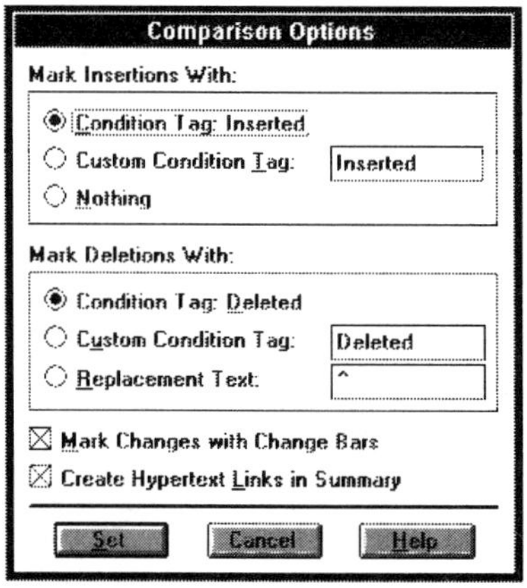

Changing Condition Indicators

By default, the condition indicators for inserted text are green and underline; those for deleted text are red and strikethrough. If you want to use something less garish, open the Conditional Text dialog box (**Esc s C**) and select **Edit Condition Tag**. In the Edit Condition Tag dialog box, type the name of the tag you want to change the indicators for, and select the style and color from the pop-up menus. Select **Set** to apply the changes. For more information on working with conditional text, consult Chapter 22.

What Is Compared

Text and Special Items—FrameMaker compares the contents of text flows with the same names on body and reference pages. In so doing, it checks for inserted or deleted text, footnotes, anchored frames, variables and their definitions, cross-references and cross-reference formats, and markers and their text.

Anchored Frames—FrameMaker compares the objects in the frame: whether the same objects are present and whether they are in the same positions. If there are any changes, the whole frame is marked as changed.

Imported Graphics—FrameMaker checks the contents, and in the case of bitmaps, the dpi resolution. It checks whether graphics have been flipped, inverted, or rotated, and compares the sizes of bounding boxes. FrameMaker also compares how graphics were imported (by copying or by reference), and, if by reference, compares the path names. If any of these elements are different, it marks the whole graphic as changed.

Equations—FrameMaker compares the size of the equation, its position in the frame, and the math expressions. If any of these elements are different, it marks the equation as changed.

Tables—FrameMaker checks the number of rows and columns, whether cells are straddled, and whether cells are rotated. If any of these elements are different, it marks the whole table as changed. If these elements are the same, but text in some cells is changed, it marks the individual cells. If the text in more than 75% of the cells is different, it marks the whole table as changed.

What Is Not Compared

FrameMaker doesn't compare master page flows and untagged flows, graphic objects and text lines not in anchored frames, anchored frame positions, footnote properties and numbers, paragraph, character, or table format tags, custom text or table formatting, or the contents of the paragraph, character, or table catalogs.

Comparing Books

Just as you can compare individual documents, you can also compare books. The comparison utility compares the components at the book level (which files are included in each book, which file with a given name is newer) and compares the contents of files whenever files with the same name are included in both books being compared. The summary lists the differences at the book level (files inserted, deleted, or replaced), followed by the differences in the contents of the common files. If you specify the creation of a composite document, a separate composite is created for each pair of common files.

APPENDIX 1

Character Sets, Character Codes, and Key Sequences

ANSI Code	Hex Code	Key Sequence	Standard Character	Hex Code	Key Sequence	Symbol Character	Dingbat Character
—	\x04	Esc hyphen D or Ctrl+hyphen	discretionary hyphen	\x04	Esc hyphen D or Ctrl+hyphen	discretionary hyphen	
—	\x05	Esc n s	suppress hyphenation	\x05	Esc n s	suppress hyphenation	
—	\x15	Esc hy-phen h	nonbreaking hyphen	\x15	Esc hy-phen h	nonbreaking hyphen	
—	\x08	tab	tab	\x08	tab	tab	
—	\x09	Shift+Enter	forced line break	\x09	Shift+Enter	forced line break	
—	\x0a	Enter	end of paragraph	\x0a	Enter	end of paragraph	
—	\x10	Esc space 1	numeric space	\x10	Esc space 1	numeric space	
—	\x11	Esc space h	nonbreaking space	\x11	Esc space h	nonbreaking space	
—	\x12	Esc space t	thin space	\x12	Esc space t	thin space	
—	\x13	Esc space n or Ctrl+ Alt+space	en space	\x13	Esc space n or Ctrl+ Alt+space	en space	

ANSI Code	Hex Code	Key Sequence	Standard Character	Hex Code	Key Sequence	Symbol Character	Dingbat Character
—	\x14	Esc space m or Ctrl+ Shift +space	em space	\x14	Esc space m or Ctrl+ Shift+space	em space	
—	\x27	Ctrl+'	'	\x27	Ctrl+'	϶	☿
—	\x60	Ctrl+`	`	\x60	Ctrl+`	‾	✿
—	\xda	Ctrl+q Shift+z	/				
—	\xde	*					
—	\xdf	*					
—	\xf5	*					
—	\xf9	Ctrl+q y					
—	\xfa	Ctrl+q z					
—	\xfd	Ctrl+q }					
—	\xfe	Ctrl+q ~					
032	\x20	space	(space)	\x20	(space)		
033	\x21	!	!	\x21	!	!	✀
034	\x22	" (smart quotes off)	"	\x22	"	∀	✁
035	\x23	#	#	\x23	#	#	✂
036	\x24	$	$	\x24	$	∃	✃
037	\x25	%	%	\x25	%	%	☎
038	\x26	&	&	\x26	&	&	✆
040	\x28	(	(	\x28	(	(	✈
041	\x29	)	)	\x29	)	)	✉
042	\x2a	*	*	\x2a	*	∗	☞

ANSI Code	Hex Code	Key Sequence	Standard Character	Hex Code	Key Sequence	Symbol Character	Dingbat Character
043	\x2b	+	+	\x2b	+	+	☞
044	\x2c	,	,	\x2c	,	,	✌
045	\x2d	-	-	\x2d	-	−	✍
046	\x2e	.	.	\x2e	.	.	✏
047	\x2f	/	/	\x2f	/	/	✒
048	\x30	0	0	\x30	0	0	✐
049	\x31	1	1	\x31	1	1	✆
050	\x32	2	2	\x32	2	2	✇
051	\x33	3	3	\x33	3	3	✓
052	\x34	4	4	\x34	4	4	✔
053	\x35	5	5	\x35	5	5	✕
054	\x36	6	6	\x36	6	6	✖
055	\x37	7	7	\x37	7	7	✗
056	\x38	8	8	\x38	8	8	✘
057	\x39	9	9	\x39	9	9	✙
058	\x3a	:	:	\x3a	:	:	✚
059	\x3b	;	;	\x3b	;	;	✛
060	\x3c	<	<	\x3c	<	<	✜
061	\x3d	=	=	\x3d	=	=	†
062	\x3e	>	>	\x3e	>	>	✞
063	\x3f	?	?	\x3f	?	?	✝
064	\x40	@	@	\x40	@	≅	✠
065	\x41	A	A	\x41	A	A	✡

ANSI Code	Hex Code	Key Sequence	Standard Character	Hex Code	Key Sequence	Symbol Character	Dingbat Character
066	\x42	B	B	\x42	B	B	✛
067	\x43	C	C	\x43	C	X	✚
068	\x44	D	D	\x44	D	Δ	❖
069	\x45	E	E	\x45	E	E	✜
070	\x46	F	F	\x46	F	Φ	◆
071	\x47	G	G	\x47	G	Γ	✦
072	\x48	H	H	\x48	H	H	★
073	\x49	I	I	\x49	I	I	☆
074	\x4a	J	J	\x4a	J	ϑ	✪
075	\x4b	K	K	\x4b	K	K	☆
076	\x4c	L	L	\x4c	L	Λ	✬
077	\x4d	M	M	\x4d	M	M	★
078	\x4e	N	N	\x4e	N	N	✺
079	\x4f	O	O	\x4f	O	O	✷
080	\x50	P	P	\x50	P	Π	✩
081	\x51	Q	Q	\x51	Q	Θ	✳
082	\x52	R	R	\x52	R	P	✹
083	\x53	S	S	\x53	S	Σ	✳
084	\x54	T	T	\x54	T	T	✳
085	\x55	U	U	\x55	U	Υ	✴
086	\x56	V	V	\x56	V	ς	✶
087	\x57	W	W	\x57	W	Ω	✷
088	\x58	X	X	\x58	X	Ξ	✸

ANSI Code	Hex Code	Key Sequence	Standard Character	Hex Code	Key Sequence	Symbol Character	Dingbat Character
089	\x59	Y	Y	\x59	Y	Ψ	✸
090	\x5a	Z	Z	\x5a	Z	Z	✸
091	\x5b	[	[	\x5b	[	[	✳
092	\x5c	\	\	\x5c	\	∴	✳
093	\x5d	]	]	\x5d	]	]	✳
094	\x5e	^	^	\x5e	^	⊥	✻
095	\x5f	_	_	\x5f	_	_	✿
097	\x61	a	a	\x61	a	α	❀
098	\x62	b	b	\x62	b	β	❁
099	\x63	c	c	\x63	c	χ	✺
0100	\x64	d	d	\x64	d	δ	✲
0101	\x65	e	e	\x65	e	ε	✵
0102	\x66	f	f	\x66	f	φ	❋
0103	\x67	g	g	\x67	g	γ	✶
0104	\x68	h	h	\x68	h	η	✳
0105	\x69	i	i	\x69	i	ι	✳
0106	\x6a	j	j	\x6a	j	φ	✳
0107	\x6b	k	k	\x6b	k	κ	✳
0108	\x6c	l	l	\x6c	l	λ	●
0109	\x6d	m	m	\x6d	m	μ	○
0110	\x6e	n	n	\x6e	n	ν	■
0111	\x6f	o	o	\x6f	o	ο	❏
0112	\x70	p	p	\x70	p	π	❐

ANSI Code	Hex Code	Key Sequence	Standard Character	Hex Code	Key Sequence	Symbol Character	Dingbat Character
0113	\x71	q	q	\x71	q	θ	❑
0114	\x72	r	r	\x72	r	ρ	❐
0115	\x73	z	z	\x73	s	σ	▲
0116	\x74	t	t	\x74	t	τ	▼
0117	\x75	u	u	\x75	u	υ	◆
0118	\x76	v	v	\x76	v	ϖ	❖
0119	\x77	w	w	\x77	w	ω	▶
0120	\x78	x	x	\x78	x	ξ	I
0121	\x79	y	y	\x79	y	ψ	I
0122	\x7a	z	z	\x7a	z	ζ	∎
0123	\x7b	{	{	\x7b	{	{	❛
0124	\x7c	|	|	\x7c	|	|	❜
0125	\x7d	}	}	\x7d	}	}	❝
0126	\x7e	~	~	\x7e	~	~	❞
0130	\xe2	Ctrl+q b	‚	—	—	Reserved	Reserved
0131	\xc4	Ctrl+q Shift+b	ƒ	—	—	Reserved	Reserved
0132	\xe3	Ctrl+q c	„	—	—	Reserved	Reserved
0133	\xc9	Ctrl+q l	…	—	—	Reserved	Reserved
0134	\xa0	Ctrl+q space	†	—	—	Reserved	Reserved
0135	\xe0	Ctrl+q `	‡	—	—	Reserved	Reserved
0136	\xf6	Ctrl+q v	ˆ	—	—	Reserved	Reserved
0137	\xe4	Ctrl+q d	‰	—	—	Reserved	Reserved
0138	\xb3	Ctrl+q 3	≥	—	—	Reserved	Reserved

ANSI Code	Hex Code	Key Sequence	Standard Character	Hex Code	Key Sequence	Symbol Character	Dingbat Character
0139	\xdc	Ctrl+q \	‹	—	—	Reserved	Reserved
0140	\xce	Ctrl+q Shift+n	Œ	—	—	Reserved	Reserved
0145	\xd4	Ctrl+q Shift+t	'	—	—	Reserved	Reserved
0146	\xd5	Ctrl+q Shift+u	'	—	—	Reserved	Reserved
0147	\xd2	Ctrl+q Shift+r or Ctrl+Alt+`	"	—	—	Reserved	Reserved
0148	\xd3	Ctrl+q Shift+s or Ctrl+Alt+'	"	—	—	Reserved	Reserved
0149	\xa5	Ctrl+q %	•	—	—	Reserved	Reserved
0150	\xd0	Ctrl+q Shift+p	–	—	—	Reserved	Reserved
0151	\xd1	Ctrl+q Shift+q	—	—	—	Reserved	Reserved
0152	\xf7	Ctrl+q w	~	—	—	Reserved	Reserved
0153	\xaa	Ctrl+q *	™	—	—	Reserved	Reserved
0154	\xf0	Ctrl+q p		—	—	Reserved	Reserved
0155	\xdd	Ctrl+q]	›	—	—	Reserved	Reserved
0156	\xcf	Ctrl+q Shift +o	œ	—	—	Reserved	Reserved
0159	\xd9	Esc % Shift+y	Ÿ	—	—	Reserved	Reserved
0161	\xc1	Ctrl+q Shift+a	¡	\xa1	Ctrl+q !	ϒ	✆
0162	\xa2	Ctrl+q "	¢	\xa2	Ctrl+q "	′	✇

ANSI Code	Hex Code	Key Sequence	Standard Character	Hex Code	Key Sequence	Symbol Character	Dingbat Character
0163	\a3	Ctrl+q #	£	\a3	Ctrl+q #	≤	❣
0164	\db	Ctrl+q [	¤	\a4	Ctrl+q $	⁄	❤
0165	\b4	Ctrl+q 4	¥	\a5	Ctrl+q %	∞	❥
0166	\ad	Ctrl+q hyphen	≠	\a6	Ctrl+q &	ƒ	♥
0167	\a4	Ctrl+q $	§	\a7	Ctrl+q '	♣	❧
0168	\ac	Ctrl+q ,	¨	\a8	Ctrl+q (	♦	♣
0169	\a9	Ctrl+q)	©	\a9	Ctrl+q)	♥	♦
0170	\bb	Ctrl+q ;	ª	\aa	Ctrl+q *	♠	♥
0171	\c7	Ctrl+q Shift+g	«	\ab	Ctrl+q +	↔	♠
0172	\c2	Ctrl+q Shift+b	¬	\ac	Ctrl+q ,	←	①
0173	\2d	- (hyphen)	-	\ad	Ctrl+q -	↑	②
0174	\a8	Ctrl+q (	®	\ae	Ctrl+q .	→	③
0175	\f8	Ctrl+q x	¯	\af	Ctrl+q /	↓	④
0176	\fb	Ctrl+q {	°	\b0	Ctrl+q 0	°	⑤
0177	\b1	Ctrl+q 1	±	\b1	Ctrl+q 1	±	⑥
0178	\b7	Ctrl+q 7	Σ	\b2	Ctrl+q 2	″	⑦
0179	\b8	Ctrl+q 8	Π	\b3	Ctrl+q 3	≥	⑧
0180	\ab	Ctrl+q +	´	\b4	Ctrl+q 4	×	⑨
0181	\b5	Ctrl+q 5	µ	\b5	Ctrl+q 5	∝	⑩
0182	\a6	Ctrl+q &	¶	\b6	Ctrl+q 6	∂	❶
0183	\e1	Ctrl+q a	·	\b7	Ctrl+q 7	•	❷
0184	\fc	Ctrl+q |	¸	\b8	Ctrl+q 8	÷	❸

ANSI Code	Hex Code	Key Sequence	Standard Character	Hex Code	Key Sequence	Symbol Character	Dingbat Character
0185	\xb6	Ctrl+q 6	∂	\xb9	Ctrl+q 9	≠	❹
0186	\xbc	Ctrl+q <	º	\xba	Ctrl+q :	≡	❺
0187	\xc8	Ctrl+q Shift+h	»	\xbb	Ctrl+q ;	≈	❻
0188	\xb9	Ctrl+q 9	π	\xbc	Ctrl+q <	…	❼
0189	\xba	Ctrl+q :	∫	\xbd	Ctrl+q =	|	❽
0190	\xbd	Ctrl+q =	Ω	\xbe	Ctrl+q >	—	❾
0191	\xc0	Ctrl+q @	¿	\xbf	Ctrl+q ?	↵	❿
0192	\xcb	Esc ` A	À	\xc0	Ctrl+q @	ℵ	①
0193	\xe7	Esc ' A	Á	\xc1	Ctrl+q Shift+a	{	②
0194	\xe5	Esc ^ A	Â	\xc2	Ctrl+q Shift+b	ℜ	③
0195	\xcc	Esc ~ A	Ã	\xc3	Ctrl+q Shift+c	℘	④
0196	\x80	Esc % A	Ä	\xc4	Ctrl+q Shift+d	⊗	⑤
0197	\x81	Esc * A	Å	\xc5	Ctrl+q Shift+e	⊕	⑥
0198	\xae	Ctrl+q	Ã	\xc6	Ctrl+q Shift+f	∅	⑦
0199	\x82	Esc , C	Ç	\xc7	Ctrl+q Shift+g	∩	⑧
0200	\xe9	Esc ` E	È	\xc8	Ctrl+q Shift+h	∪	⑨
0201	\x83	Esc ' E	É	\xc9	Ctrl+q Shift+i	⊃	⑩
0202	\xe6	Esc ^ E	Ê	\xca	Ctrl+q Shift+j	⊇	❶

ANSI Code	Hex Code	Key Sequence	Standard Character	Hex Code	Key Sequence	Symbol Character	Dingbat Character
0203	\xe8	Esc % E	Ë	\xcb	Esc ' A	⊄	❷
0204	\xed	Esc ` I	Ì	\xcc	Esc ~ A	⊂	❸
0205	\xea	Esc ' I	Í	\xcd	Esc ~ O	⊆	❹
0206	\xeb	Esc ^ I	Î	\xce	Ctrl+q Shift+n	∈	❺
0207	\xec	Esc % I	Ï	\xcf	Ctrl+q Shift+o	∉	❻
0208	\xc3	Ctrl+q Shift+c	√	\xd0	Ctrl+q Shift+p	∠	❼
0209	\x84	Esc ~ N	Ñ	\xd1	Ctrl+q Shift+q	∇	❽
0210	\xf1	Esc ` O	Ò	\xd2	Ctrl+q Shift+r	®	❾
0211	\xee	Esc ' O	Ó	\xd3	Ctrl+q Shift+s	©	❿
0212	\xef	Esc ^ O	Ô	\xd4	Ctrl+q Shift+t	™	→
0213	\xcd	Esc ~ O	Õ	\xd5	Ctrl+q Shift+u	Π	→
0214	\x85	Esc % O	Ö	\xd6	Ctrl+q Shift+v	√	↔
0215	\xb0	Ctrl+q 0	∞	\xd7	Ctrl+q Shift+w	·	↕
0216	\xaf	Ctrl+q /	Ø	\xd8	Esc % y	¬	↘
0217	\xf4	Esc ` U	Ù	\xd9	Esc % Y	∧	➡
0218	\xf2	Esc ' U	Ú	\xda	Ctrl+q Shift+z	∨	↗
0219	\xf3	Esc ^ U	Û	\xdb	Ctrl+q [	⇔	➥
0220	\x86	Esc % U	Ü	\xdc	Ctrl+q \	⇐	✿

ANSI Code	Hex Code	Key Sequence	Standard Character	Hex Code	Key Sequence	Symbol Character	Dingbat Character
0221	\xc5	Ctrl+q Shift+e	≈	\xdd	Ctrl+q]	⇑	☜
0222	\xd7	Ctrl+q Shift+w	◊	\xde	Ctrl+q ^	⇒	→
0223	\xa7	Ctrl+q '	_	\xdf	Ctrl+q _	⇓	➡
0224	\x88	Esc ` a	à	\xe0	Ctrl+q `	◊	➡
0225	\x87	Esc ' a	á	\xe1	Ctrl+q a	〈	➡
0226	\x89	Esc ^ a	â	\xe2	Ctrl+q b	®	➢
0227	\x8b	Esc ~ a	ã	\xe3	Ctrl+q c	©	➣
0228	\x8a	Esc % a	ä	\xe4	Ctrl+q d	™	➤
0229	\x8c	Esc * a	å	\xe5	Esc ^ A	Σ	➥
0230	\xbe	Ctrl+q >	æ	\xe6	Esc ^ E	⎛	➦
0231	\x8d	Esc , c	ç	\xe7	Esc ' A	⎜	➧
0232	\x8f	Esc ` e	è	\xe8	Esc % E	⎝	➨
0233	\x8e	Esc ' e	é	\xe9	Esc ` E	⎡	⇨
0234	\x90	Esc ^ e	ê	\xea	Esc ' I	⎢	⇨
0235	\x91	Esc % e	ë	\xeb	Esc ^ I	⎣	⇦
0236	\x93	Esc ` i	ì	\xec	Esc % I	⎧	⇦
0237	\x92	Esc ' i	í	\xed	Esc ` I	⎨	⇨
0238	\x94	Esc ^ i	î	\xee	Esc ' O	⎩	⇨
0239	\x95	Esc % i	ï	\xef	Esc ^ O	⎪	⇨
0240	\xb2	Ctrl+q 2	≤	\xf0	—	Reserved	Reserved
0241	\x96	Esc ~ n	ñ	\xf1	Esc ` O	〉	⇨
0242	\x98	Esc ` o	ò	\xf2	Esc ' U	∫	⊃

ANSI Code	Hex Code	Key Sequence	Standard Character	Hex Code	Key Sequence	Symbol Character	Dingbat Character
0243	\x97	Esc ' o	ó	\xf3	Esc ^ U	⌠	⇒→
0244	\x99	Esc ^ o	ô	\xf4	Esc ` U	|	↘
0245	\x9b	Esc ~ o	õ	\xf5	Ctrl+q u	⌡	⇒→
0246	\x9a	Esc % o	ö	\xf6	Ctrl+q v	⟩	↗
0247	\xd6	Ctrl+q Shift+v	÷	\xf7	Ctrl+q w	|	↘
0248	\xbf	Ctrl+q ?	ø	\xf8	Ctrl+q x	⟩	⇒→
0249	\x9d	Esc ` u	ù	\xf9	Ctrl+q y	⌉	↗
0250	\x9c	Esc ' u	ú	\xfa	Ctrl+q z	|	→
0251	\x9e	Esc ^ u	û	\xfb	Ctrl+q {	⌋	↔
0252	\x9f	Esc % u	ü	\xfc	Ctrl+q |	⟩	⇒⇒
0253	\xc6	Ctrl+q Shift+f	ý	\xfd	Ctrl+q }	⎰	⇒⇒
0254	\xca	Ctrl+q Shift+j	þ	\xfe	Ctrl+q ~	⌡	⇒⇒
0255	\xd8	Esc % y	ÿ	\xff			

INDEX